WALKIN'
BUTTERFLY 2
CHIHIRO TAMAKI

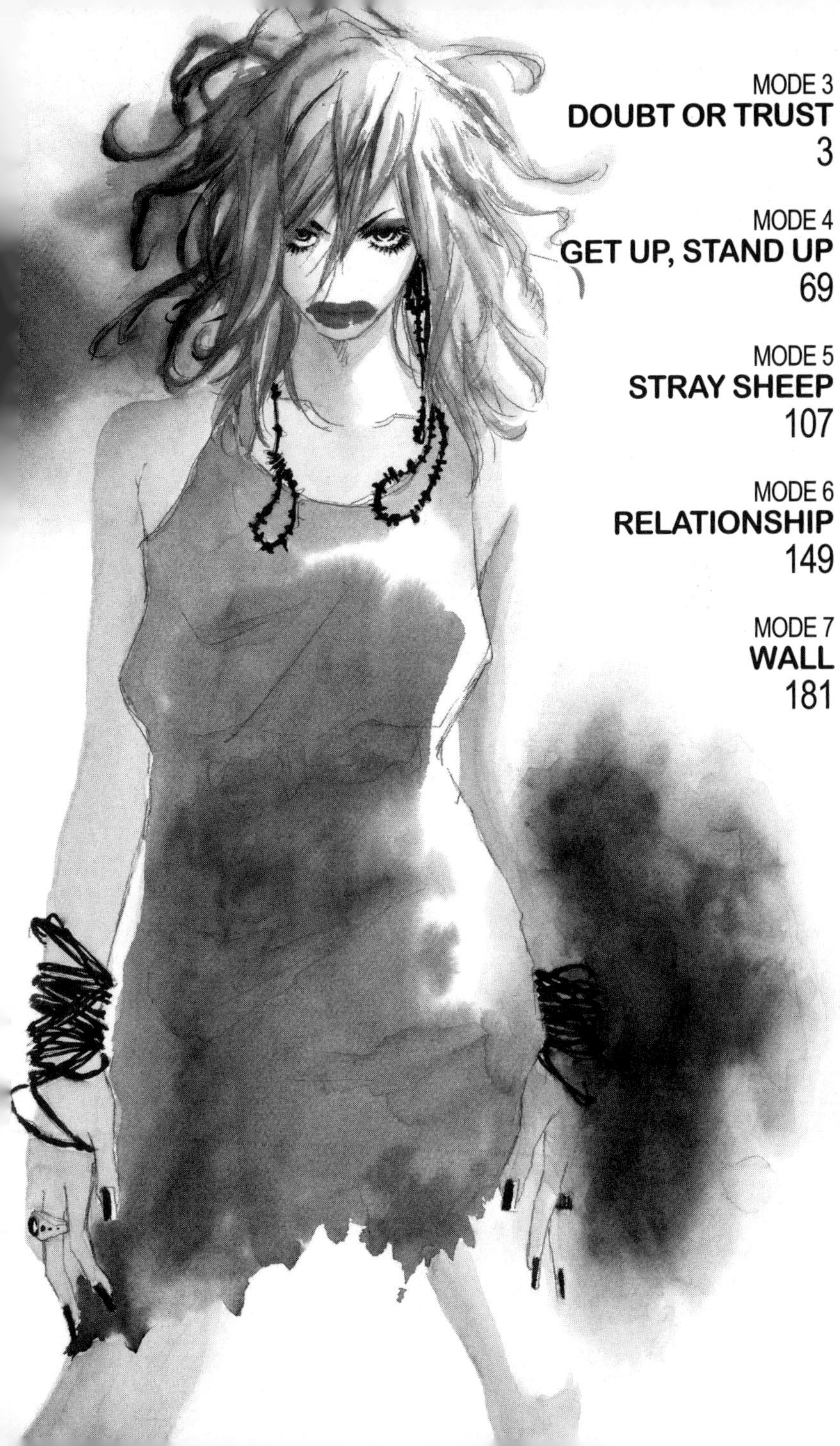

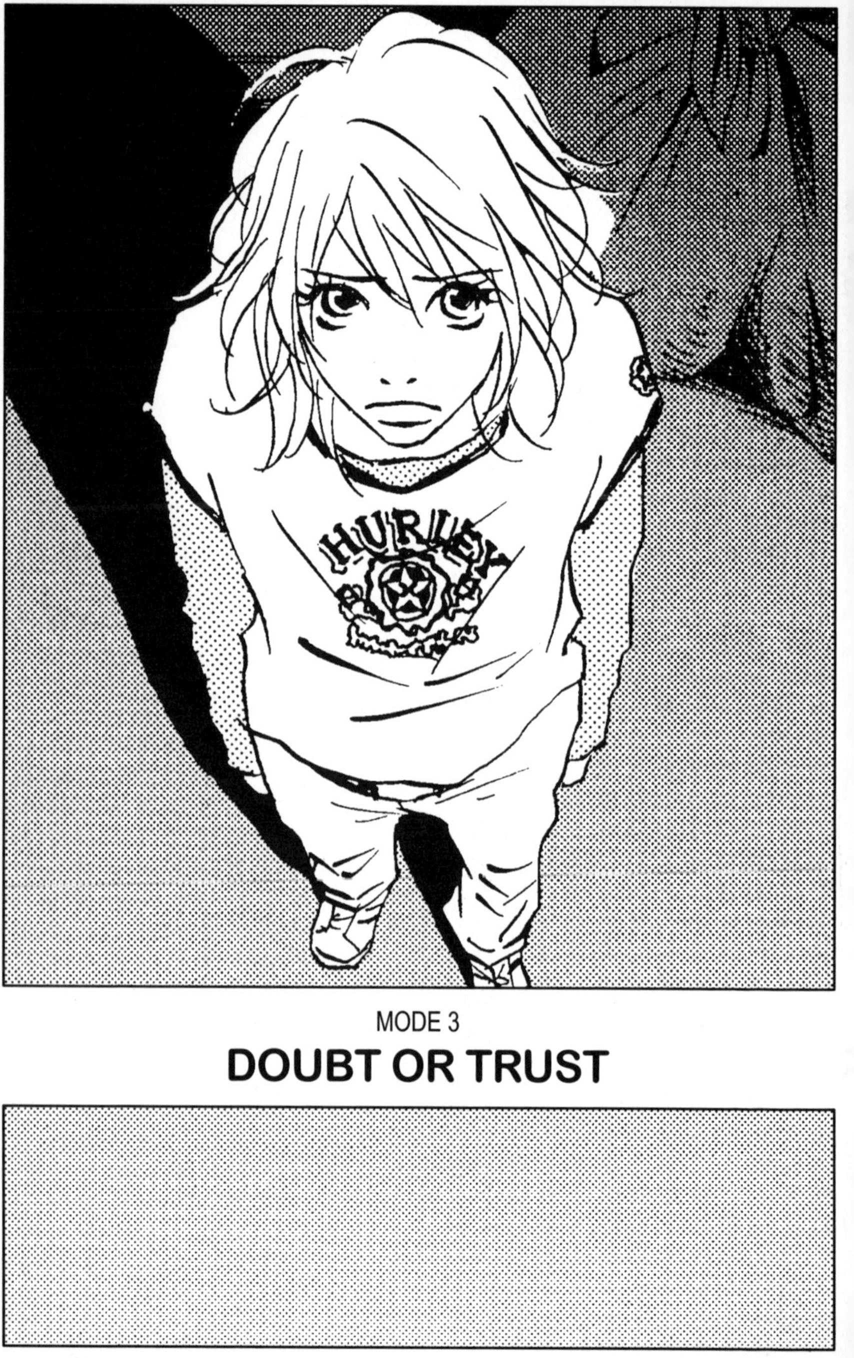
HURLEY

MODE 3

DOUBT OR TRUST

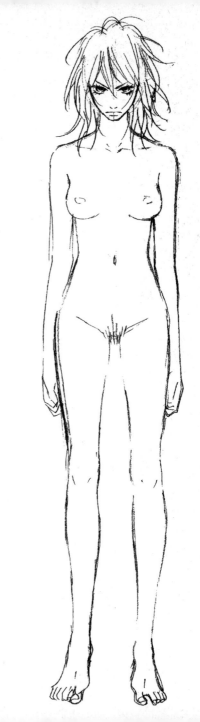

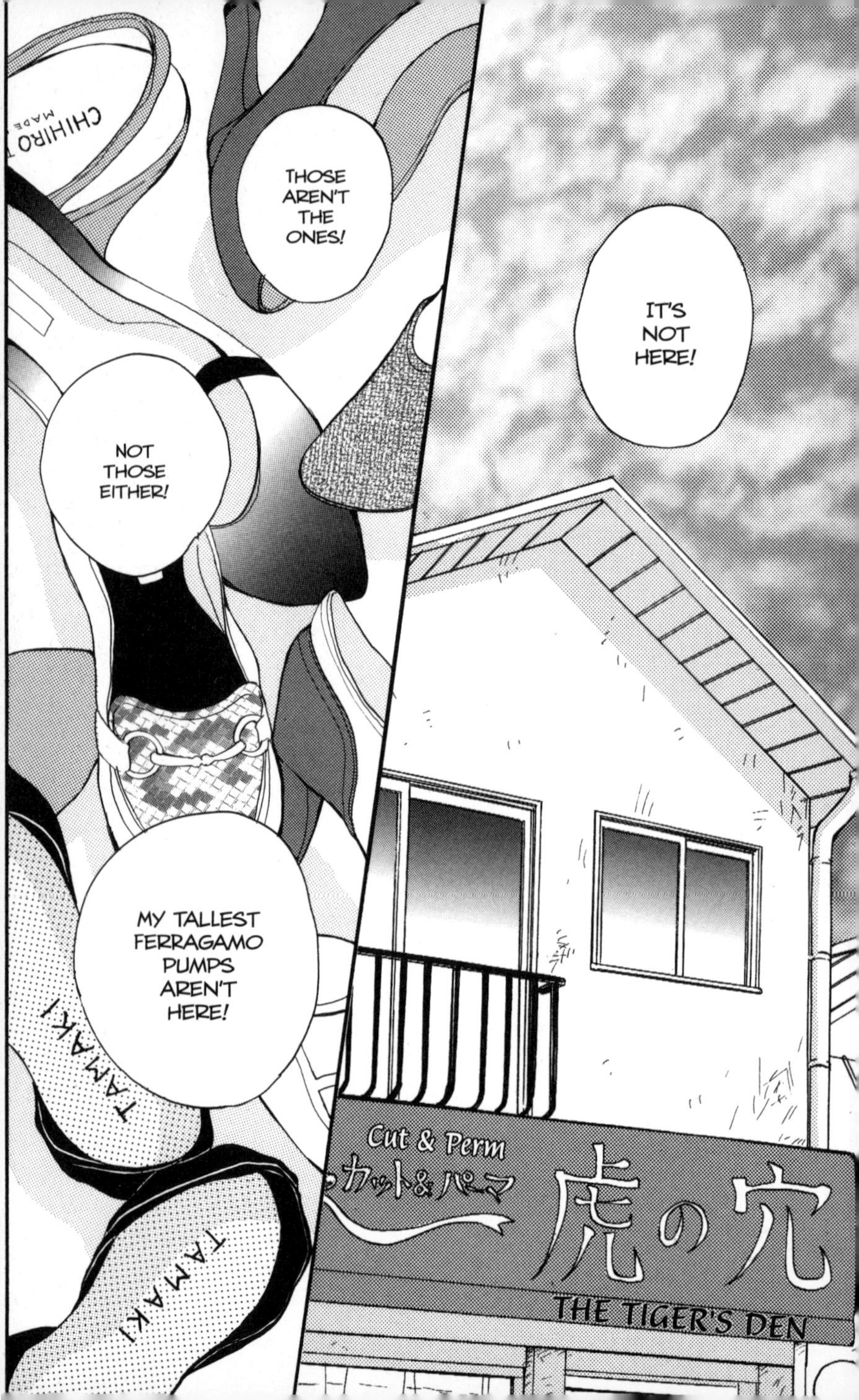
IT'S NOT HERE!
Cut & Perm
カット&パーマ
虎の穴
THE TIGER'S DEN
THOSE AREN'T THE ONES!
NOT THOSE EITHER!
MY TALLEST FERRAGAMO PUMPS AREN'T HERE!
TAMAKI
TAMAKI

OH... I'M GOING TO BE LATE FOR THE RECEPTION. WHY NOW?!

WHERE COULD THEY...?

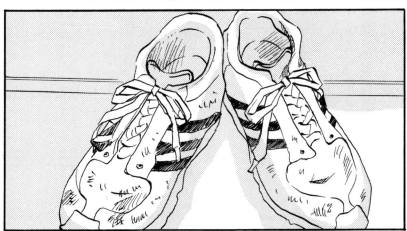

IT COULDN'T POSSIBLY BE... THAT IDIOT, MICHIKO.

...
...

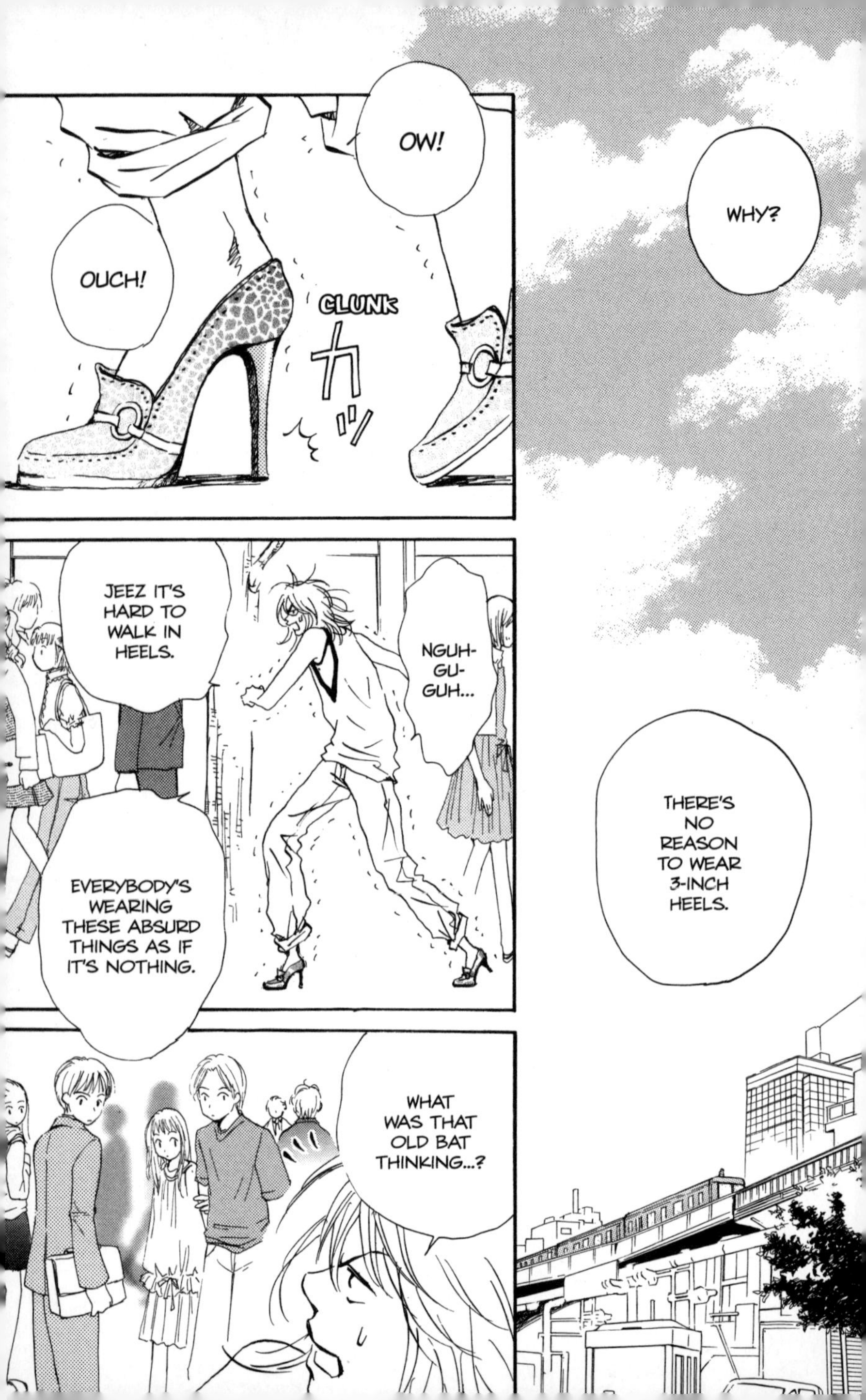
WHY?
THERE'S NO REASON TO WEAR 3-INCH HEELS.
OW!
OUCH!
CLUNK
カッ
NGUH-GU-GUH...
JEEZ IT'S HARD TO WALK IN HEELS.
EVERYBODY'S WEARING THESE ABSURD THINGS AS IF IT'S NOTHING.
WHAT WAS THAT OLD BAT THINKING...?

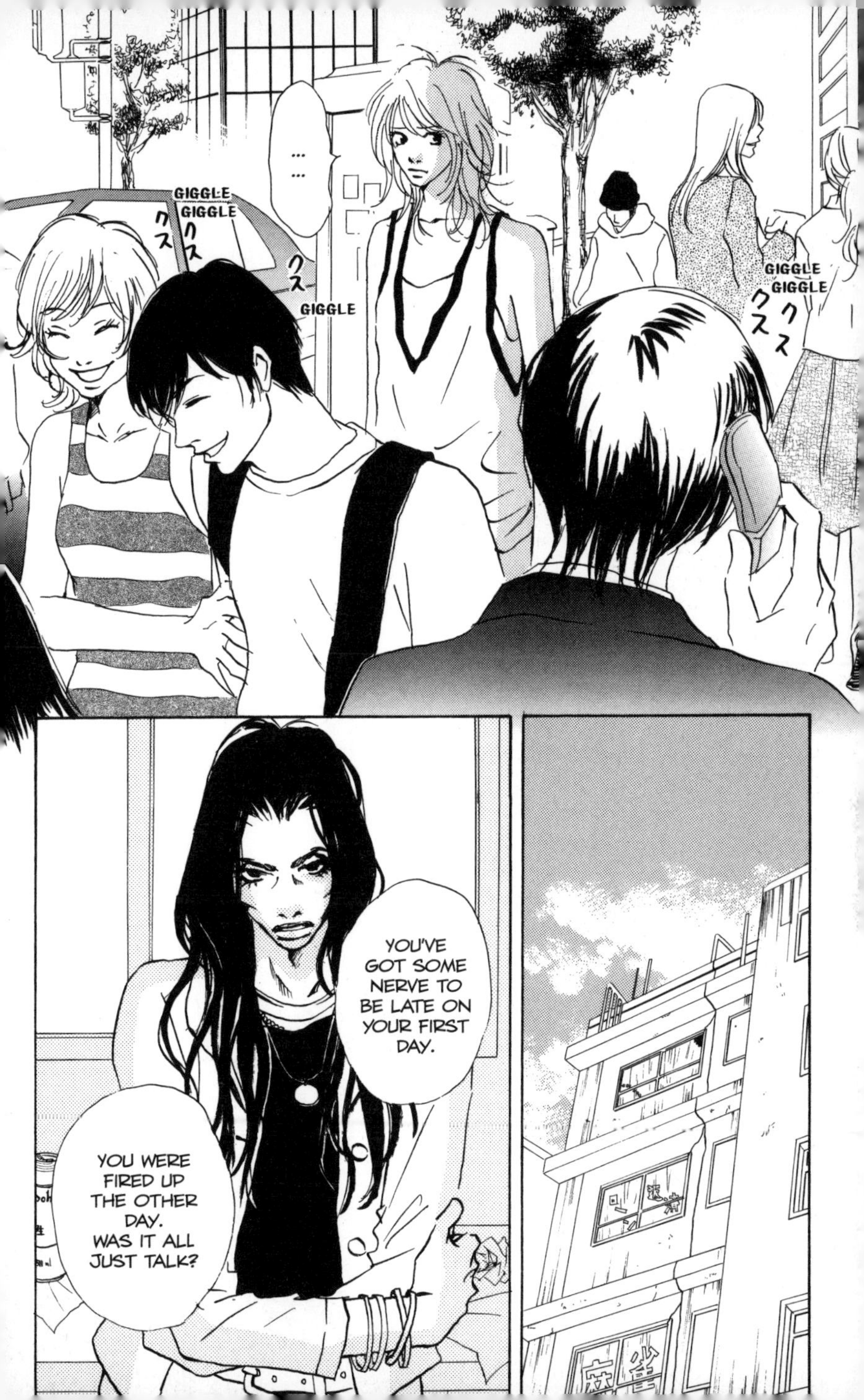

GIGGLE GIGGLE
クスクス
...
...
GIGGLE GIGGLE
クスクス
クス
GIGGLE
YOU'VE GOT SOME NERVE TO BE LATE ON YOUR FIRST DAY.
YOU WERE FIRED UP THE OTHER DAY. WAS IT ALL JUST TALK?

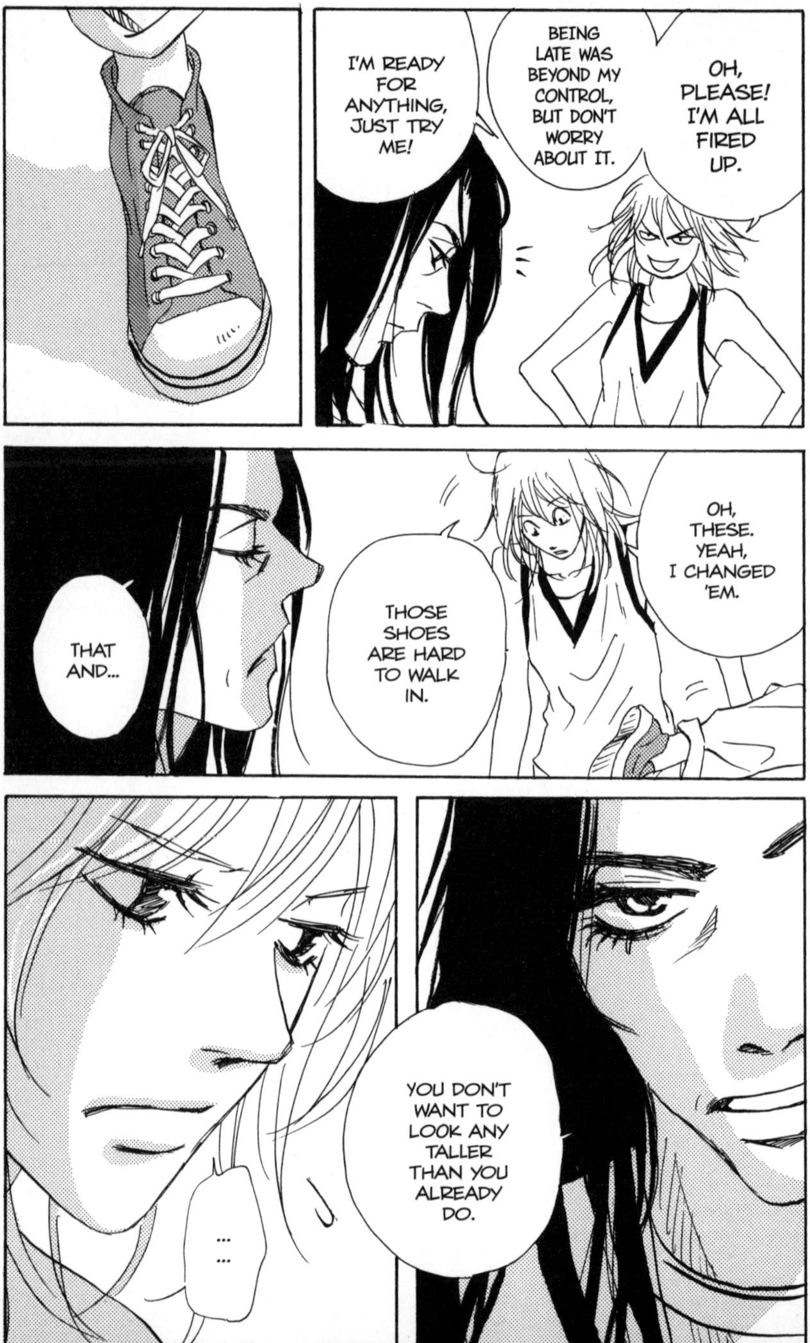
OH, PLEASE! I'M ALL FIRED UP.
BEING LATE WAS BEYOND MY CONTROL, BUT DON'T WORRY ABOUT IT.
I'M READY FOR ANYTHING, JUST TRY ME!
OH, THESE. YEAH, I CHANGED 'EM.
THOSE SHOES ARE HARD TO WALK IN.
THAT AND...
YOU DON'T WANT TO LOOK ANY TALLER THAN YOU ALREADY DO.
... ...

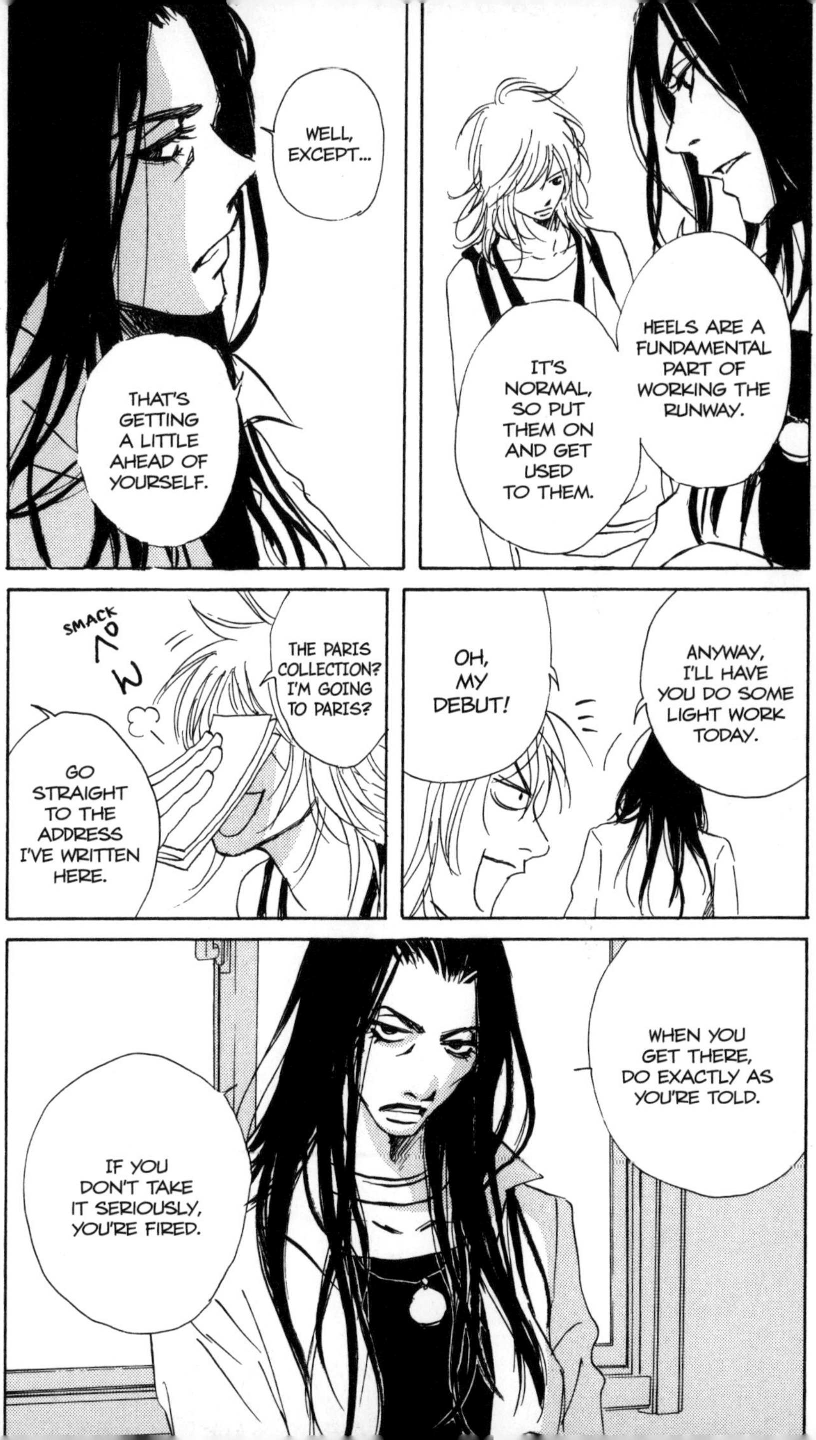
HEELS ARE A FUNDAMENTAL PART OF WORKING THE RUNWAY.
IT'S NORMAL, SO PUT THEM ON AND GET USED TO THEM.
WELL, EXCEPT...
THAT'S GETTING A LITTLE AHEAD OF YOURSELF.
ANYWAY, I'LL HAVE YOU DO SOME LIGHT WORK TODAY.
OH, MY DEBUT!
THE PARIS COLLECTION? I'M GOING TO PARIS?
SMACK
GO STRAIGHT TO THE ADDRESS I'VE WRITTEN HERE.
WHEN YOU GET THERE, DO EXACTLY AS YOU'RE TOLD.
IF YOU DON'T TAKE IT SERIOUSLY, YOU'RE FIRED.

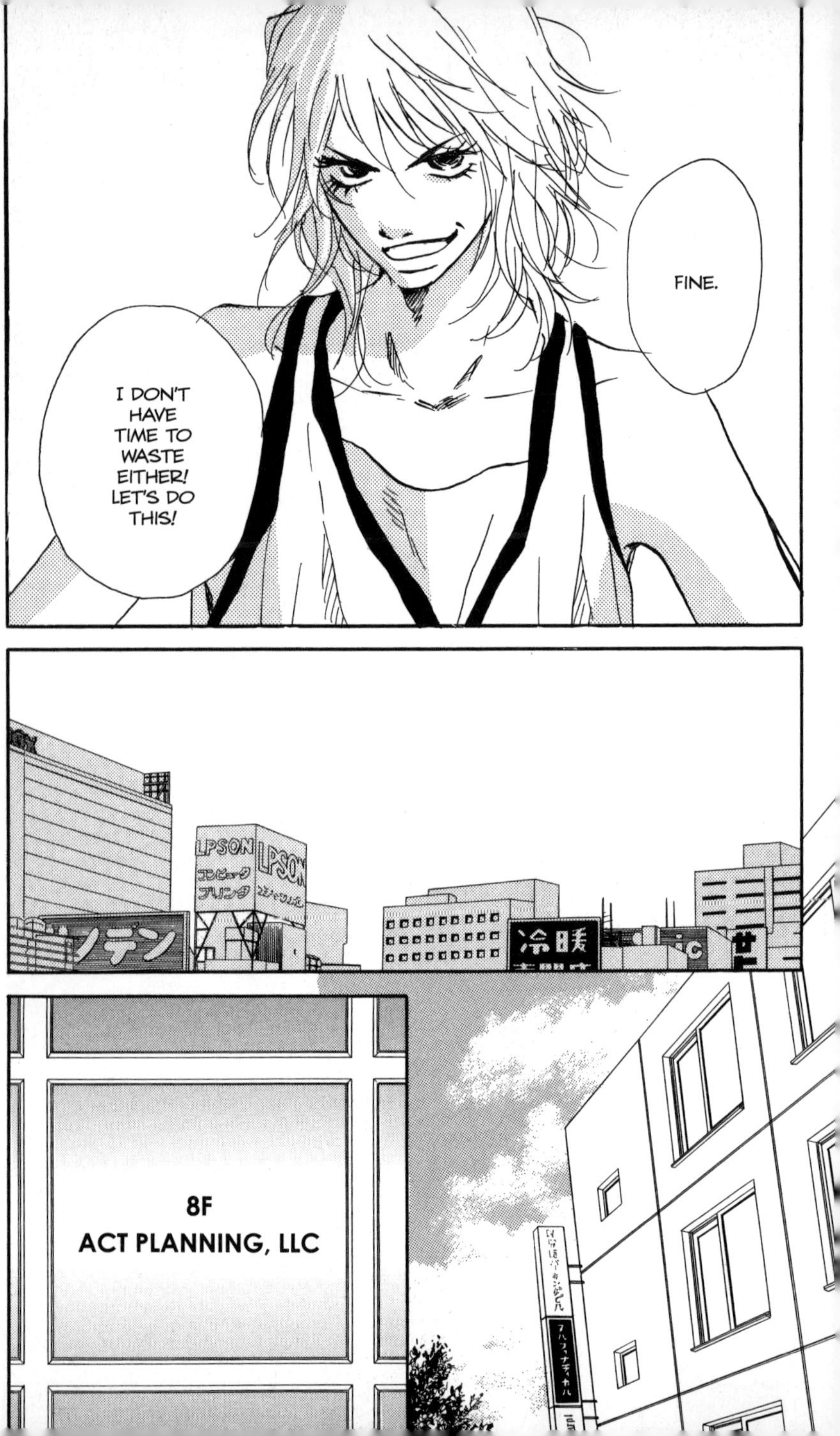
FINE.
I DON'T HAVE TIME TO WASTE EITHER! LET'S DO THIS!
LPSON
8F
ACT PLANNING, LLC

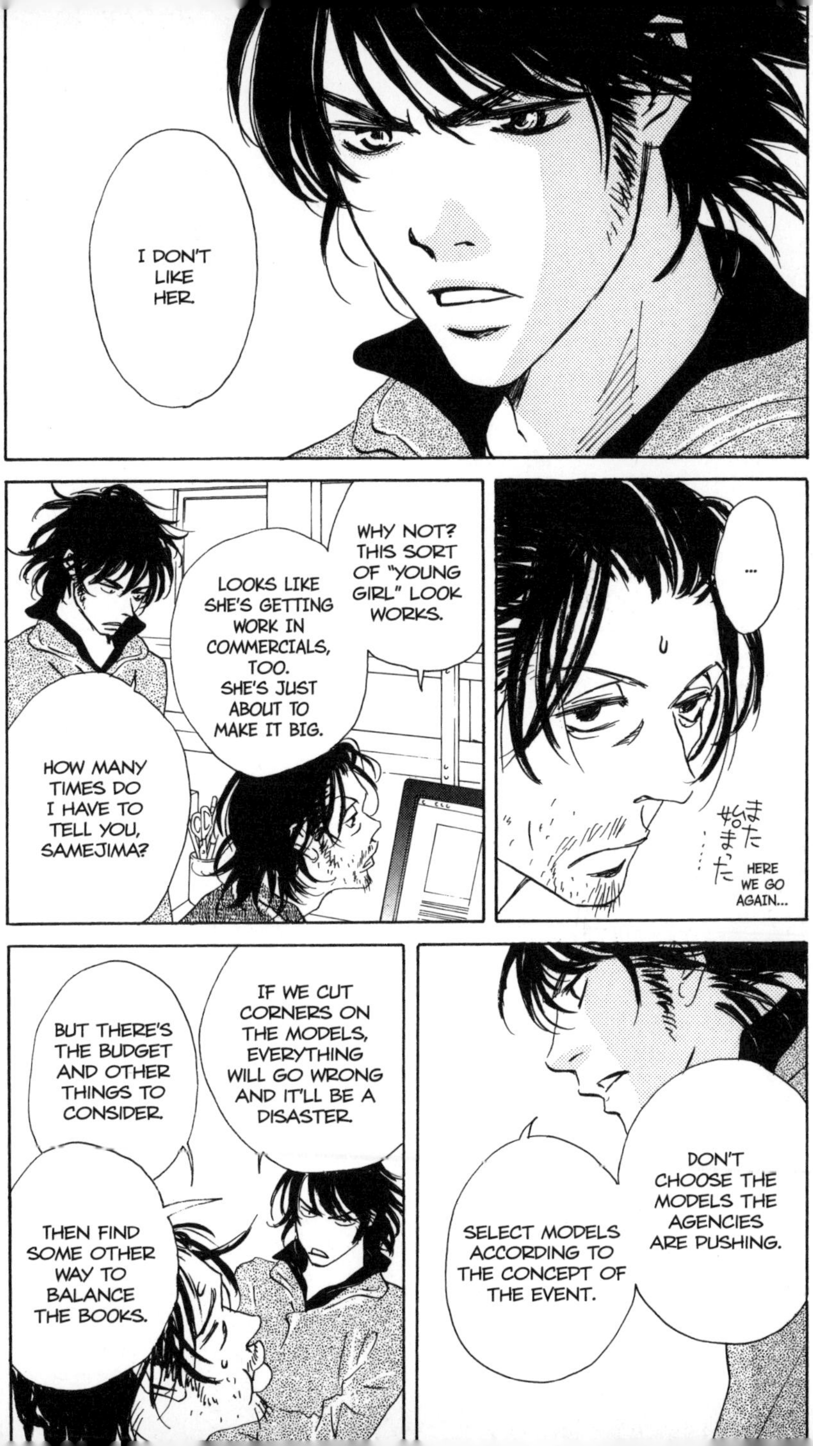
I DON'T LIKE HER.
...
また始まった……
HERE WE GO AGAIN...
WHY NOT? THIS SORT OF "YOUNG GIRL" LOOK WORKS.
LOOKS LIKE SHE'S GETTING WORK IN COMMERCIALS, TOO. SHE'S JUST ABOUT TO MAKE IT BIG.
HOW MANY TIMES DO I HAVE TO TELL YOU, SAMEJIMA?
DON'T CHOOSE THE MODELS THE AGENCIES ARE PUSHING.
SELECT MODELS ACCORDING TO THE CONCEPT OF THE EVENT.
IF WE CUT CORNERS ON THE MODELS, EVERYTHING WILL GO WRONG AND IT'LL BE A DISASTER.
BUT THERE'S THE BUDGET AND OTHER THINGS TO CONSIDER.
THEN FIND SOME OTHER WAY TO BALANCE THE BOOKS.

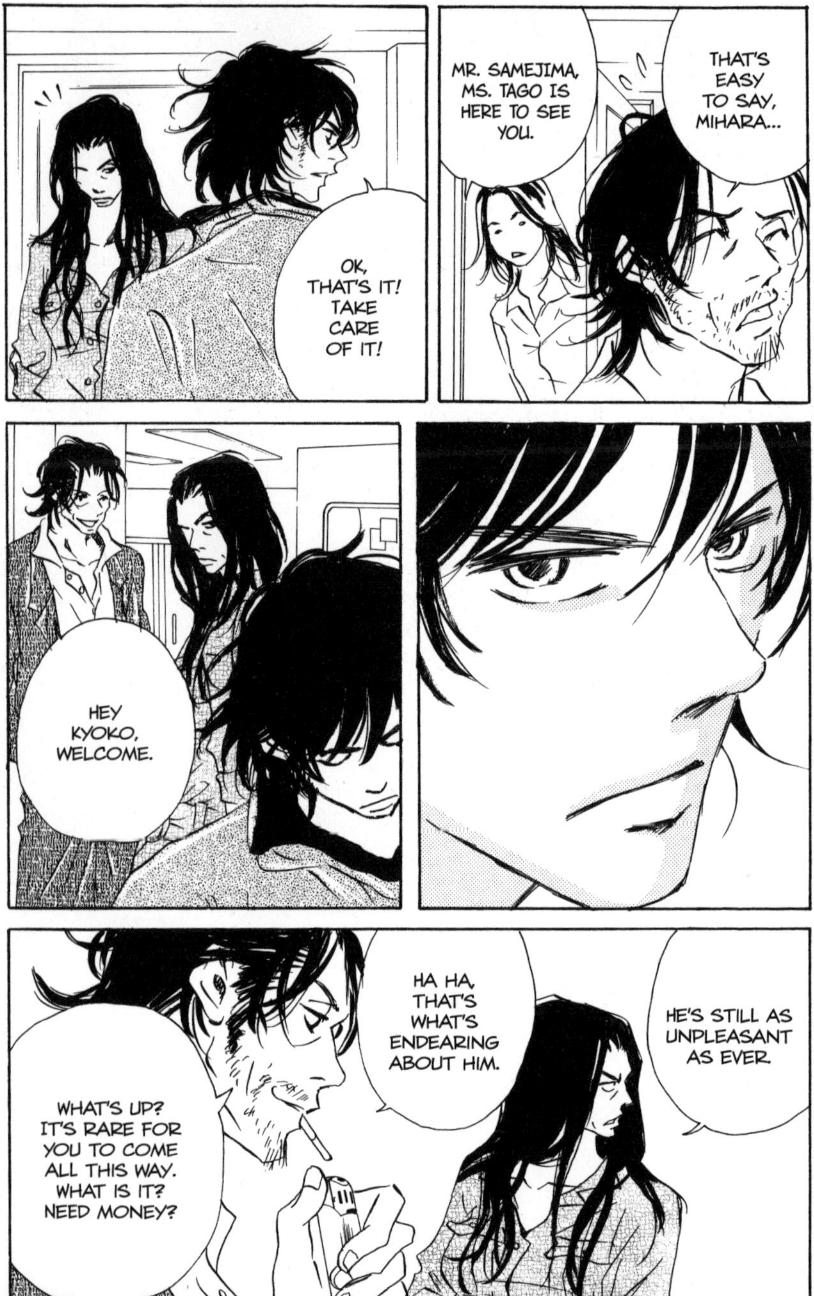
THAT'S EASY TO SAY, MIHARA...
MR. SAMEJIMA, MS. TAGO IS HERE TO SEE YOU.
OK, THAT'S IT! TAKE CARE OF IT!
HEY KYOKO, WELCOME.
HE'S STILL AS UNPLEASANT AS EVER.
HA HA, THAT'S WHAT'S ENDEARING ABOUT HIM.
WHAT'S UP? IT'S RARE FOR YOU TO COME ALL THIS WAY. WHAT IS IT? NEED MONEY?

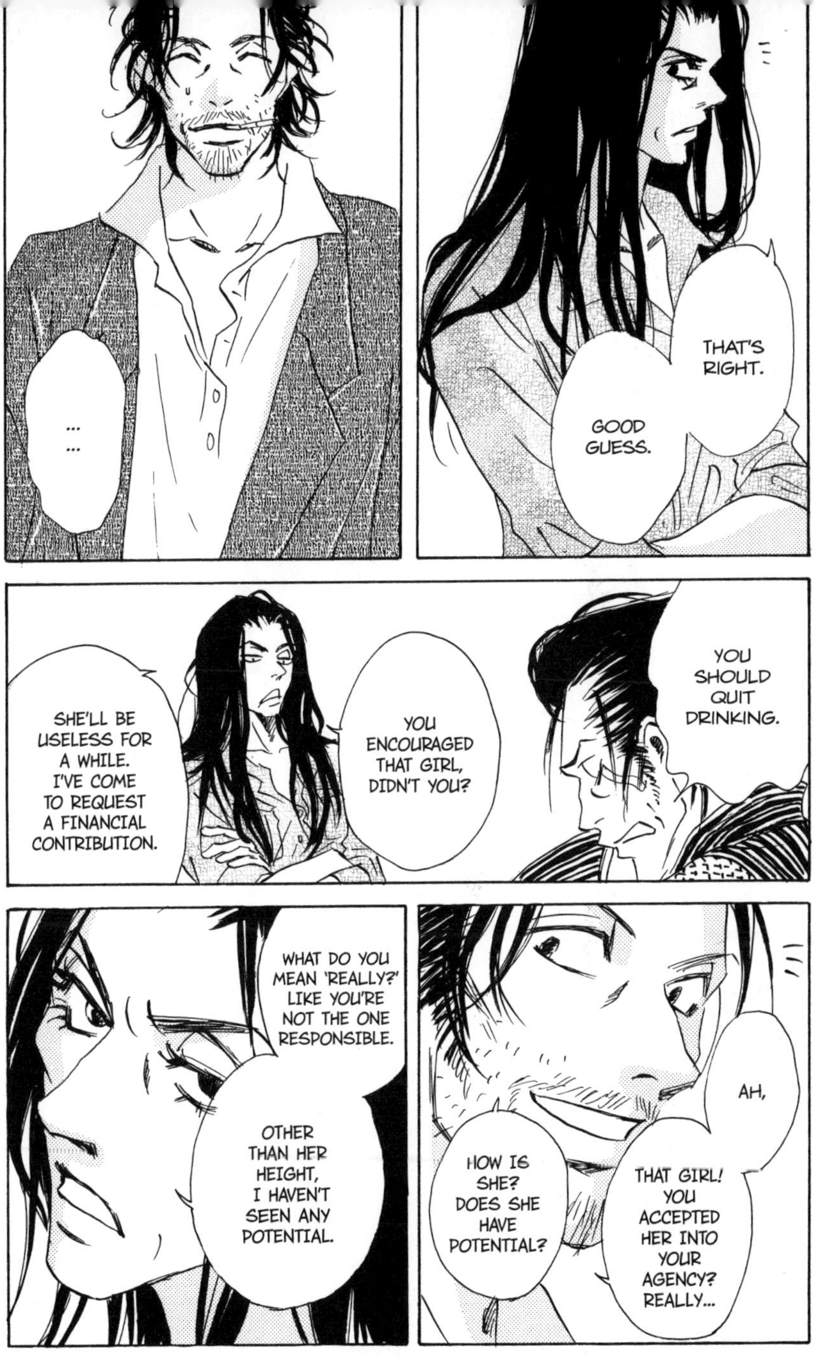
THAT'S RIGHT.
GOOD GUESS.
......
YOU SHOULD QUIT DRINKING.
YOU ENCOURAGED THAT GIRL, DIDN'T YOU?
SHE'LL BE USELESS FOR A WHILE. I'VE COME TO REQUEST A FINANCIAL CONTRIBUTION.
AH,
THAT GIRL! YOU ACCEPTED HER INTO YOUR AGENCY? REALLY...
HOW IS SHE? DOES SHE HAVE POTENTIAL?
WHAT DO YOU MEAN 'REALLY?' LIKE YOU'RE NOT THE ONE RESPONSIBLE.
OTHER THAN HER HEIGHT, I HAVEN'T SEEN ANY POTENTIAL.

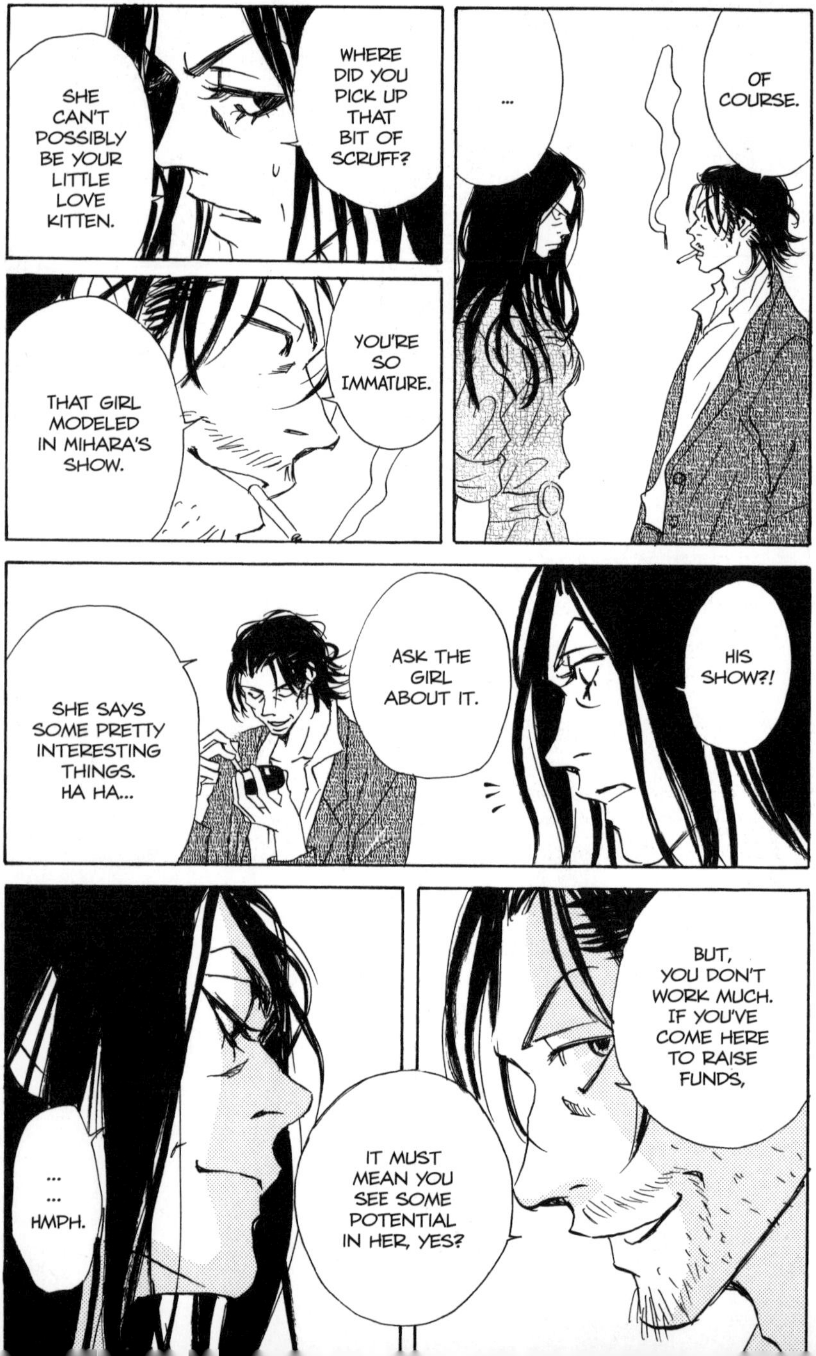
OF COURSE.
...
WHERE DID YOU PICK UP THAT BIT OF SCRUFF?
SHE CAN'T POSSIBLY BE YOUR LITTLE LOVE KITTEN.
YOU'RE SO IMMATURE.
THAT GIRL MODELED IN MIHARA'S SHOW.
HIS SHOW?!
ASK THE GIRL ABOUT IT.
SHE SAYS SOME PRETTY INTERESTING THINGS. HA HA...
BUT, YOU DON'T WORK MUCH. IF YOU'VE COME HERE TO RAISE FUNDS,
IT MUST MEAN YOU SEE SOME POTENTIAL IN HER, YES?
... ... HMPH.

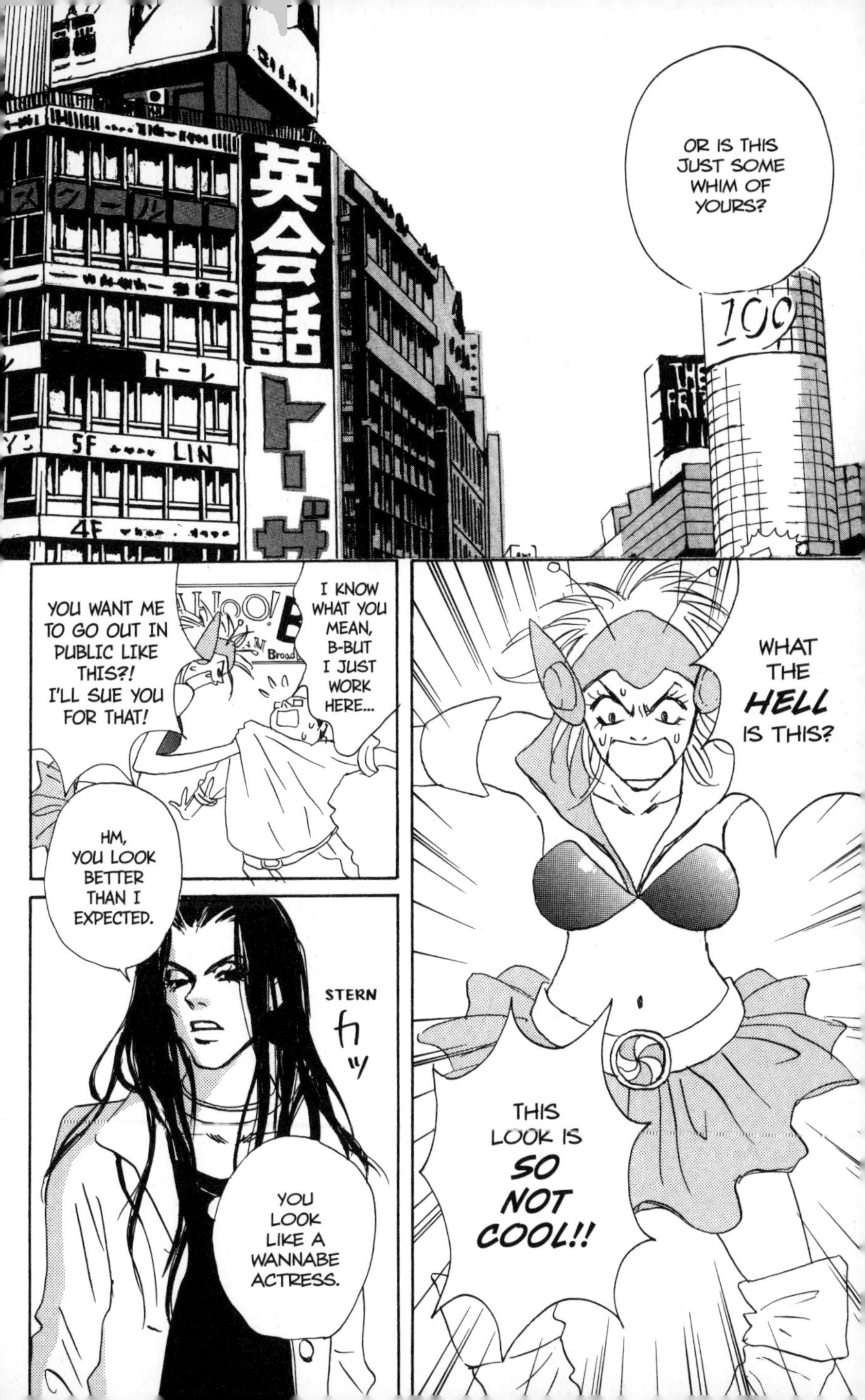

OR IS THIS JUST SOME WHIM OF YOURS?
WHAT THE **HELL** IS THIS?
THIS LOOK IS **SO NOT COOL!!**
YOU WANT ME TO GO OUT IN PUBLIC LIKE THIS?! I'LL SUE YOU FOR THAT!
I KNOW WHAT YOU MEAN, B-BUT I JUST WORK HERE...
HM, YOU LOOK BETTER THAN I EXPECTED.
STERN
カッ
YOU LOOK LIKE A WANNABE ACTRESS.

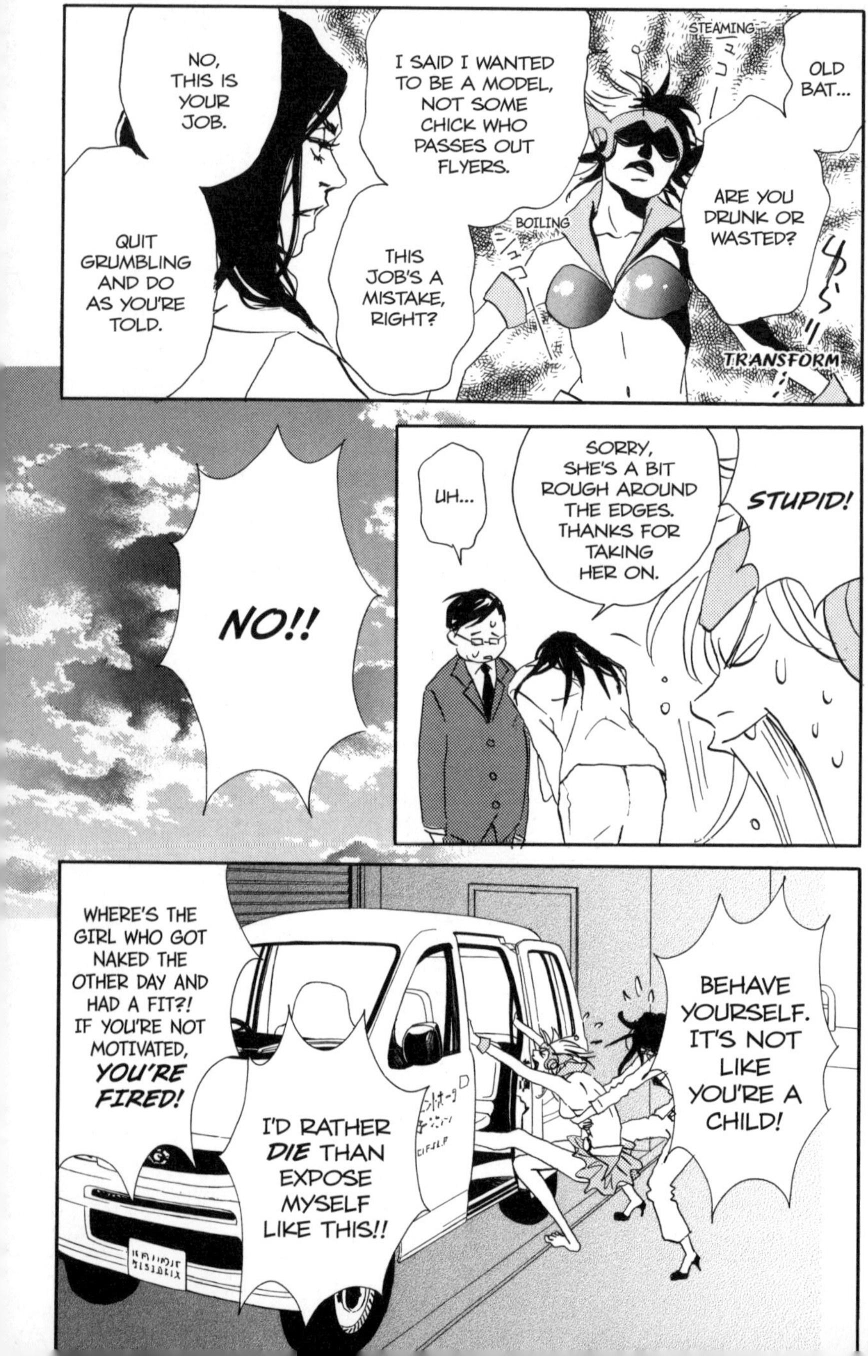
OLD BAT...
STEAMING
ARE YOU DRUNK OR WASTED?
TRANSFORM
I SAID I WANTED TO BE A MODEL, NOT SOME CHICK WHO PASSES OUT FLYERS.
BOILING
THIS JOB'S A MISTAKE, RIGHT?
NO, THIS IS YOUR JOB.
QUIT GRUMBLING AND DO AS YOU'RE TOLD.
STUPID!
SORRY, SHE'S A BIT ROUGH AROUND THE EDGES. THANKS FOR TAKING HER ON.
UH...
NO!!
BEHAVE YOURSELF. IT'S NOT LIKE YOU'RE A CHILD!
WHERE'S THE GIRL WHO GOT NAKED THE OTHER DAY AND HAD A FIT?! IF YOU'RE NOT MOTIVATED, YOU'RE FIRED!
I'D RATHER DIE THAN EXPOSE MYSELF LIKE THIS!!

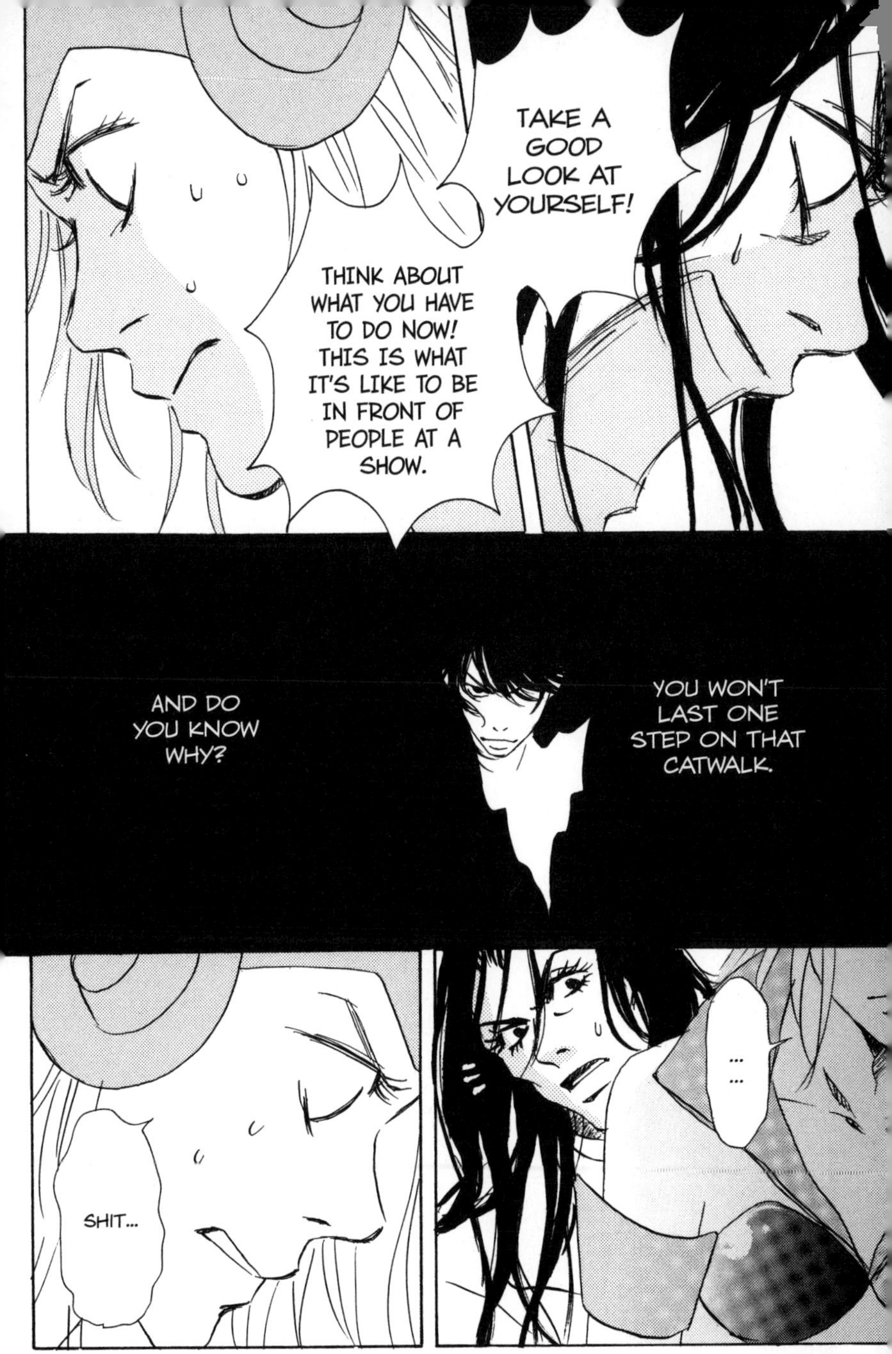
TAKE A GOOD LOOK AT YOURSELF!
THINK ABOUT WHAT YOU HAVE TO DO NOW! THIS IS WHAT IT'S LIKE TO BE IN FRONT OF PEOPLE AT A SHOW.
YOU WON'T LAST ONE STEP ON THAT CATWALK.
AND DO YOU KNOW WHY?
......
SHIT...

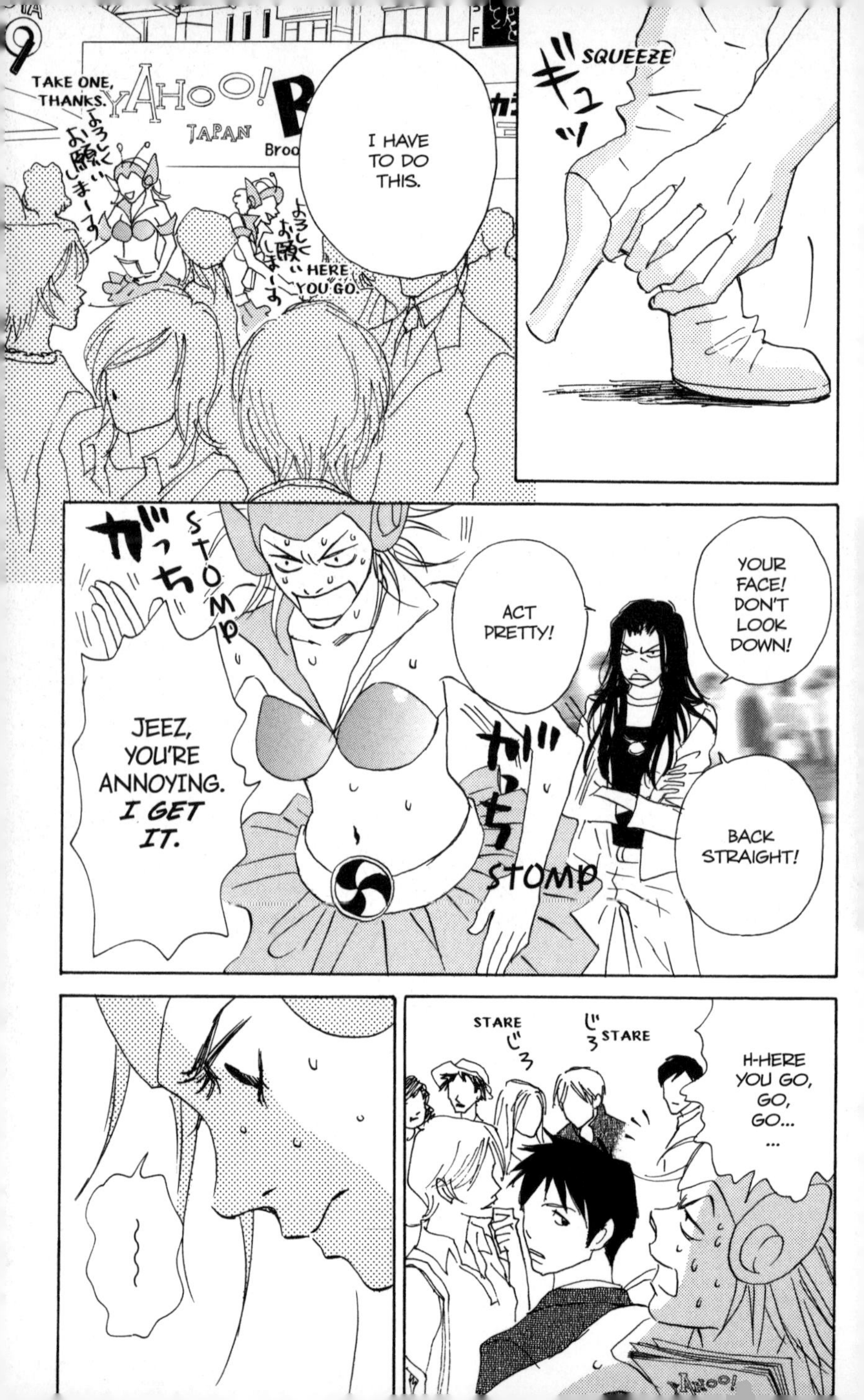
ギュッ
SQUEEZE
I HAVE TO DO THIS.
HERE YOU GO.
よろしくお願いしまーす
YAHOO! JAPAN
TAKE ONE, THANKS.
よろしくお願いしまーす
YOUR FACE! DON'T LOOK DOWN!
BACK STRAIGHT!
ACT PRETTY!
がっち
STOMP
がっち
STOMP
JEEZ, YOU'RE ANNOYING. *I GET IT.*
H-HERE YOU GO, GO, GO... ...
じろ
STARE
じろ
STARE
YAHOO!

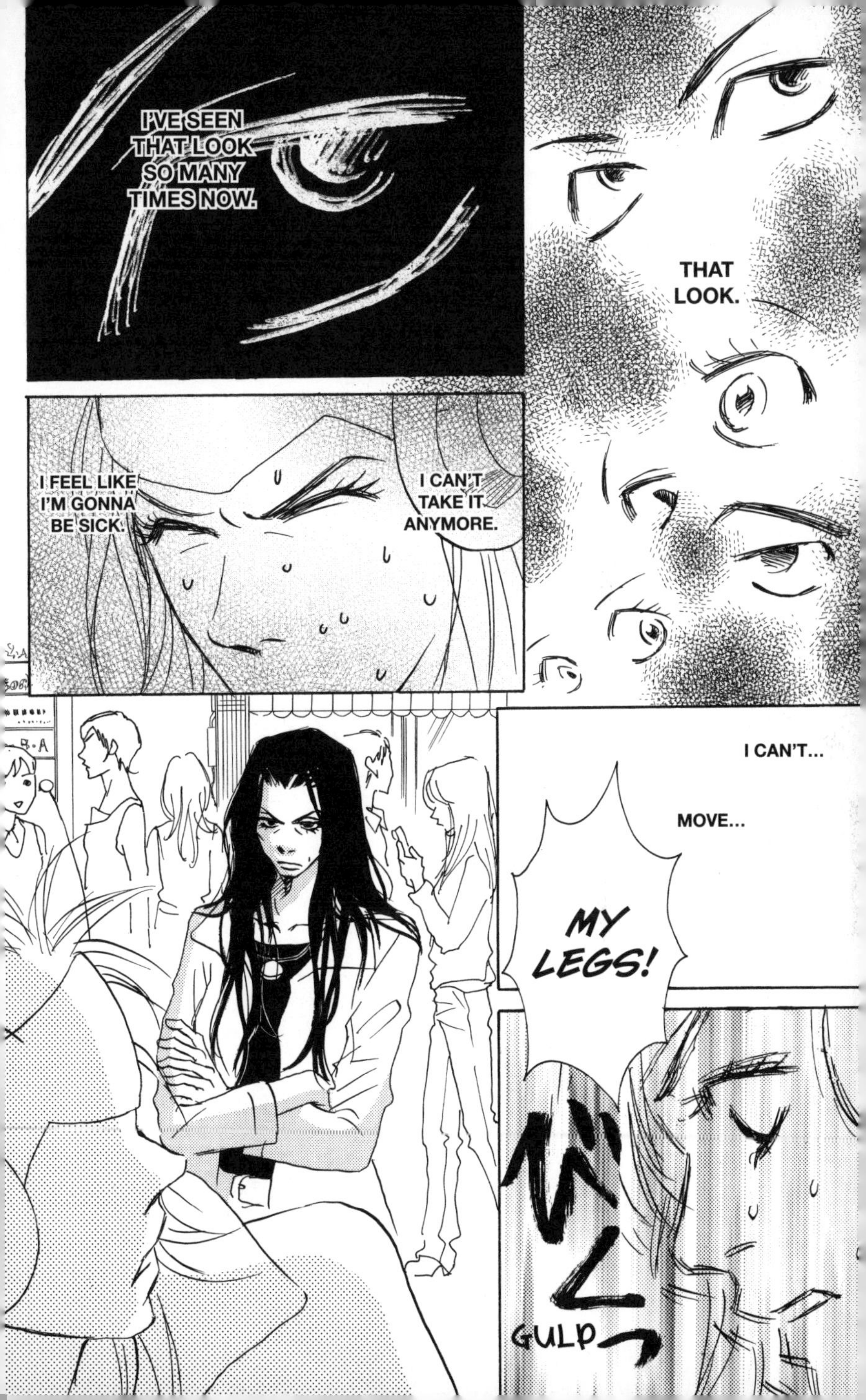
THAT LOOK.
I'VE SEEN THAT LOOK SO MANY TIMES NOW.
I CAN'T TAKE IT ANYMORE.
I FEEL LIKE I'M GONNA BE SICK.
I CAN'T...
MOVE...
MY LEGS!
GULP

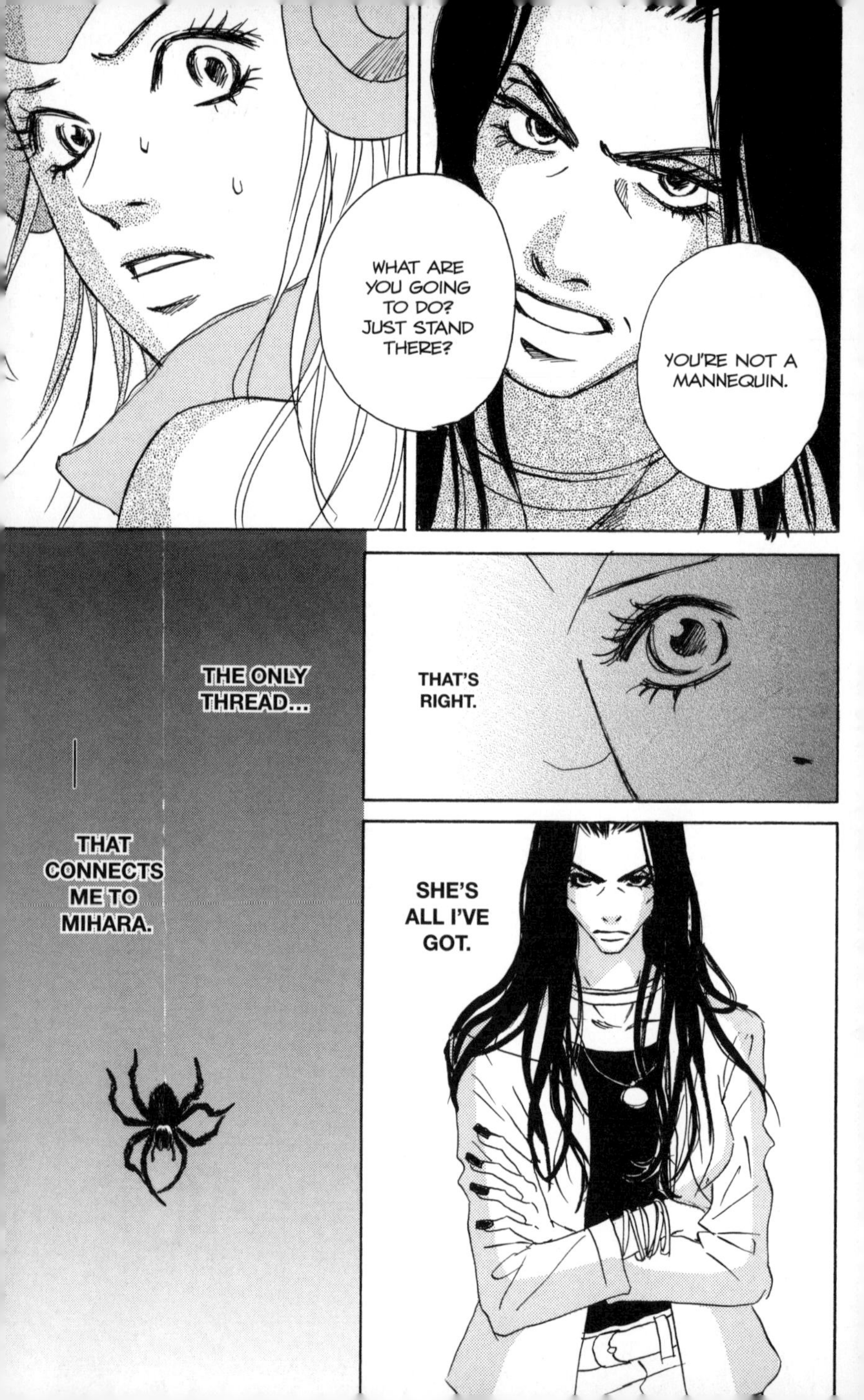
WHAT ARE YOU GOING TO DO? JUST STAND THERE?
YOU'RE NOT A MANNEQUIN.
THAT'S RIGHT.
SHE'S ALL I'VE GOT.
THE ONLY THREAD...
THAT CONNECTS ME TO MIHARA.

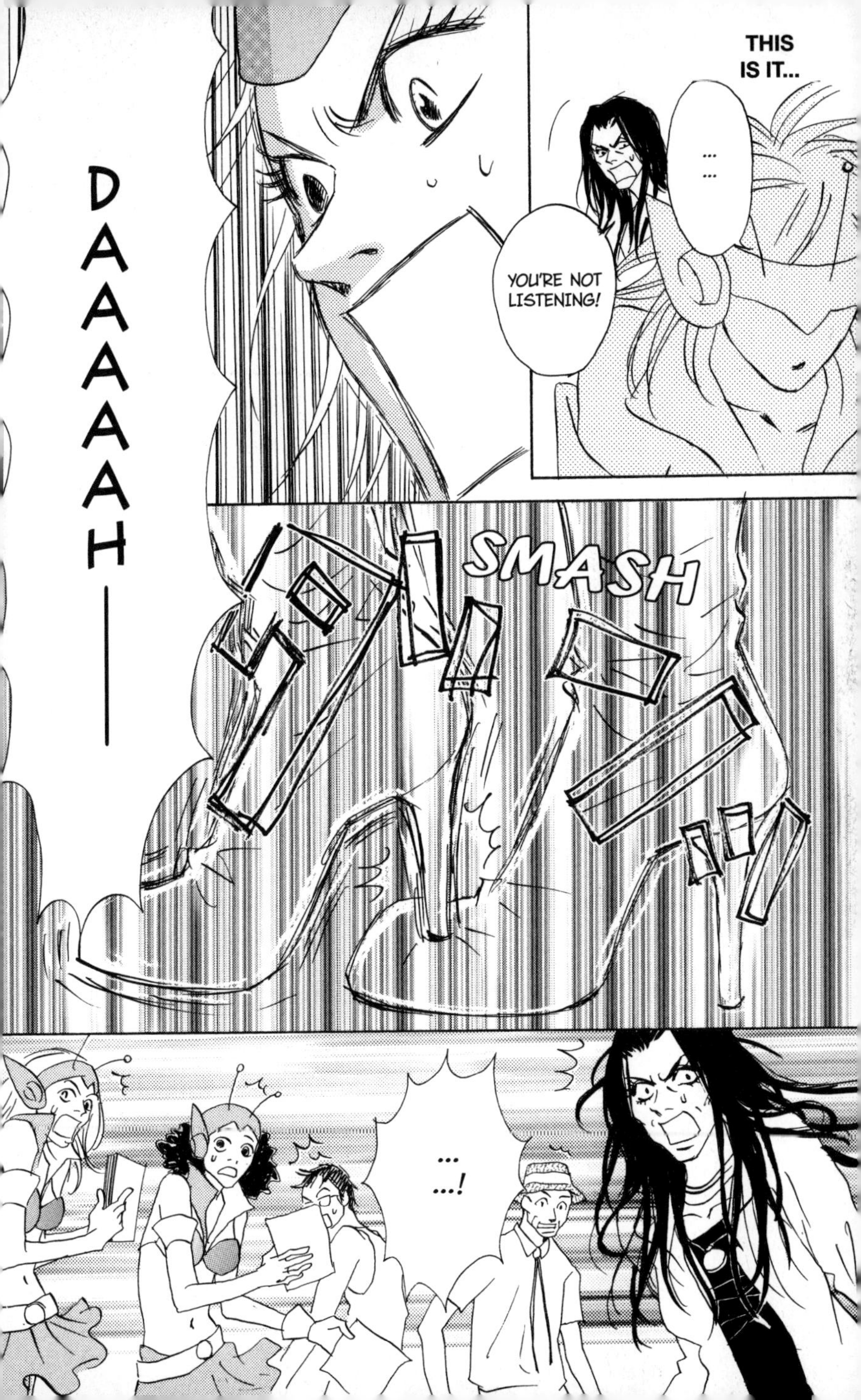
THIS IS IT...
... ...
YOU'RE NOT LISTENING!
DAAAAAH—
SMASH
... ...!

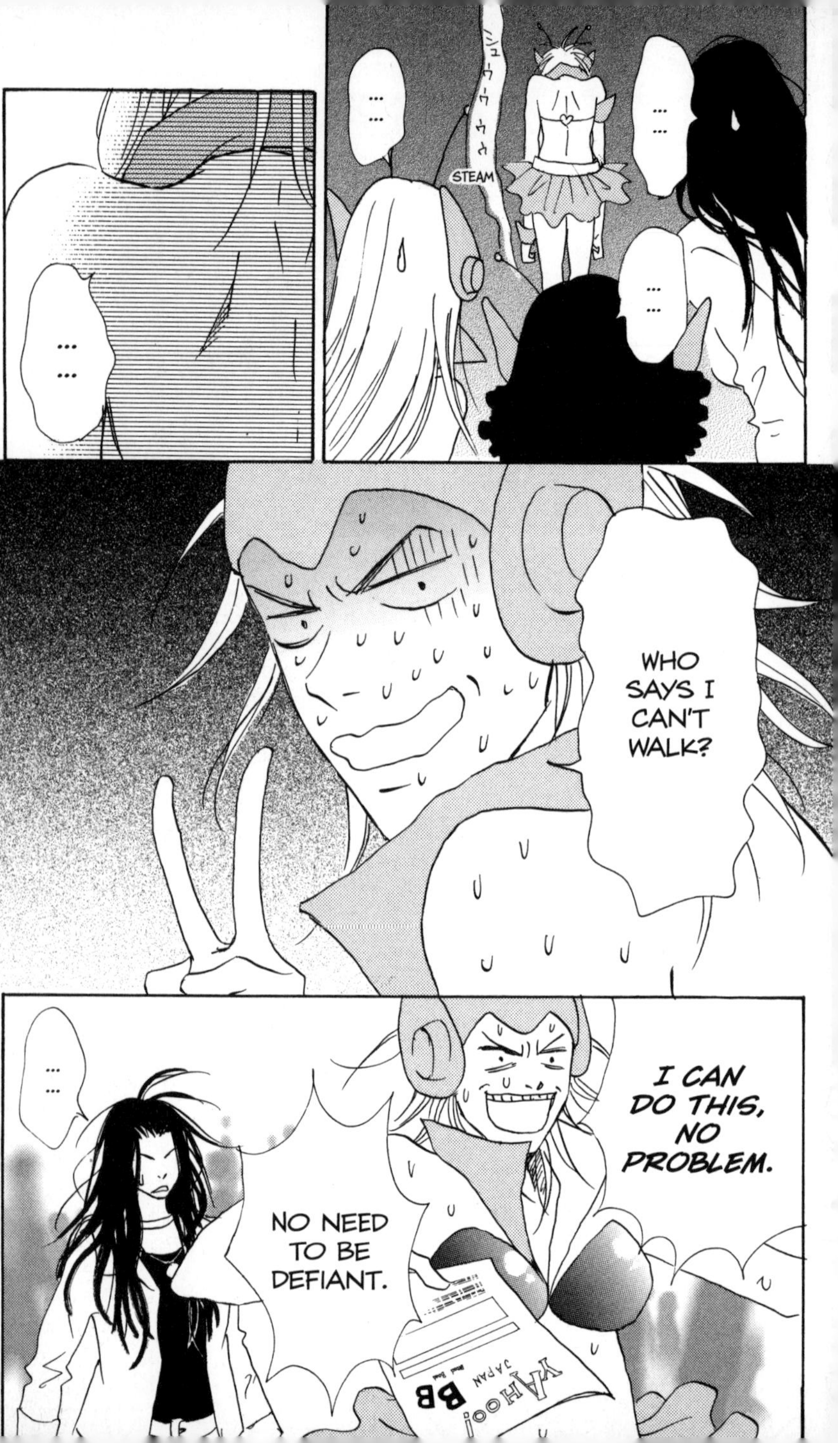

... ...
... ...
STEAM
... ...
... ...
WHO SAYS I CAN'T WALK?
I CAN DO THIS, NO PROBLEM.
NO NEED TO BE DEFIANT.
... ...

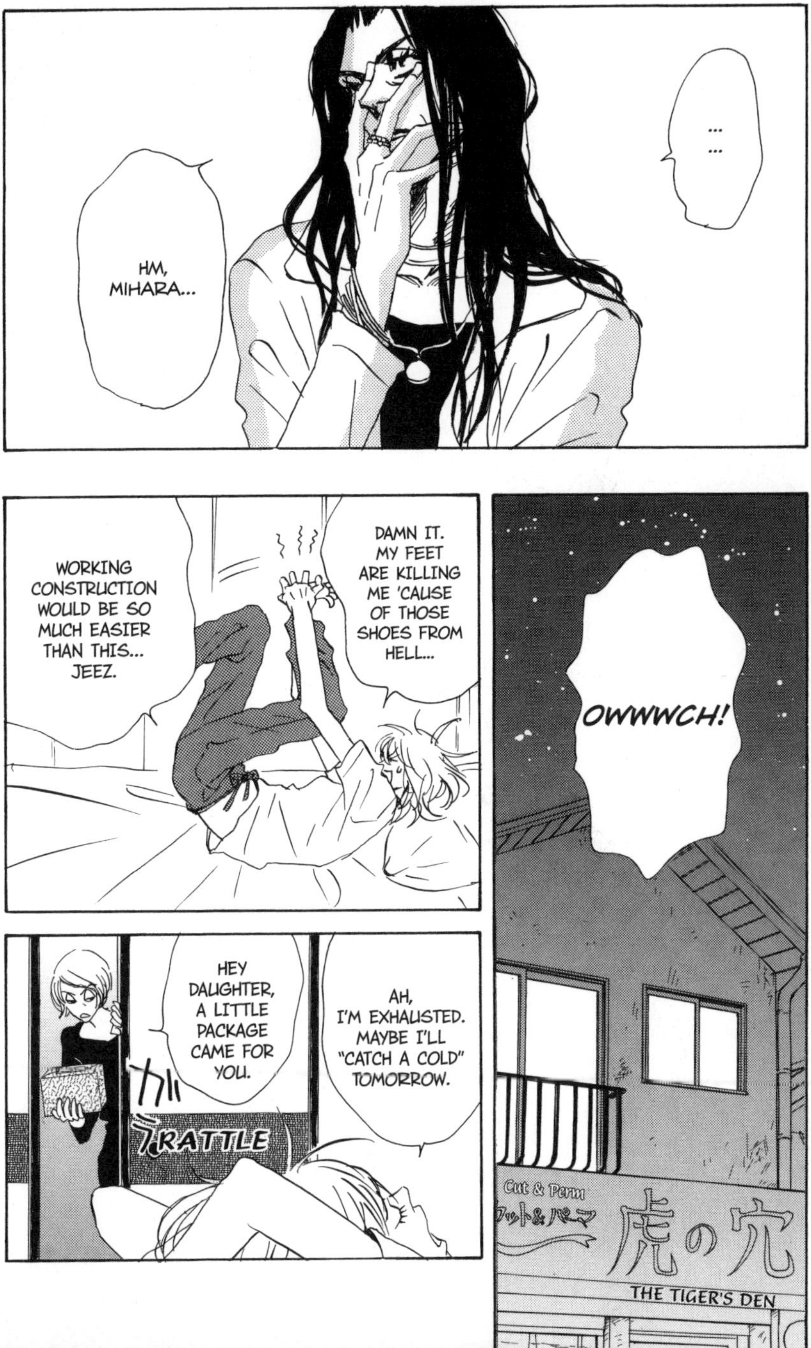

...
...
HM, MIHARA...
OWWWCH!
Cut & Perm
虎の穴
THE TIGER'S DEN
DAMN IT. MY FEET ARE KILLING ME 'CAUSE OF THOSE SHOES FROM HELL...
WORKING CONSTRUCTION WOULD BE SO MUCH EASIER THAN THIS... JEEZ.
AH, I'M EXHAUSTED. MAYBE I'LL "CATCH A COLD" TOMORROW.
HEY DAUGHTER, A LITTLE PACKAGE CAME FOR YOU.
RATTLE

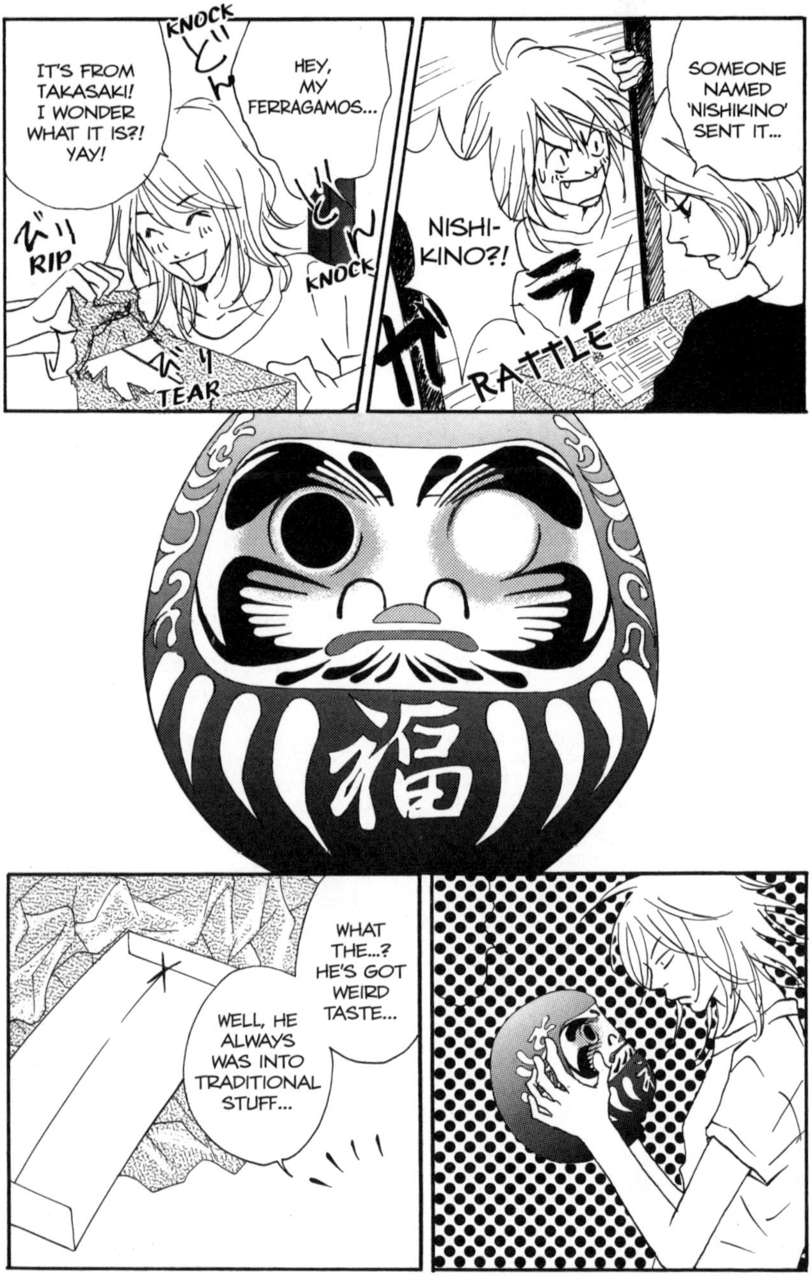
SOMEONE NAMED 'NISHIKINO' SENT IT...
NISHI-KINO?!
RATTLE
KNOCK
HEY, MY FERRAGAMOS...
IT'S FROM TAKASAKI! I WONDER WHAT IT IS?! YAY!
KNOCK
RIP
TEAR
福
WHAT THE...? HE'S GOT WEIRD TASTE...
WELL, HE ALWAYS WAS INTO TRADITIONAL STUFF...

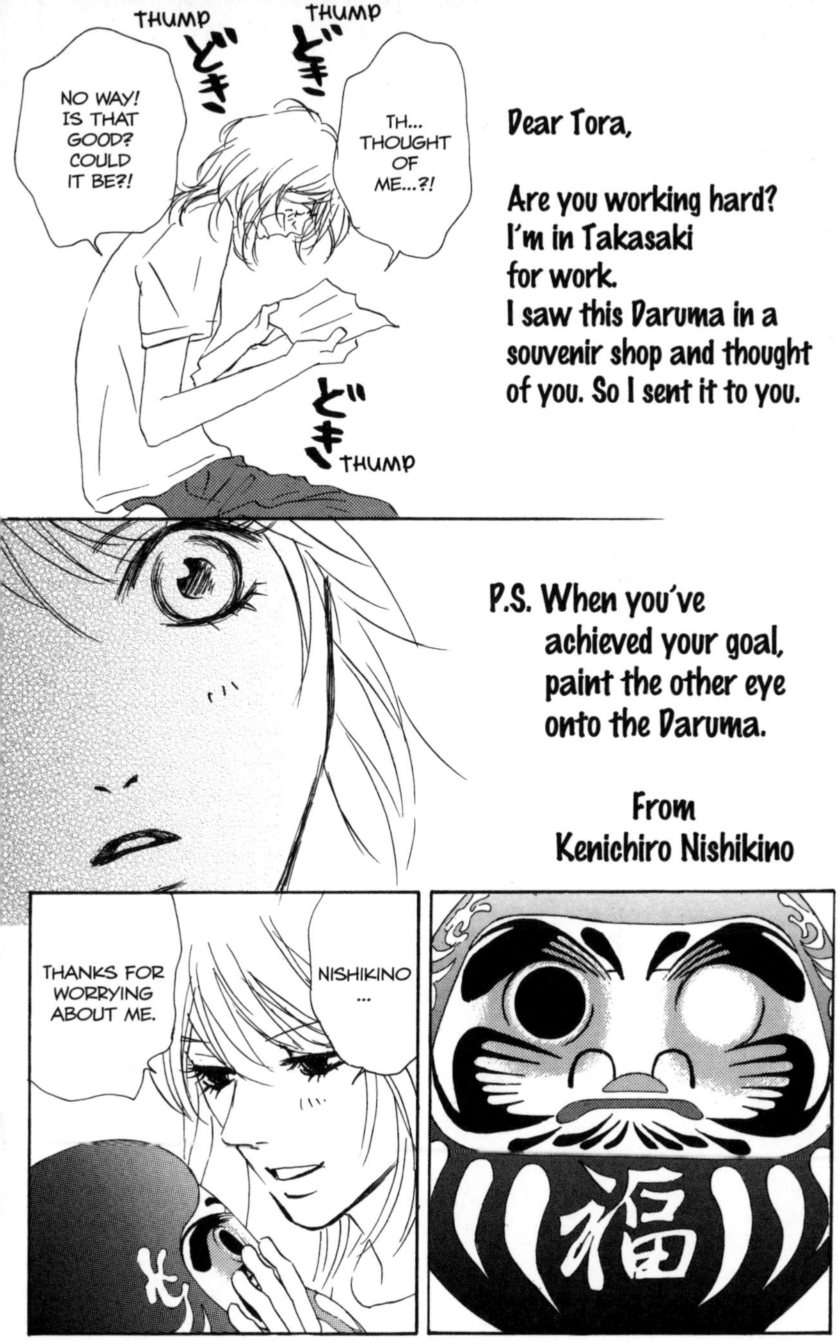
Dear Tora,
Are you working hard? I'm in Takasaki for work. I saw this Daruma in a souvenir shop and thought of you. So I sent it to you.
THUMP
TH... THOUGHT OF ME...?!
THUMP
NO WAY! IS THAT GOOD? COULD IT BE?!
THUMP
P.S. When you've achieved your goal, paint the other eye onto the Daruma.
From Kenichiro Nishikino
NISHIKINO ...
THANKS FOR WORRYING ABOUT ME.

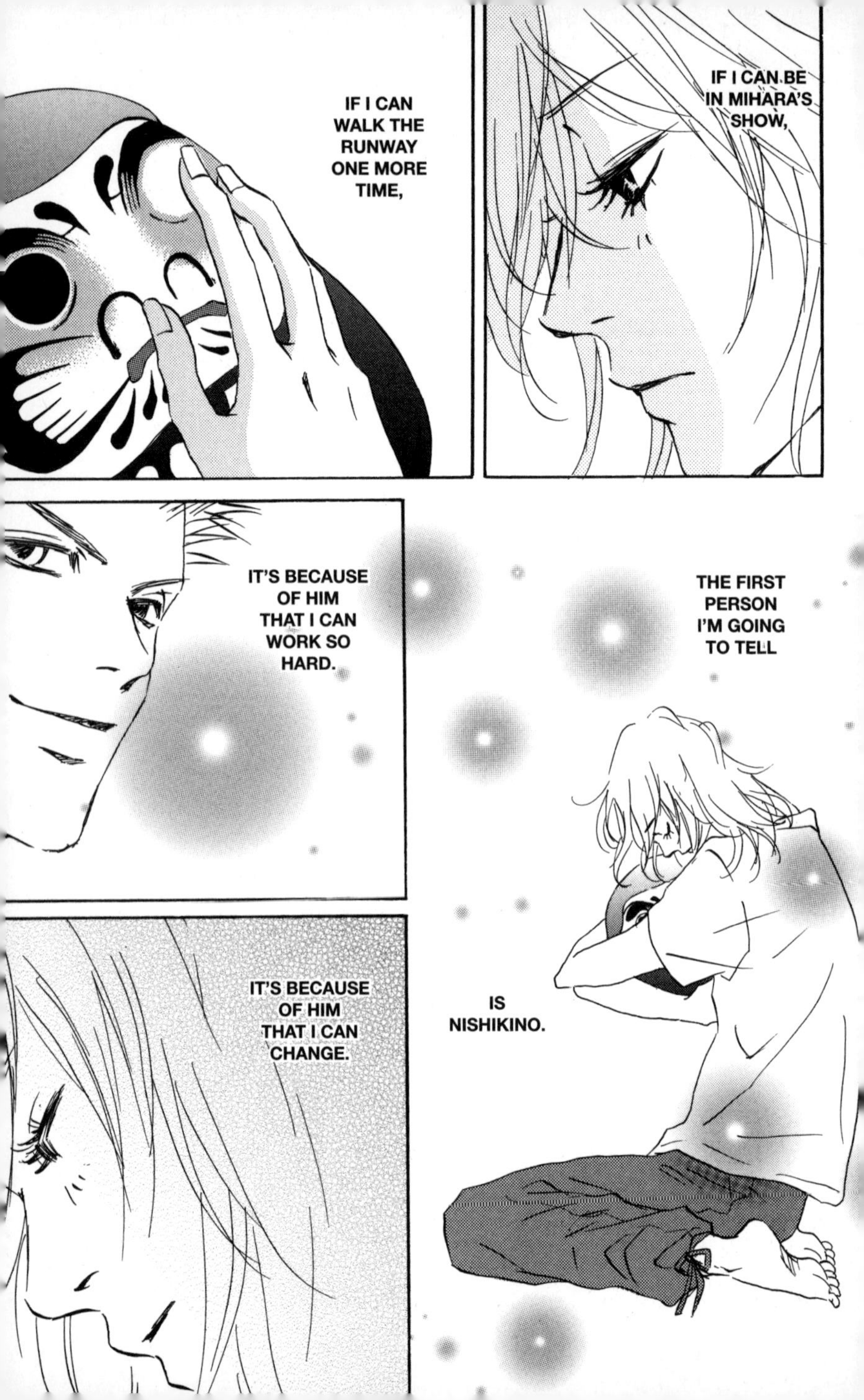
IF I CAN BE IN MIHARA'S SHOW,
IF I CAN WALK THE RUNWAY ONE MORE TIME,
THE FIRST PERSON I'M GOING TO TELL
IS NISHIKINO.
IT'S BECAUSE OF HIM THAT I CAN WORK SO HARD.
IT'S BECAUSE OF HIM THAT I CAN CHANGE.

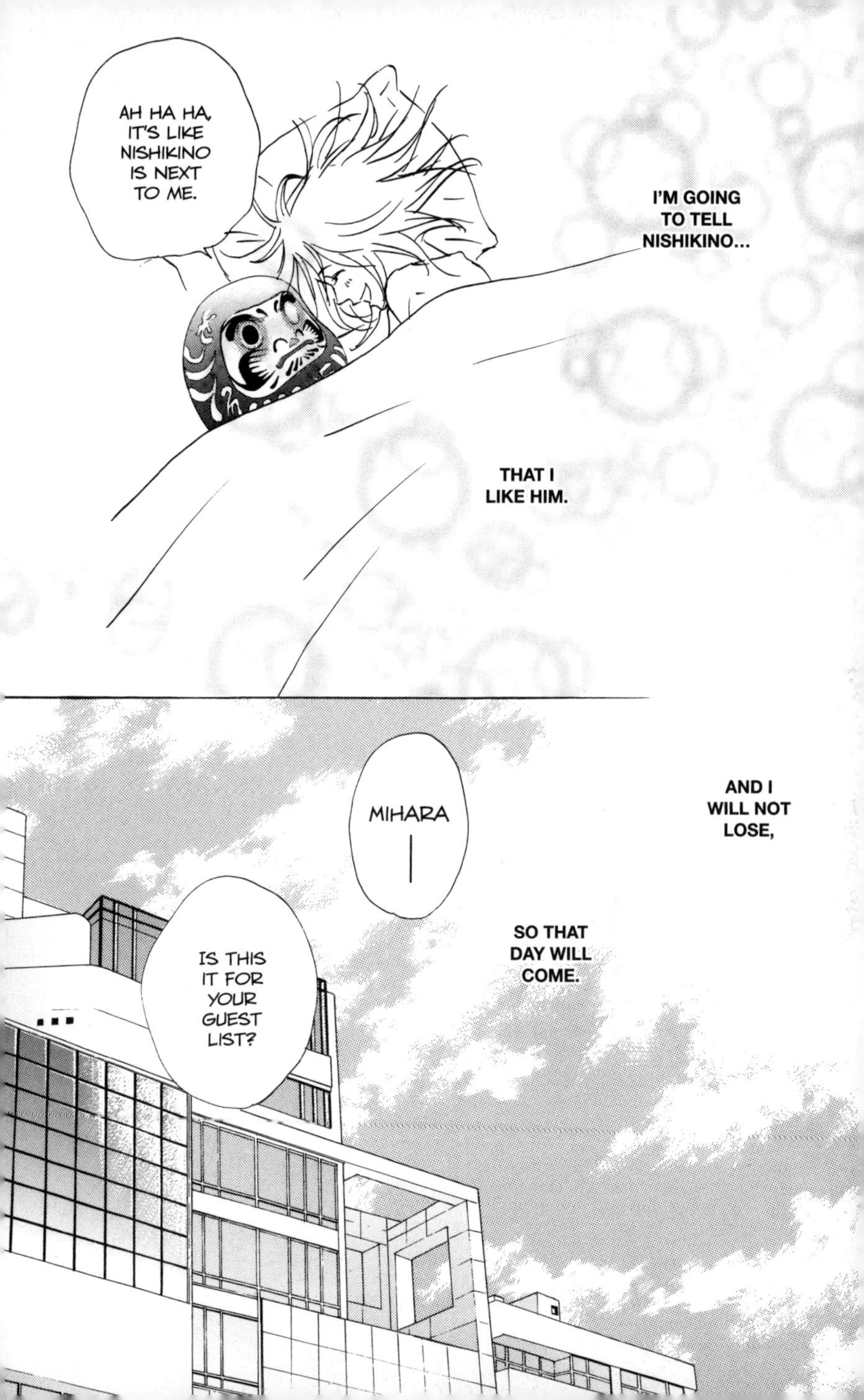
I'M GOING TO TELL NISHIKINO...
AH HA HA, IT'S LIKE NISHIKINO IS NEXT TO ME.
THAT I LIKE HIM.
AND I WILL NOT LOSE,
SO THAT DAY WILL COME.
MIHARA—
IS THIS IT FOR YOUR GUEST LIST?

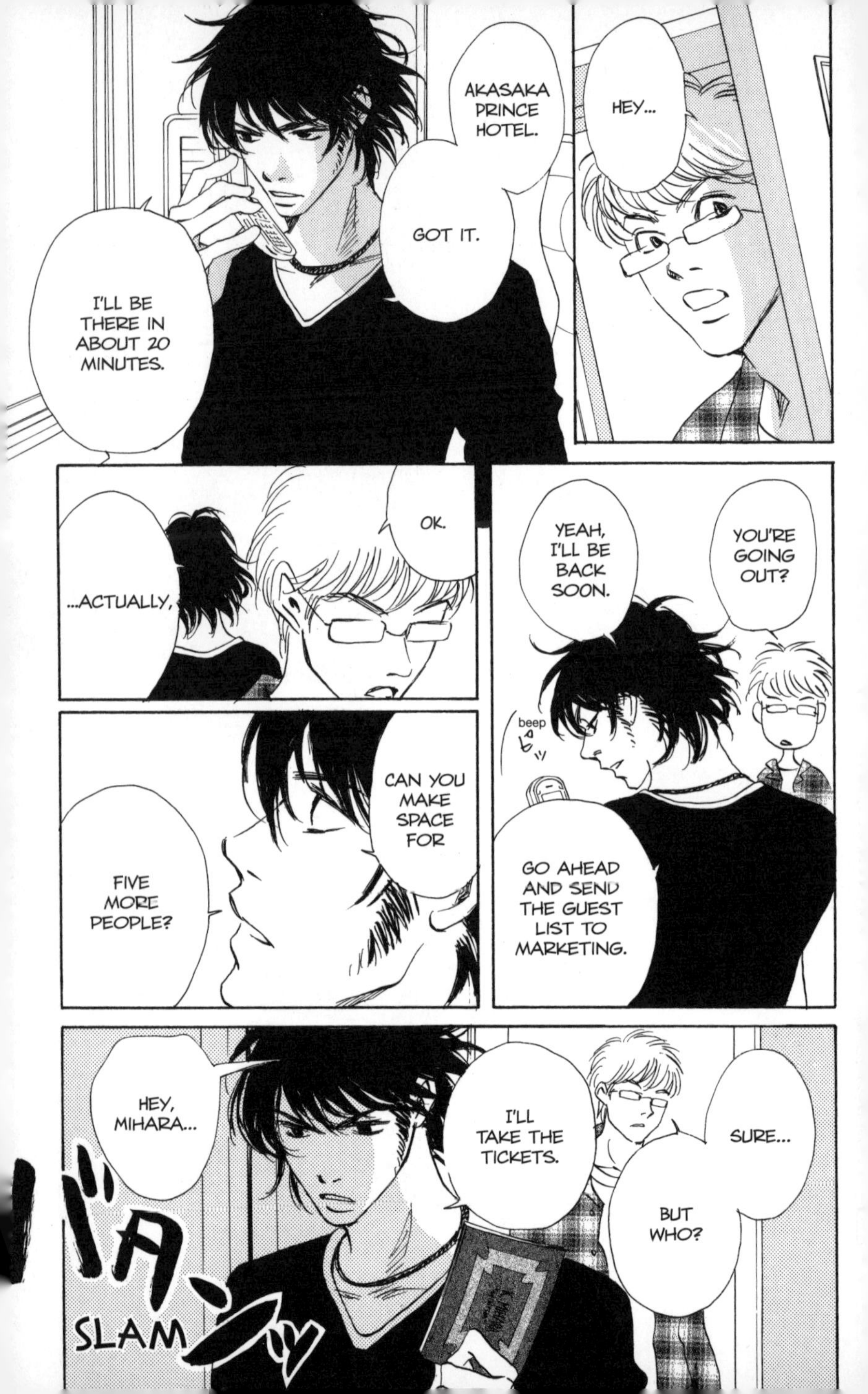
HEY...
AKASAKA PRINCE HOTEL.
GOT IT.
I'LL BE THERE IN ABOUT 20 MINUTES.
YOU'RE GOING OUT?
YEAH, I'LL BE BACK SOON.
beep
ピッ
GO AHEAD AND SEND THE GUEST LIST TO MARKETING.
OK.
...ACTUALLY,
CAN YOU MAKE SPACE FOR
FIVE MORE PEOPLE?
SURE...
BUT WHO?
I'LL TAKE THE TICKETS.
HEY, MIHARA...
バン
SLAM

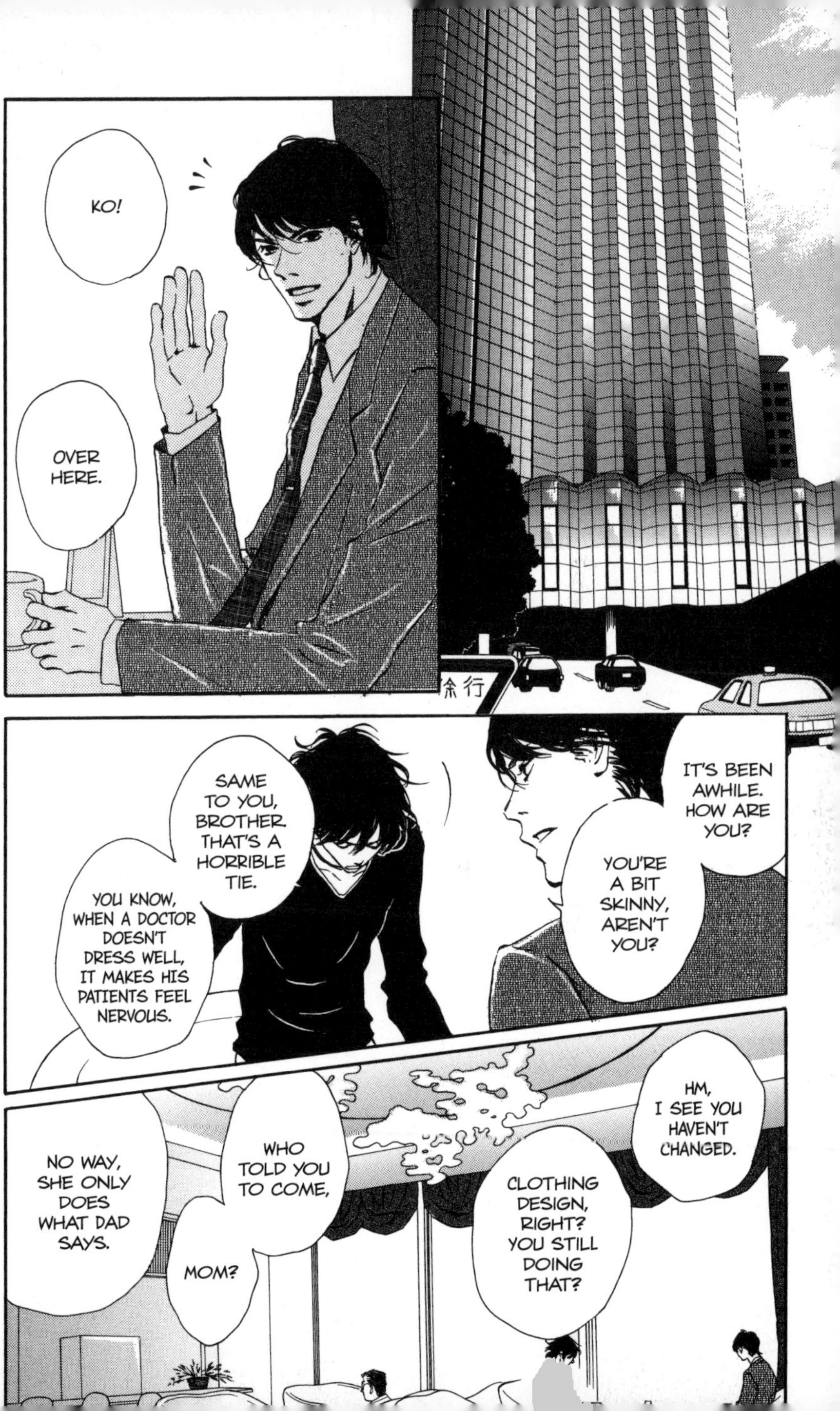
徐行
KO!
OVER HERE.
IT'S BEEN AWHILE. HOW ARE YOU?
YOU'RE A BIT SKINNY, AREN'T YOU?
SAME TO YOU, BROTHER. THAT'S A HORRIBLE TIE.
YOU KNOW, WHEN A DOCTOR DOESN'T DRESS WELL, IT MAKES HIS PATIENTS FEEL NERVOUS.
HM, I SEE YOU HAVEN'T CHANGED.
CLOTHING DESIGN, RIGHT? YOU STILL DOING THAT?
WHO TOLD YOU TO COME,
MOM?
NO WAY, SHE ONLY DOES WHAT DAD SAYS.

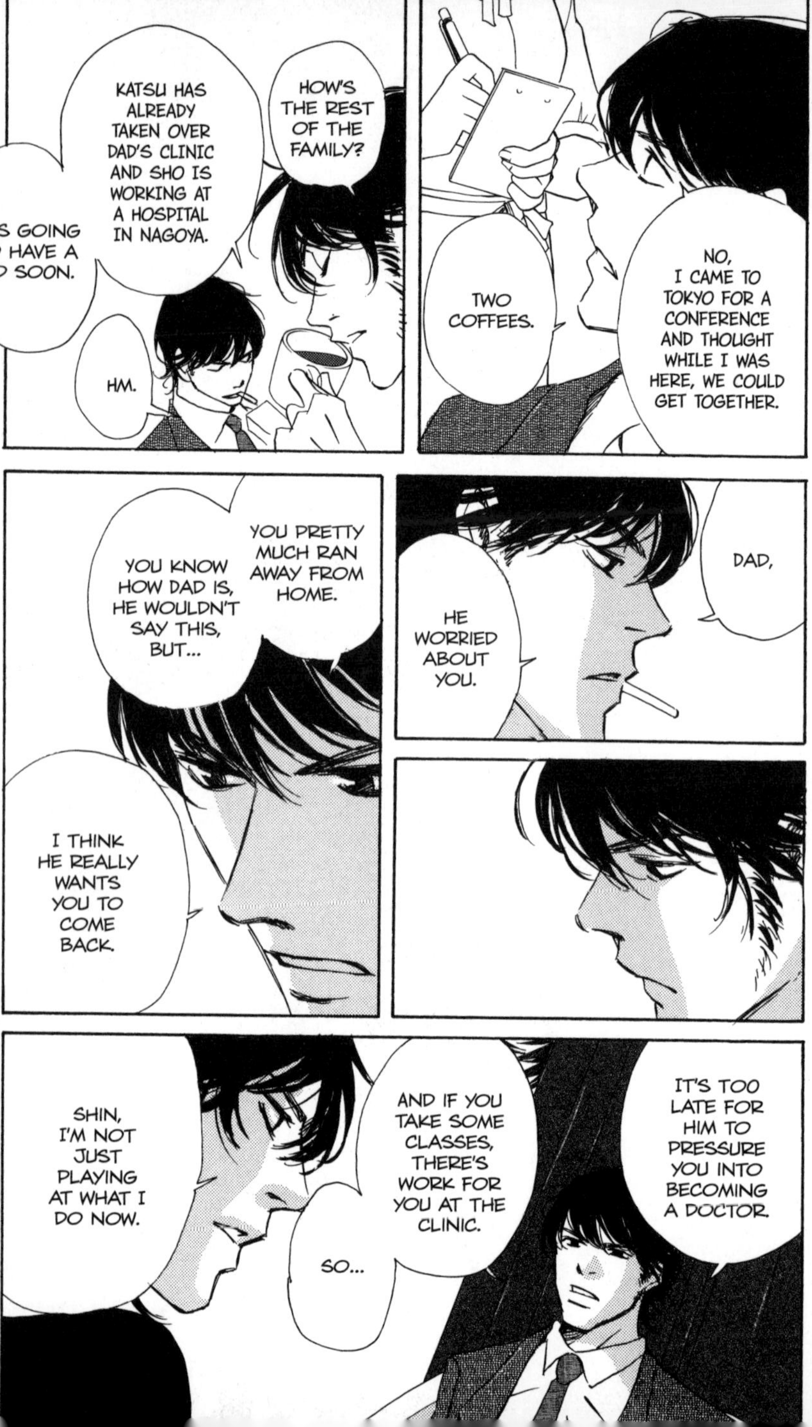
NO, I CAME TO TOKYO FOR A CONFERENCE AND THOUGHT WHILE I WAS HERE, WE COULD GET TOGETHER.
TWO COFFEES.
HOW'S THE REST OF THE FAMILY?
KATSU HAS ALREADY TAKEN OVER DAD'S CLINIC AND SHO IS WORKING AT A HOSPITAL IN NAGOYA.
HE'S GOING TO HAVE A KID SOON.
HM.
DAD,
HE WORRIED ABOUT YOU.
YOU PRETTY MUCH RAN AWAY FROM HOME.
YOU KNOW HOW DAD IS, HE WOULDN'T SAY THIS, BUT...
I THINK HE REALLY WANTS YOU TO COME BACK.
IT'S TOO LATE FOR HIM TO PRESSURE YOU INTO BECOMING A DOCTOR.
AND IF YOU TAKE SOME CLASSES, THERE'S WORK FOR YOU AT THE CLINIC.
SO...
SHIN, I'M NOT JUST PLAYING AT WHAT I DO NOW.

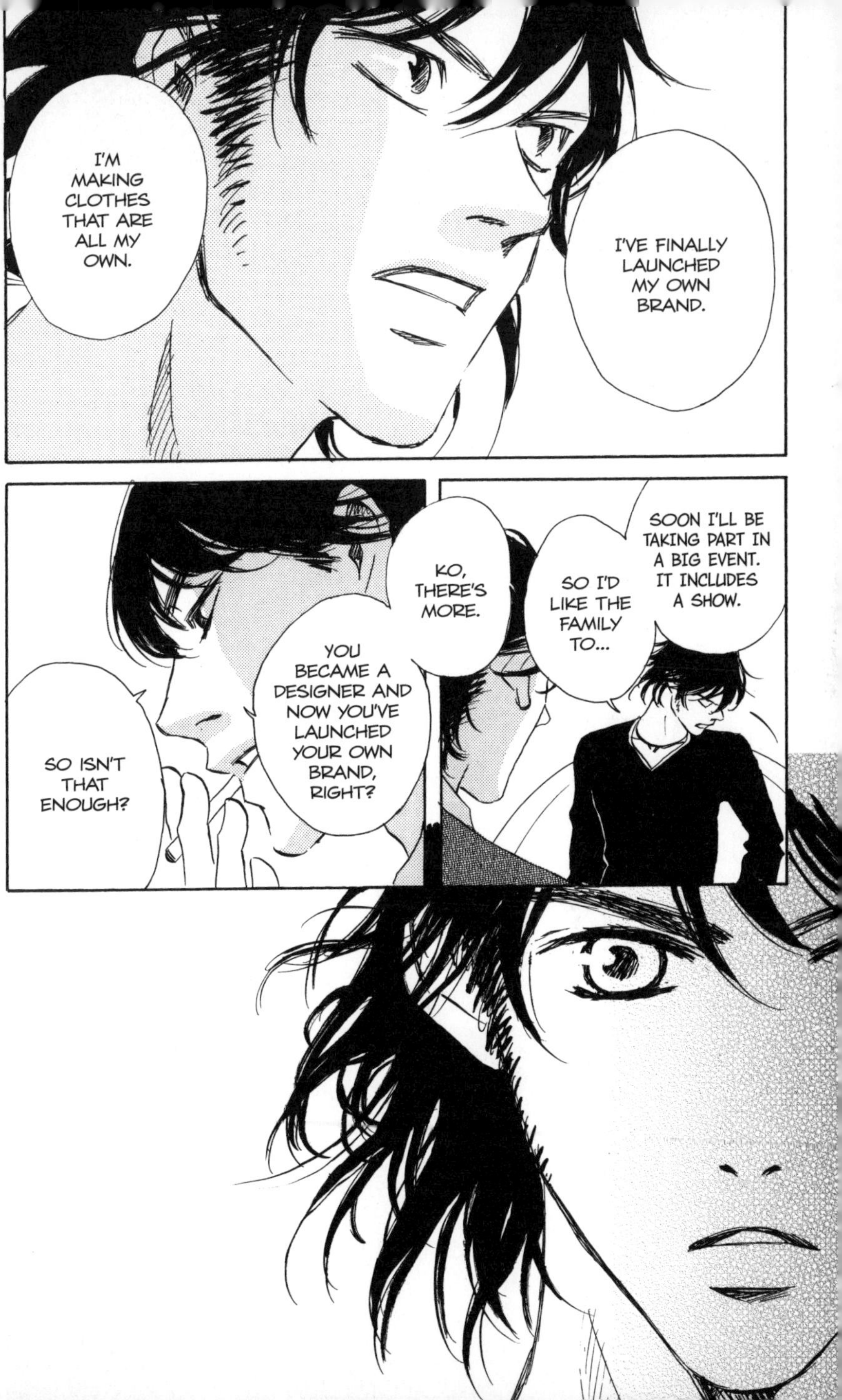
I'VE FINALLY LAUNCHED MY OWN BRAND.
I'M MAKING CLOTHES THAT ARE ALL MY OWN.
SOON I'LL BE TAKING PART IN A BIG EVENT. IT INCLUDES A SHOW.
SO I'D LIKE THE FAMILY TO...
KO, THERE'S MORE.
YOU BECAME A DESIGNER AND NOW YOU'VE LAUNCHED YOUR OWN BRAND, RIGHT?
SO ISN'T THAT ENOUGH?

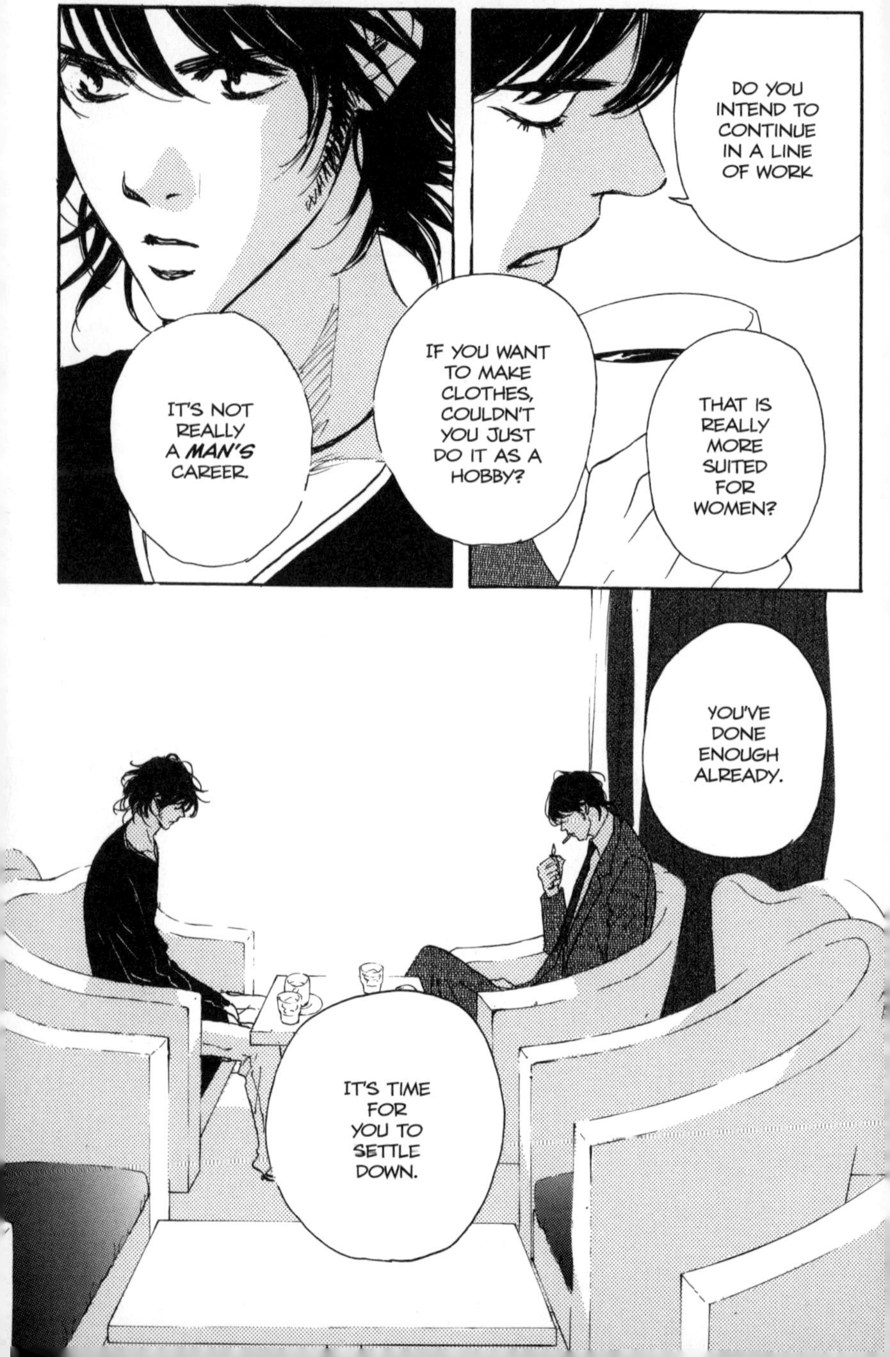
DO YOU INTEND TO CONTINUE IN A LINE OF WORK
THAT IS REALLY MORE SUITED FOR WOMEN?
IF YOU WANT TO MAKE CLOTHES, COULDN'T YOU JUST DO IT AS A HOBBY?
IT'S NOT REALLY A **MAN'S** CAREER.
YOU'VE DONE ENOUGH ALREADY.
IT'S TIME FOR YOU TO SETTLE DOWN.

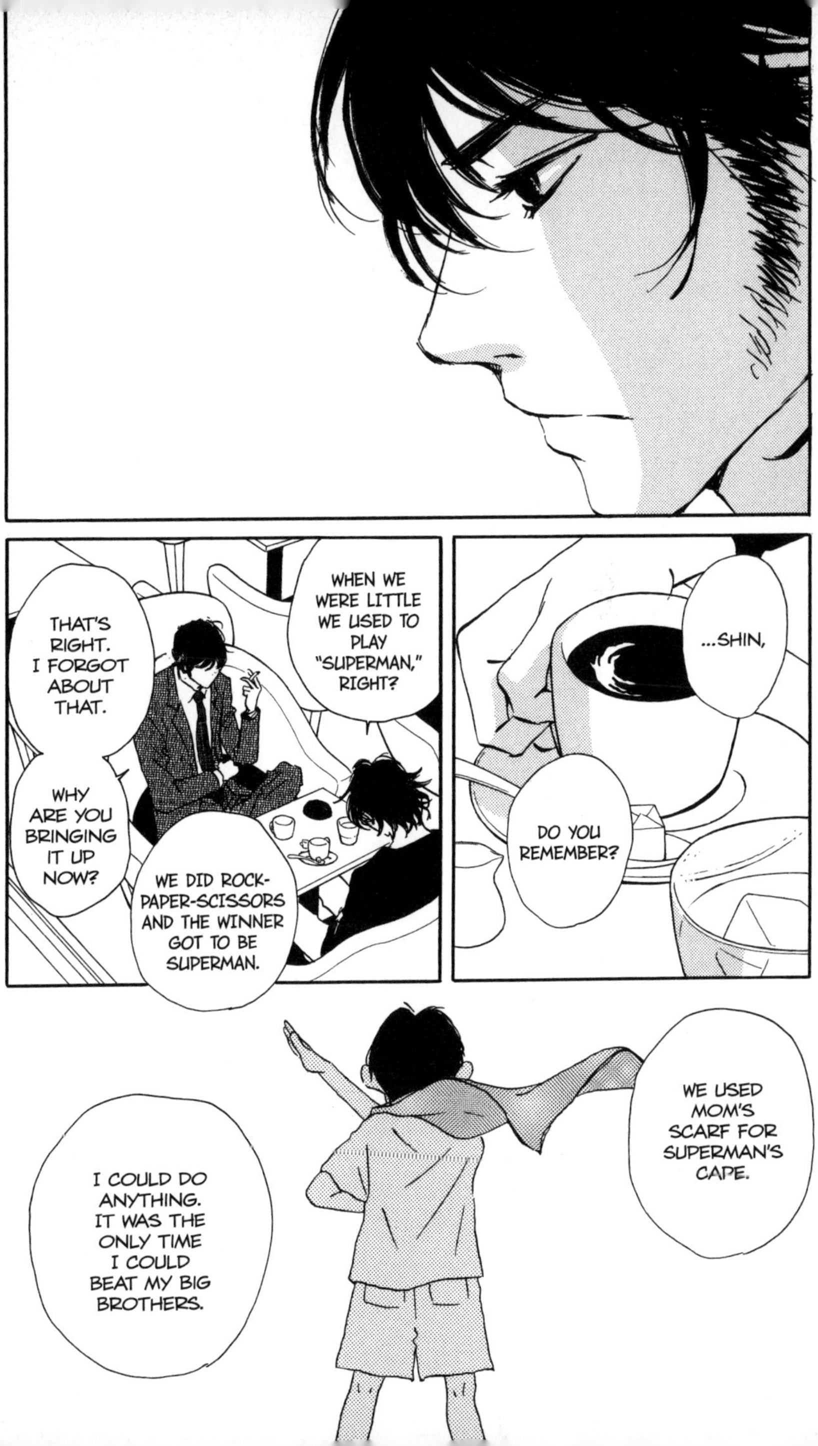
...SHIN,
DO YOU REMEMBER?
WHEN WE WERE LITTLE WE USED TO PLAY "SUPERMAN," RIGHT?
THAT'S RIGHT. I FORGOT ABOUT THAT.
WHY ARE YOU BRINGING IT UP NOW?
WE DID ROCK-PAPER-SCISSORS AND THE WINNER GOT TO BE SUPERMAN.
WE USED MOM'S SCARF FOR SUPERMAN'S CAPE.
I COULD DO ANYTHING. IT WAS THE ONLY TIME I COULD BEAT MY BIG BROTHERS.

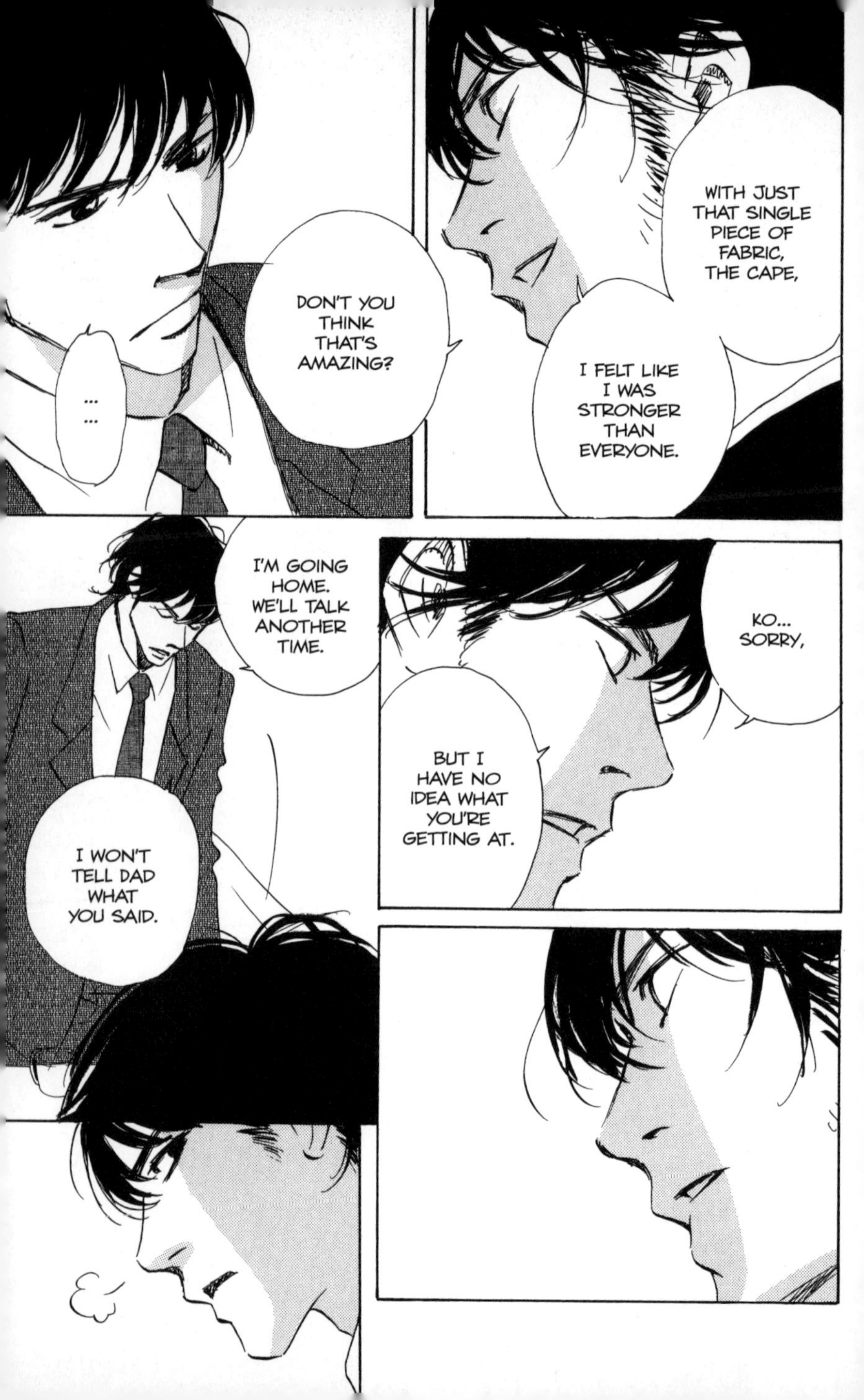
WITH JUST THAT SINGLE PIECE OF FABRIC, THE CAPE,
I FELT LIKE I WAS STRONGER THAN EVERYONE.
DON'T YOU THINK THAT'S AMAZING?
... ...
KO... SORRY,
BUT I HAVE NO IDEA WHAT YOU'RE GETTING AT.
I'M GOING HOME. WE'LL TALK ANOTHER TIME.
I WON'T TELL DAD WHAT YOU SAID.

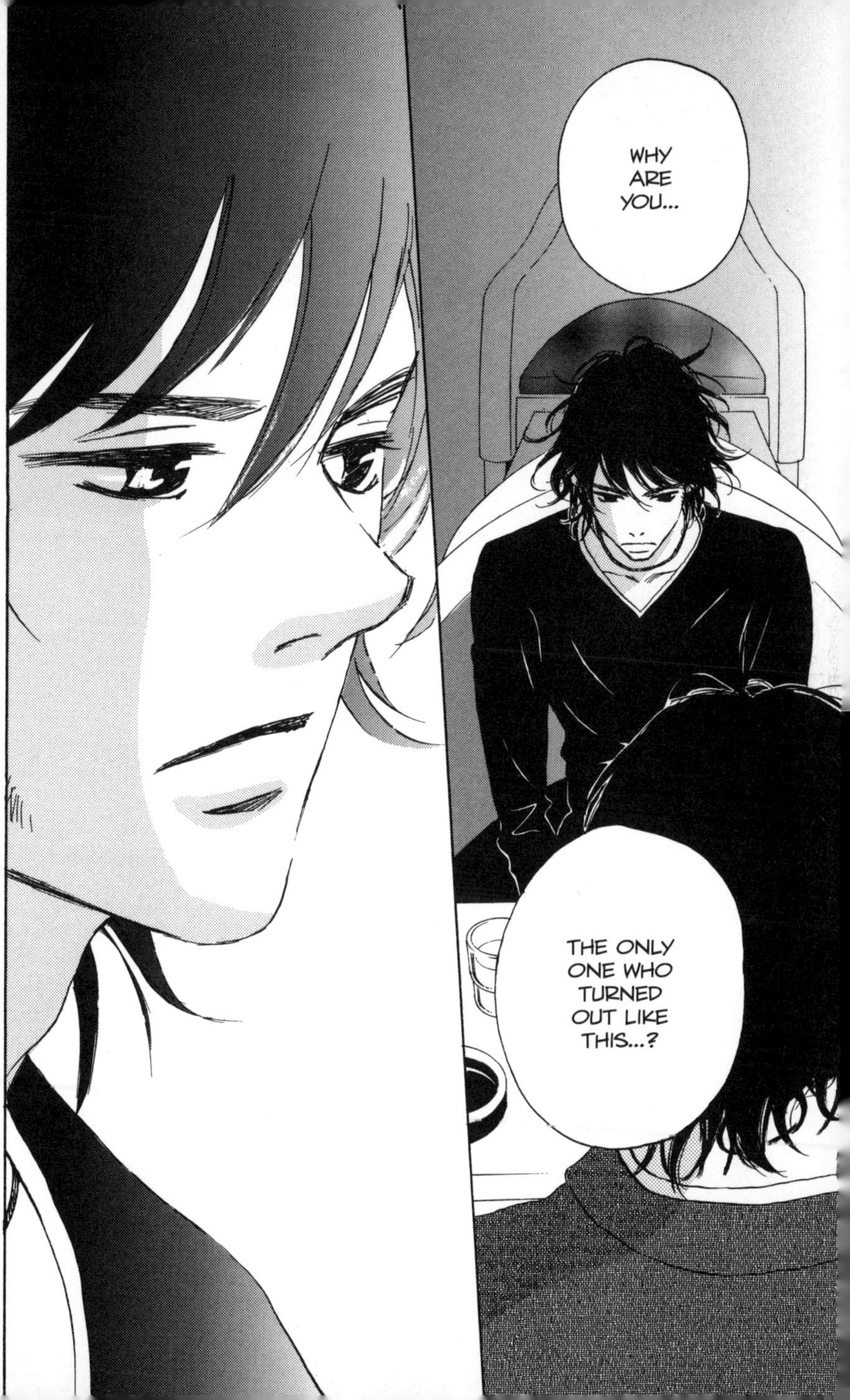
WHY ARE YOU...
THE ONLY ONE WHO TURNED OUT LIKE THIS...?

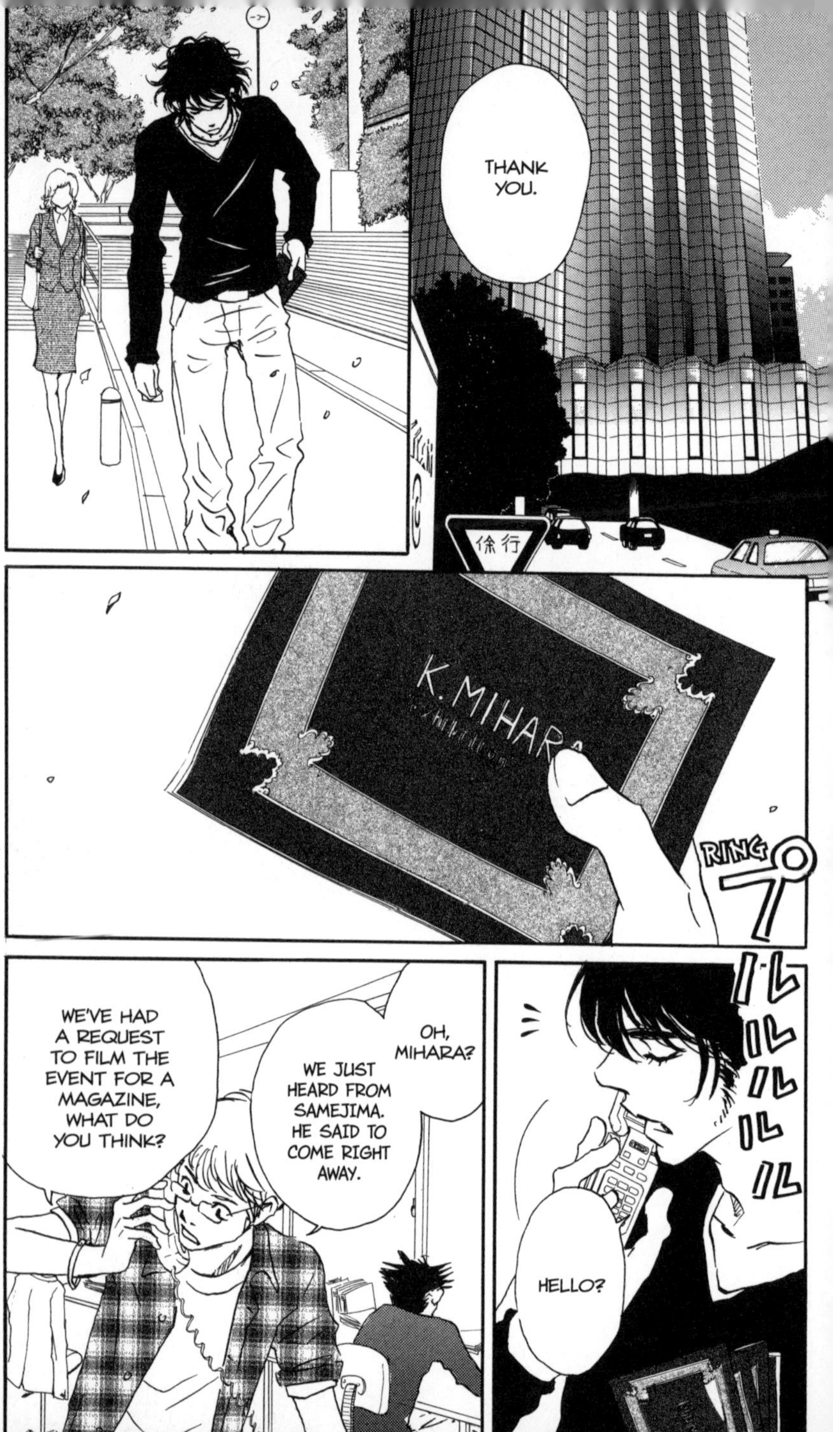
THANK YOU.
徐行
K. MIHARA
RING
ルルルル
HELLO?
OH, MIHARA?
WE JUST HEARD FROM SAMEJIMA. HE SAID TO COME RIGHT AWAY.
WE'VE HAD A REQUEST TO FILM THE EVENT FOR A MAGAZINE, WHAT DO YOU THINK?

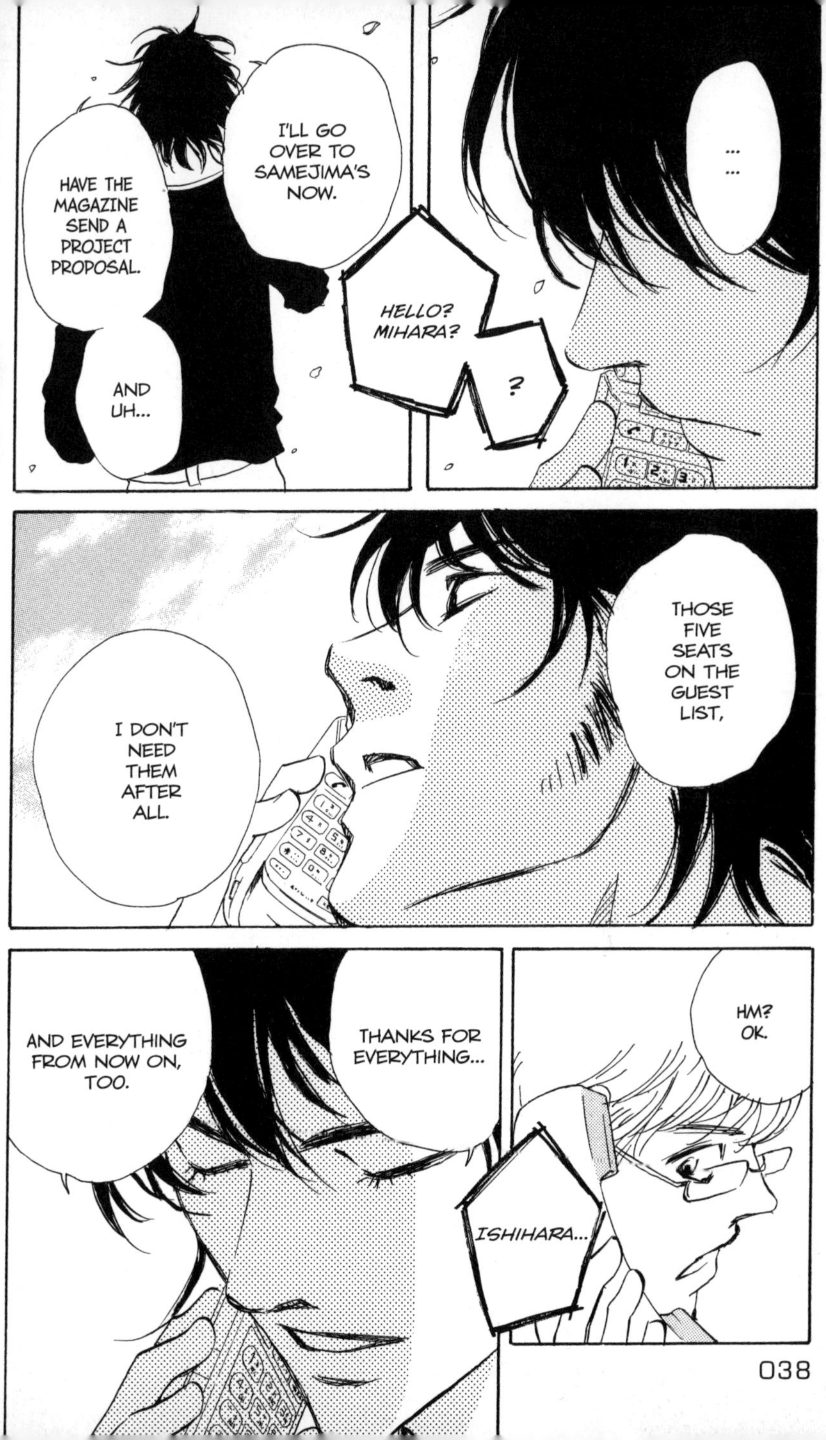
... ...
HELLO? MIHARA?
?
I'LL GO OVER TO SAMEJIMA'S NOW.
HAVE THE MAGAZINE SEND A PROJECT PROPOSAL.
AND UH...
THOSE FIVE SEATS ON THE GUEST LIST,
I DON'T NEED THEM AFTER ALL.
HM? OK.
ISHIHARA...
THANKS FOR EVERYTHING...
AND EVERYTHING FROM NOW ON, TOO.

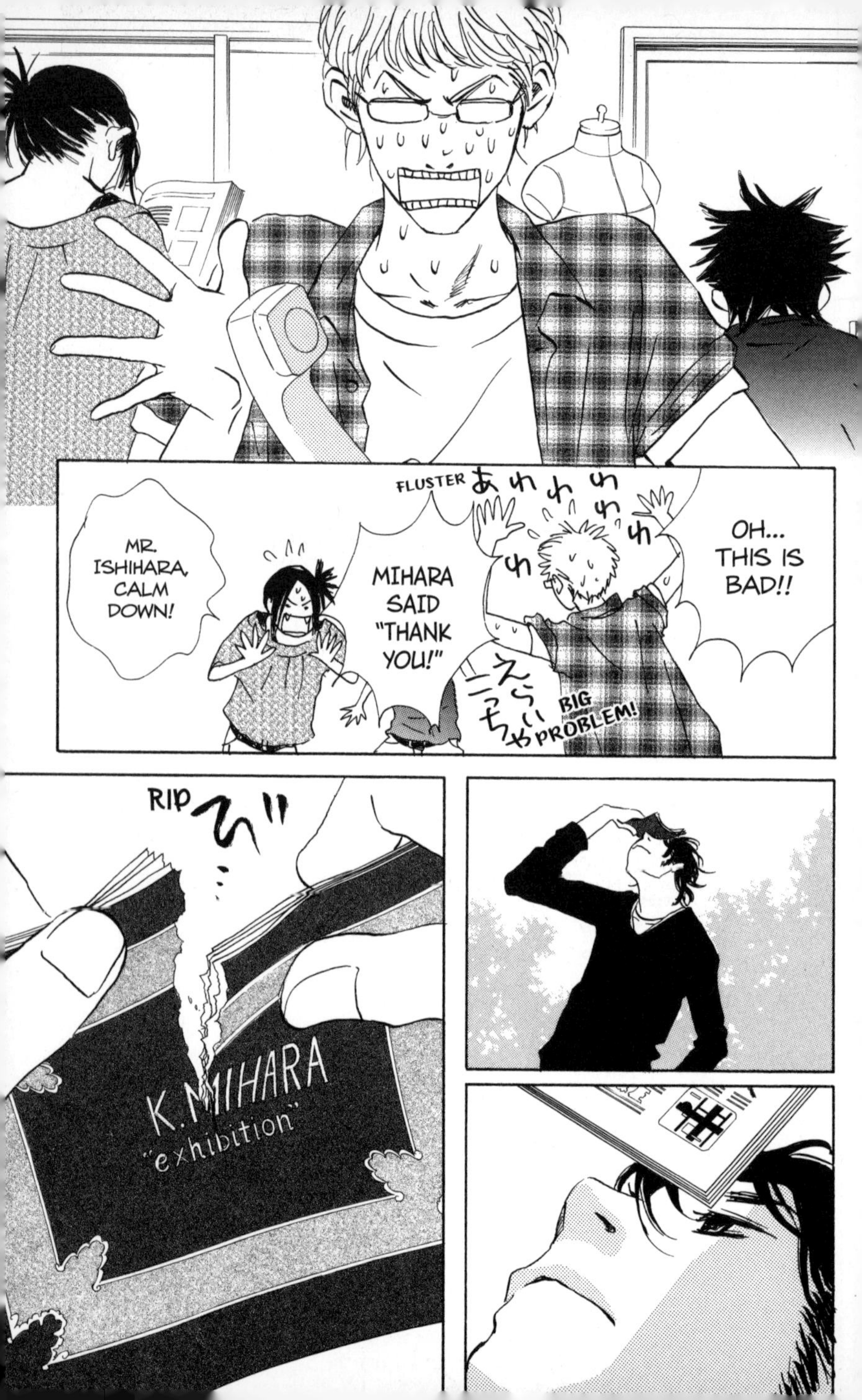
OH... THIS IS BAD!!
FLUSTER
えらいこっちゃ
BIG PROBLEM!
MIHARA SAID "THANK YOU!"
MR. ISHIHARA, CALM DOWN!
RIP
びり
K. MIHARA
"exhibition"

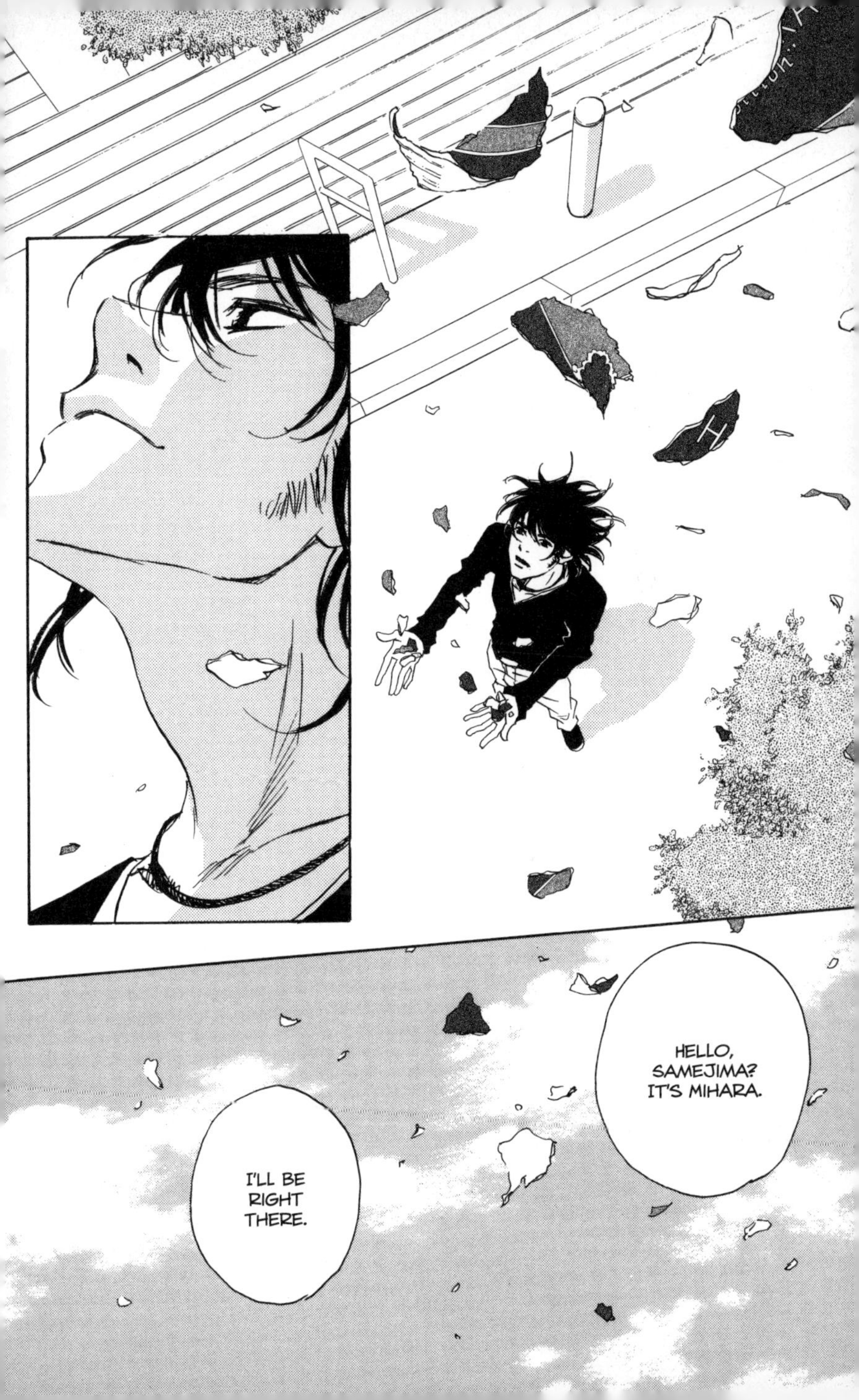
HELLO, SAMEJIMA? IT'S MIHARA.
I'LL BE RIGHT THERE.

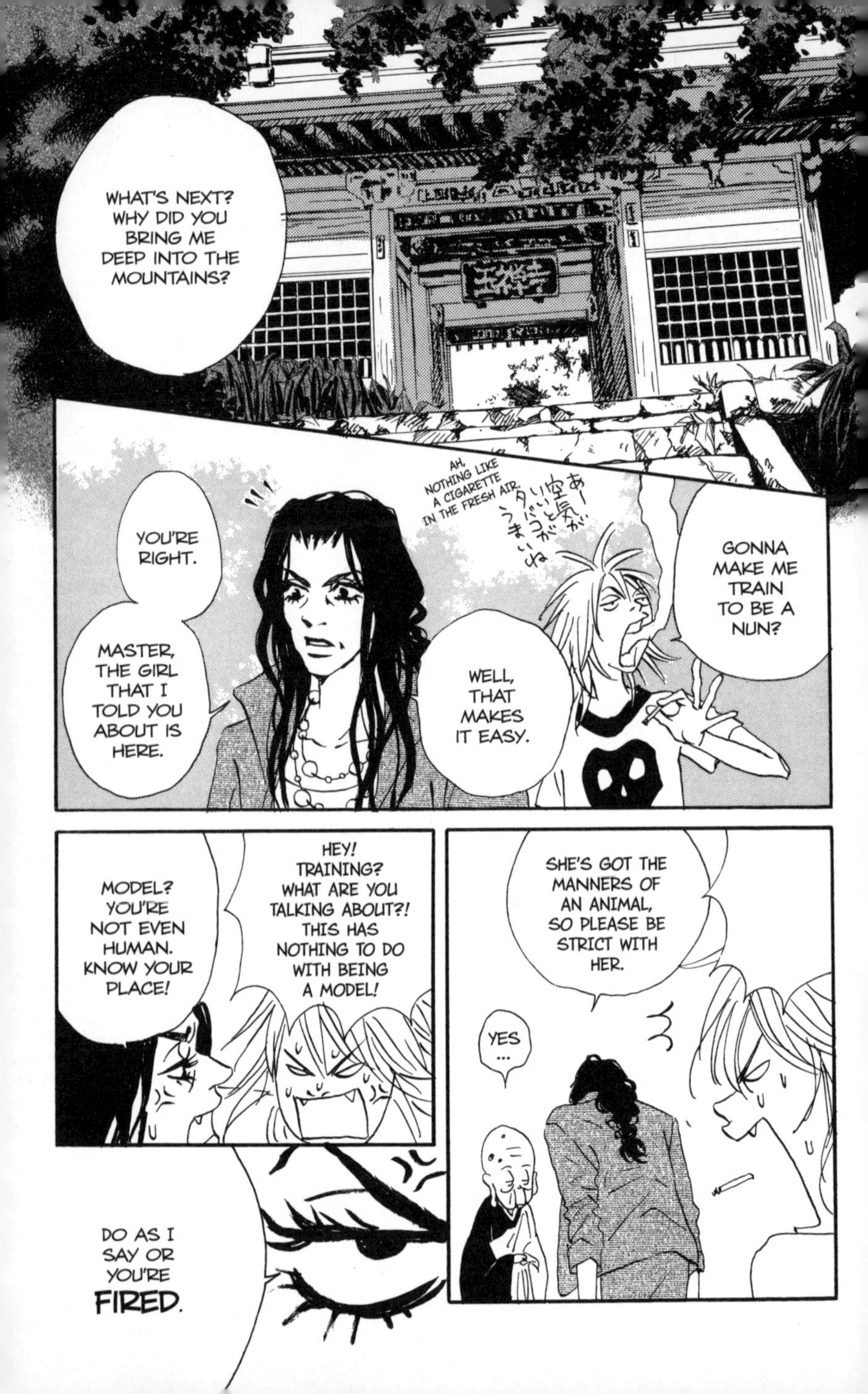
WHAT'S NEXT? WHY DID YOU BRING ME DEEP INTO THE MOUNTAINS?
GONNA MAKE ME TRAIN TO BE A NUN?
AH, NOTHING LIKE A CIGARETTE IN THE FRESH AIR.
あー空気がいいとタバコがうまいね
WELL, THAT MAKES IT EASY.
YOU'RE RIGHT.
MASTER, THE GIRL THAT I TOLD YOU ABOUT IS HERE.
SHE'S GOT THE MANNERS OF AN ANIMAL, SO PLEASE BE STRICT WITH HER.
YES ...
HEY! TRAINING? WHAT ARE YOU TALKING ABOUT?! THIS HAS NOTHING TO DO WITH BEING A MODEL!
MODEL? YOU'RE NOT EVEN HUMAN. KNOW YOUR PLACE!
DO AS I SAY OR YOU'RE **FIRED**.

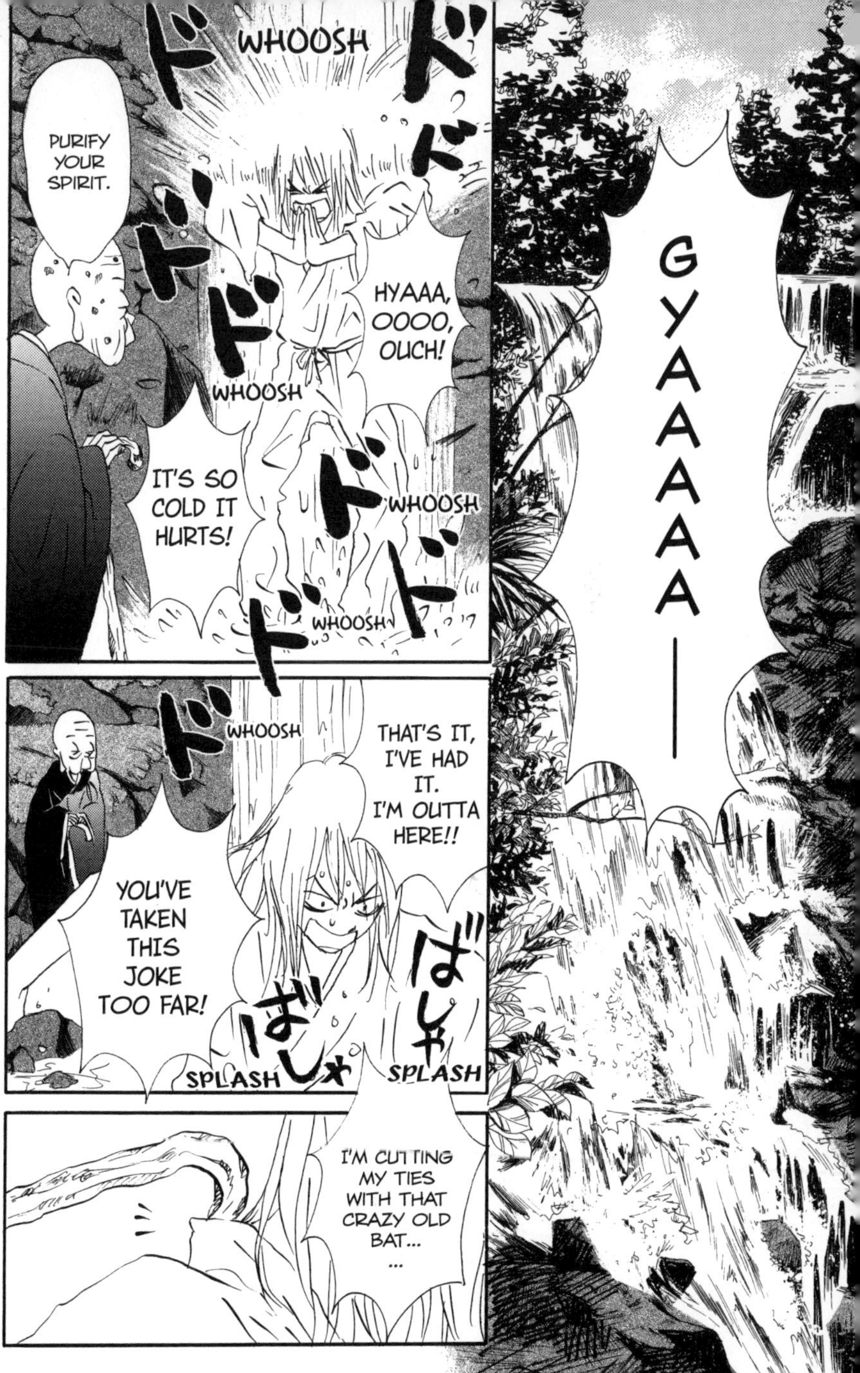

GYAAAAA—
WHOOSH
ドドドド
HYAAA, OOOO, OUCH!
PURIFY YOUR SPIRIT.
WHOOSH
WHOOSH
IT'S SO COLD IT HURTS!
WHOOSH
WHOOSH
THAT'S IT, I'VE HAD IT. I'M OUTTA HERE!!
YOU'VE TAKEN THIS JOKE TOO FAR!
ばしゃ
SPLASH
ばしゃ
SPLASH
I'M CUTTING MY TIES WITH THAT CRAZY OLD BAT... ...

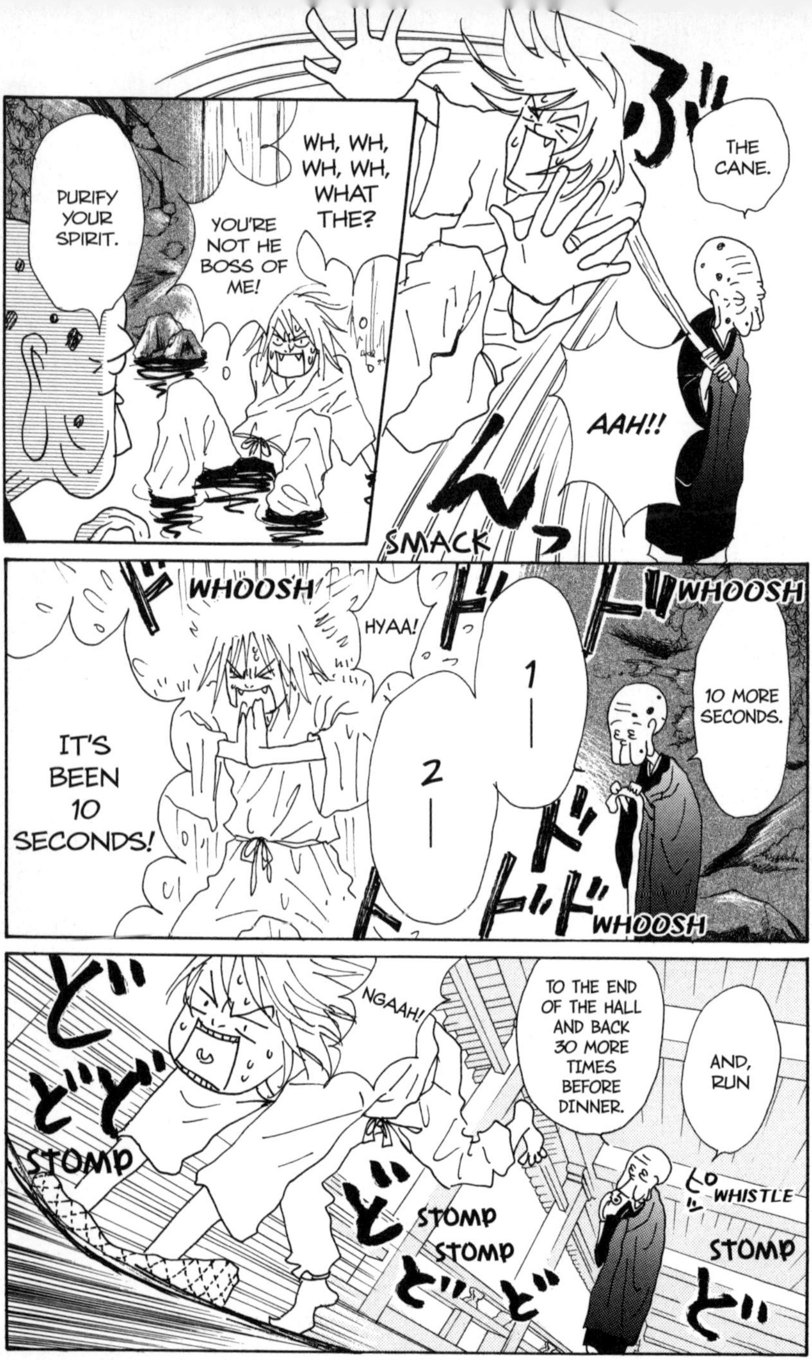

ぶ"
THE CANE.
AAH!!
ん
SMACK
WH, WH, WH, WH, WHAT THE?
PURIFY YOUR SPIRIT.
YOU'RE NOT HE BOSS OF ME!
WHOOSH
10 MORE SECONDS.
1 | 2 |
HYAA!
WHOOSH
IT'S BEEN 10 SECONDS!
WHOOSH
AND, RUN
TO THE END OF THE HALL AND BACK 30 MORE TIMES BEFORE DINNER.
NGAAH!
ピッ WHISTLE
STOMP
STOMP STOMP
STOMP

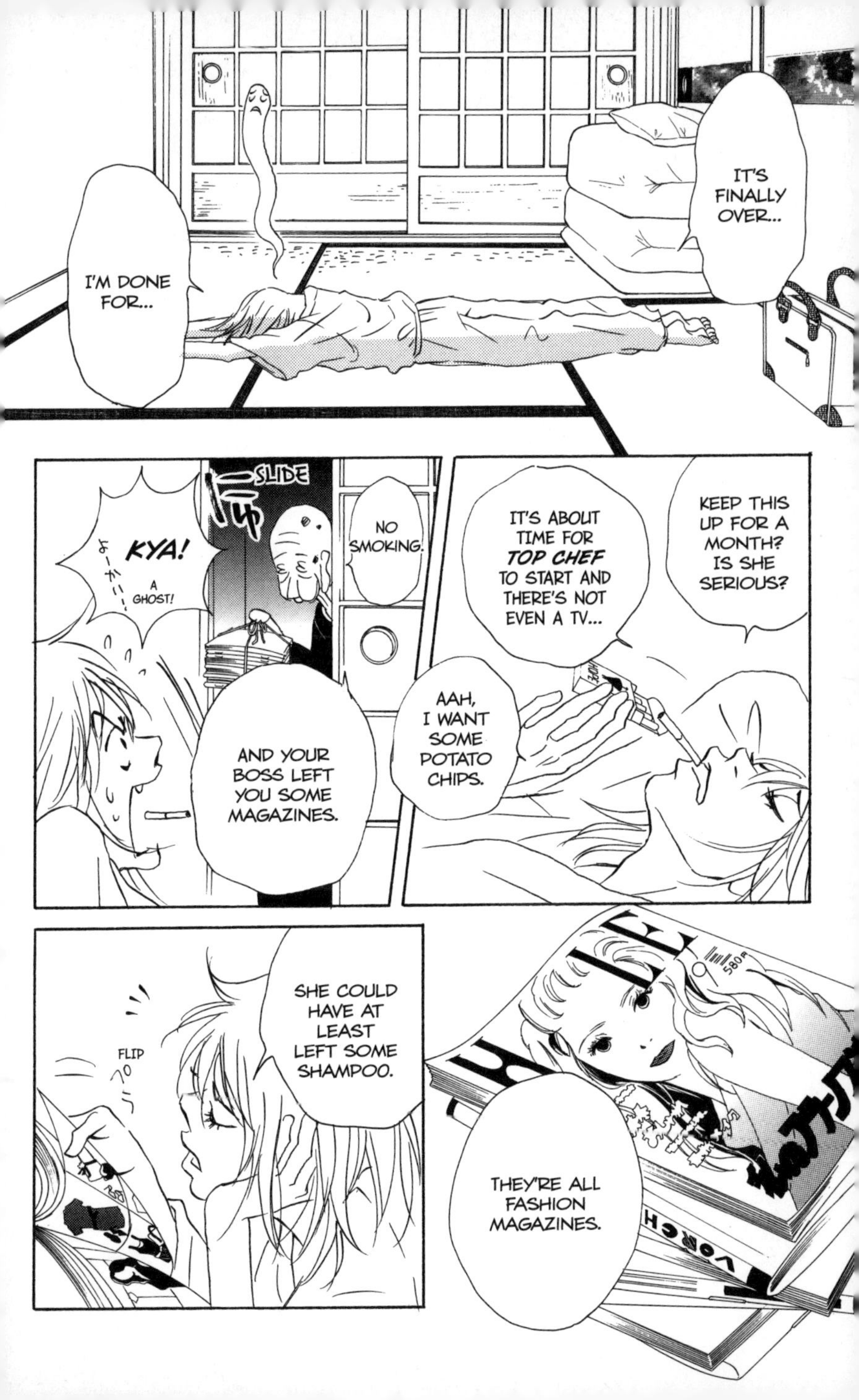
IT'S FINALLY OVER...
I'M DONE FOR...
KEEP THIS UP FOR A MONTH? IS SHE SERIOUS?
IT'S ABOUT TIME FOR TOP CHEF TO START AND THERE'S NOT EVEN A TV...
AAH, I WANT SOME POTATO CHIPS.
SLIDE
NO SMOKING.
KYA!
A GHOST!
AND YOUR BOSS LEFT YOU SOME MAGAZINES.
THEY'RE ALL FASHION MAGAZINES.
SHE COULD HAVE AT LEAST LEFT SOME SHAMPOO.
FLIP

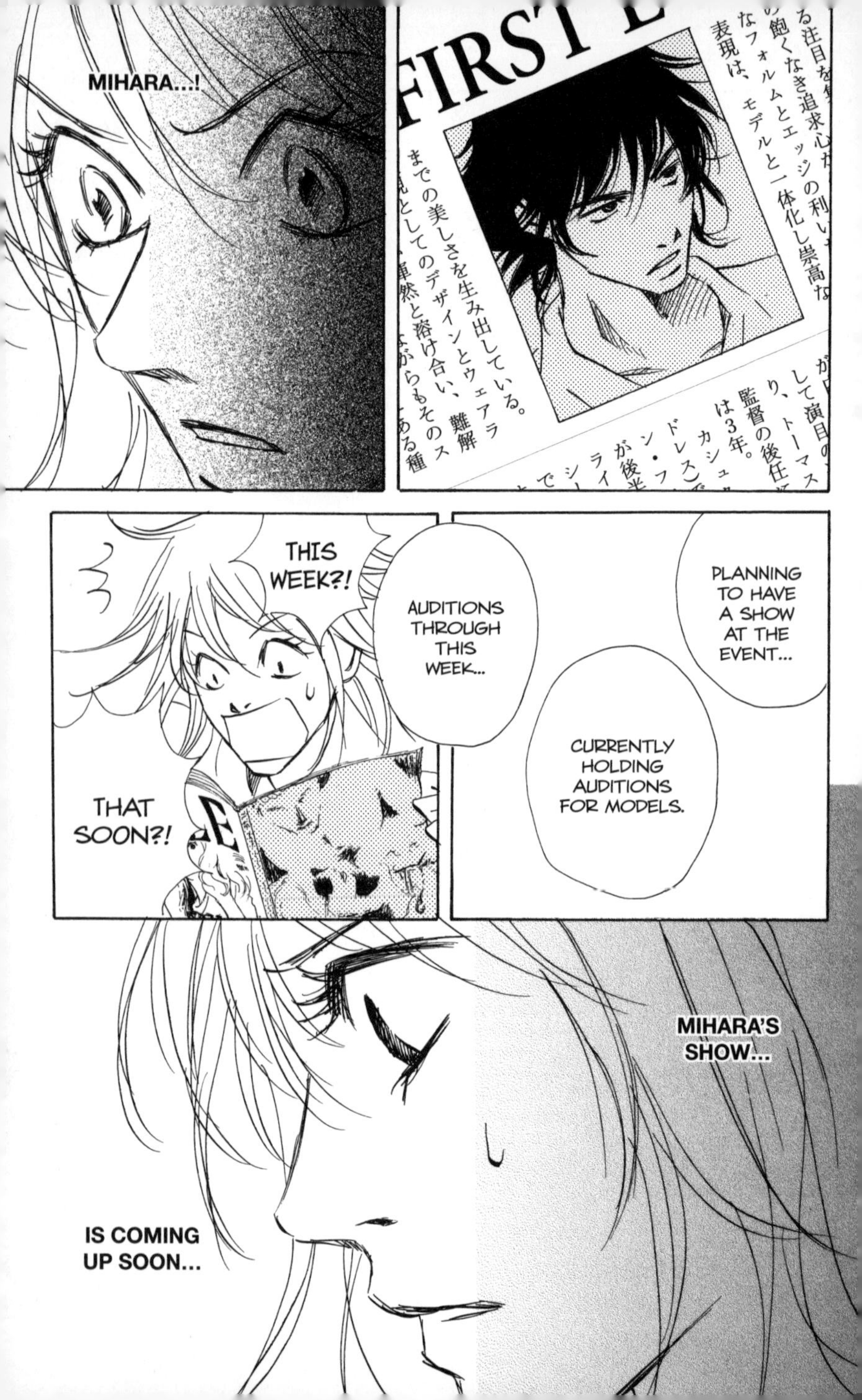
FIRST E
る注目を
の飽くなき追求心が
なフォルムとエッジの利い
表現は、モデルと一体化し崇高な
までの美しさを生み出している。
としてのデザインとウェアラ
難解
は3年。
MIHARA...!
PLANNING TO HAVE A SHOW AT THE EVENT...
CURRENTLY HOLDING AUDITIONS FOR MODELS.
AUDITIONS THROUGH THIS WEEK...
THIS WEEK?!
THAT SOON?!
MIHARA'S SHOW...
IS COMING UP SOON...

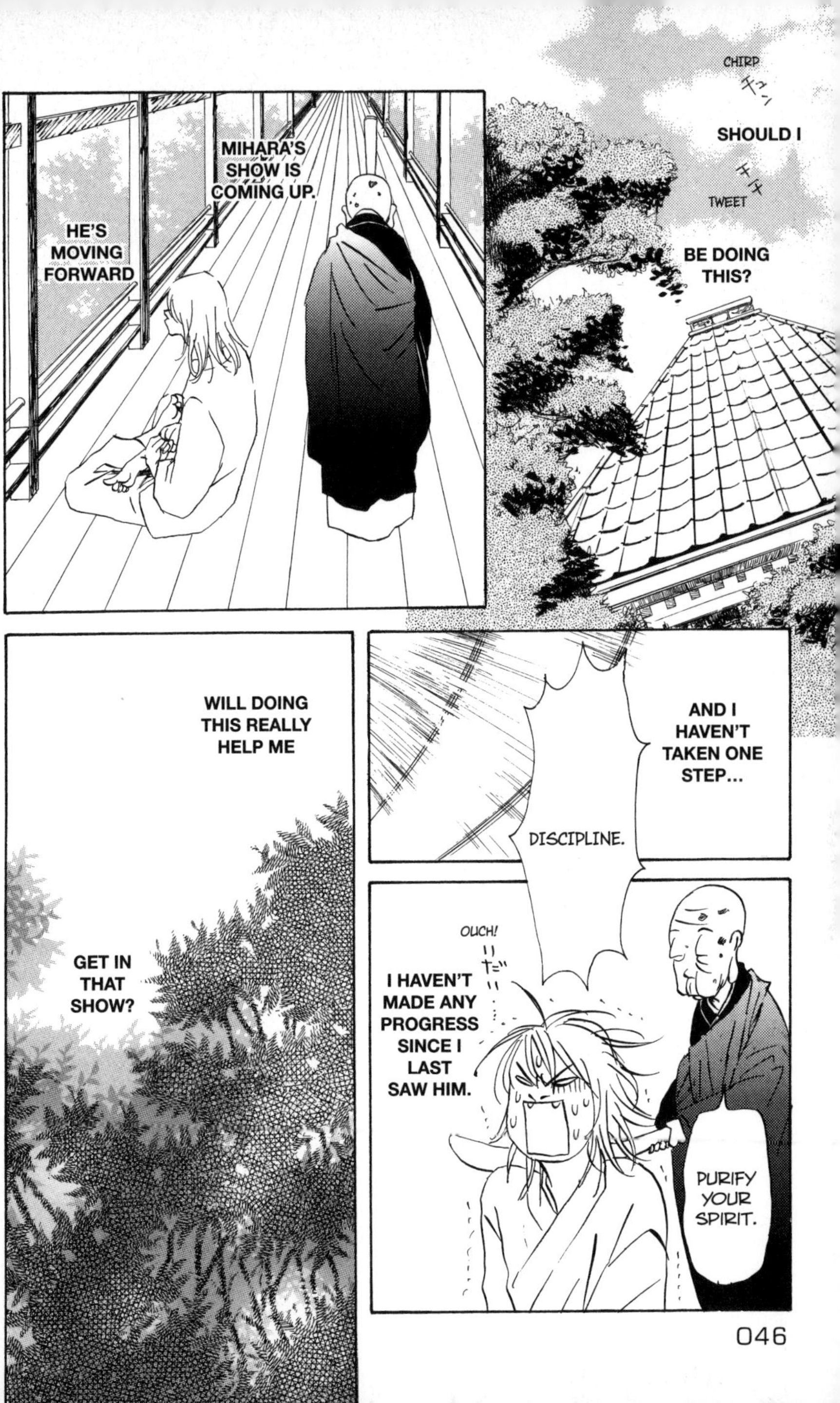
CHIRP
SHOULD I
TWEET
BE DOING THIS?
MIHARA'S SHOW IS COMING UP.
HE'S MOVING FORWARD
AND I HAVEN'T TAKEN ONE STEP...
DISCIPLINE.
PURIFY YOUR SPIRIT.
OUCH!
I HAVEN'T MADE ANY PROGRESS SINCE I LAST SAW HIM.
WILL DOING THIS REALLY HELP ME
GET IN THAT SHOW?

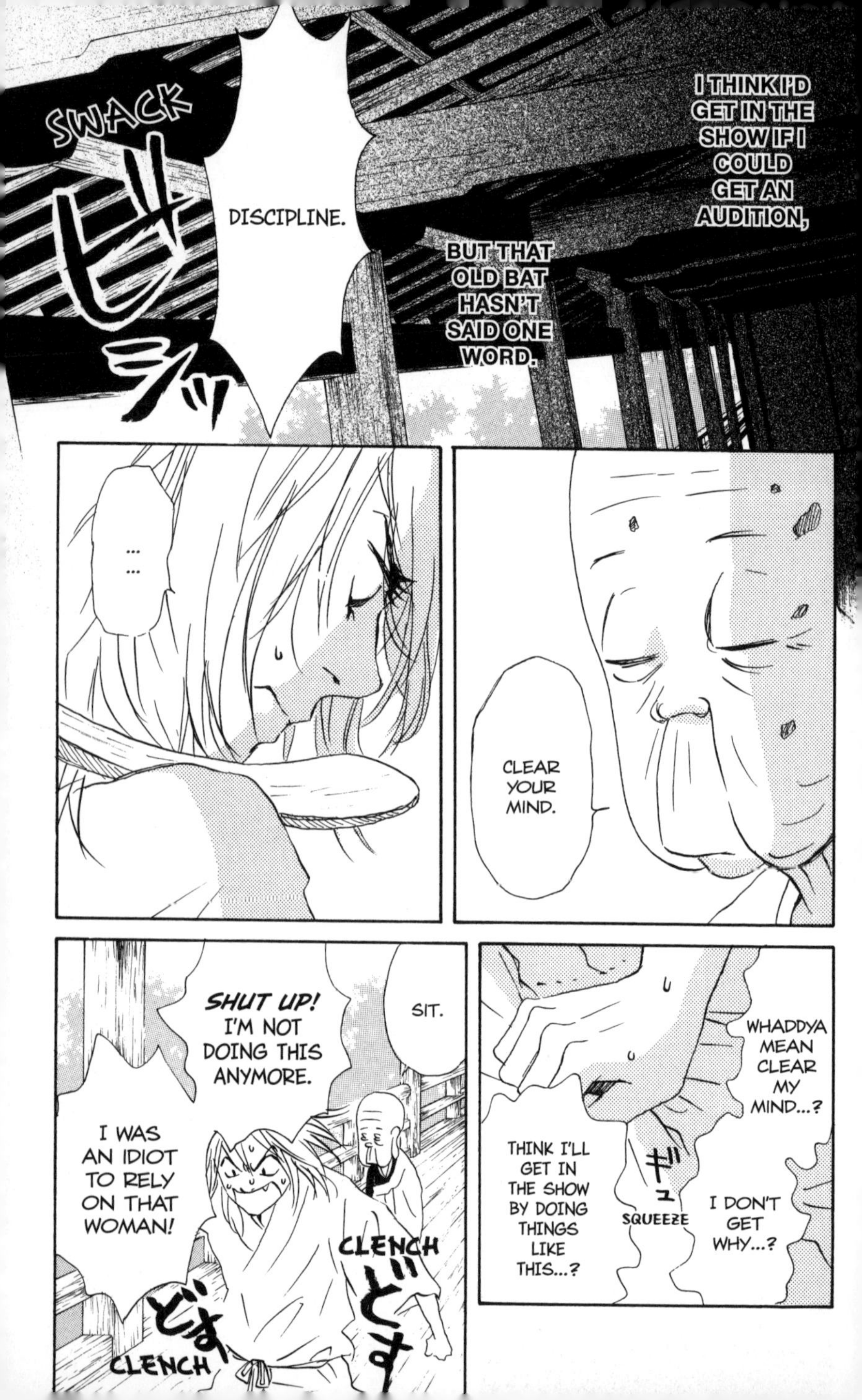
I THINK I'D GET IN THE SHOW IF I COULD GET AN AUDITION,
BUT THAT OLD BAT HASN'T SAID ONE WORD.
DISCIPLINE.
SWACK
CLEAR YOUR MIND.
......
WHADDYA MEAN CLEAR MY MIND...?
I DON'T GET WHY...?
SQUEEZE
THINK I'LL GET IN THE SHOW BY DOING THINGS LIKE THIS...?
SIT.
SHUT UP! I'M NOT DOING THIS ANYMORE.
I WAS AN IDIOT TO RELY ON THAT WOMAN!
どすっ
CLENCH
どす
CLENCH

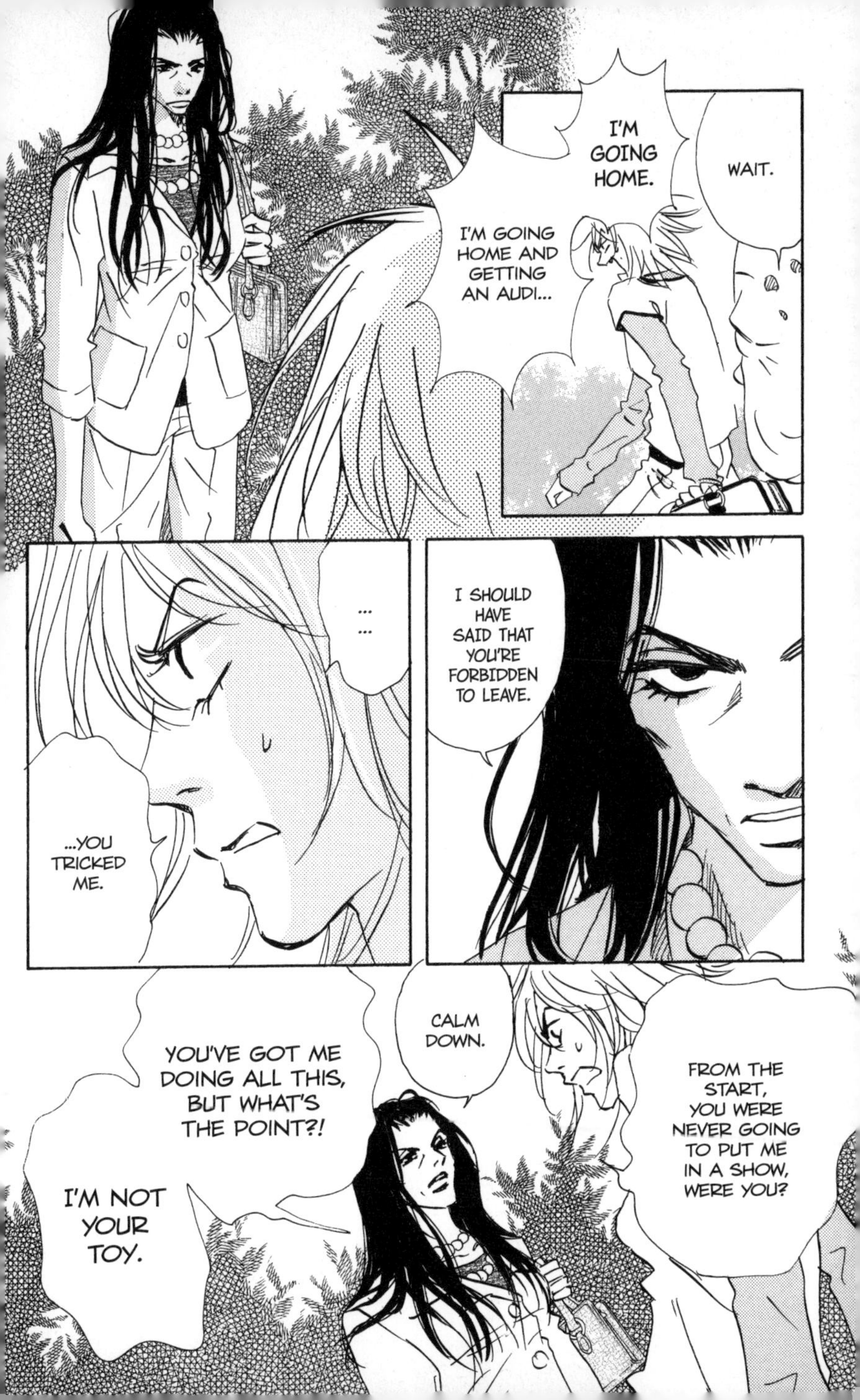
I'M GOING HOME.
WAIT.
I'M GOING HOME AND GETTING AN AUDI...
I SHOULD HAVE SAID THAT YOU'RE FORBIDDEN TO LEAVE.
... ...
...YOU TRICKED ME.
FROM THE START, YOU WERE NEVER GOING TO PUT ME IN A SHOW, WERE YOU?
CALM DOWN.
YOU'VE GOT ME DOING ALL THIS, BUT WHAT'S THE POINT?!
I'M NOT YOUR TOY.

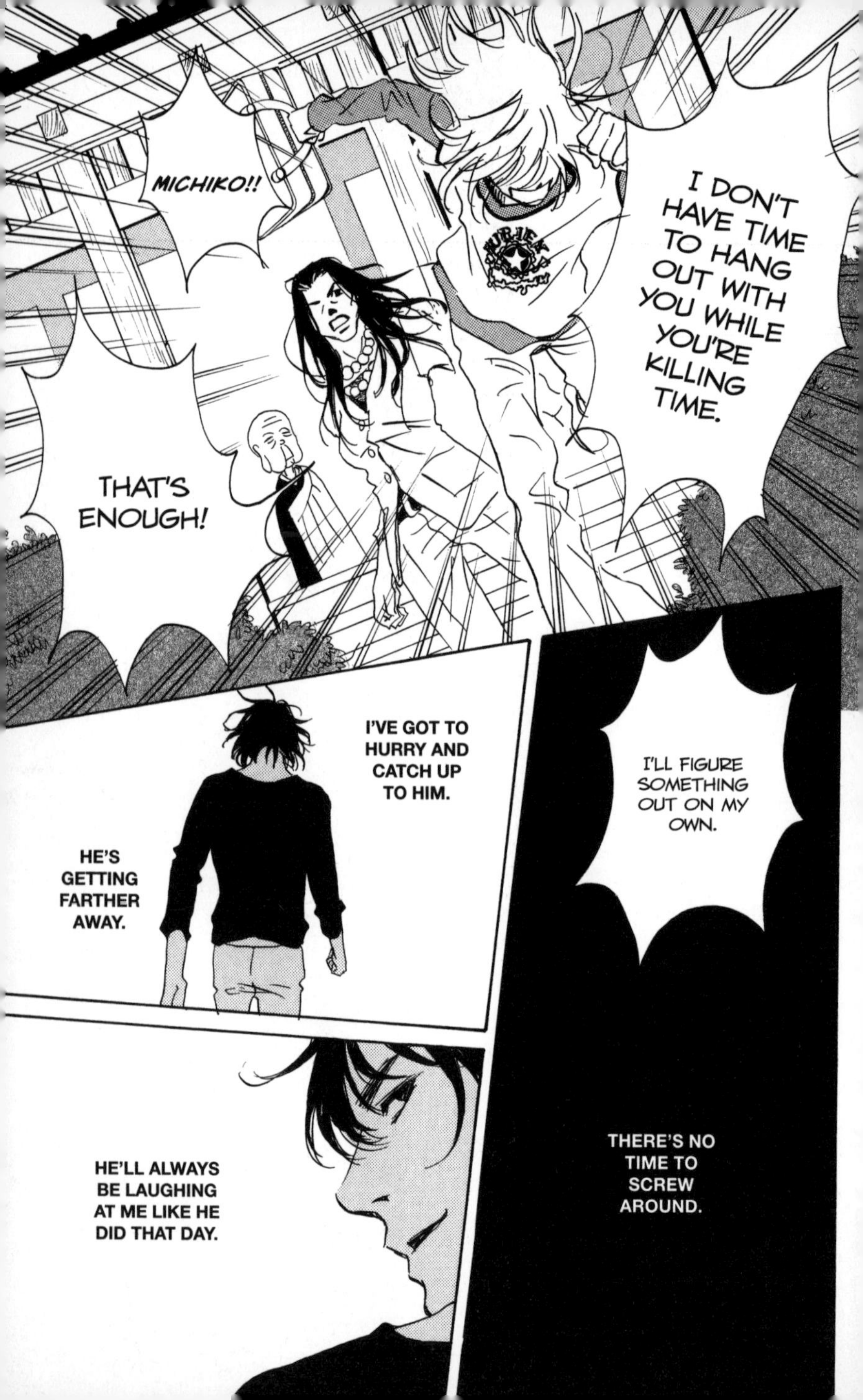
I DON'T HAVE TIME TO HANG OUT WITH YOU WHILE YOU'RE KILLING TIME.
MICHIKO!!
THAT'S ENOUGH!
I'LL FIGURE SOMETHING OUT ON MY OWN.
THERE'S NO TIME TO SCREW AROUND.
I'VE GOT TO HURRY AND CATCH UP TO HIM.
HE'S GETTING FARTHER AWAY.
HE'LL ALWAYS BE LAUGHING AT ME LIKE HE DID THAT DAY.

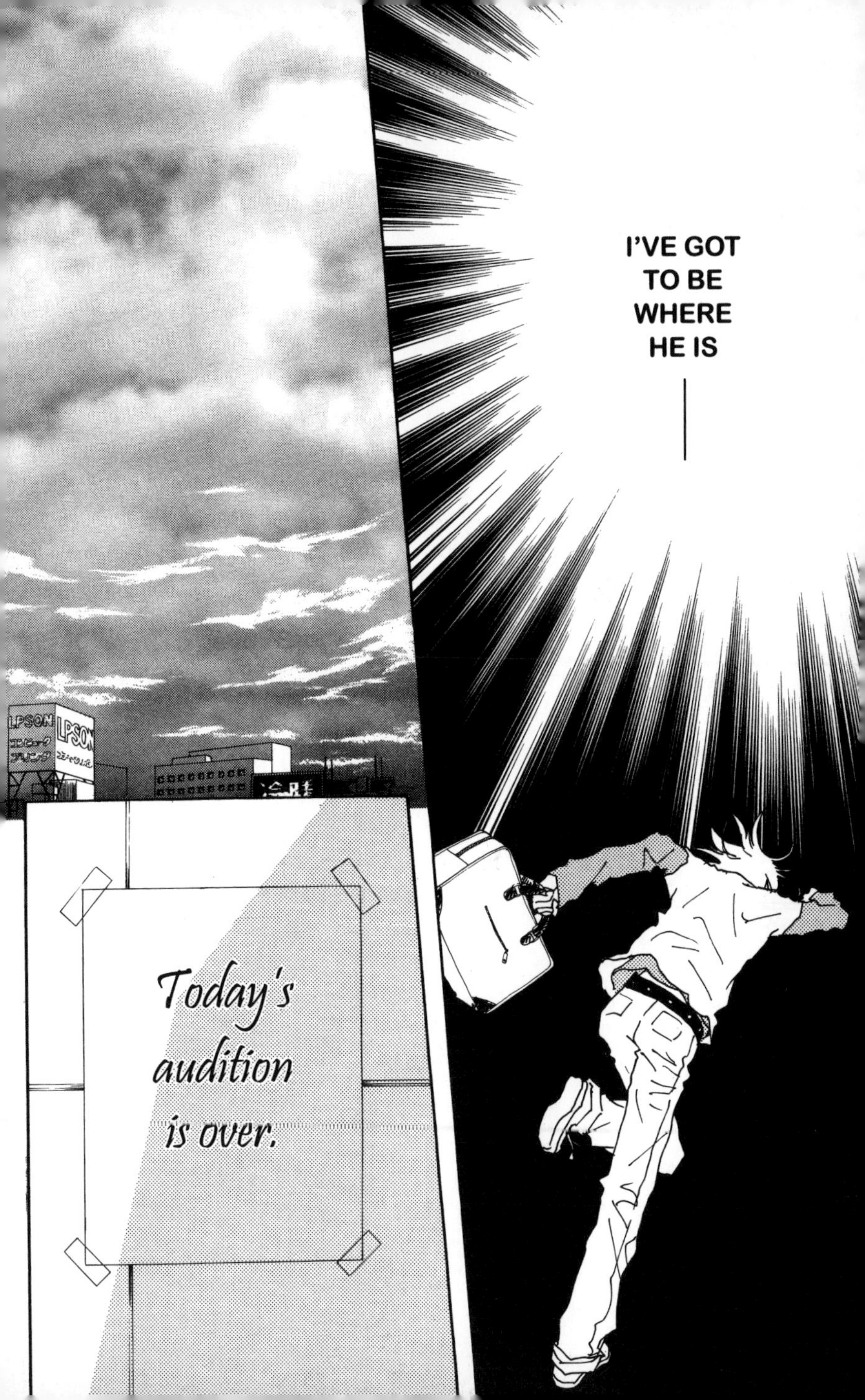
I'VE GOT TO BE WHERE HE IS —
LPSON
Today's audition is over.

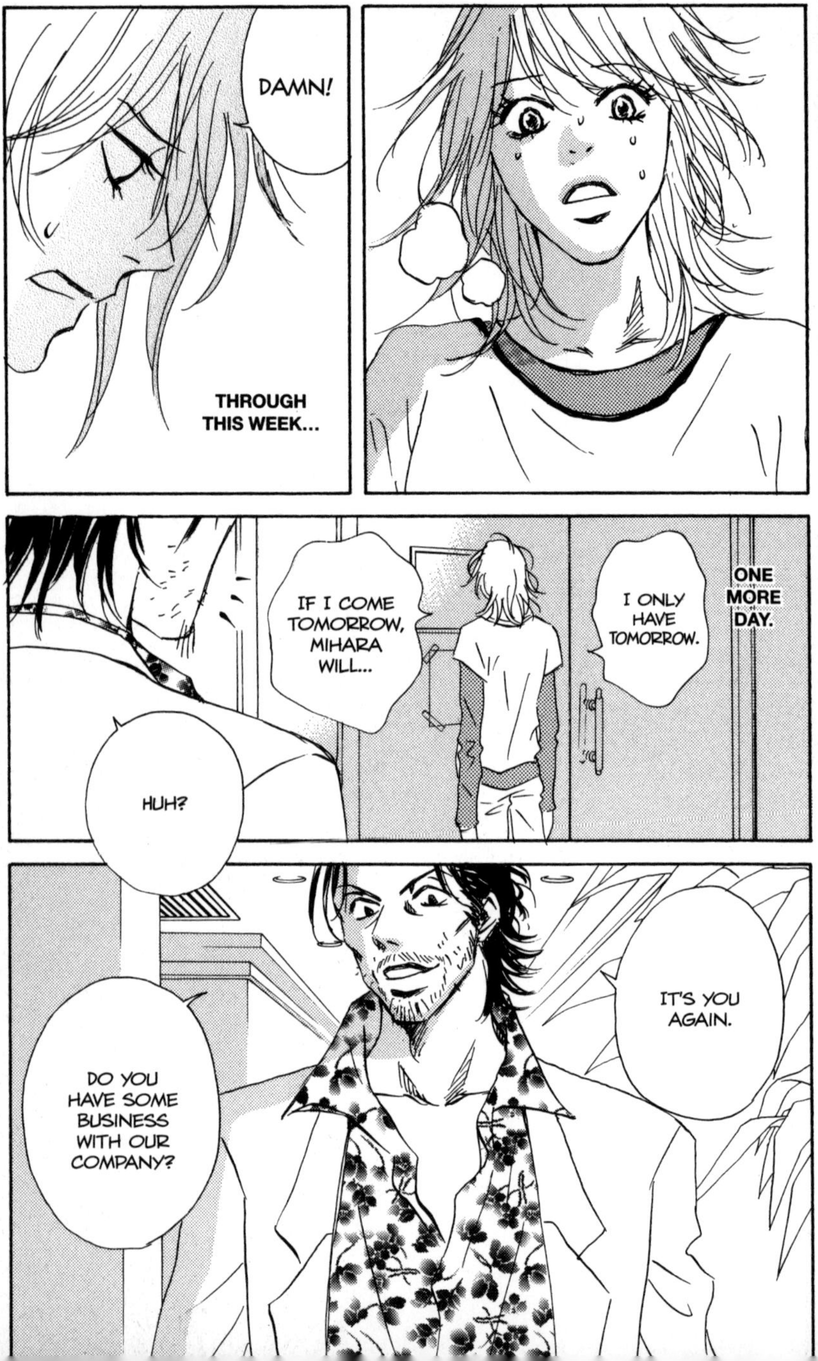
DAMN!
THROUGH THIS WEEK...
ONE MORE DAY.
I ONLY HAVE TOMORROW.
IF I COME TOMORROW, MIHARA WILL...
HUH?
IT'S YOU AGAIN.
DO YOU HAVE SOME BUSINESS WITH OUR COMPANY?

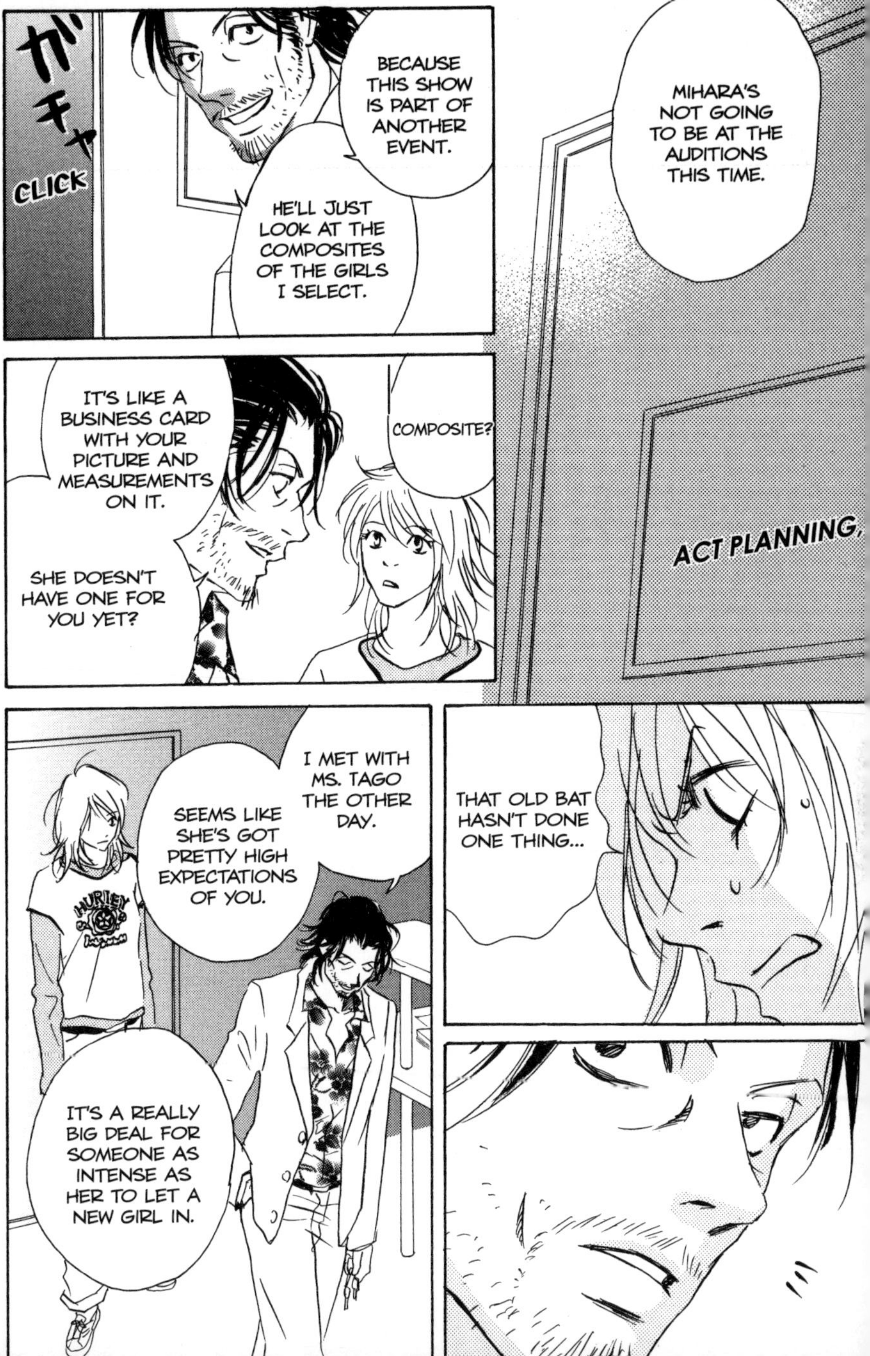
MIHARA'S NOT GOING TO BE AT THE AUDITIONS THIS TIME.
ACT PLANNING,
ガチャ
CLICK
BECAUSE THIS SHOW IS PART OF ANOTHER EVENT.
HE'LL JUST LOOK AT THE COMPOSITES OF THE GIRLS I SELECT.
COMPOSITE?
IT'S LIKE A BUSINESS CARD WITH YOUR PICTURE AND MEASUREMENTS ON IT.
SHE DOESN'T HAVE ONE FOR YOU YET?
THAT OLD BAT HASN'T DONE ONE THING...
I MET WITH MS. TAGO THE OTHER DAY.
SEEMS LIKE SHE'S GOT PRETTY HIGH EXPECTATIONS OF YOU.
IT'S A REALLY BIG DEAL FOR SOMEONE AS INTENSE AS HER TO LET A NEW GIRL IN.

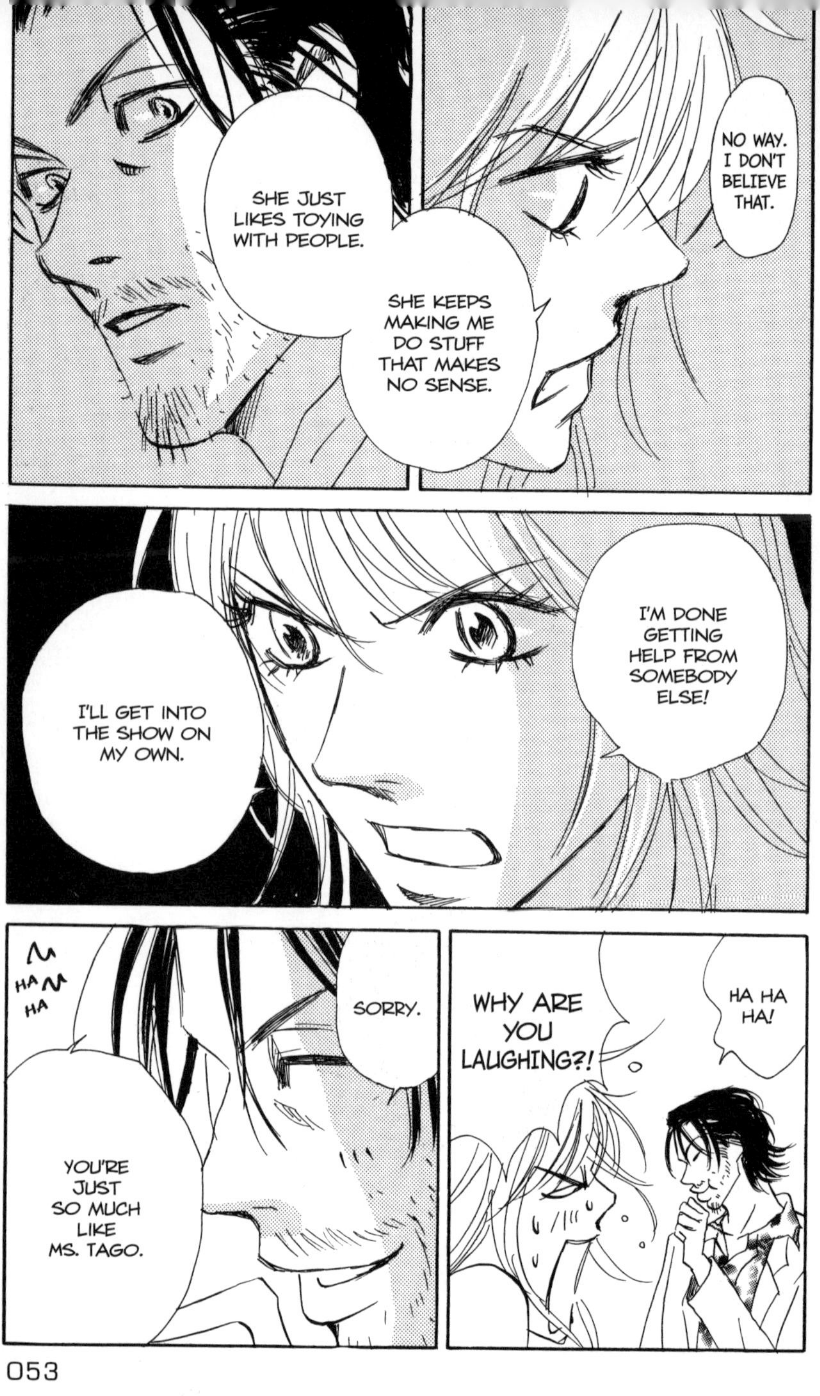
NO WAY. I DON'T BELIEVE THAT.
SHE KEEPS MAKING ME DO STUFF THAT MAKES NO SENSE.
SHE JUST LIKES TOYING WITH PEOPLE.
I'M DONE GETTING HELP FROM SOMEBODY ELSE!
I'LL GET INTO THE SHOW ON MY OWN.
HA HA HA!
WHY ARE YOU LAUGHING?!
SORRY.
HA HA HA
YOU'RE JUST SO MUCH LIKE MS. TAGO.

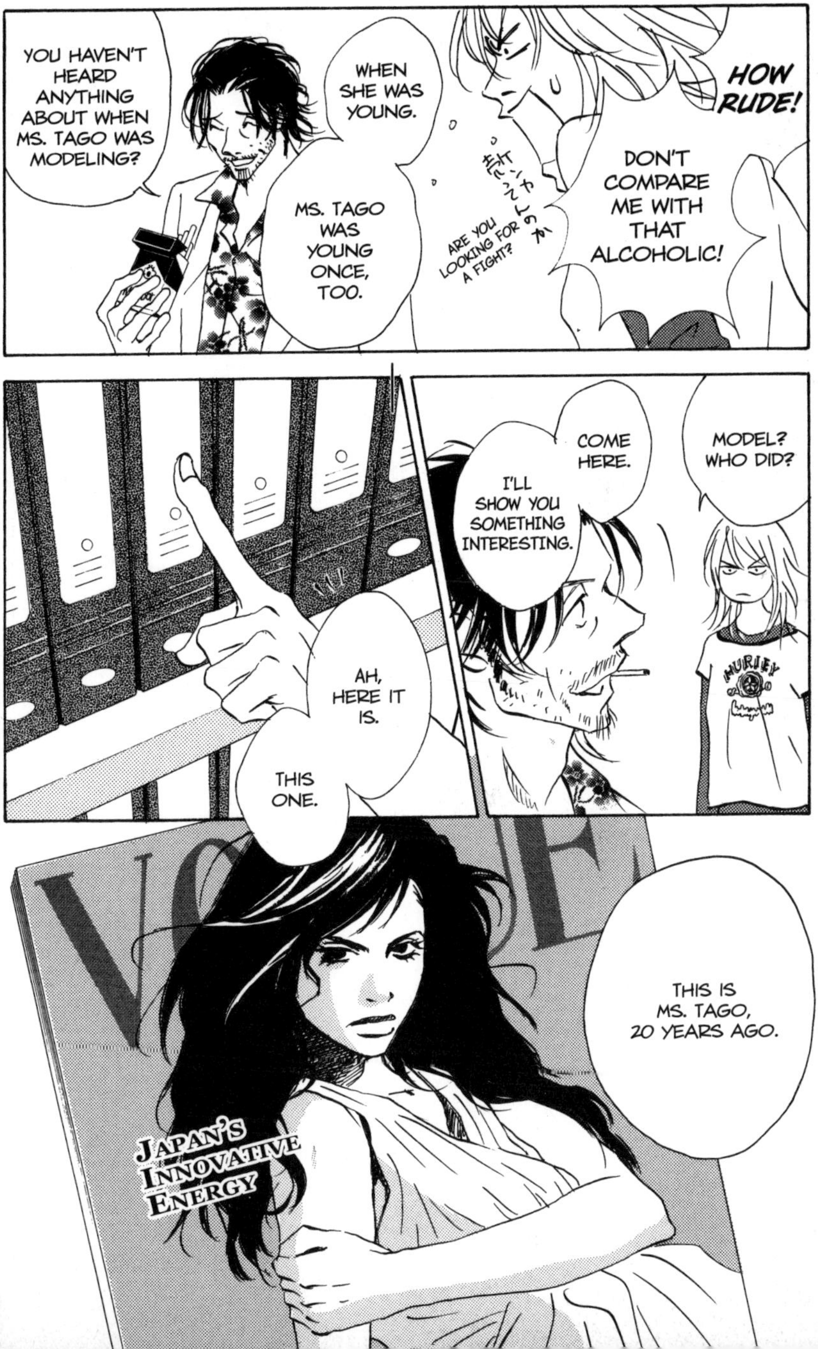
HOW RUDE!
DON'T COMPARE ME WITH THAT ALCOHOLIC!
ARE YOU LOOKING FOR A FIGHT?
WHEN SHE WAS YOUNG.
MS. TAGO WAS YOUNG ONCE, TOO.
YOU HAVEN'T HEARD ANYTHING ABOUT WHEN MS. TAGO WAS MODELING?
MODEL? WHO DID?
COME HERE.
I'LL SHOW YOU SOMETHING INTERESTING.
AH, HERE IT IS.
THIS ONE.
THIS IS MS. TAGO, 20 YEARS AGO.
JAPAN'S INNOVATIVE ENERGY

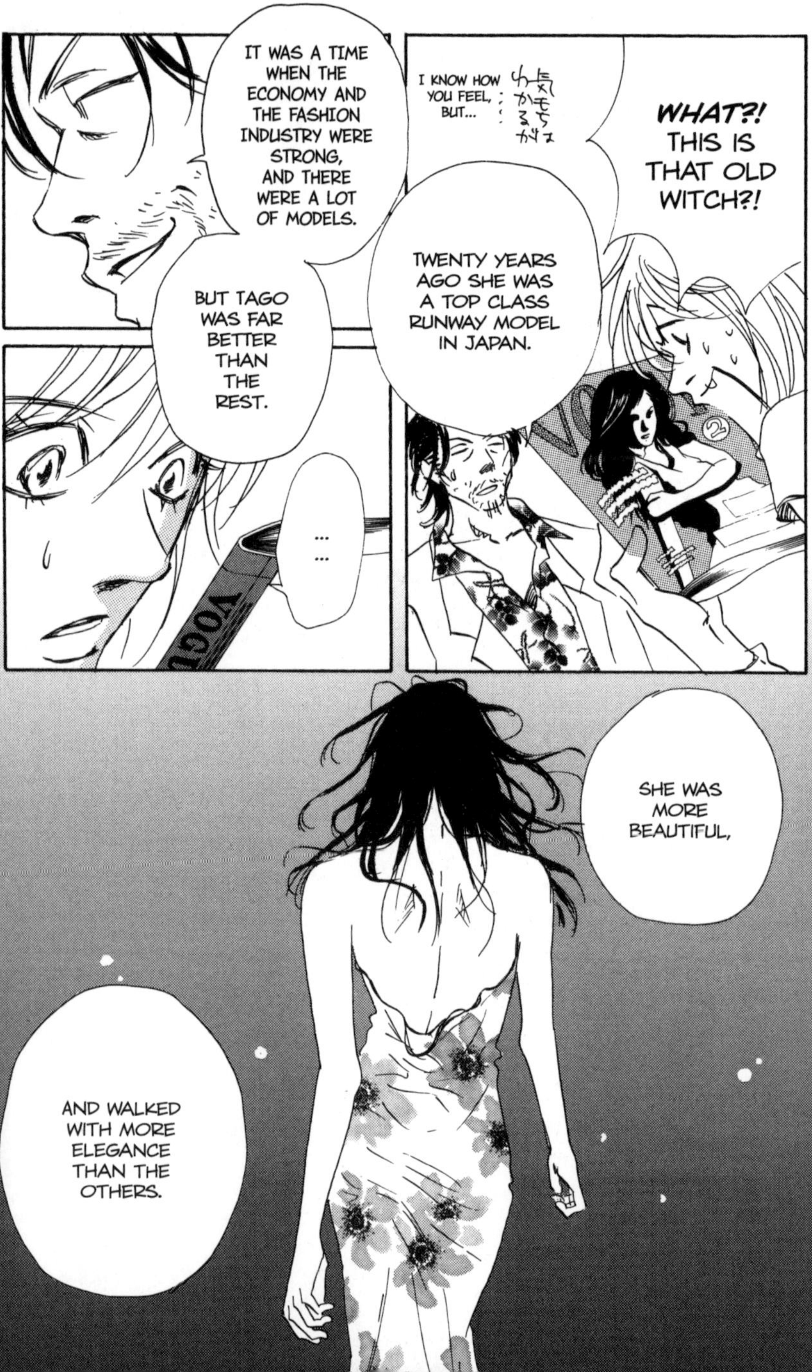
WHAT?! THIS IS THAT OLD WITCH?!
I KNOW HOW YOU FEEL, BUT...
TWENTY YEARS AGO SHE WAS A TOP CLASS RUNWAY MODEL IN JAPAN.
IT WAS A TIME WHEN THE ECONOMY AND THE FASHION INDUSTRY WERE STRONG, AND THERE WERE A LOT OF MODELS.
BUT TAGO WAS FAR BETTER THAN THE REST.
... ...
SHE WAS MORE BEAUTIFUL,
AND WALKED WITH MORE ELEGANCE THAN THE OTHERS.

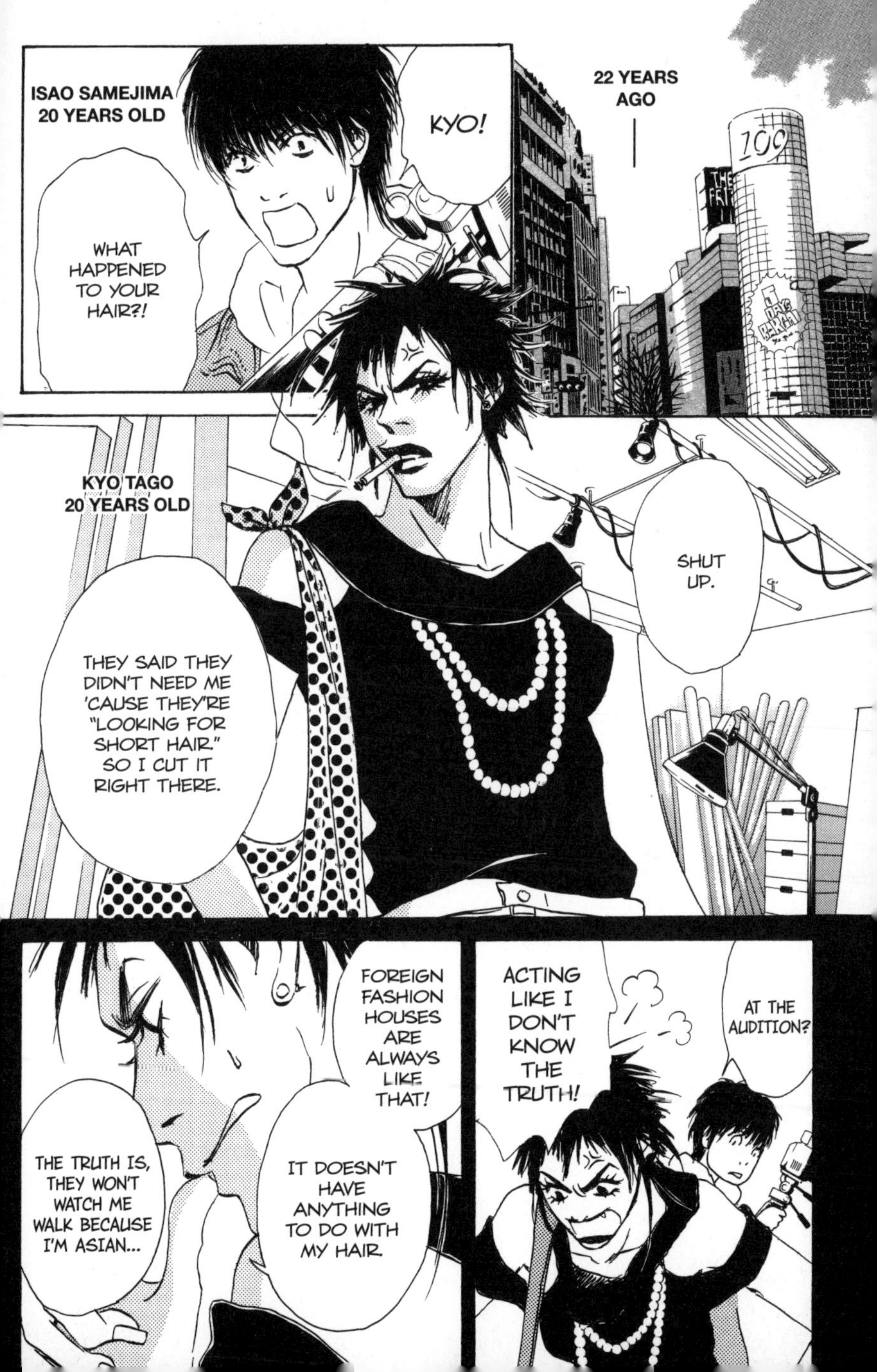
22 YEARS AGO
KYO!
ISAO SAMEJIMA 20 YEARS OLD
WHAT HAPPENED TO YOUR HAIR?!
SHUT UP.
KYO TAGO 20 YEARS OLD
THEY SAID THEY DIDN'T NEED ME 'CAUSE THEY'RE "LOOKING FOR SHORT HAIR." SO I CUT IT RIGHT THERE.
AT THE AUDITION?
ACTING LIKE I DON'T KNOW THE TRUTH!
FOREIGN FASHION HOUSES ARE ALWAYS LIKE THAT!
IT DOESN'T HAVE ANYTHING TO DO WITH MY HAIR.
THE TRUTH IS, THEY WON'T WATCH ME WALK BECAUSE I'M ASIAN...

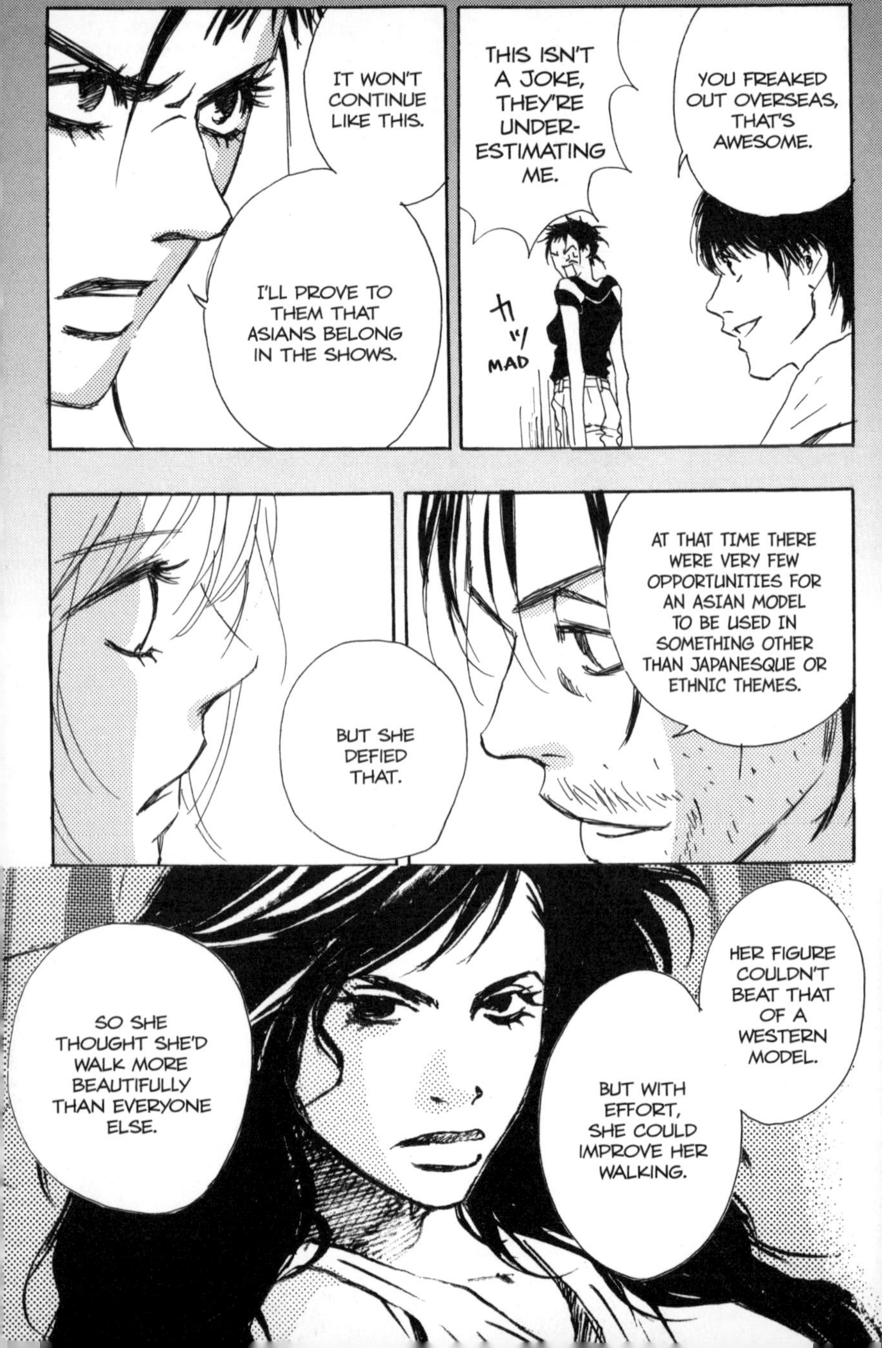
YOU FREAKED OUT OVERSEAS, THAT'S AWESOME.
THIS ISN'T A JOKE, THEY'RE UNDER-ESTIMATING ME.
MAD
IT WON'T CONTINUE LIKE THIS.
I'LL PROVE TO THEM THAT ASIANS BELONG IN THE SHOWS.
AT THAT TIME THERE WERE VERY FEW OPPORTUNITIES FOR AN ASIAN MODEL TO BE USED IN SOMETHING OTHER THAN JAPANESQUE OR ETHNIC THEMES.
BUT SHE DEFIED THAT.
HER FIGURE COULDN'T BEAT THAT OF A WESTERN MODEL.
BUT WITH EFFORT, SHE COULD IMPROVE HER WALKING.
SO SHE THOUGHT SHE'D WALK MORE BEAUTIFULLY THAN EVERYONE ELSE.

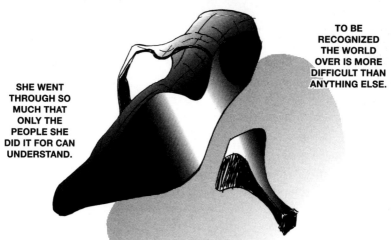

TO BE RECOGNIZED THE WORLD OVER IS MORE DIFFICULT THAN ANYTHING ELSE.

SHE WENT THROUGH SO MUCH THAT ONLY THE PEOPLE SHE DID IT FOR CAN UNDERSTAND.

AND THEN SHE ATTAINED THAT BEAUTIFUL WALK

A BEAUTY THAT SHE COULD ONLY REACH THROUGH WILL AND DETERMINATION.

...
...

THERE'S AN ARTICLE ABOUT HER APPEARANCE IN PARIS.

LET'S SEE... WHICH ONE IS IT?

UM, ABOUT HER WALK...
...

HOW DID
SHE DO
IT?

IT'S POSSIBLE
THAT THE VIDEO
SHE TOOK
TO STUDY FROM
IS STILL IN
HER OFFICE.

**MODELS AREN'T
JUST DOLLS
WHO STAND
AND WALK
AROUND.**

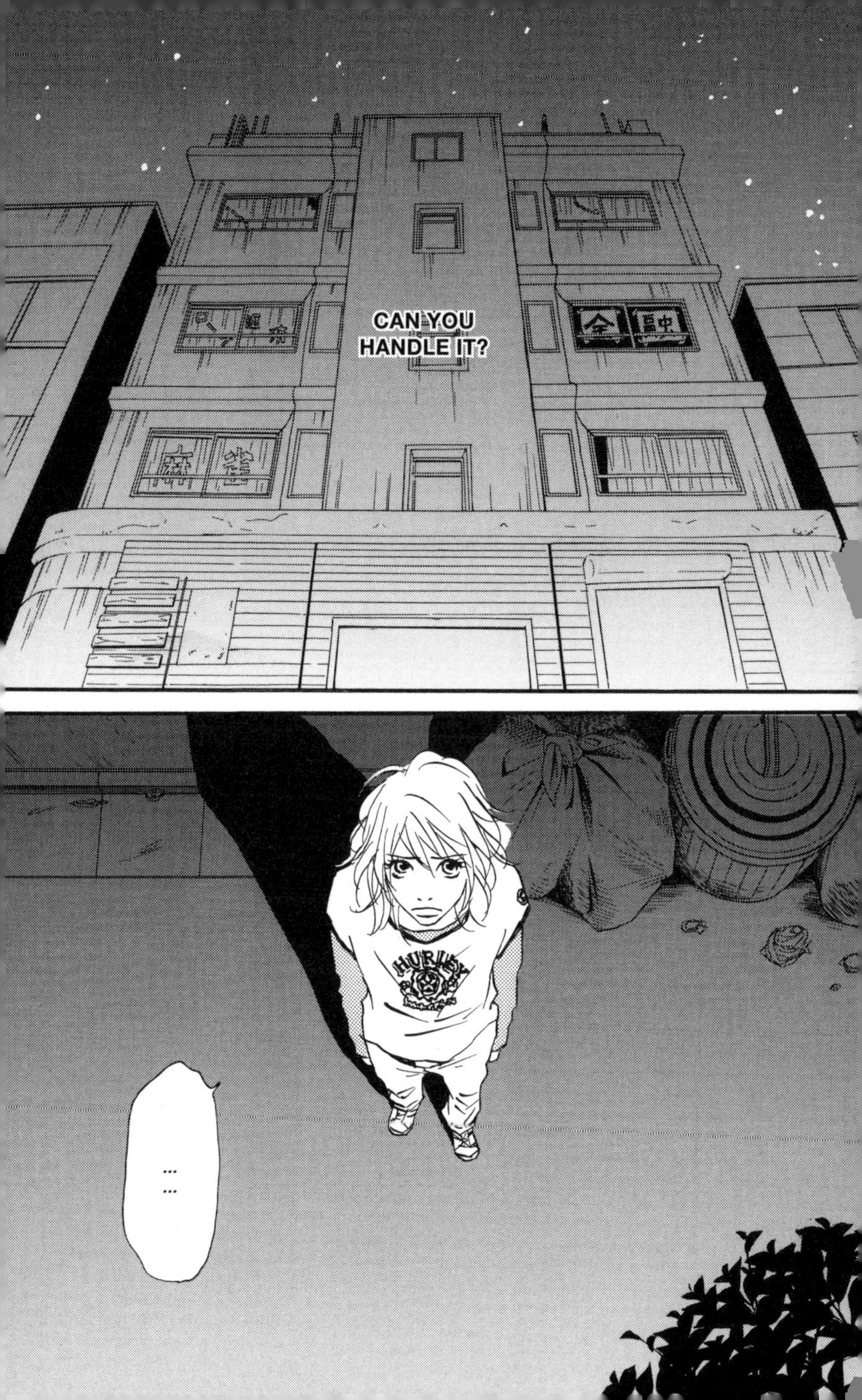
CAN YOU HANDLE IT?
……

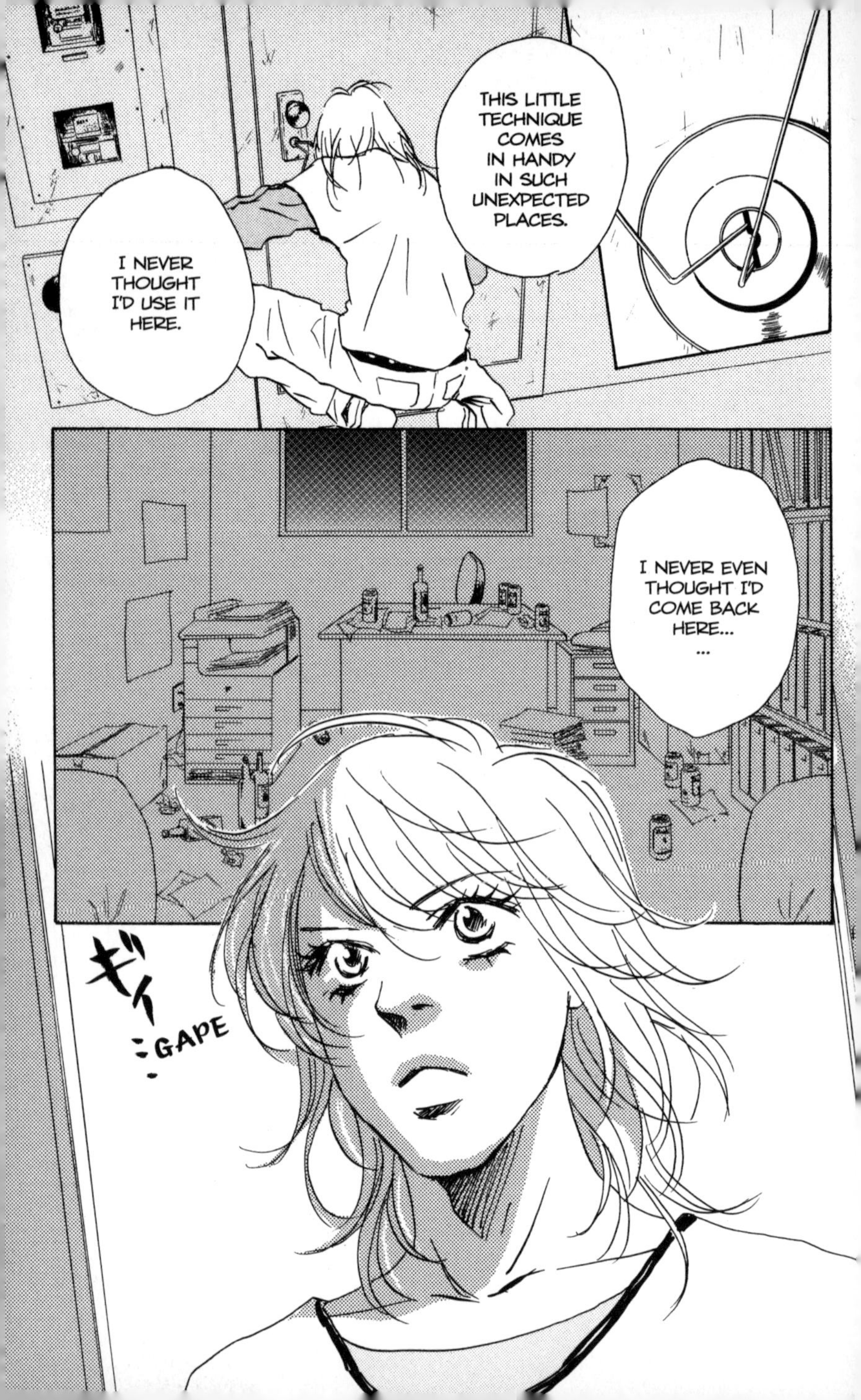
THIS LITTLE TECHNIQUE COMES IN HANDY IN SUCH UNEXPECTED PLACES.
I NEVER THOUGHT I'D USE IT HERE.
I NEVER EVEN THOUGHT I'D COME BACK HERE... ...
ギイ
GAPE

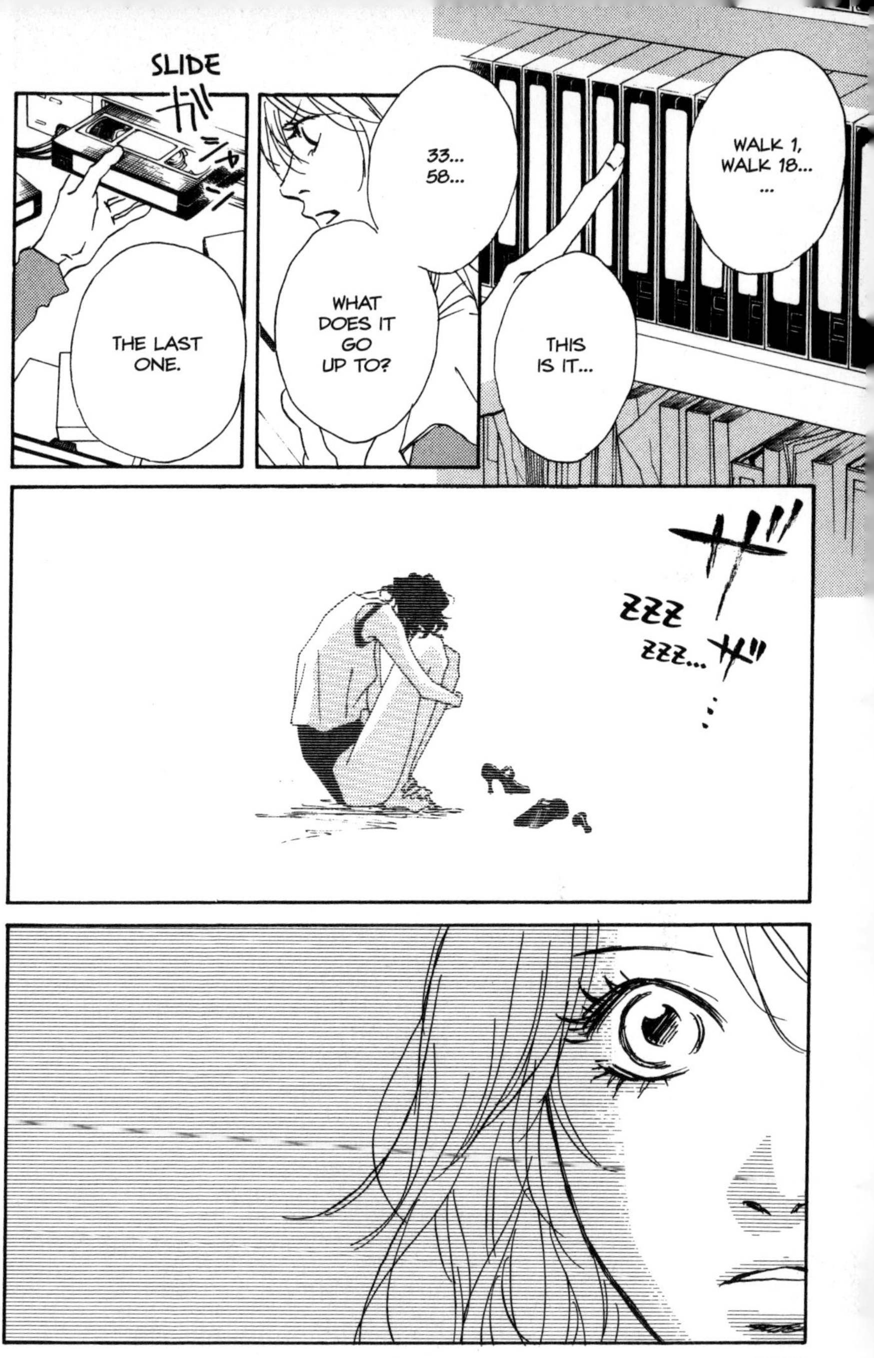

WALK 1, WALK 18... ...
33... 58...
THIS IS IT...
WHAT DOES IT GO UP TO?
SLIDE
THE LAST ONE.
ZZZ
ZZZ...

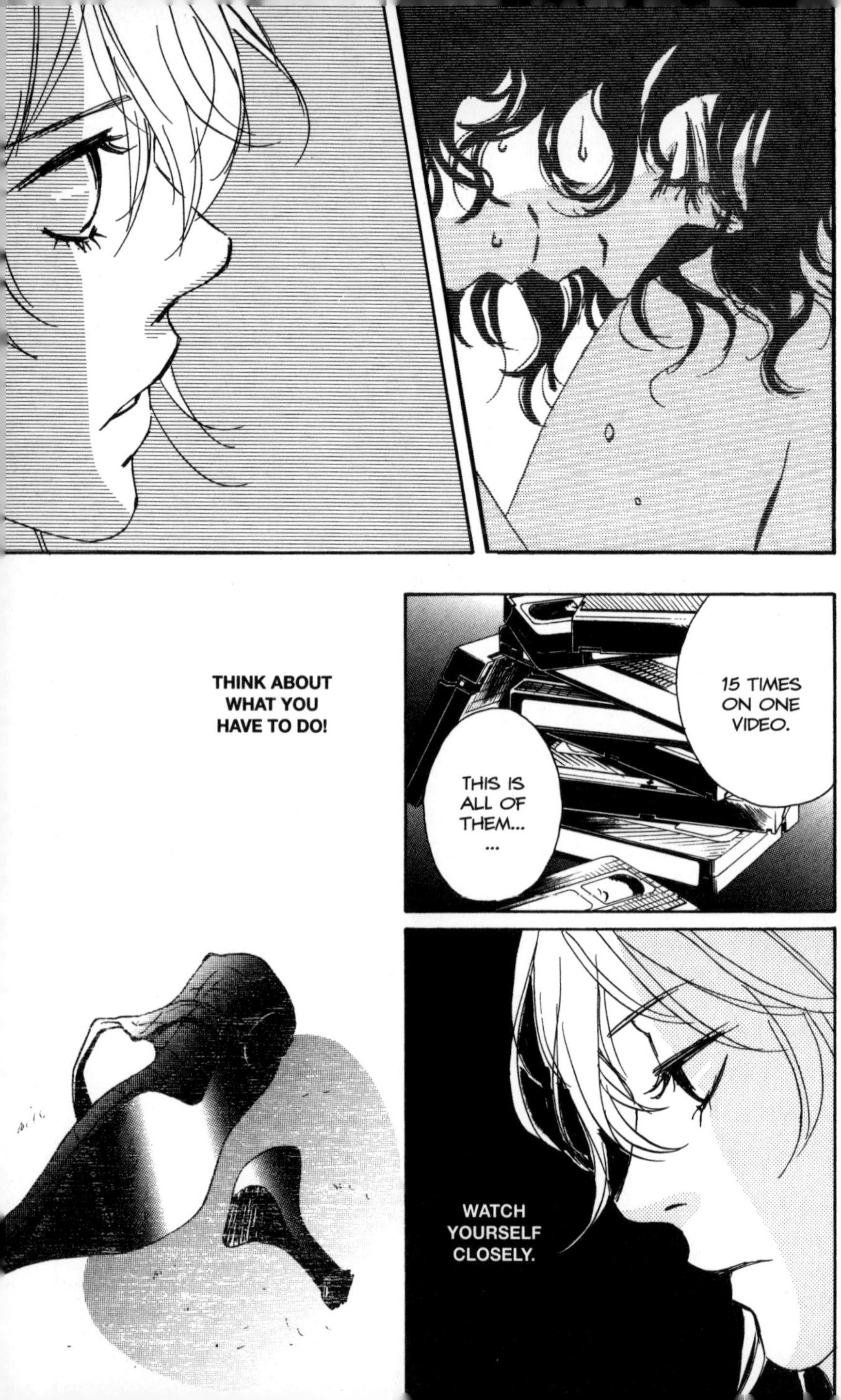
15 TIMES ON ONE VIDEO.
THIS IS ALL OF THEM... ...
THINK ABOUT WHAT YOU HAVE TO DO!
WATCH YOURSELF CLOSELY.

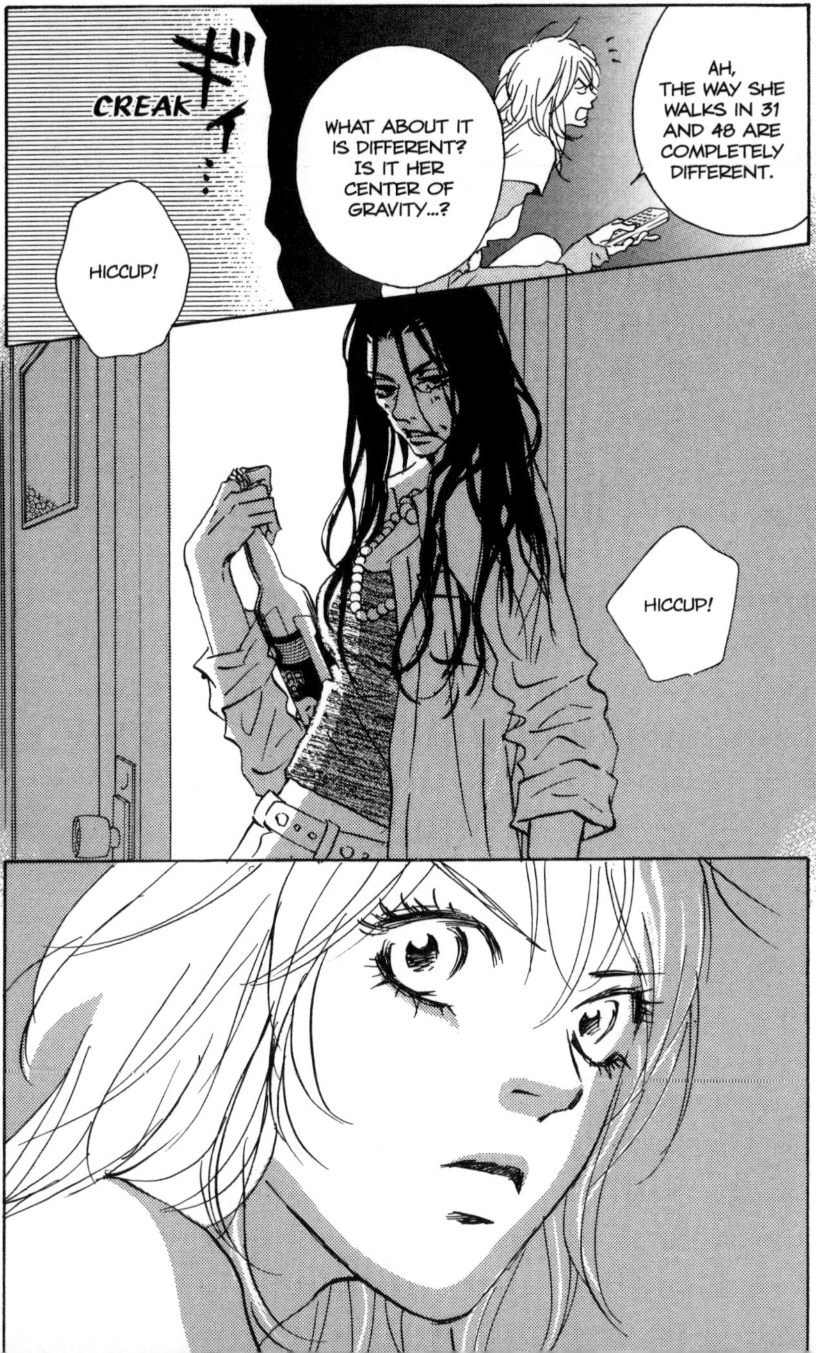
AH, THE WAY SHE WALKS IN 31 AND 48 ARE COMPLETELY DIFFERENT.
WHAT ABOUT IT IS DIFFERENT? IS IT HER CENTER OF GRAVITY...?
ギィ…
CREAK
HICCUP!
HICCUP!

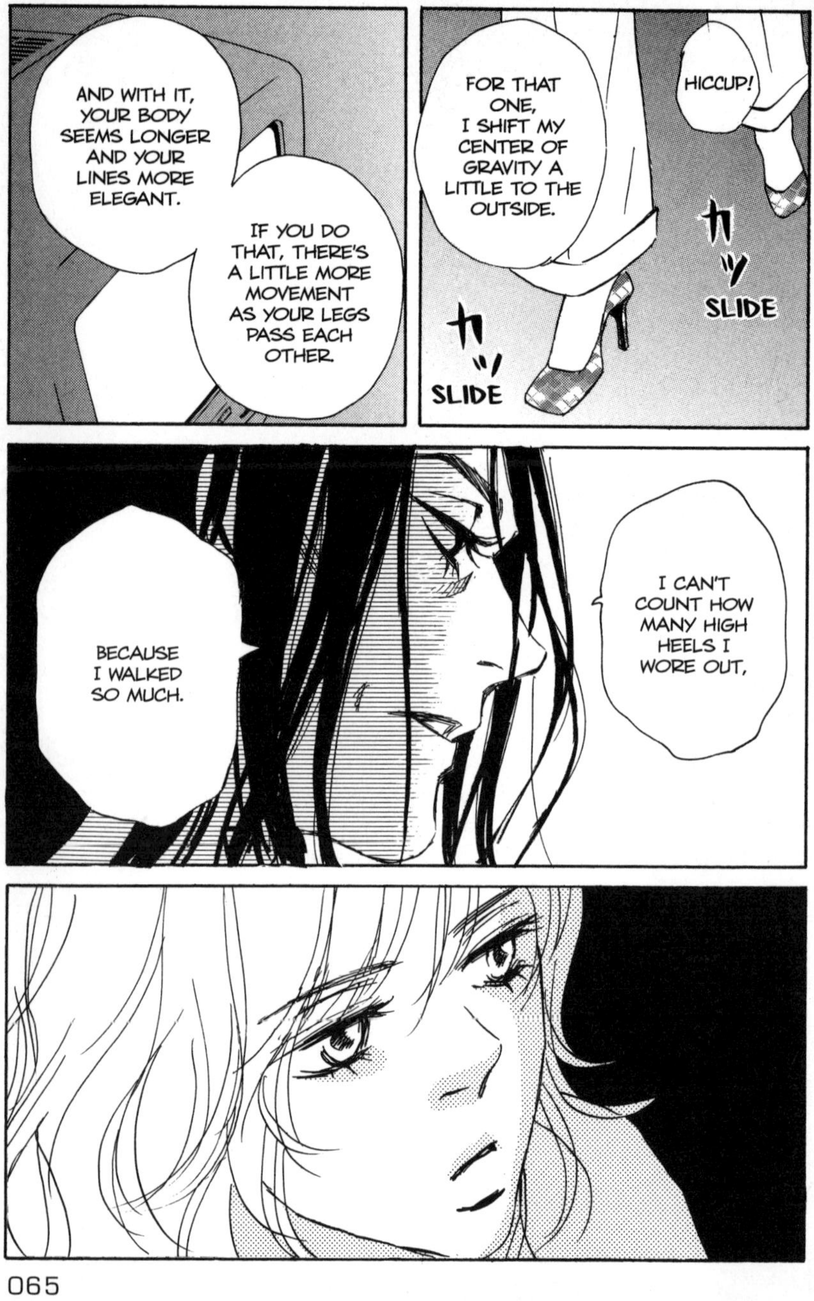
HICCUP!
FOR THAT ONE, I SHIFT MY CENTER OF GRAVITY A LITTLE TO THE OUTSIDE.
カッ SLIDE
カッ SLIDE
AND WITH IT, YOUR BODY SEEMS LONGER AND YOUR LINES MORE ELEGANT.
IF YOU DO THAT, THERE'S A LITTLE MORE MOVEMENT AS YOUR LEGS PASS EACH OTHER.
I CAN'T COUNT HOW MANY HIGH HEELS I WORE OUT,
BECAUSE I WALKED SO MUCH.

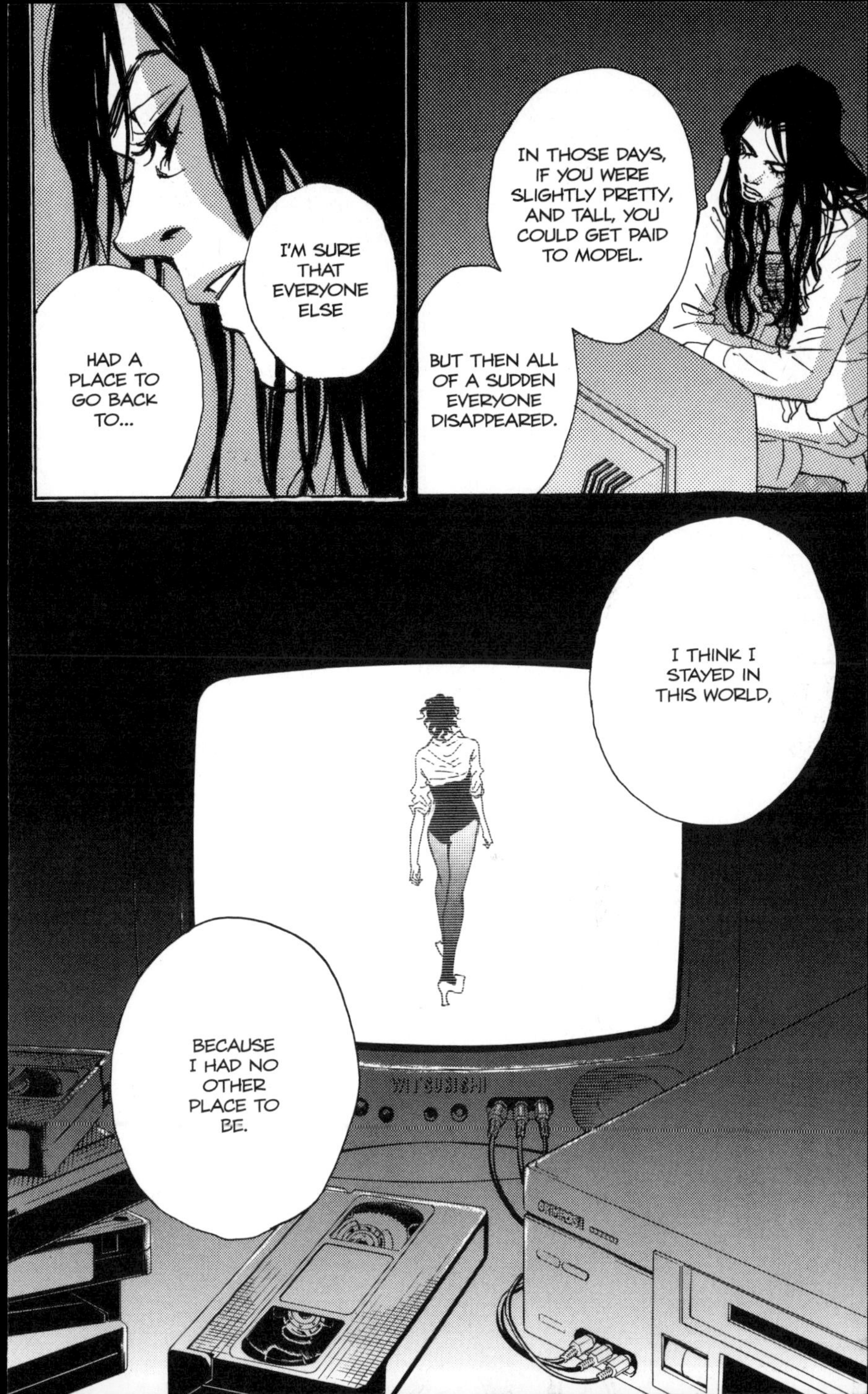
IN THOSE DAYS, IF YOU WERE SLIGHTLY PRETTY, AND TALL, YOU COULD GET PAID TO MODEL.
BUT THEN ALL OF A SUDDEN EVERYONE DISAPPEARED.
I'M SURE THAT EVERYONE ELSE
HAD A PLACE TO GO BACK TO...
I THINK I STAYED IN THIS WORLD,
BECAUSE I HAD NO OTHER PLACE TO BE.

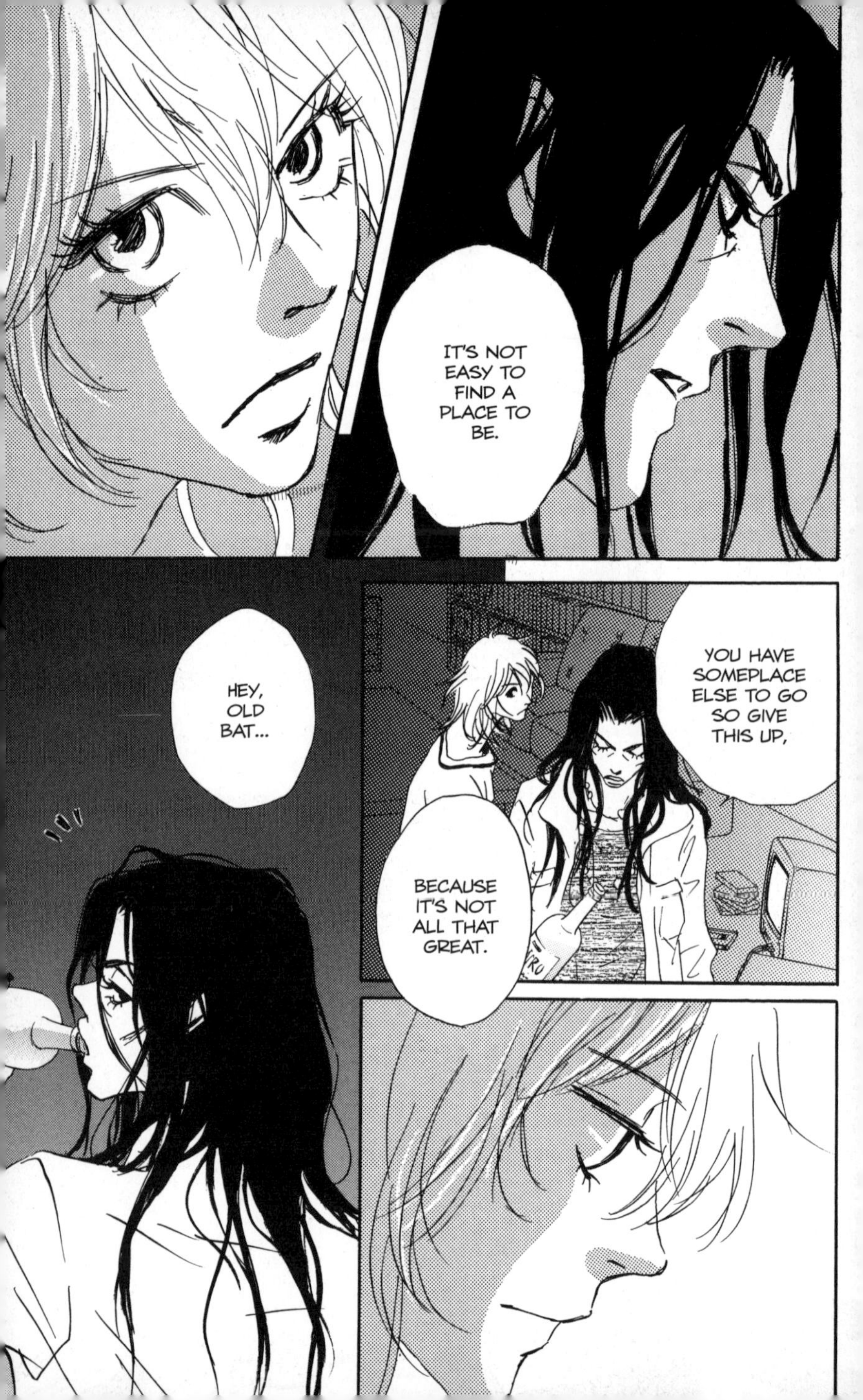
IT'S NOT EASY TO FIND A PLACE TO BE.
YOU HAVE SOMEPLACE ELSE TO GO SO GIVE THIS UP,
BECAUSE IT'S NOT ALL THAT GREAT.
HEY, OLD BAT...

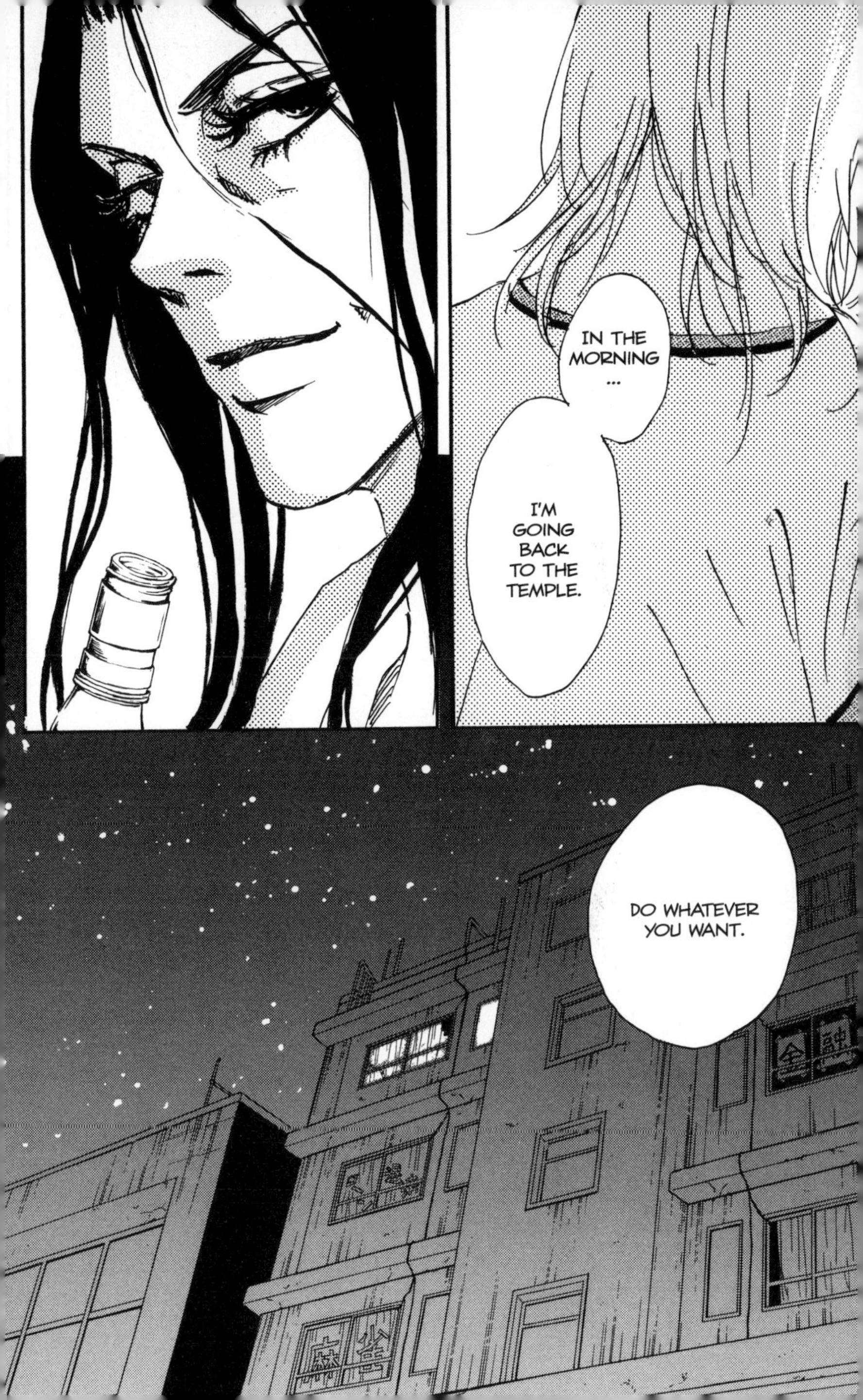
IN THE MORNING ...
I'M GOING BACK TO THE TEMPLE.
DO WHATEVER YOU WANT.

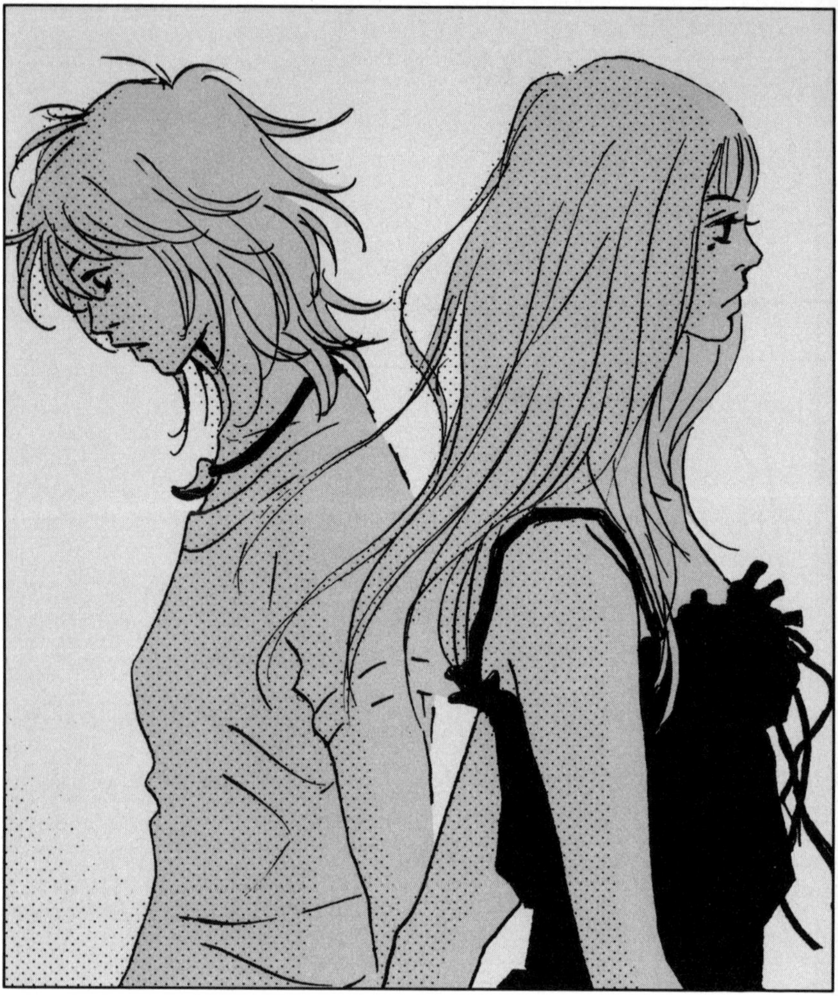

MODE 4

GET UP, STAND UP

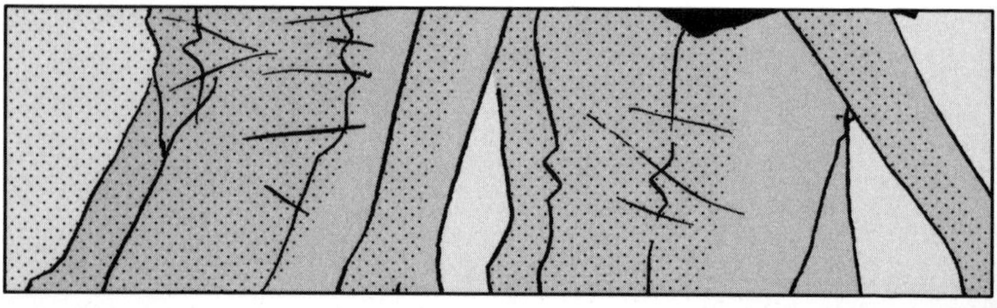

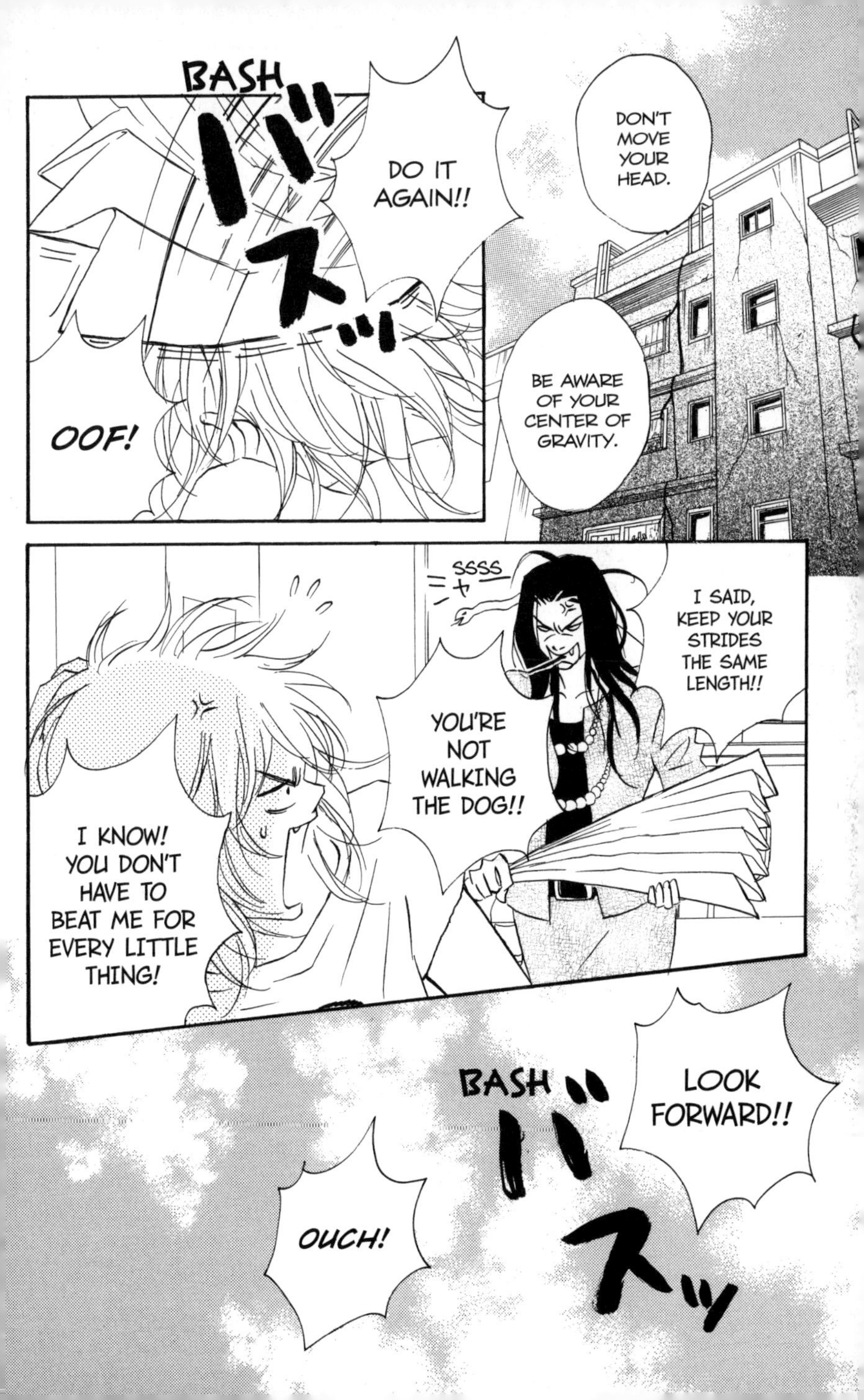
DON'T MOVE YOUR HEAD.
BE AWARE OF YOUR CENTER OF GRAVITY.
BASH
DO IT AGAIN!!
OOF!
I SAID, KEEP YOUR STRIDES THE SAME LENGTH!!
SSSS
YOU'RE NOT WALKING THE DOG!!
I KNOW! YOU DON'T HAVE TO BEAT ME FOR EVERY LITTLE THING!
LOOK FORWARD!!
BASH
OUCH!

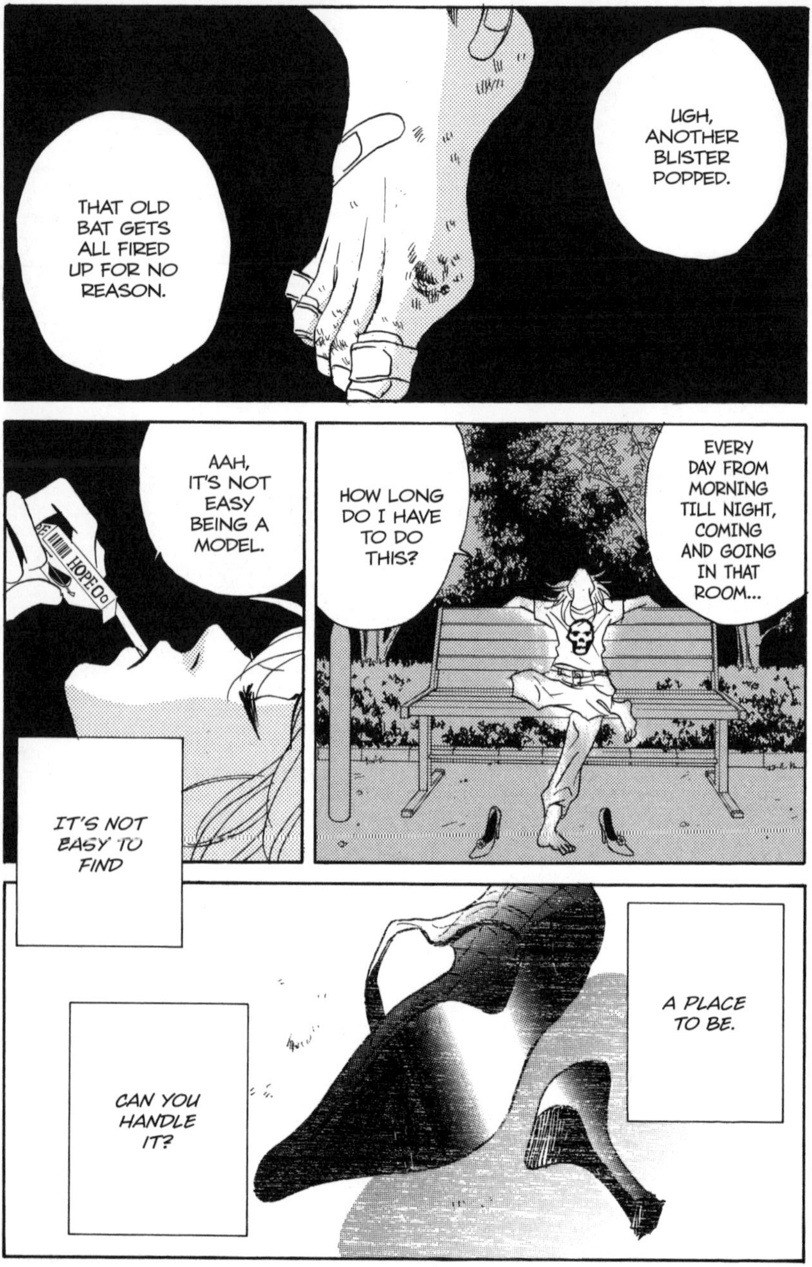
UGH, ANOTHER BLISTER POPPED.
THAT OLD BAT GETS ALL FIRED UP FOR NO REASON.
EVERY DAY FROM MORNING TILL NIGHT, COMING AND GOING IN THAT ROOM...
HOW LONG DO I HAVE TO DO THIS?
AAH, IT'S NOT EASY BEING A MODEL.
IT'S NOT EASY TO FIND
A PLACE TO BE.
CAN YOU HANDLE IT?

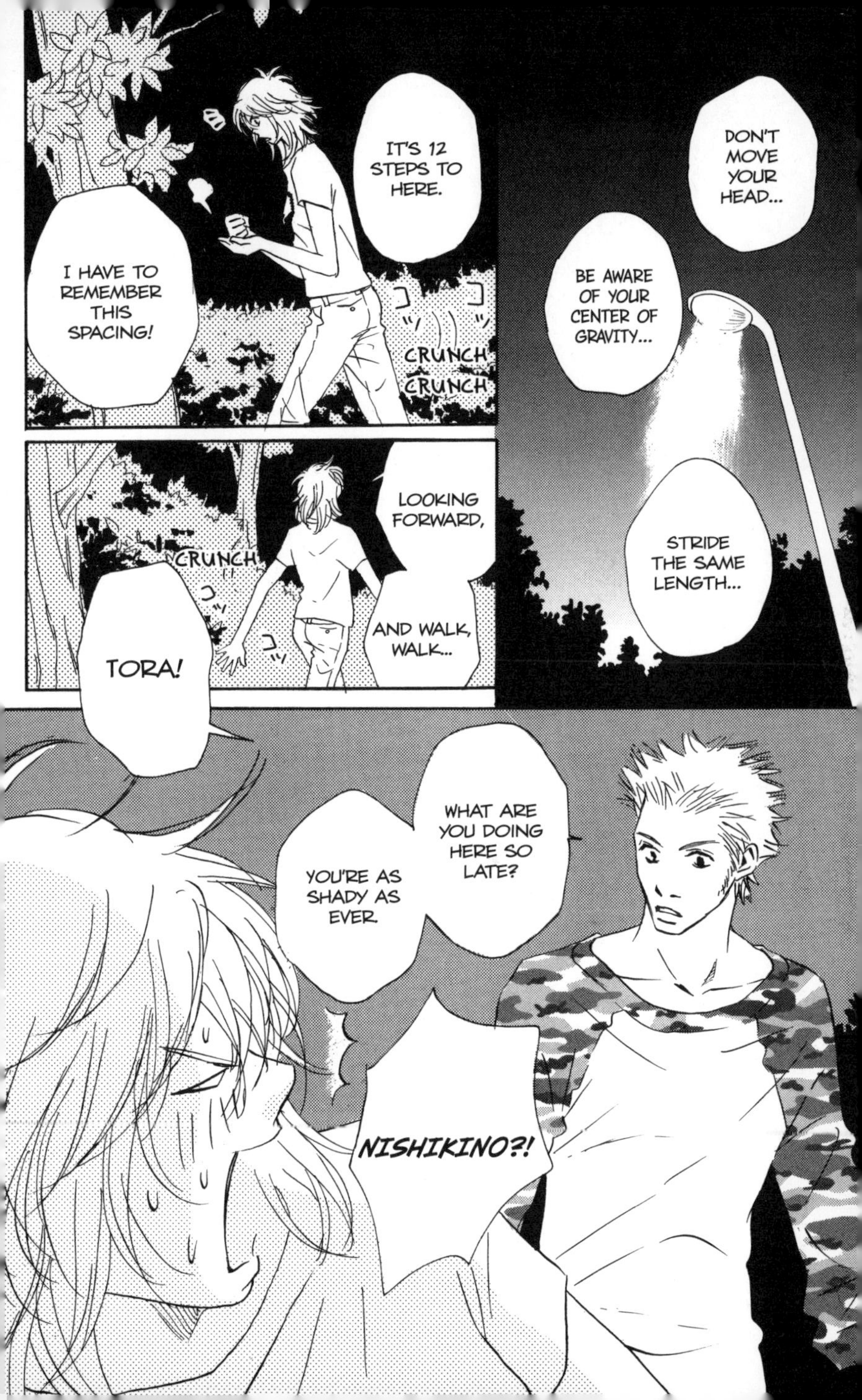
DON'T MOVE YOUR HEAD...
BE AWARE OF YOUR CENTER OF GRAVITY...
STRIDE THE SAME LENGTH...
IT'S 12 STEPS TO HERE.
I HAVE TO REMEMBER THIS SPACING!
CRUNCH
CRUNCH
LOOKING FORWARD,
AND WALK, WALK...
CRUNCH
TORA!
WHAT ARE YOU DOING HERE SO LATE?
YOU'RE AS SHADY AS EVER.
NISHIKINO?!

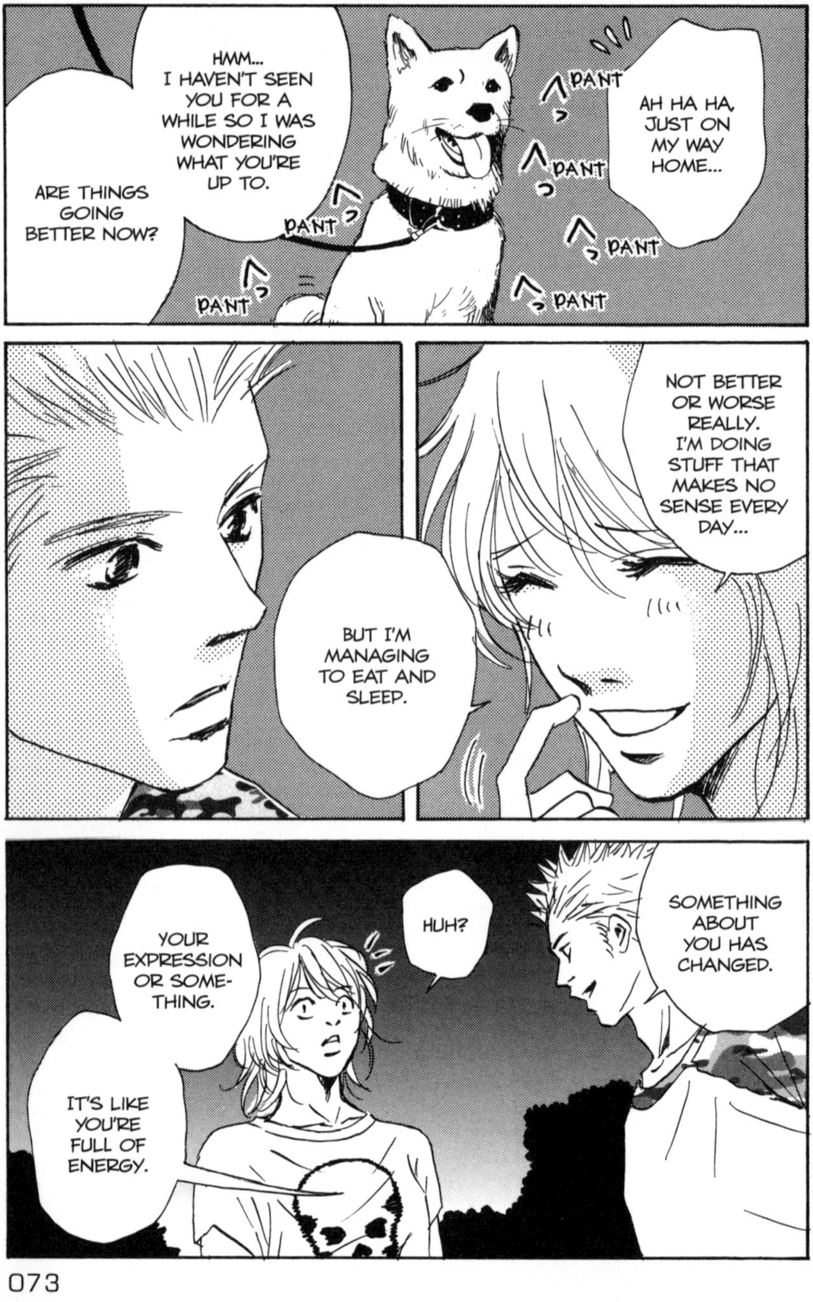
AH HA HA, JUST ON MY WAY HOME...
PANT PANT PANT PANT PANT PANT
HMM... I HAVEN'T SEEN YOU FOR A WHILE SO I WAS WONDERING WHAT YOU'RE UP TO.
ARE THINGS GOING BETTER NOW?
NOT BETTER OR WORSE REALLY. I'M DOING STUFF THAT MAKES NO SENSE EVERY DAY...
BUT I'M MANAGING TO EAT AND SLEEP.
SOMETHING ABOUT YOU HAS CHANGED.
HUH?
YOUR EXPRESSION OR SOME-THING.
IT'S LIKE YOU'RE FULL OF ENERGY.

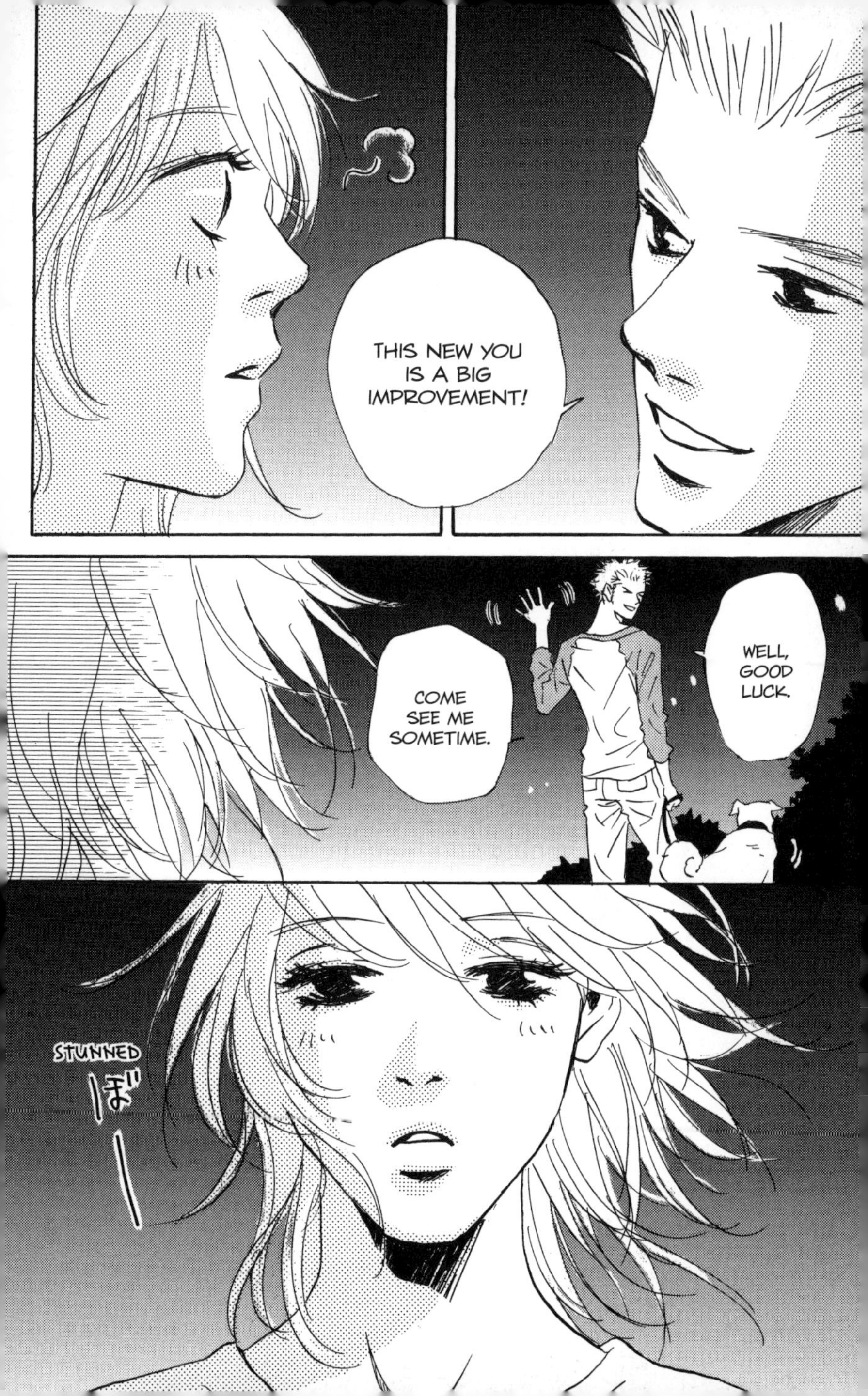
THIS NEW YOU IS A BIG IMPROVEMENT!
WELL, GOOD LUCK.
COME SEE ME SOMETIME.
STUNNED
ぼーー

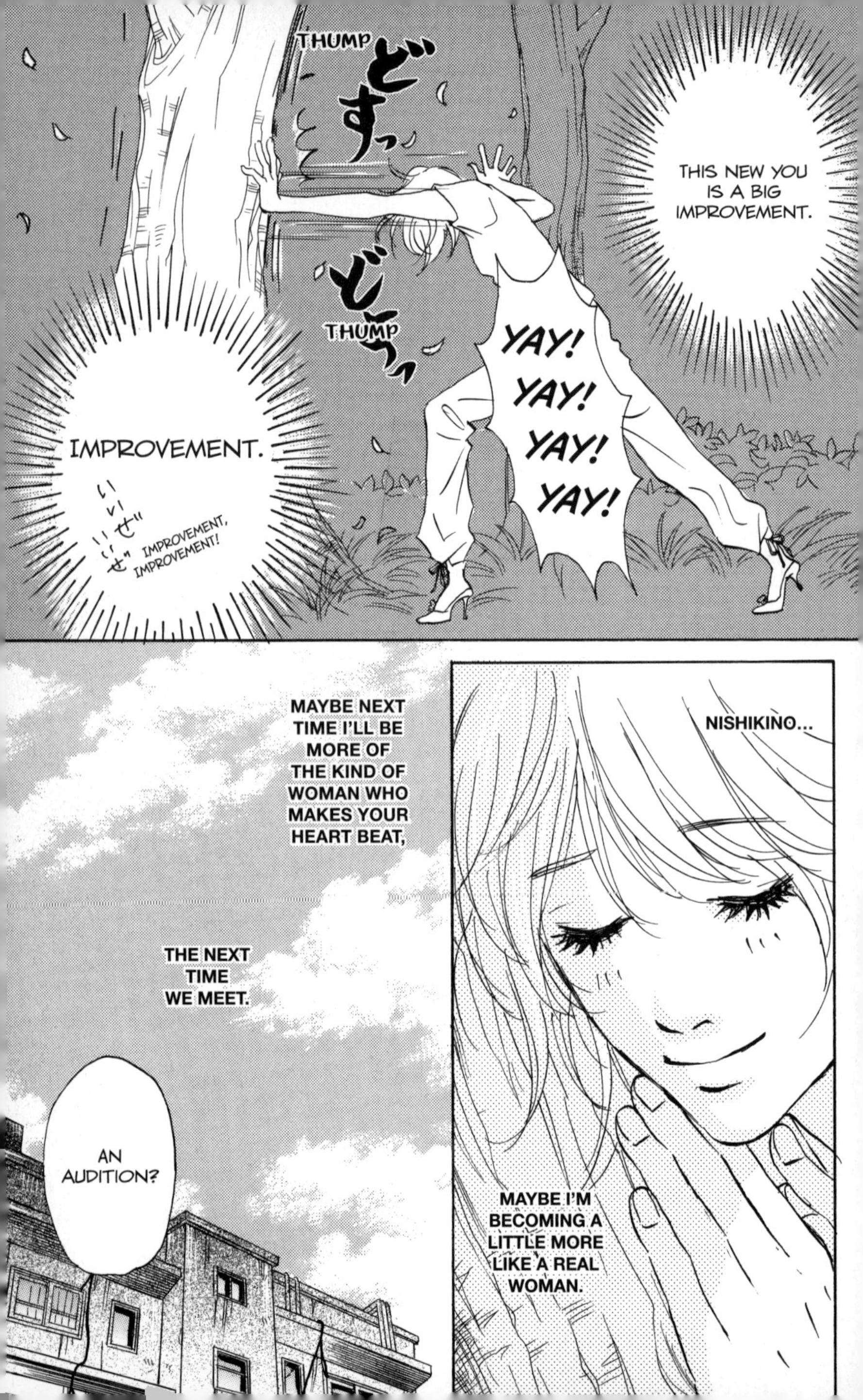
THIS NEW YOU IS A BIG IMPROVEMENT.
THUMP
どすっ
THUMP
YAY! YAY! YAY! YAY!
IMPROVEMENT.
IMPROVEMENT, IMPROVEMENT!
NISHIKINO...
MAYBE I'M BECOMING A LITTLE MORE LIKE A REAL WOMAN.
MAYBE NEXT TIME I'LL BE MORE OF THE KIND OF WOMAN WHO MAKES YOUR HEART BEAT,
THE NEXT TIME WE MEET.
AN AUDITION?

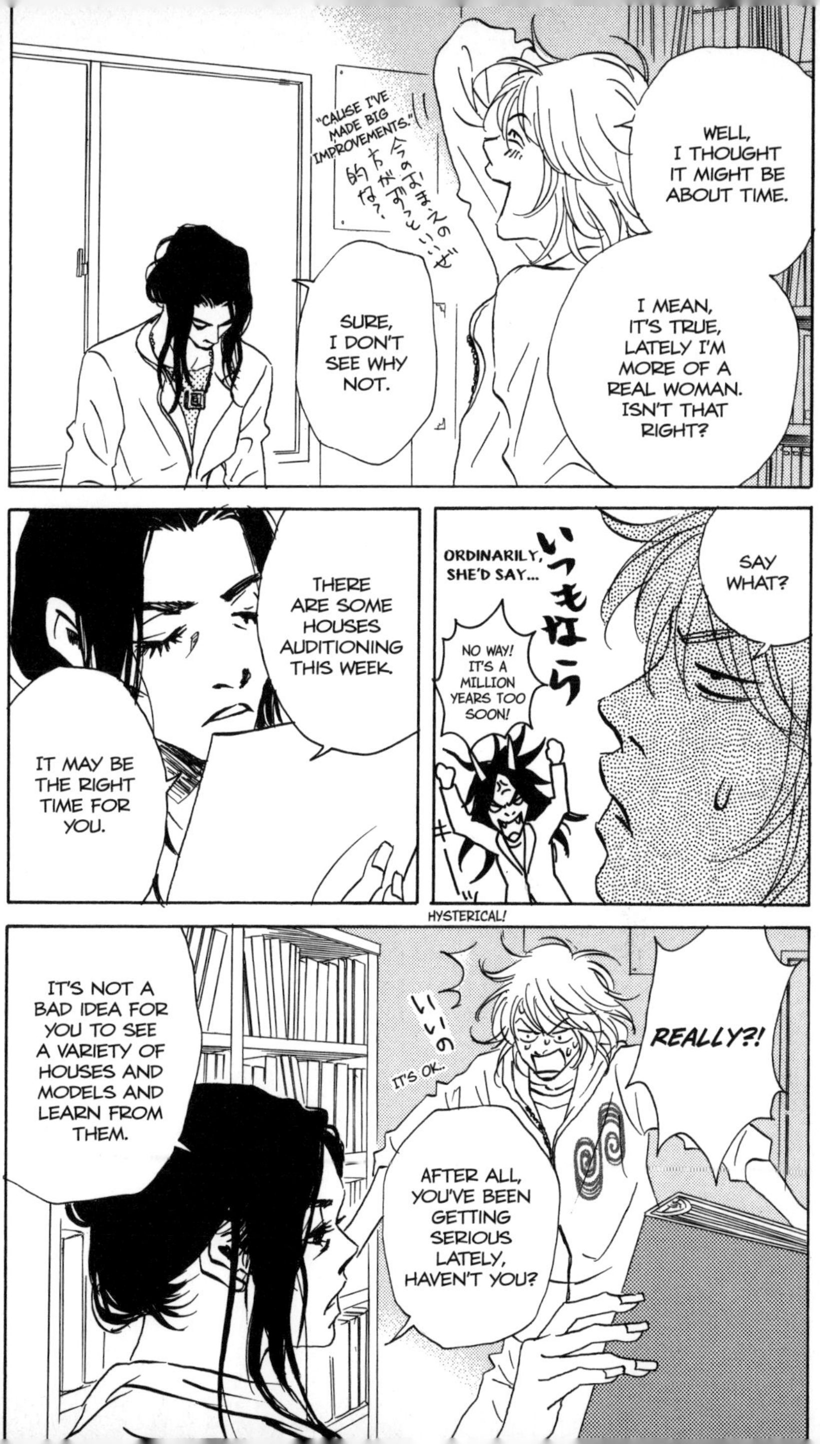
WELL, I THOUGHT IT MIGHT BE ABOUT TIME.
I MEAN, IT'S TRUE, LATELY I'M MORE OF A REAL WOMAN. ISN'T THAT RIGHT?
今のおまえのほうがずっといいぜ的な?
"CAUSE I'VE MADE BIG IMPROVEMENTS."
SURE, I DON'T SEE WHY NOT.
SAY WHAT?
いつもなら
ORDINARILY, SHE'D SAY...
NO WAY! IT'S A MILLION YEARS TOO SOON!
HYSTERICAL!
THERE ARE SOME HOUSES AUDITIONING THIS WEEK.
IT MAY BE THE RIGHT TIME FOR YOU.
REALLY?!
いいの
IT'S OK.
AFTER ALL, YOU'VE BEEN GETTING SERIOUS LATELY, HAVEN'T YOU?
IT'S NOT A BAD IDEA FOR YOU TO SEE A VARIETY OF HOUSES AND MODELS AND LEARN FROM THEM.

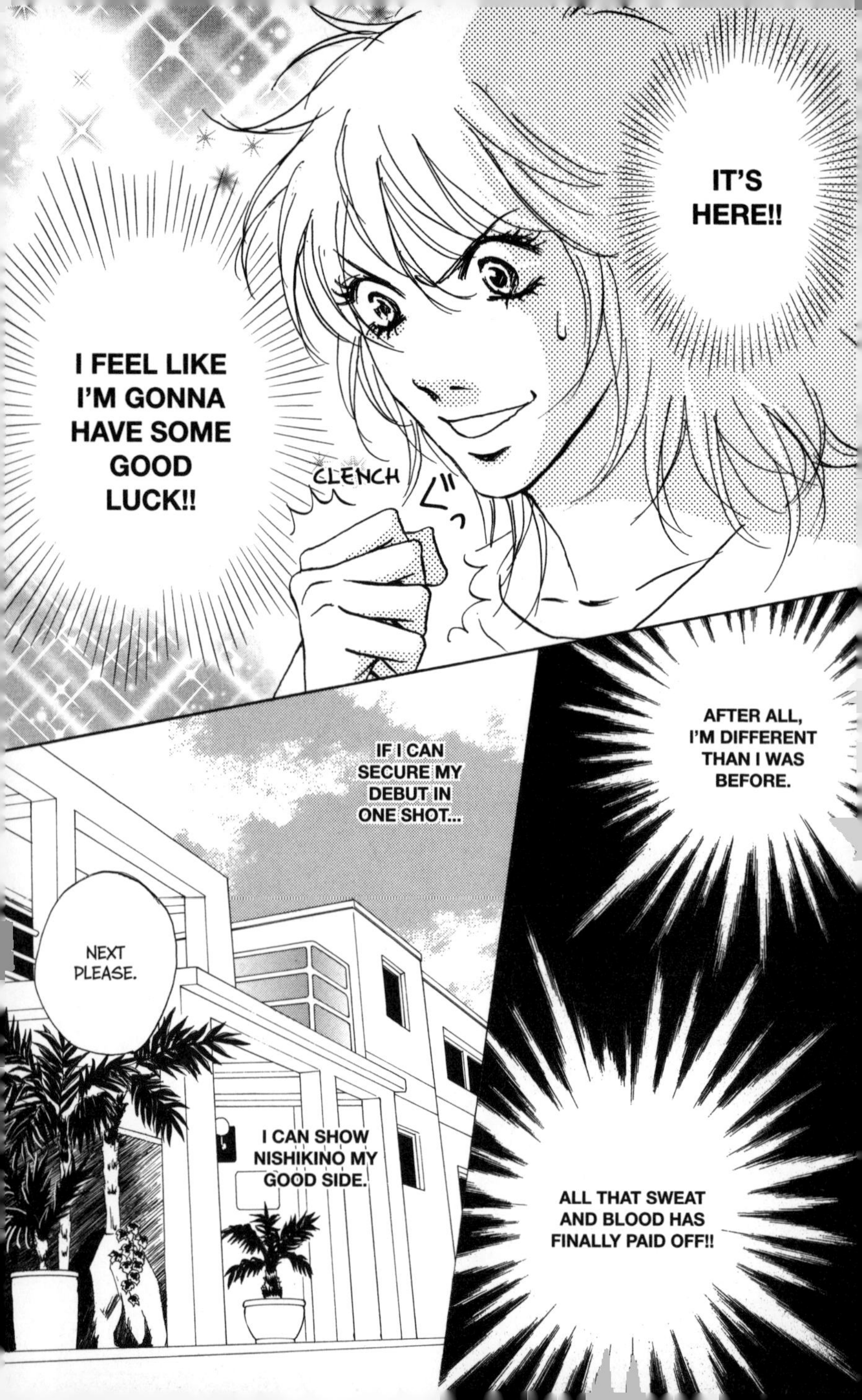
IT'S HERE!!
I FEEL LIKE I'M GONNA HAVE SOME GOOD LUCK!!
CLENCH
AFTER ALL, I'M DIFFERENT THAN I WAS BEFORE.
ALL THAT SWEAT AND BLOOD HAS FINALLY PAID OFF!!
IF I CAN SECURE MY DEBUT IN ONE SHOT...
I CAN SHOW NISHIKINO MY GOOD SIDE.
NEXT PLEASE.

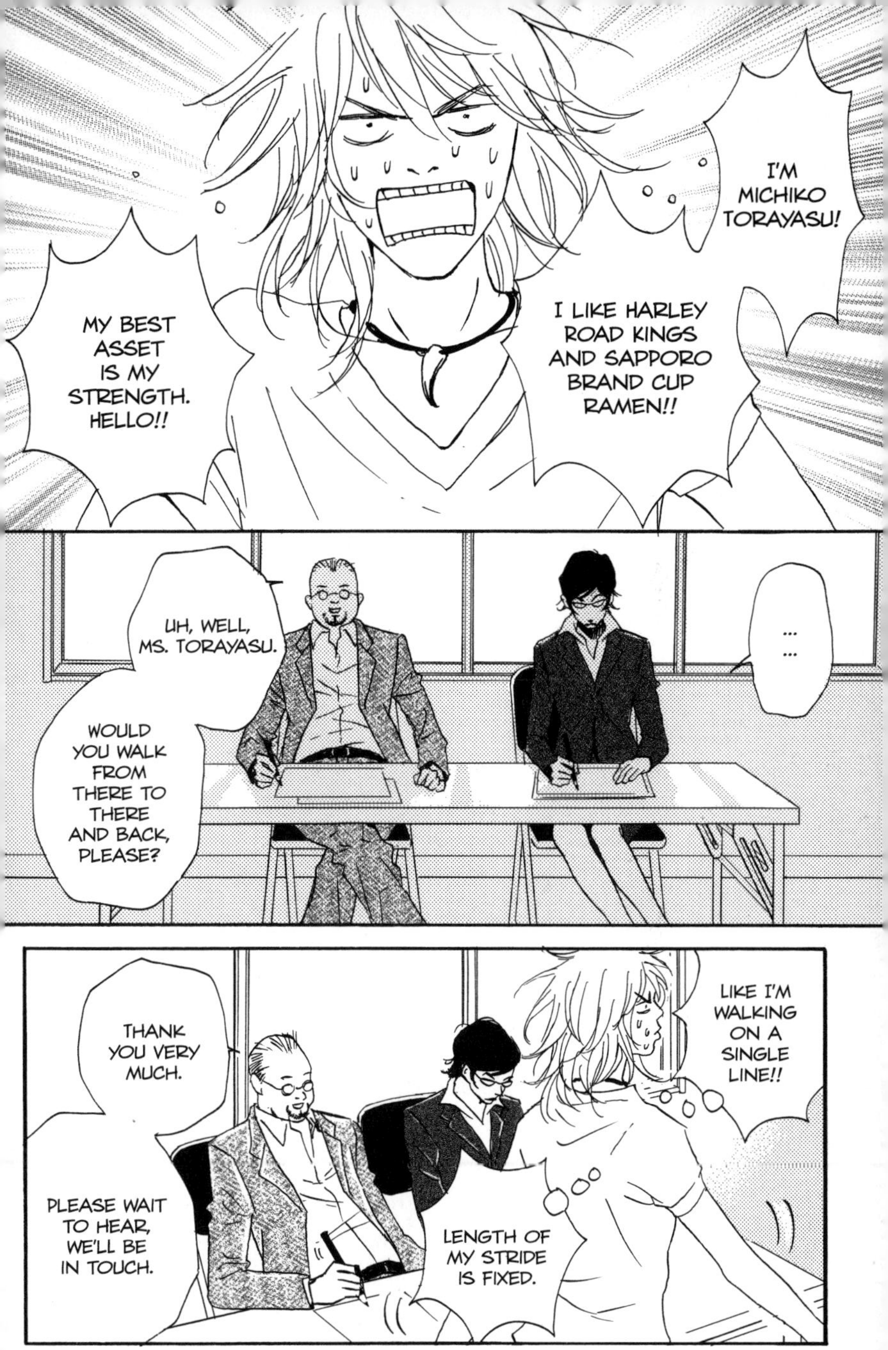
I'M MICHIKO TORAYASU!
I LIKE HARLEY ROAD KINGS AND SAPPORO BRAND CUP RAMEN!!
MY BEST ASSET IS MY STRENGTH. HELLO!!
... ...
UH, WELL, MS. TORAYASU.
WOULD YOU WALK FROM THERE TO THERE AND BACK, PLEASE?
LIKE I'M WALKING ON A SINGLE LINE!!
LENGTH OF MY STRIDE IS FIXED.
THANK YOU VERY MUCH.
PLEASE WAIT TO HEAR, WE'LL BE IN TOUCH.

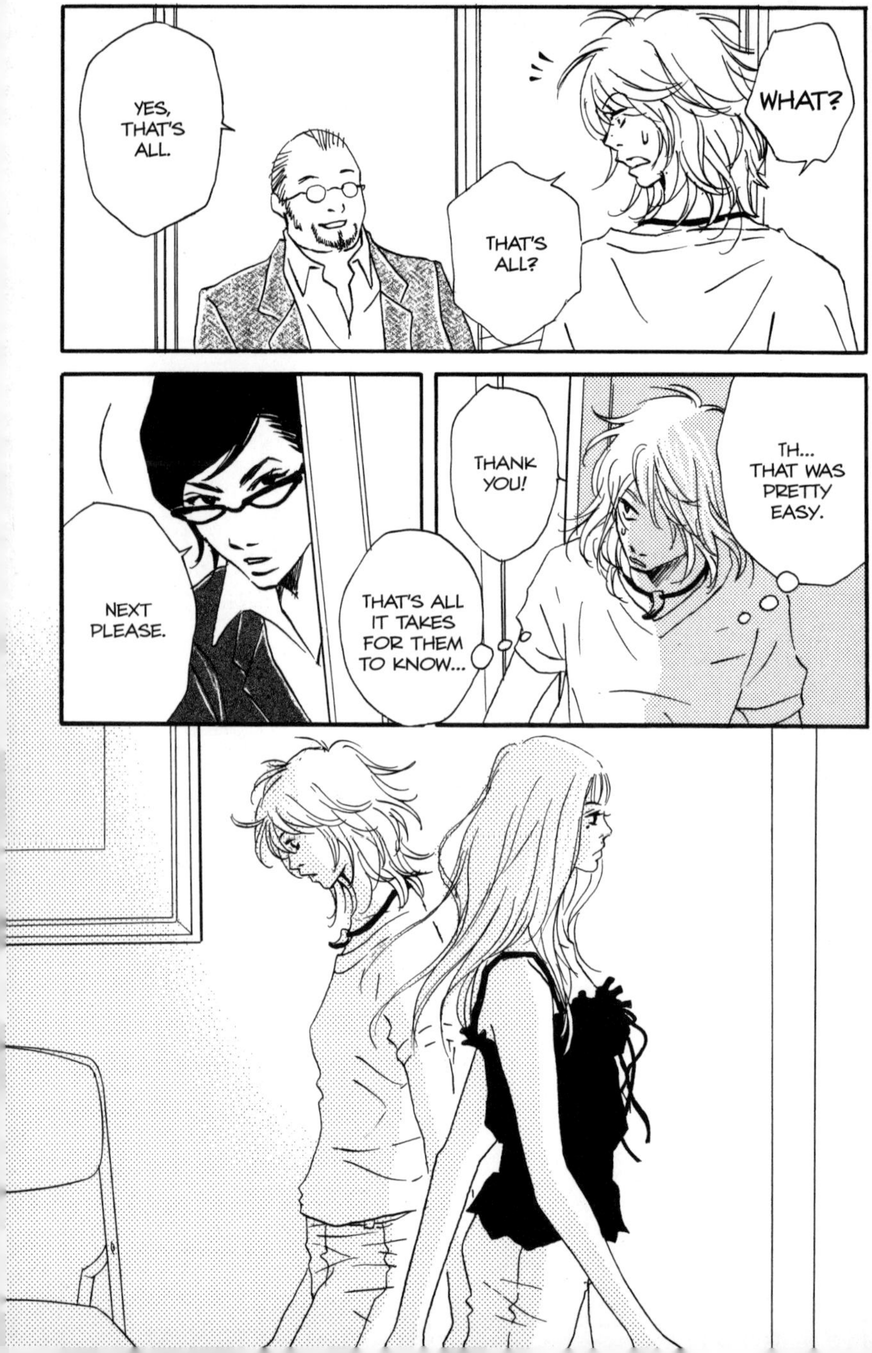
WHAT?
THAT'S ALL?
YES, THAT'S ALL.
TH... THAT WAS PRETTY EASY.
THANK YOU!
THAT'S ALL IT TAKES FOR THEM TO KNOW...
NEXT PLEASE.

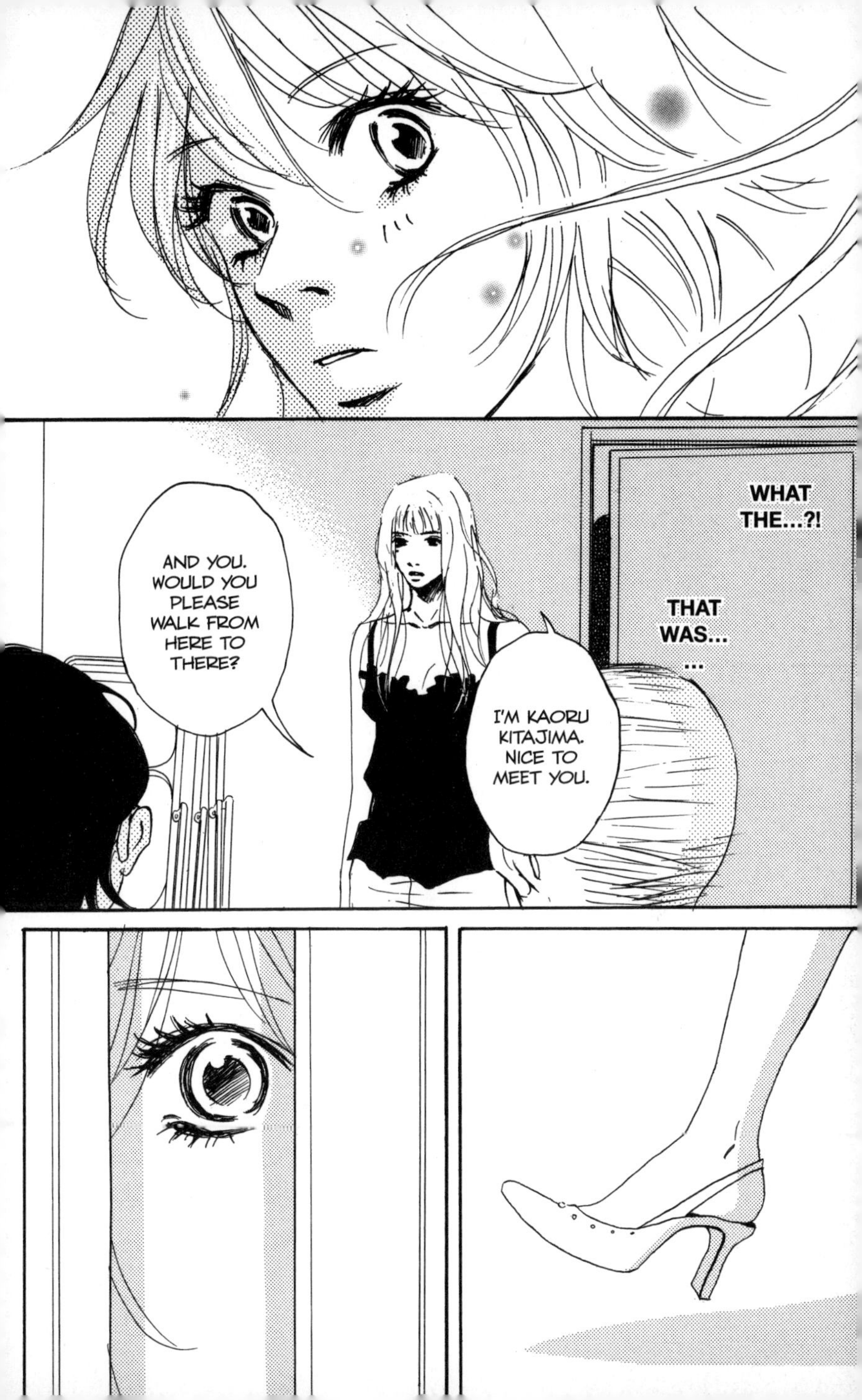
WHAT THE...?!
THAT WAS... ...
I'M KAORU KITAJIMA. NICE TO MEET YOU.
AND YOU. WOULD YOU PLEASE WALK FROM HERE TO THERE?

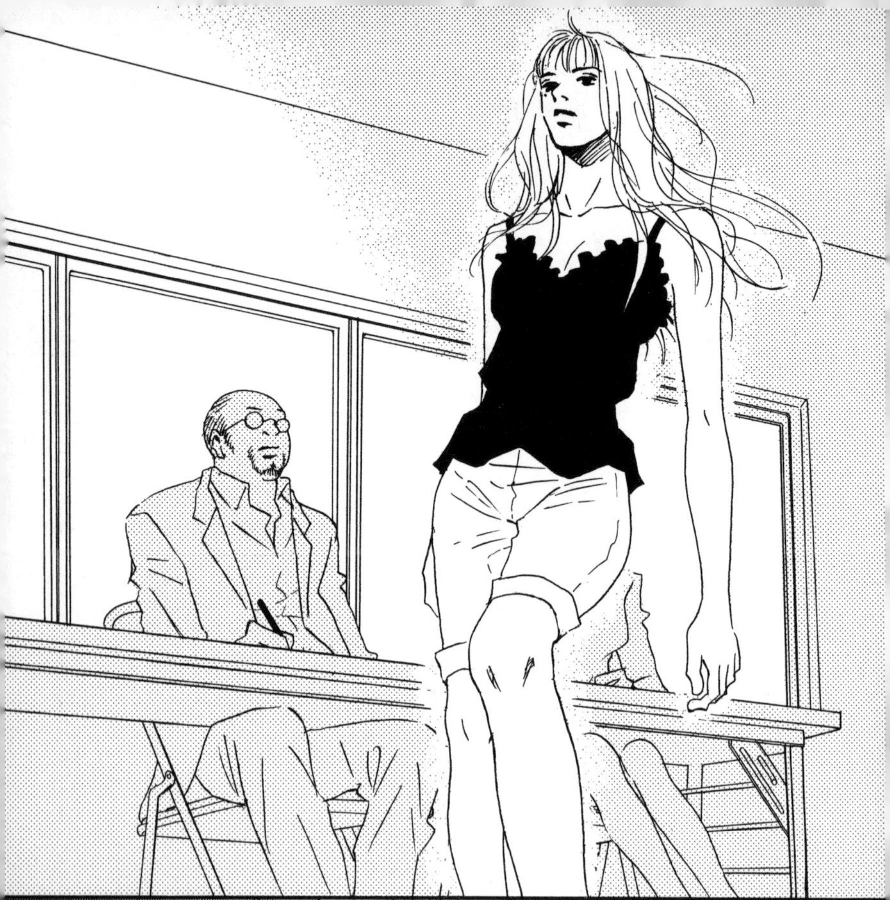
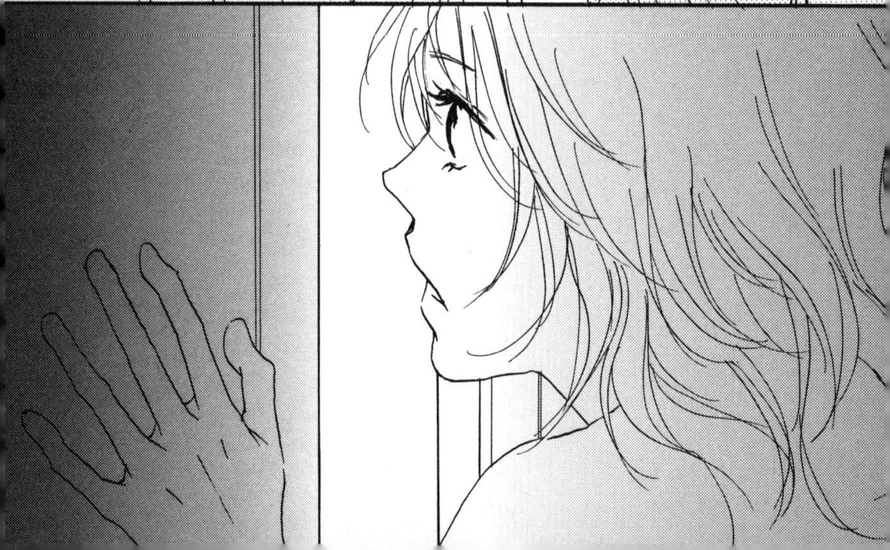

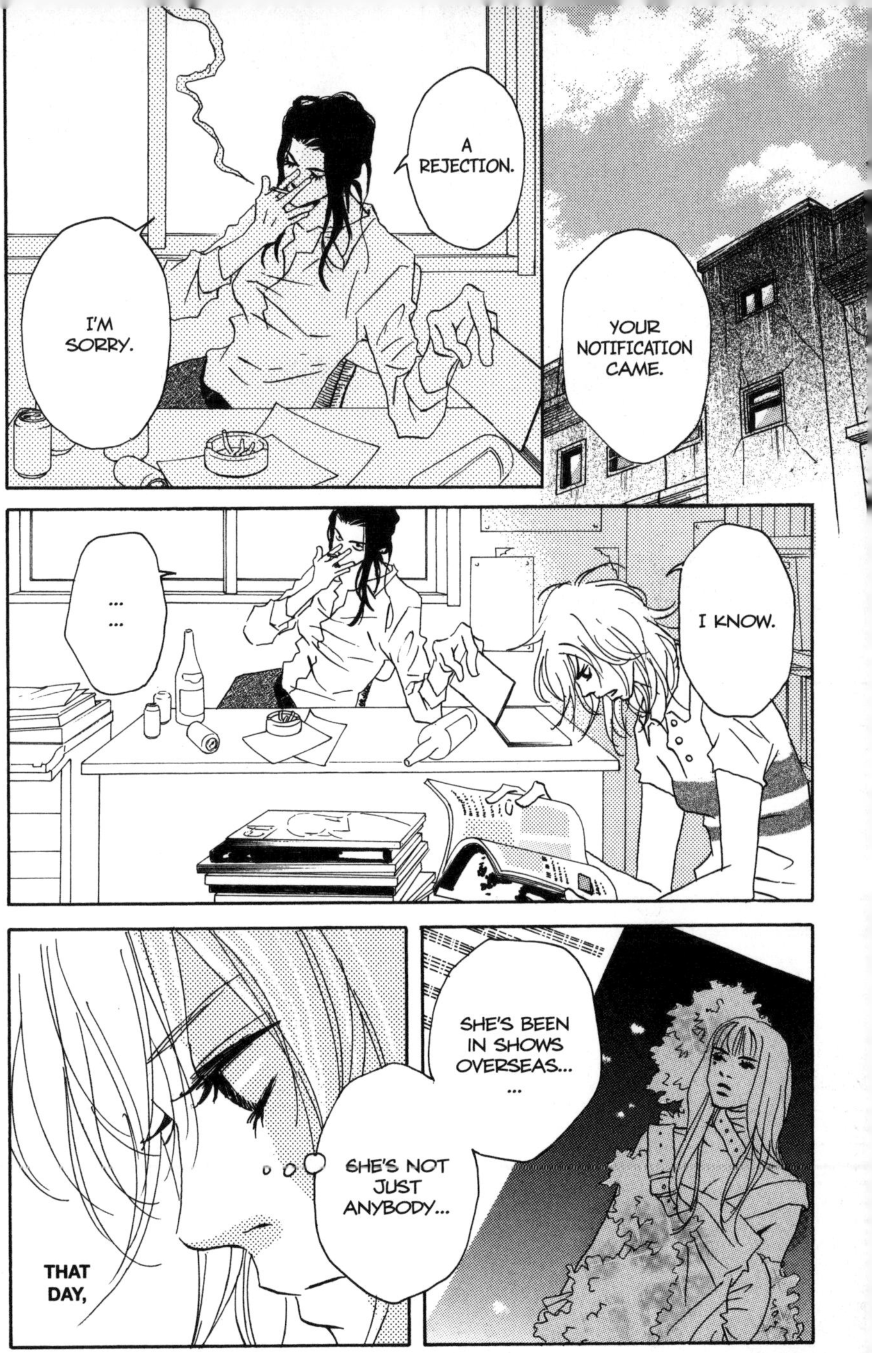
YOUR NOTIFICATION CAME.
A REJECTION.
I'M SORRY.
I KNOW.
...
...
SHE'S BEEN IN SHOWS OVERSEAS... ...
SHE'S NOT JUST ANYBODY...
THAT DAY,

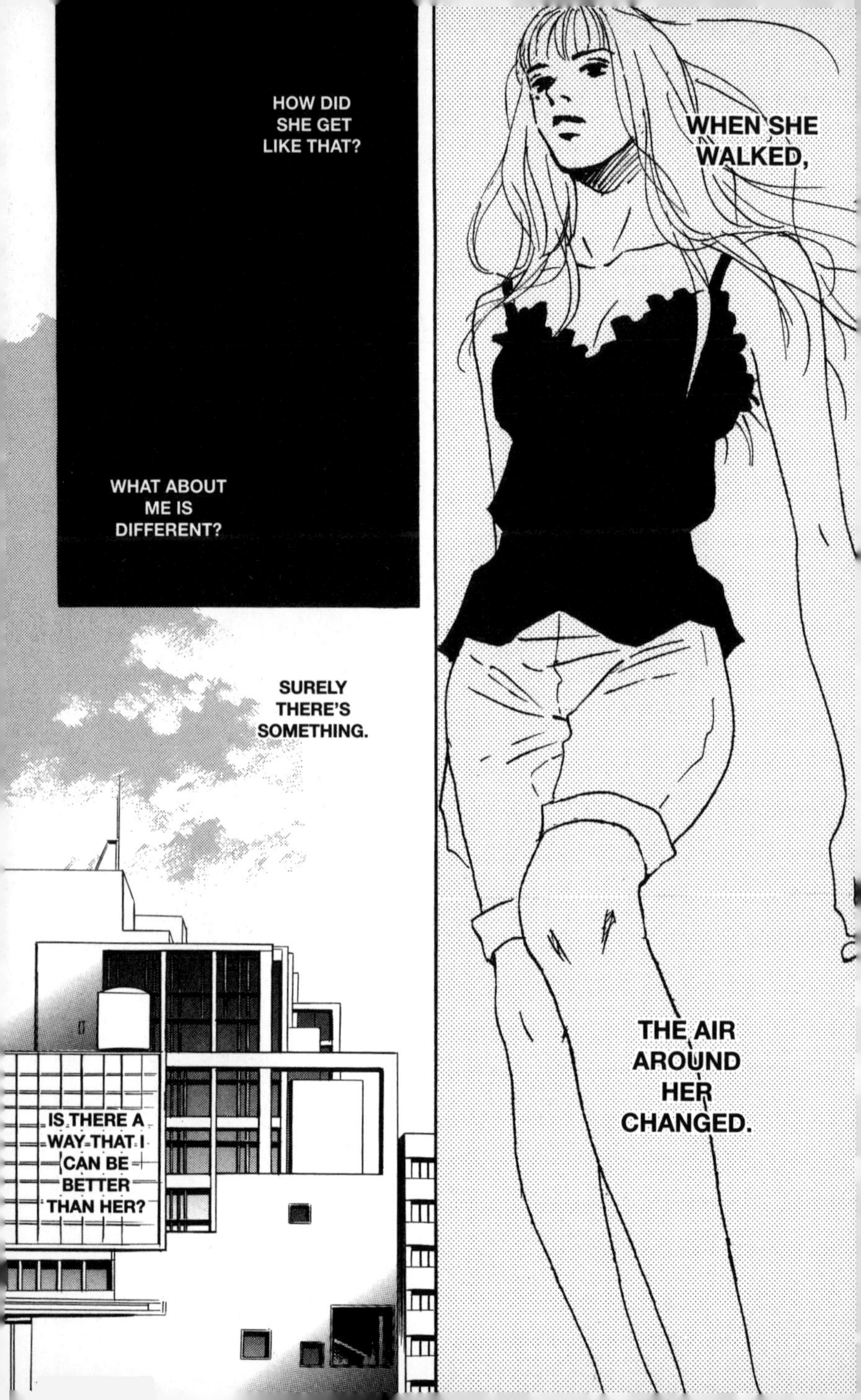
WHEN SHE WALKED,
THE AIR AROUND HER CHANGED.
HOW DID SHE GET LIKE THAT?
WHAT ABOUT ME IS DIFFERENT?
SURELY THERE'S SOMETHING.
IS THERE A WAY THAT I CAN BE BETTER THAN HER?

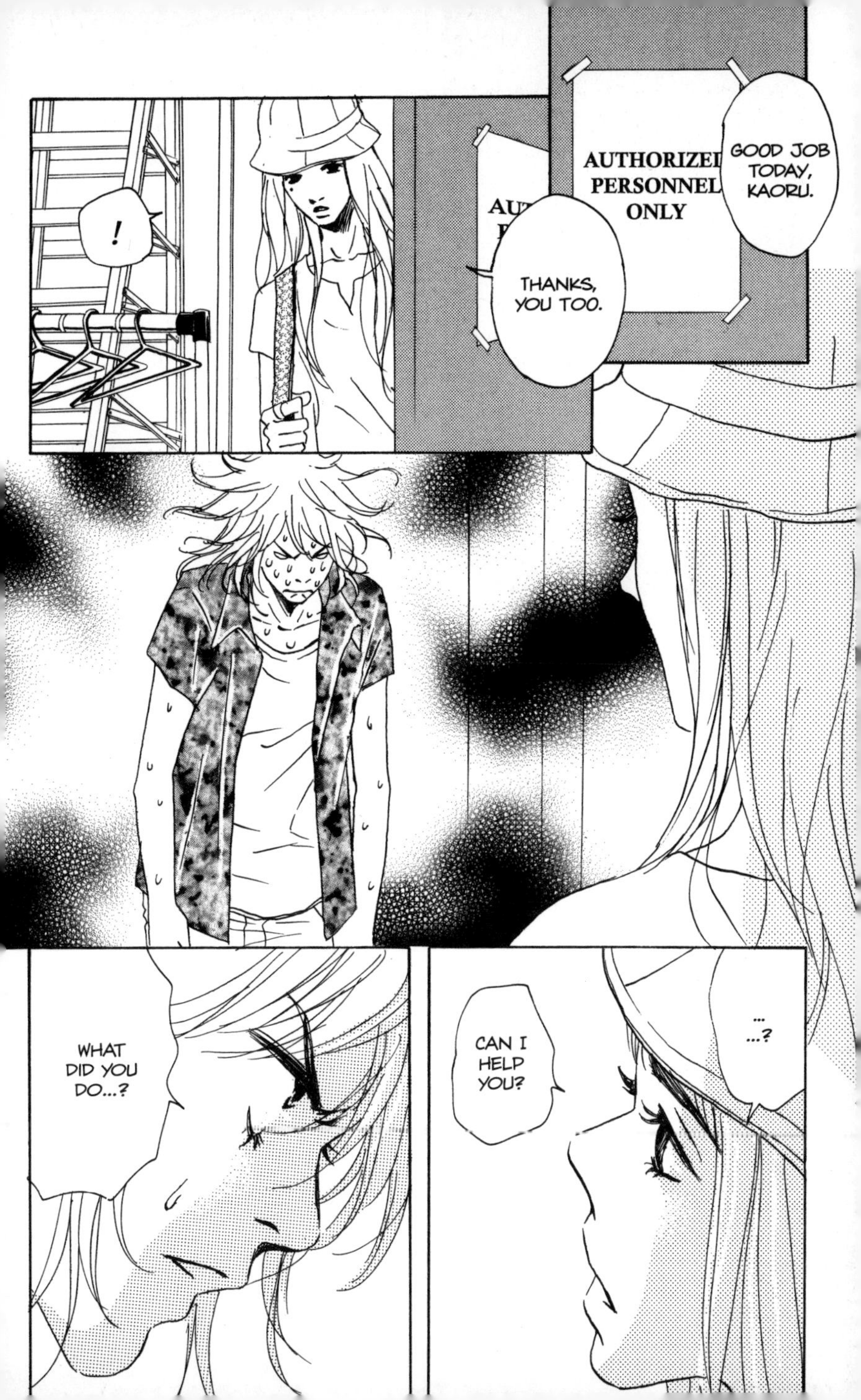
AUTHORIZED PERSONNEL ONLY
GOOD JOB TODAY, KAORU.
THANKS, YOU TOO.
!
...
...?
CAN I HELP YOU?
WHAT DID YOU DO...?

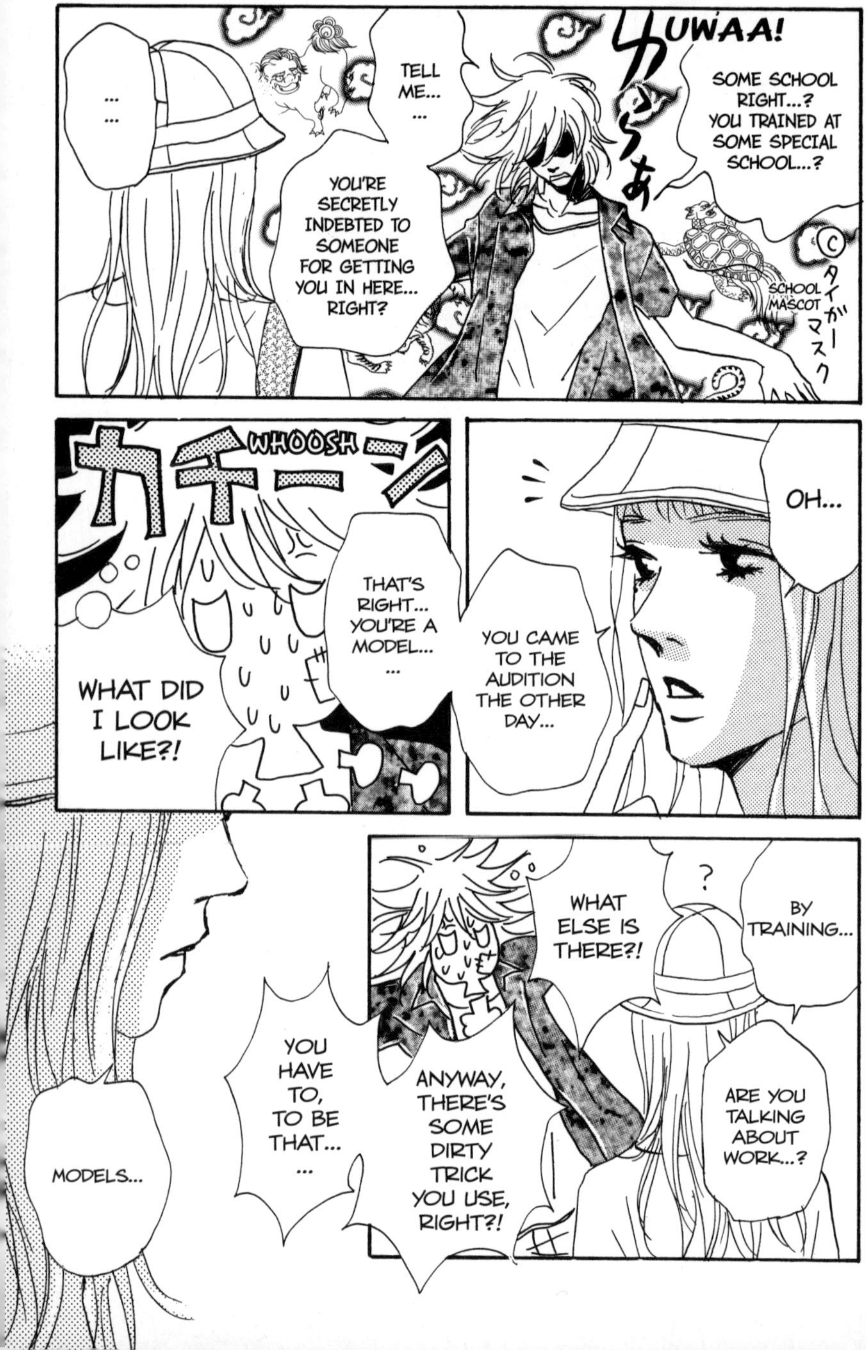
UWAA!
ゆらあ
SOME SCHOOL RIGHT...? YOU TRAINED AT SOME SPECIAL SCHOOL...?
© タイガーマスク
SCHOOL MASCOT
TELL ME... ...
YOU'RE SECRETLY INDEBTED TO SOMEONE FOR GETTING YOU IN HERE... RIGHT?
... ...
OH...
YOU CAME TO THE AUDITION THE OTHER DAY...
THAT'S RIGHT... YOU'RE A MODEL... ...
カチーン
WHOOSH
WHAT DID I LOOK LIKE?!
BY TRAINING...
?
WHAT ELSE IS THERE?!
ARE YOU TALKING ABOUT WORK...?
ANYWAY, THERE'S SOME DIRTY TRICK YOU USE, RIGHT?!
YOU HAVE TO, TO BE THAT... ...
MODELS...

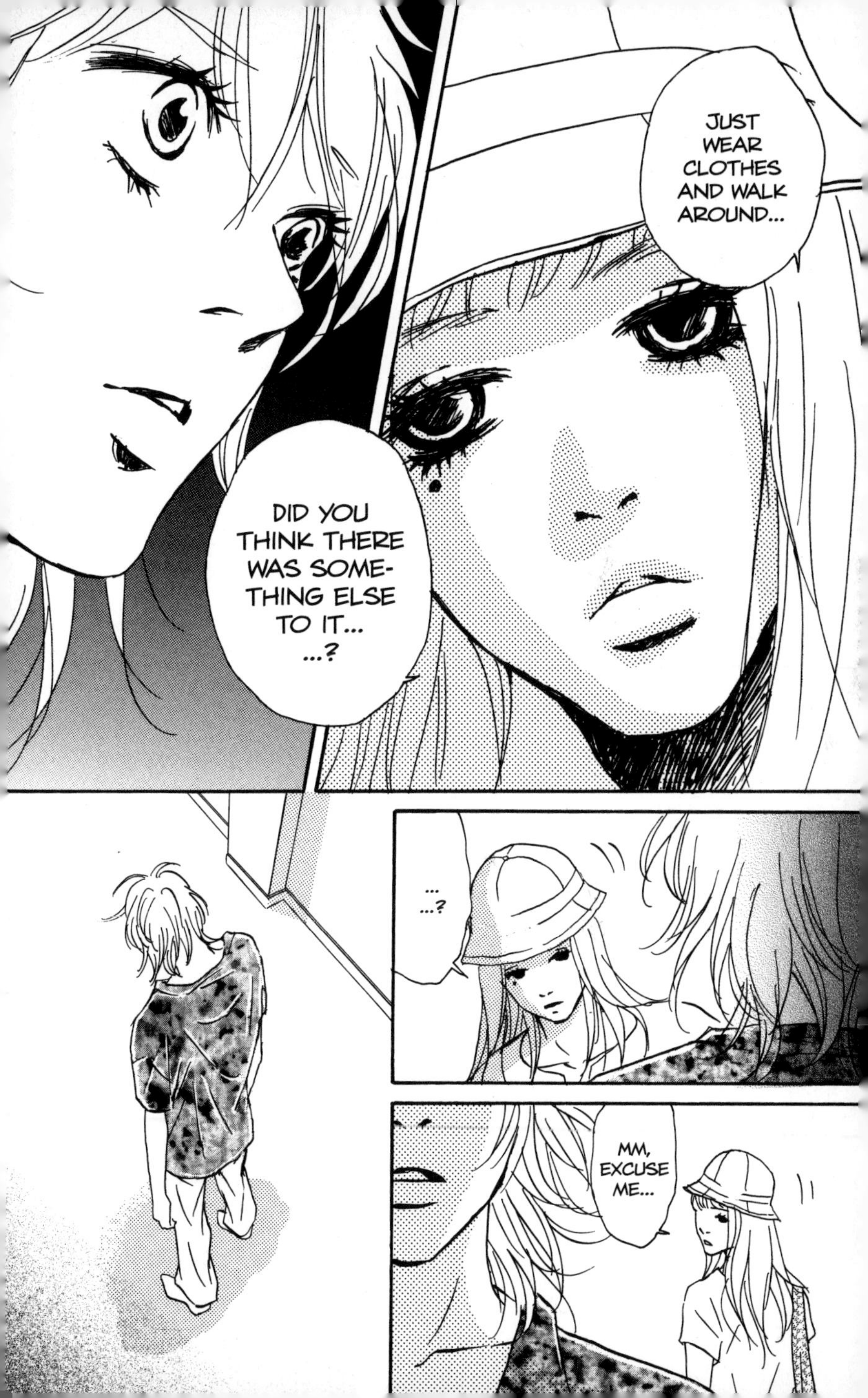
JUST WEAR CLOTHES AND WALK AROUND...
DID YOU THINK THERE WAS SOME-THING ELSE TO IT... ...?
... ...?
MM, EXCUSE ME...

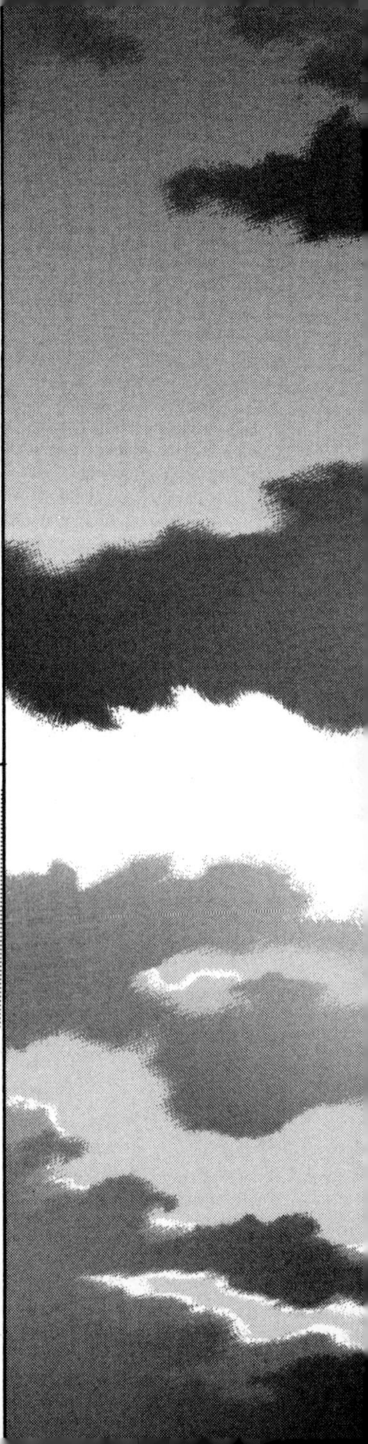

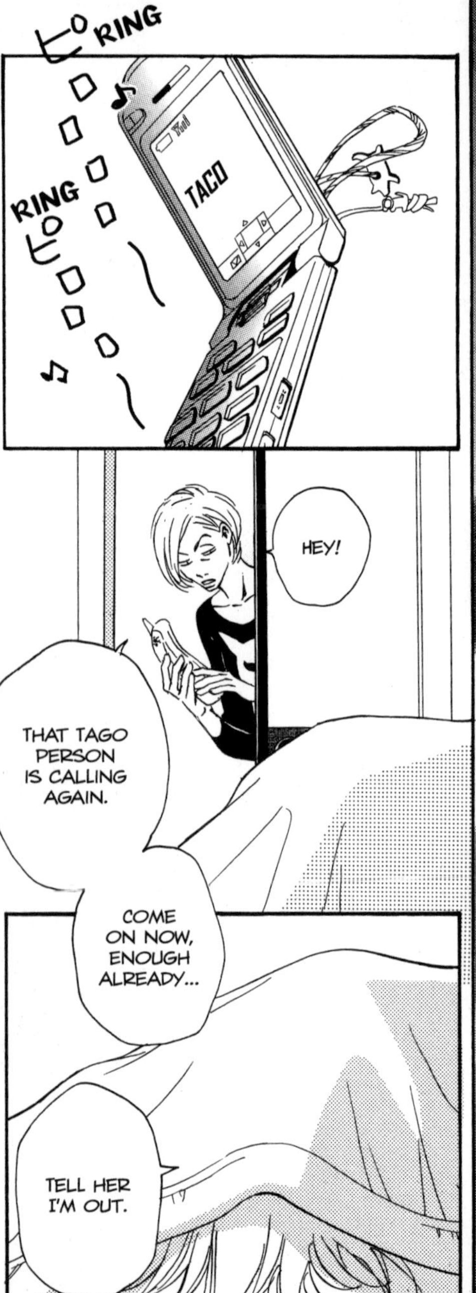
RING
RING
TACO
HEY!
THAT TAGO PERSON IS CALLING AGAIN.
COME ON NOW, ENOUGH ALREADY...
TELL HER I'M OUT.

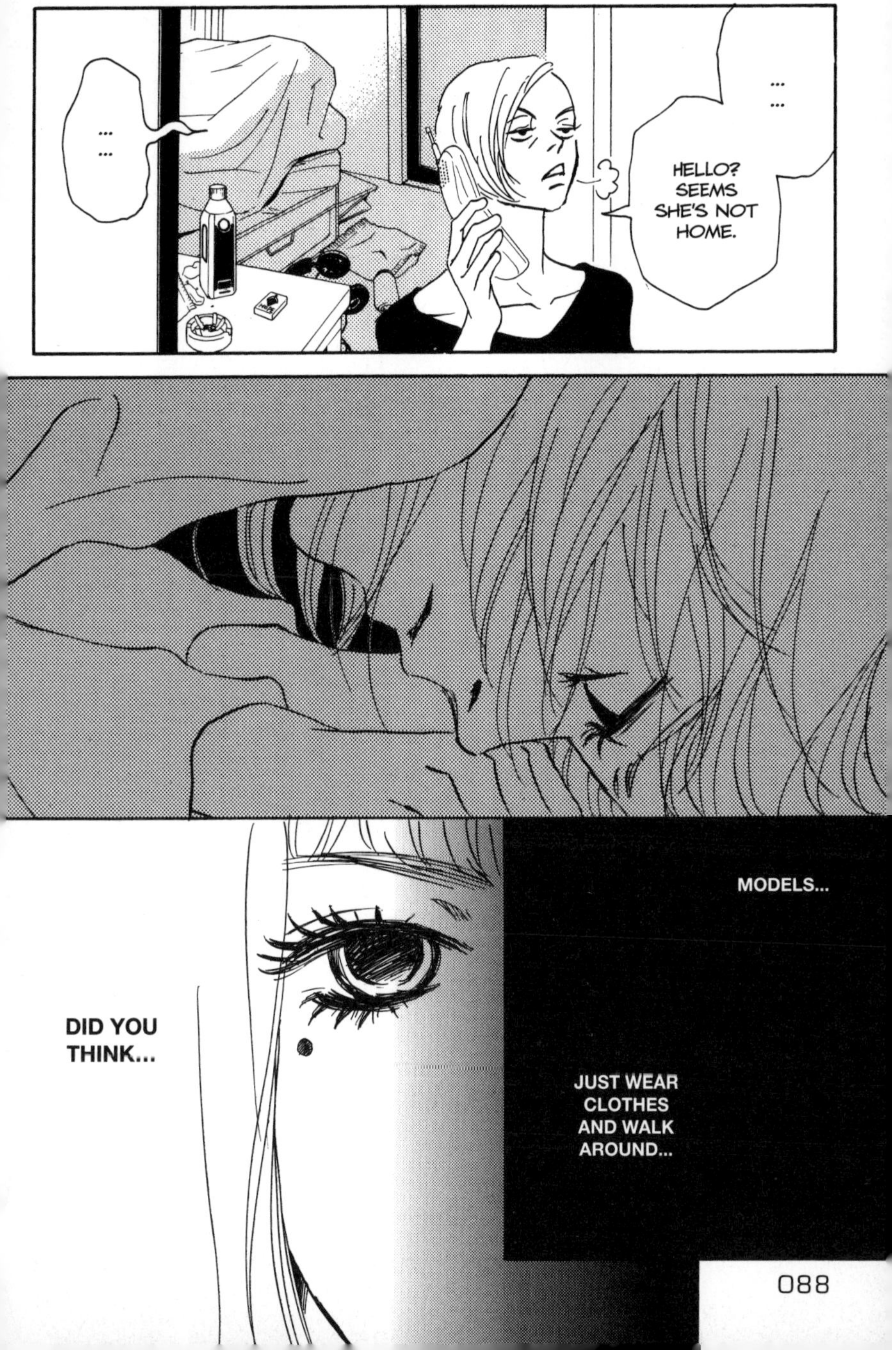
...
...
HELLO? SEEMS SHE'S NOT HOME.
...
...
MODELS...
JUST WEAR CLOTHES AND WALK AROUND...
DID YOU THINK...

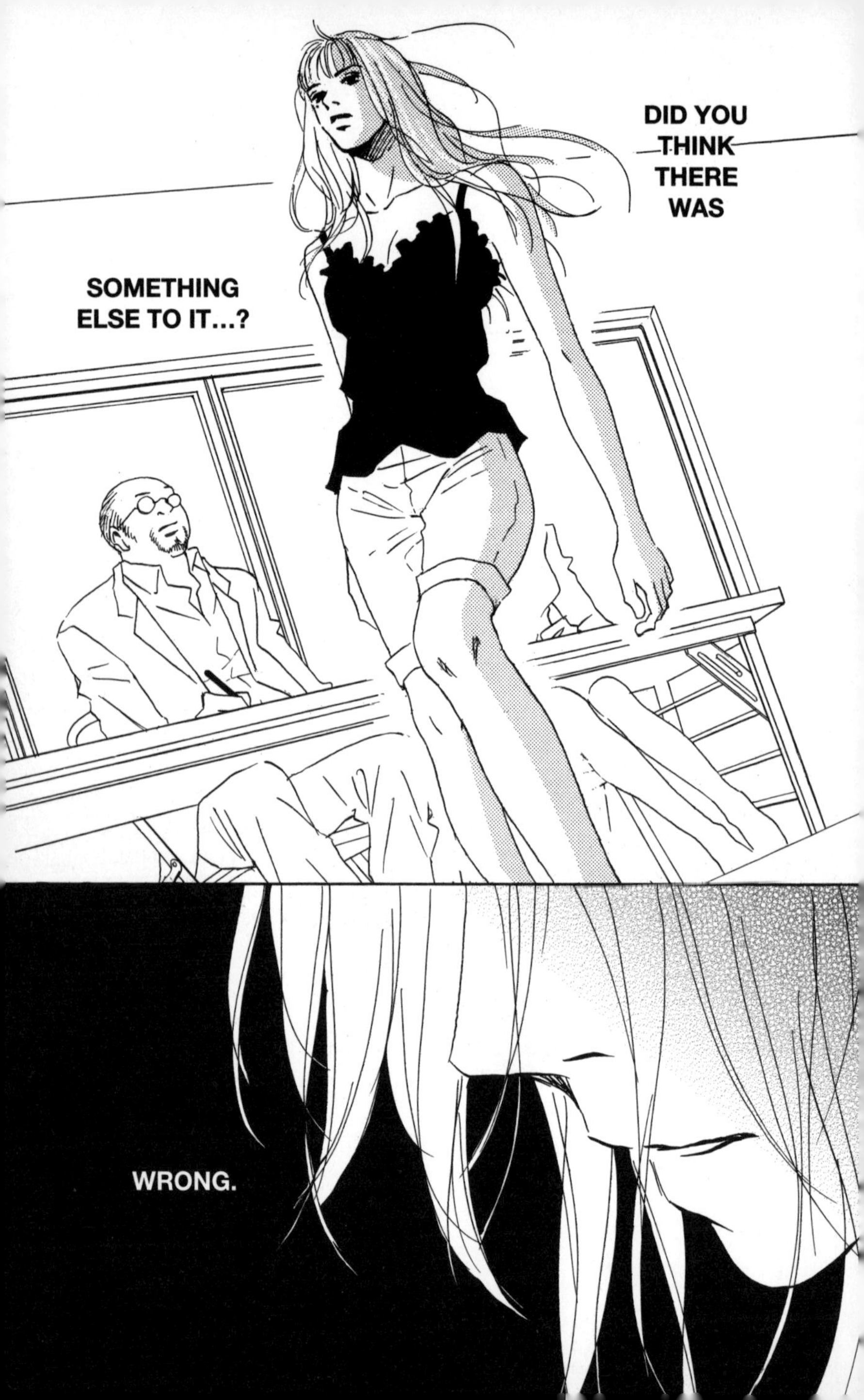
DID YOU THINK THERE WAS
SOMETHING ELSE TO IT...?
WRONG.

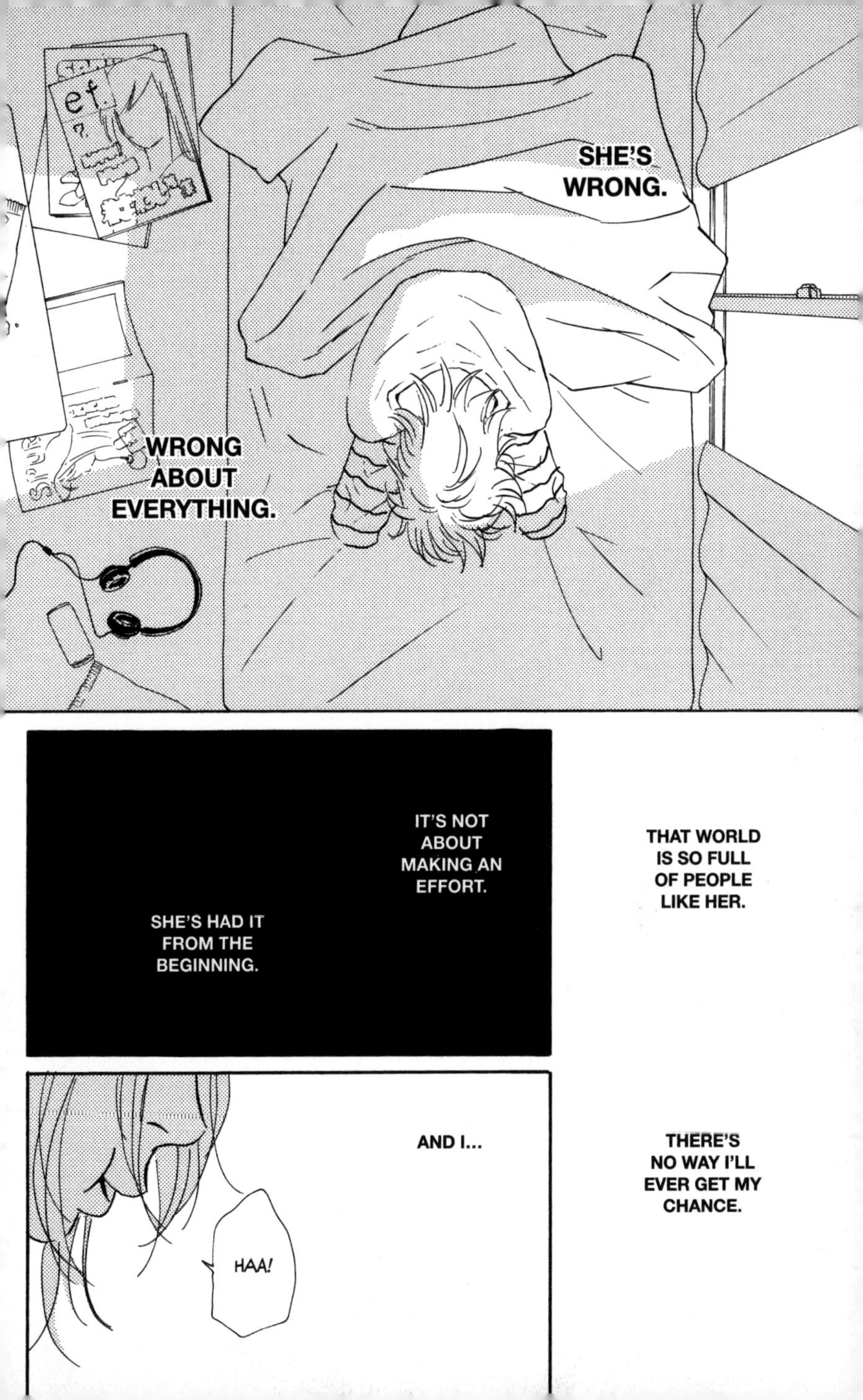
SHE'S WRONG.
WRONG ABOUT EVERYTHING.
THAT WORLD IS SO FULL OF PEOPLE LIKE HER.
IT'S NOT ABOUT MAKING AN EFFORT.
SHE'S HAD IT FROM THE BEGINNING.
THERE'S NO WAY I'LL EVER GET MY CHANCE.
AND I...
HAA!

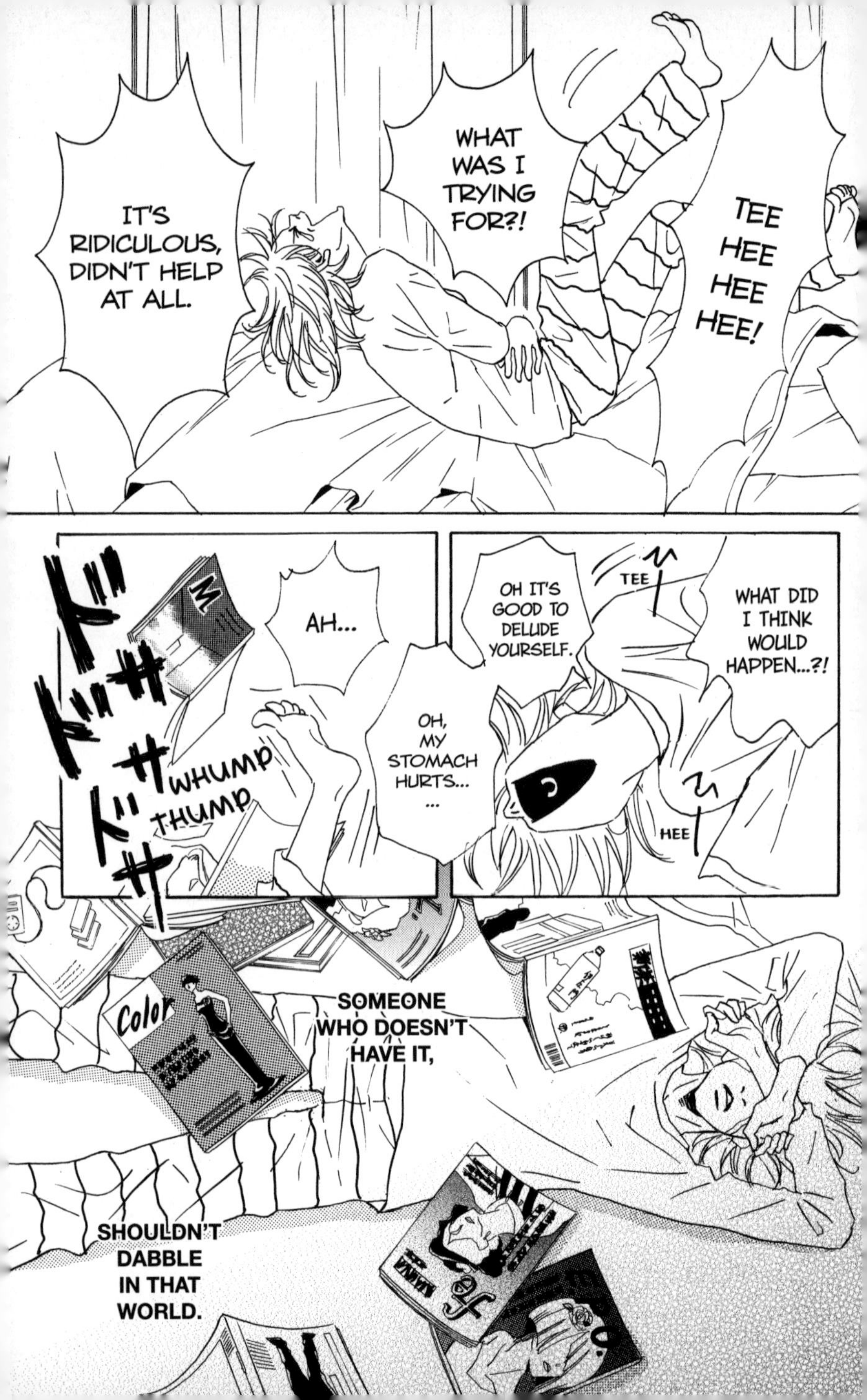
TEE HEE HEE HEE!
WHAT WAS I TRYING FOR?!
IT'S RIDICULOUS, DIDN'T HELP AT ALL.
WHAT DID I THINK WOULD HAPPEN...?!
TEE
HEE
OH IT'S GOOD TO DELUDE YOURSELF.
OH, MY STOMACH HURTS... ...
AH...
WHUMP THUMP
Color
SOMEONE WHO DOESN'T HAVE IT,
SHOULDN'T DABBLE IN THAT WORLD.

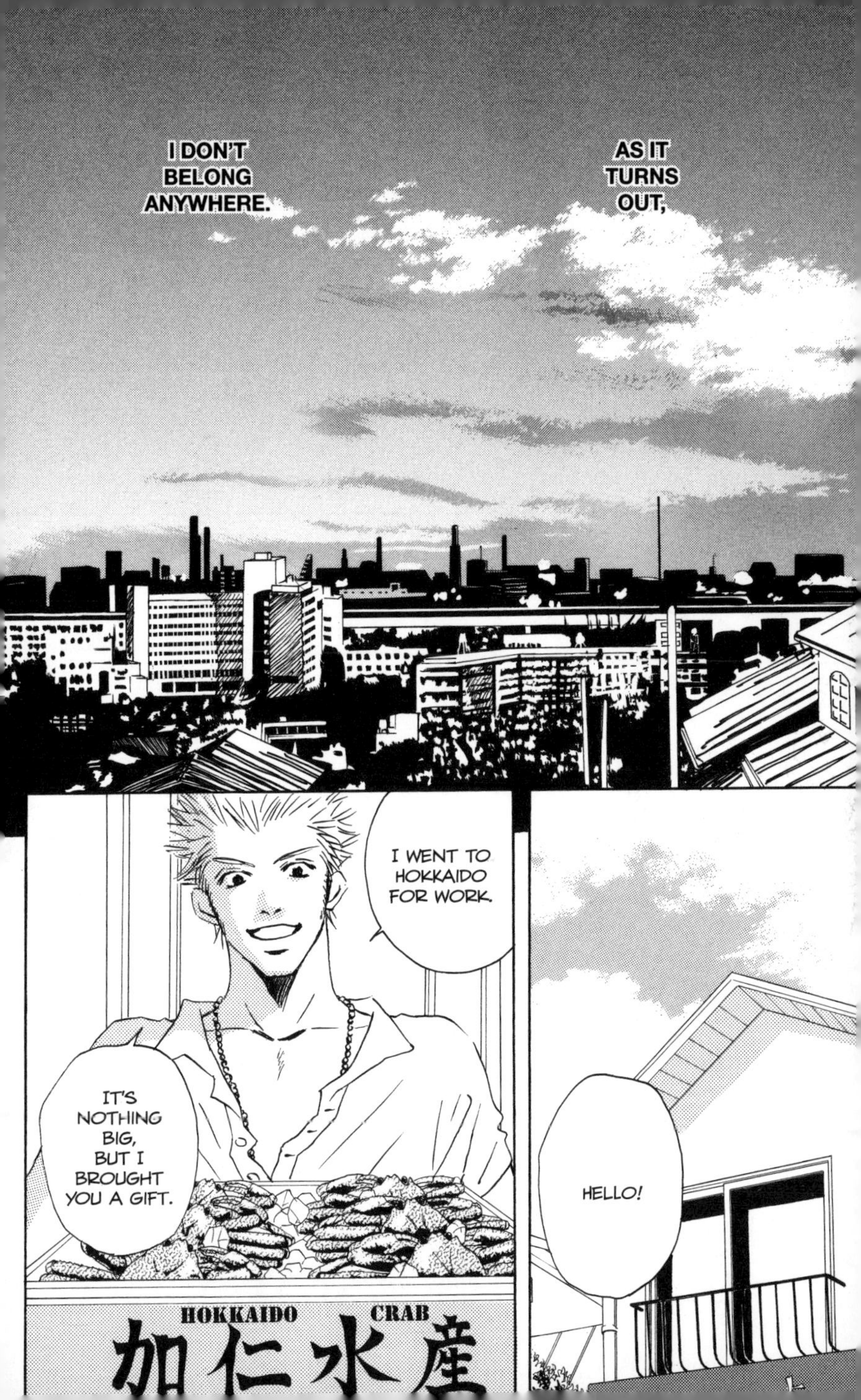
AS IT TURNS OUT,
I DON'T BELONG ANYWHERE.
HELLO!
I WENT TO HOKKAIDO FOR WORK.
IT'S NOTHING BIG, BUT I BROUGHT YOU A GIFT.
HOKKAIDO CRAB
加仁水産

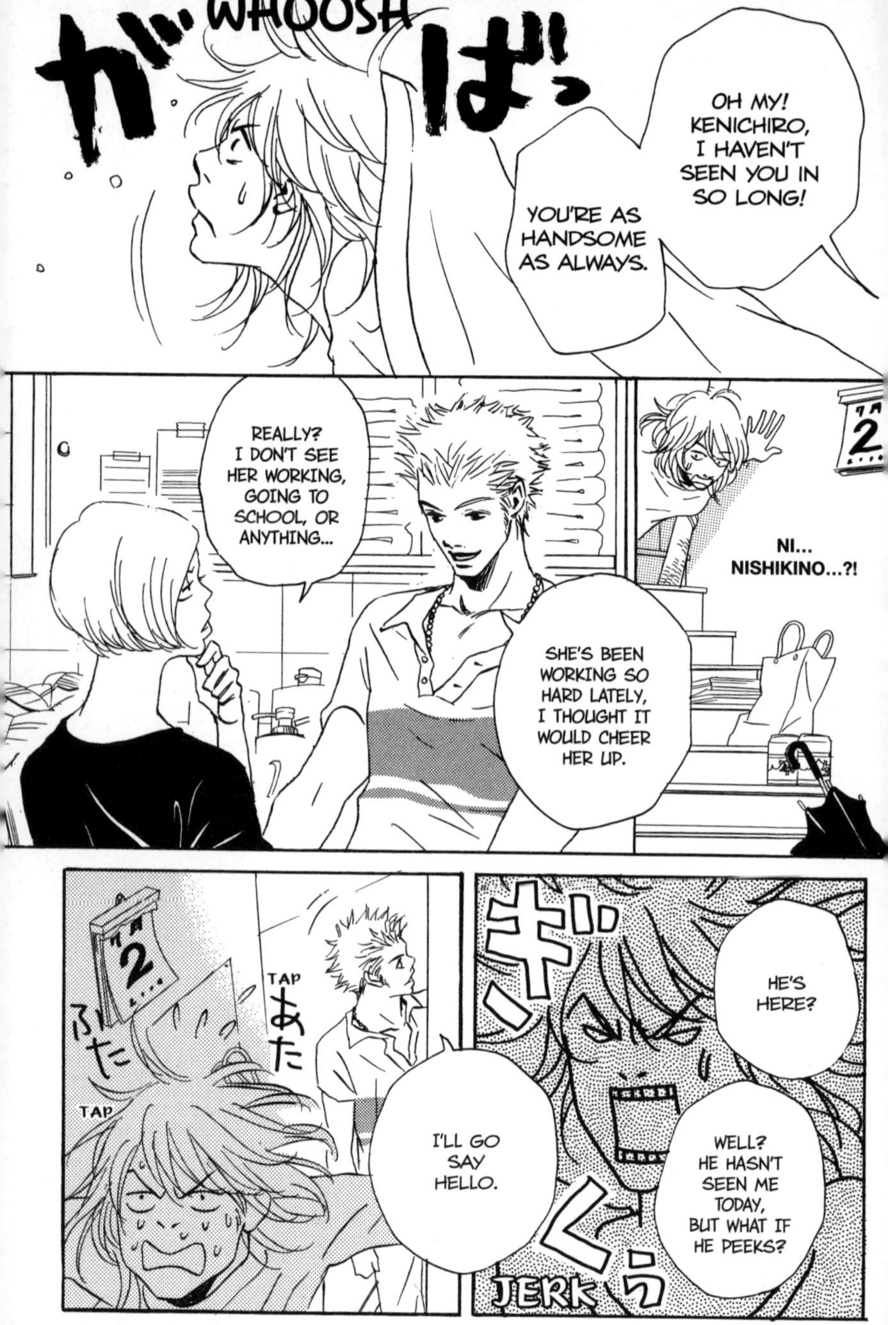
OH MY! KENICHIRO, I HAVEN'T SEEN YOU IN SO LONG!
YOU'RE AS HANDSOME AS ALWAYS.
がばっ
WHOOSH
NI... NISHIKINO...?!
SHE'S BEEN WORKING SO HARD LATELY, I THOUGHT IT WOULD CHEER HER UP.
REALLY? I DON'T SEE HER WORKING, GOING TO SCHOOL, OR ANYTHING...
ギくう
JERK
HE'S HERE?
WELL? HE HASN'T SEEN ME TODAY, BUT WHAT IF HE PEEKS?
I'LL GO SAY HELLO.
あた
TAP
ふた
TAP

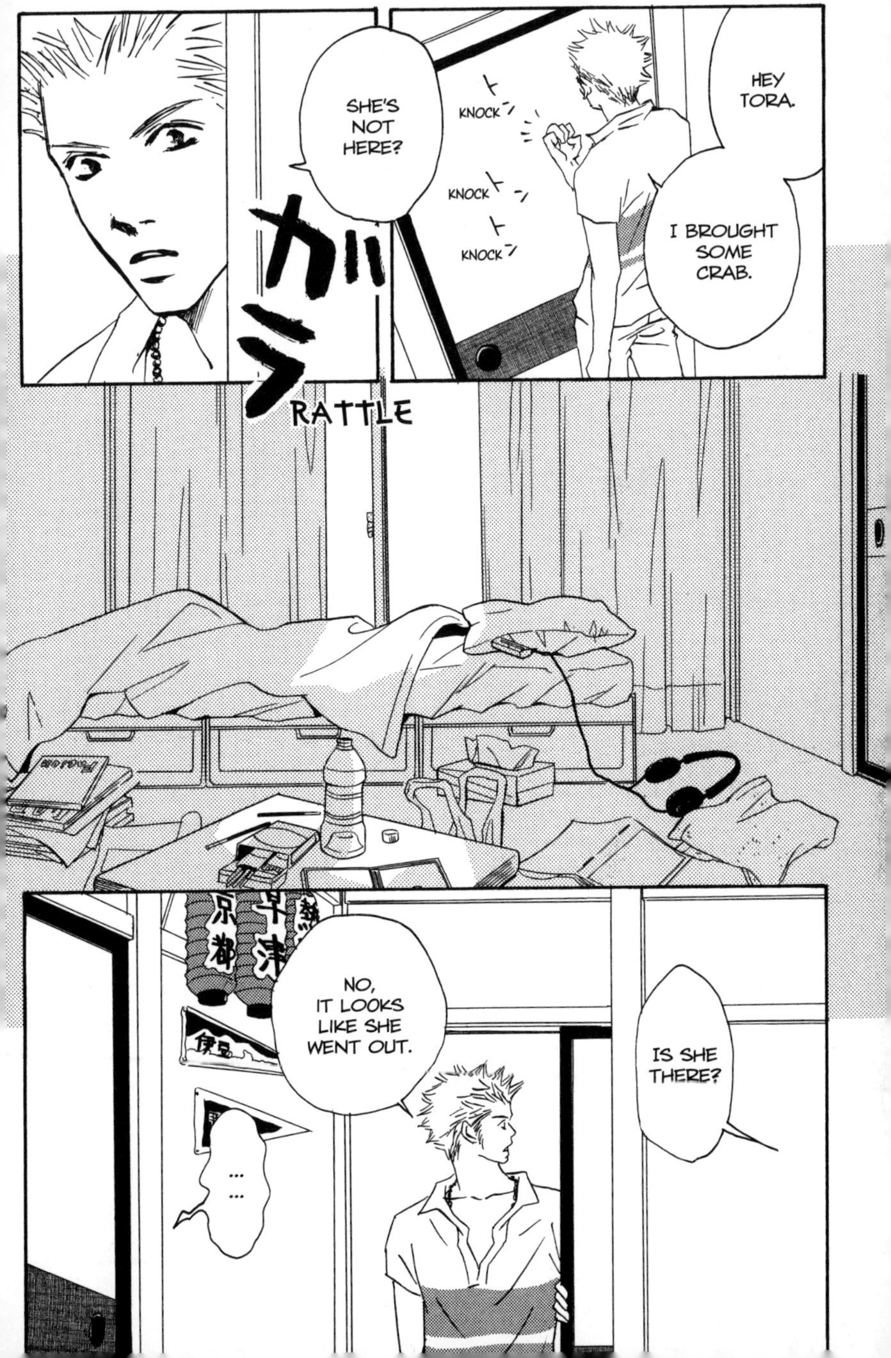
HEY TORA.
I BROUGHT SOME CRAB.
KNOCK
KNOCK
KNOCK
SHE'S NOT HERE?
ガラ
RATTLE
IS SHE THERE?
NO, IT LOOKS LIKE SHE WENT OUT.
... ...

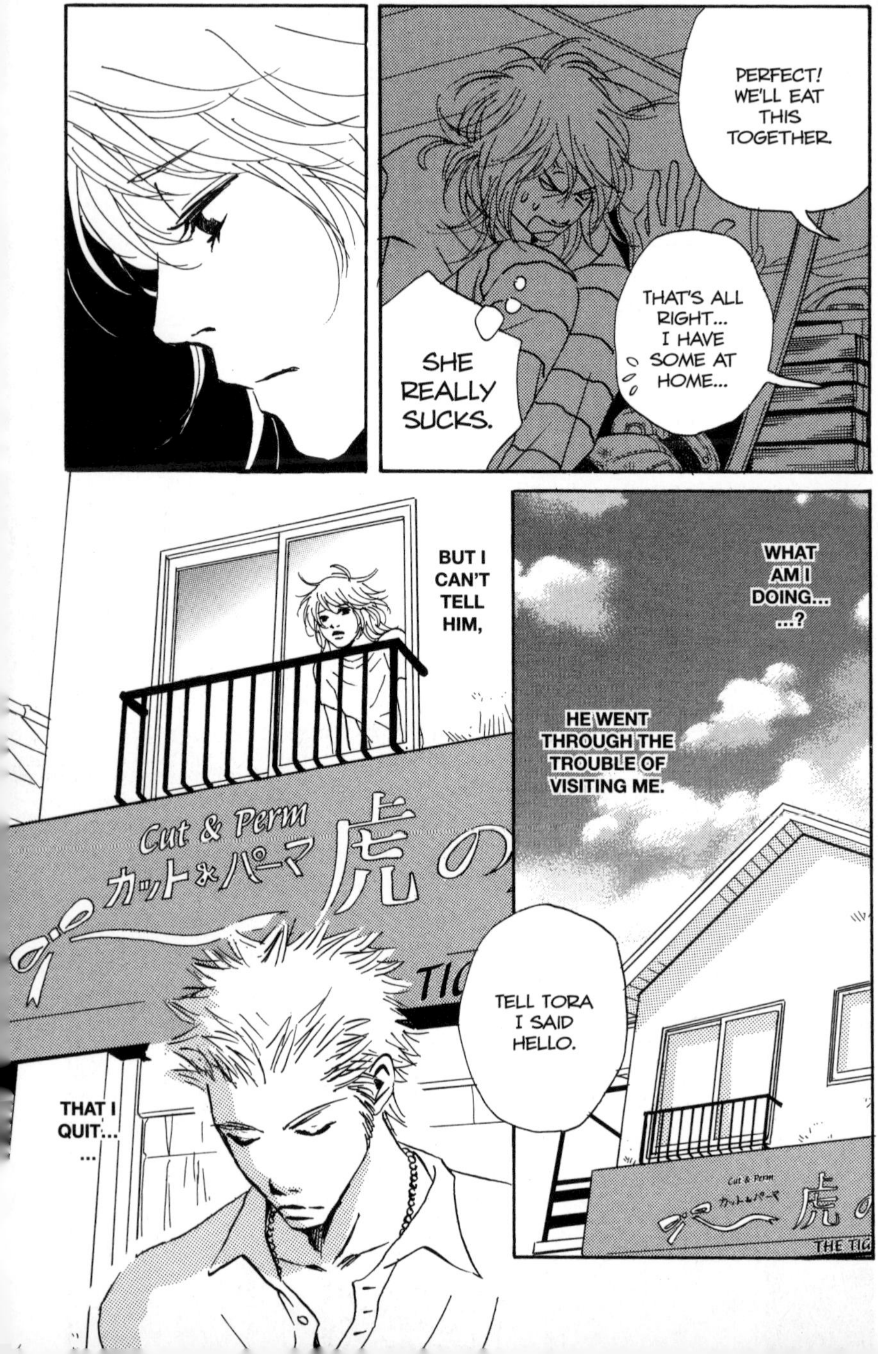
PERFECT! WE'LL EAT THIS TOGETHER.
THAT'S ALL RIGHT... I HAVE SOME AT HOME...
SHE REALLY SUCKS.
WHAT AM I DOING... ...?
HE WENT THROUGH THE TROUBLE OF VISITING ME.
TELL TORA I SAID HELLO.
Cut & Perm
カット&パーマ
虎の
BUT I CAN'T TELL HIM,
THAT I QUIT... ...
Cut & Perm
カット&パーマ
虎の

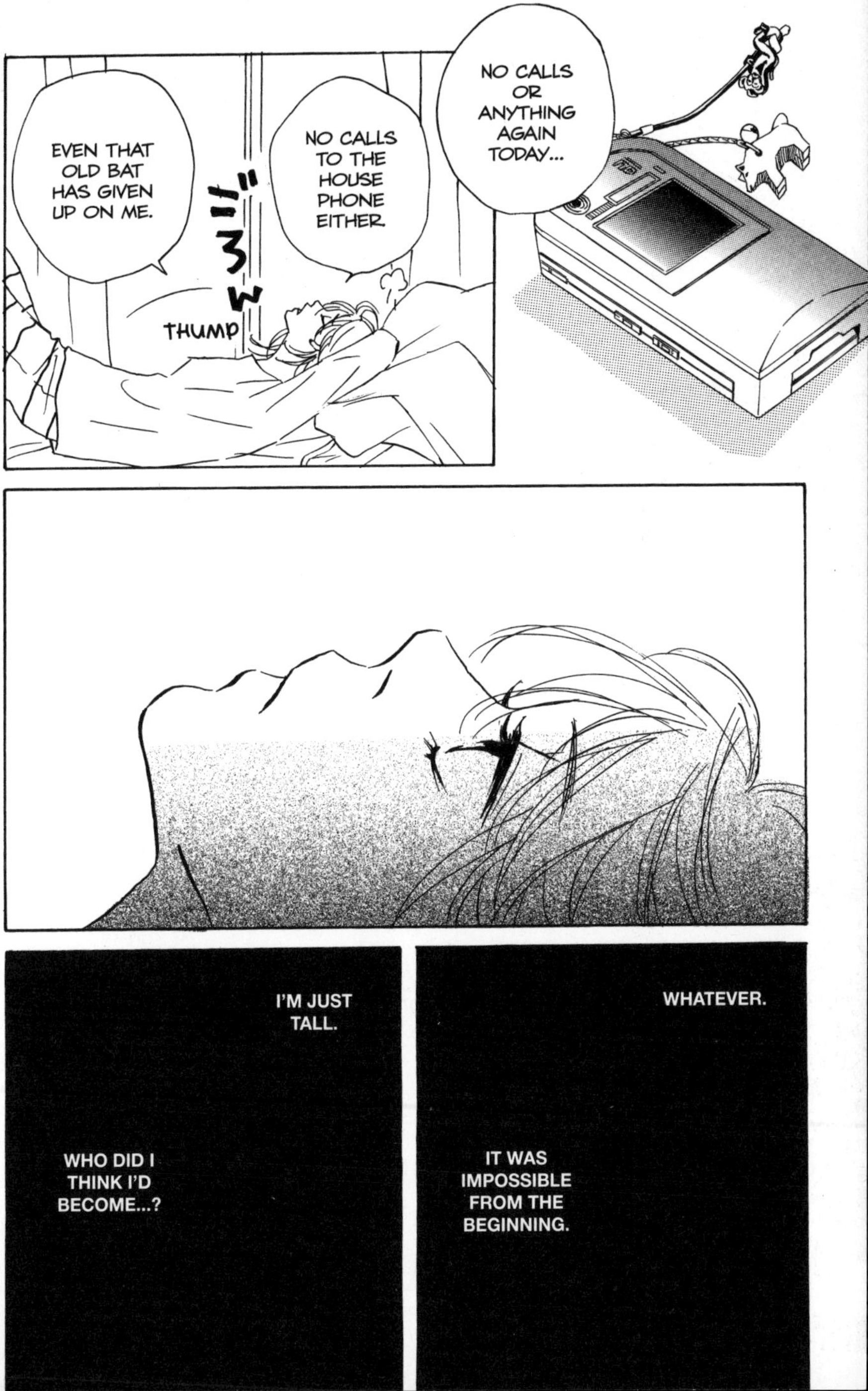
NO CALLS OR ANYTHING AGAIN TODAY...
NO CALLS TO THE HOUSE PHONE EITHER.
EVEN THAT OLD BAT HAS GIVEN UP ON ME.
THUMP
WHATEVER.
IT WAS IMPOSSIBLE FROM THE BEGINNING.
I'M JUST TALL.
WHO DID I THINK I'D BECOME...?

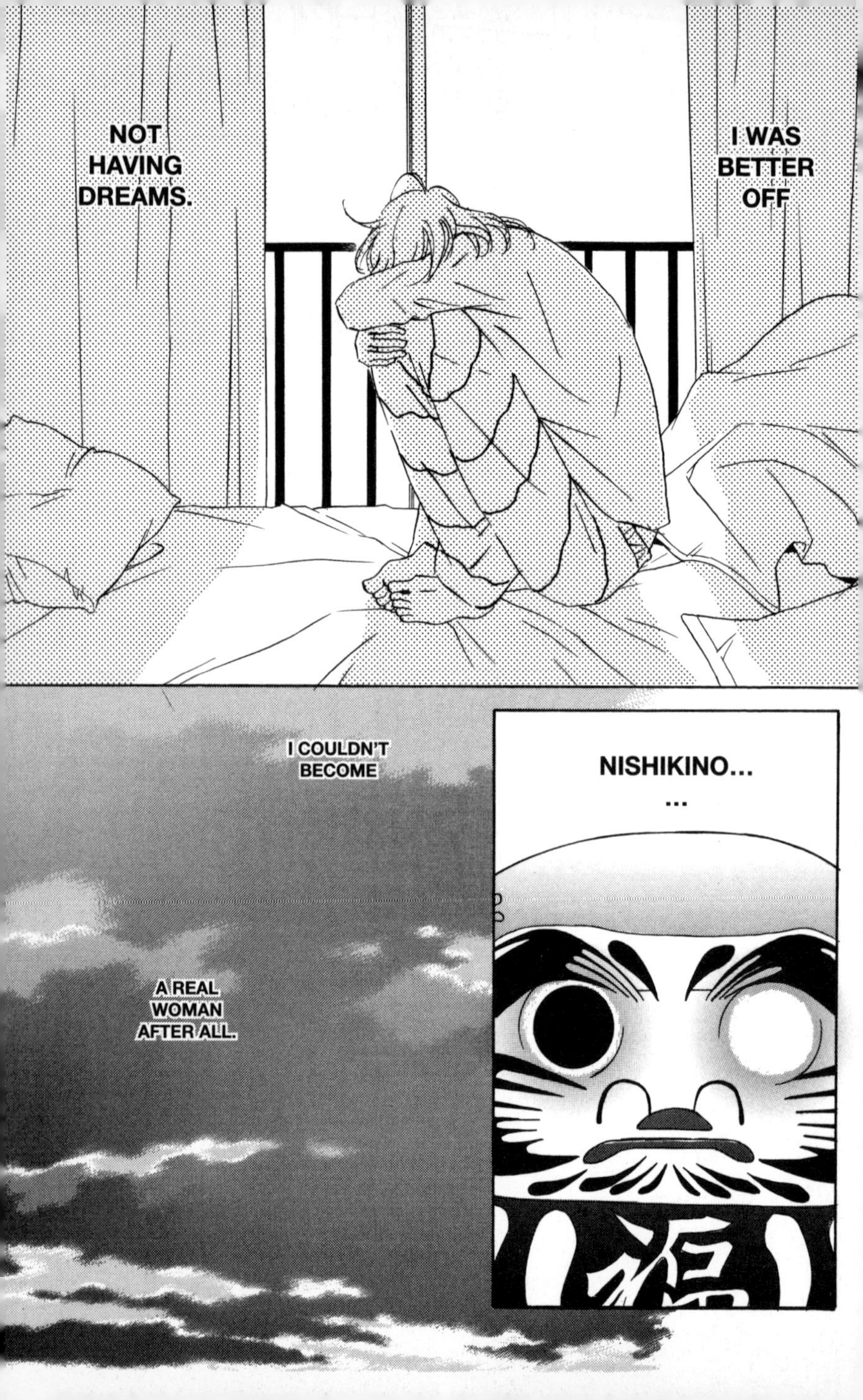
I WAS BETTER OFF
NOT HAVING DREAMS.
NISHIKINO...
...
I COULDN'T BECOME
A REAL WOMAN AFTER ALL.

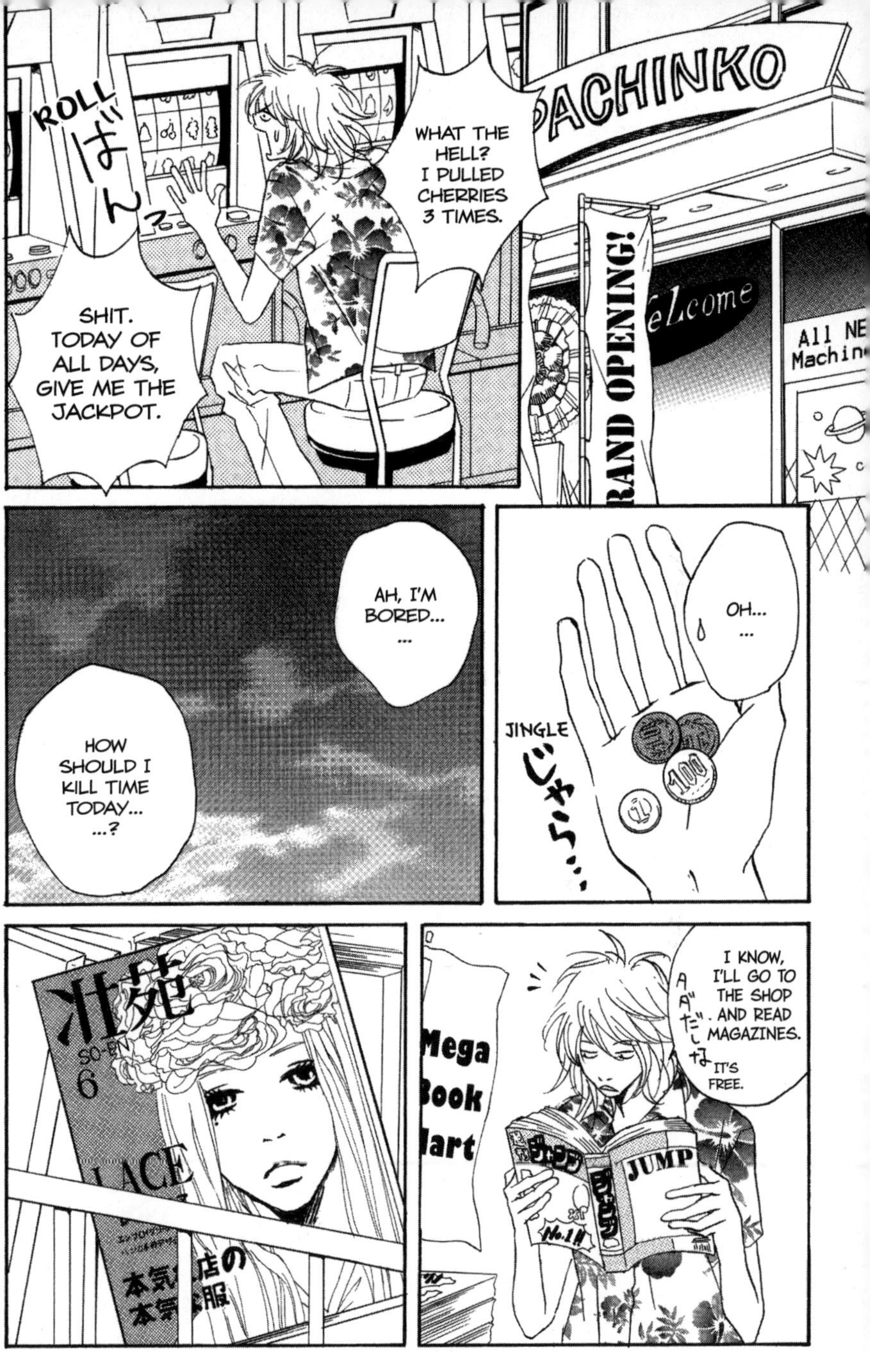
PACHINKO
WHAT THE HELL? I PULLED CHERRIES 3 TIMES.
ROLL
ばん
SHIT. TODAY OF ALL DAYS, GIVE ME THE JACKPOT.
RAND OPENING!
eLcome
OH... ...
JINGLE
じゃら…
AH, I'M BORED... ...
HOW SHOULD I KILL TIME TODAY... ...?
I KNOW, I'LL GO TO THE SHOP AND READ MAGAZINES.
IT'S FREE.
Mega
JUMP
No.1!!
SO-EN
6

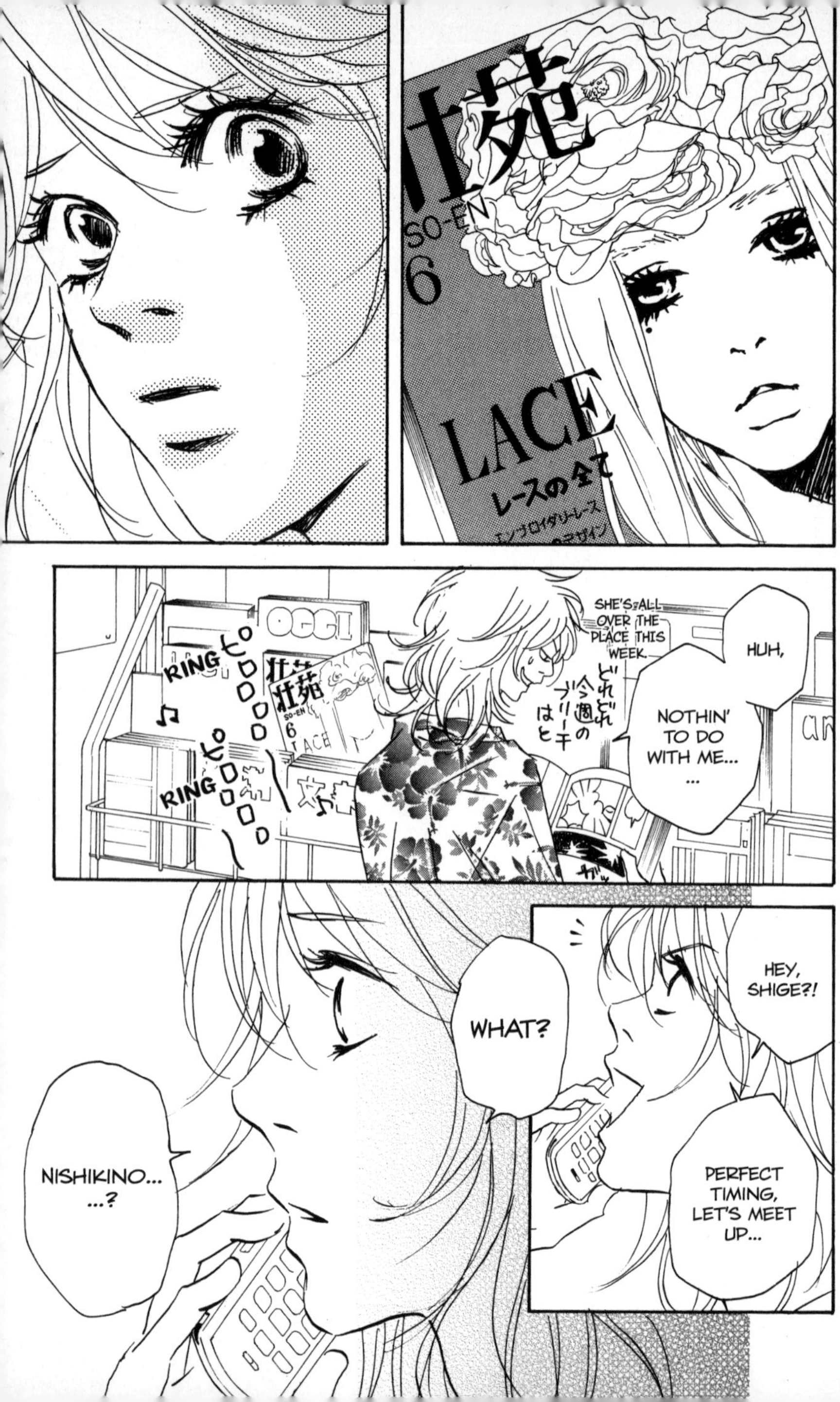
荘苑
SO-EN
6
LACE
レースの全て
HUH,
NOTHIN' TO DO WITH ME... ...
SHE'S ALL OVER THE PLACE THIS WEEK.
どれどれ今週のブリーチはと
OGGI
RING
RING
HEY, SHIGE?!
PERFECT TIMING, LET'S MEET UP...
WHAT?
NISHIKINO... ...?

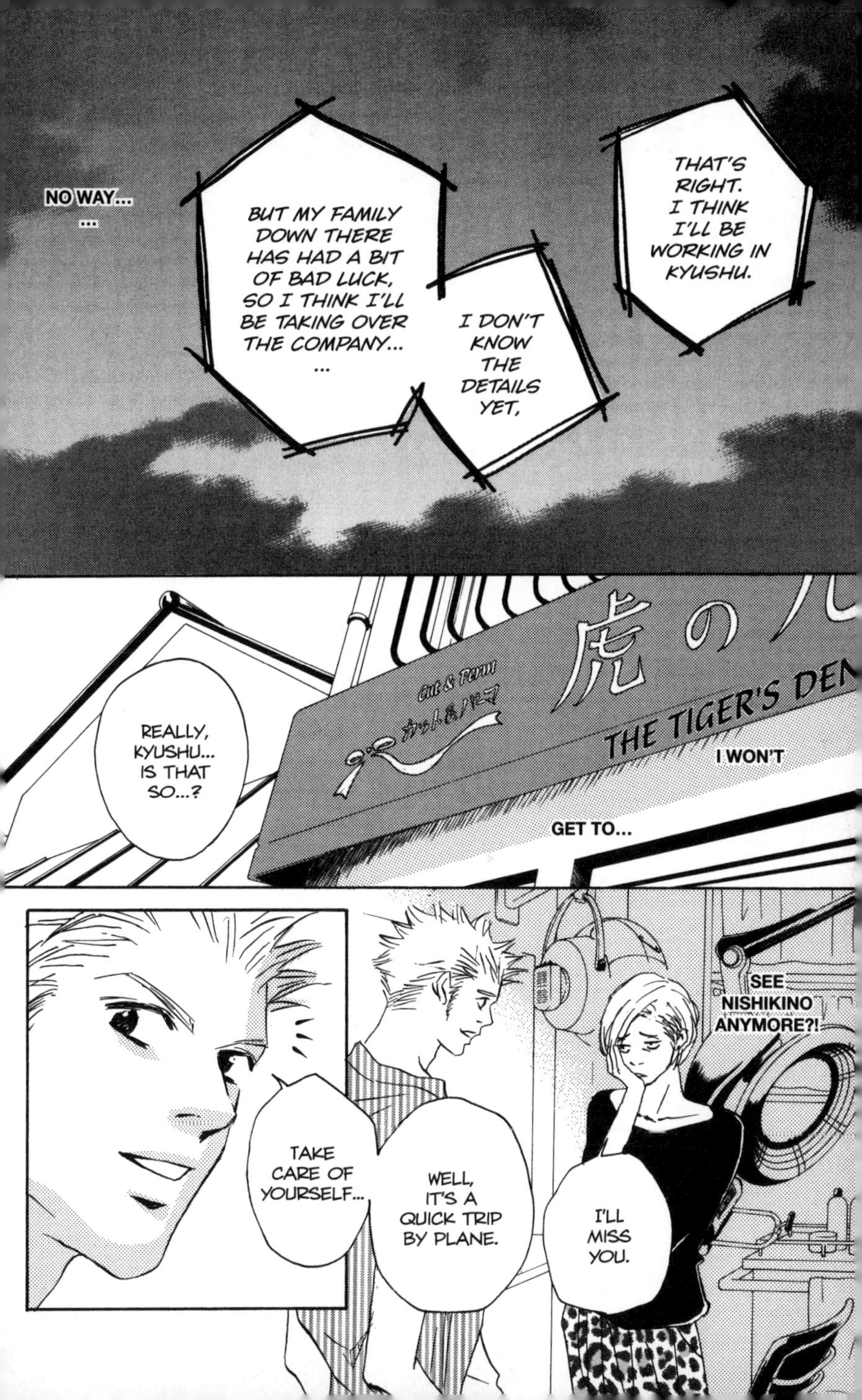
THAT'S RIGHT. I THINK I'LL BE WORKING IN KYUSHU.
I DON'T KNOW THE DETAILS YET,
BUT MY FAMILY DOWN THERE HAS HAD A BIT OF BAD LUCK, SO I THINK I'LL BE TAKING OVER THE COMPANY... ...
NO WAY... ...
虎の
Cut & Perm
カット&パーマ
THE TIGER'S DEN
I WON'T
GET TO...
REALLY, KYUSHU... IS THAT SO...?
SEE NISHIKINO ANYMORE?!
I'LL MISS YOU.
WELL, IT'S A QUICK TRIP BY PLANE.
TAKE CARE OF YOURSELF...

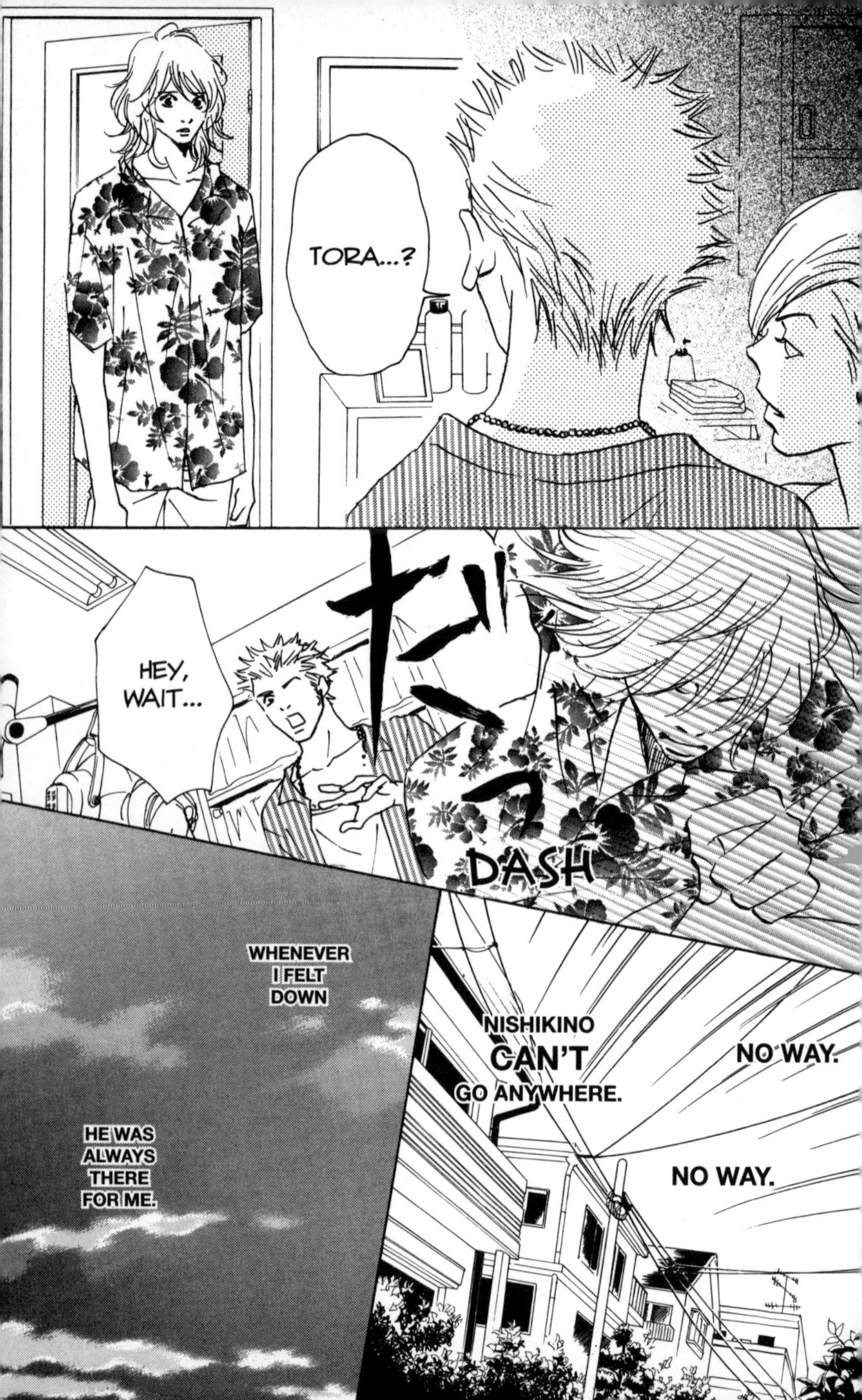
TORA...?
HEY, WAIT...
DASH
NO WAY.
NISHIKINO CAN'T GO ANYWHERE.
NO WAY.
WHENEVER I FELT DOWN
HE WAS ALWAYS THERE FOR ME.

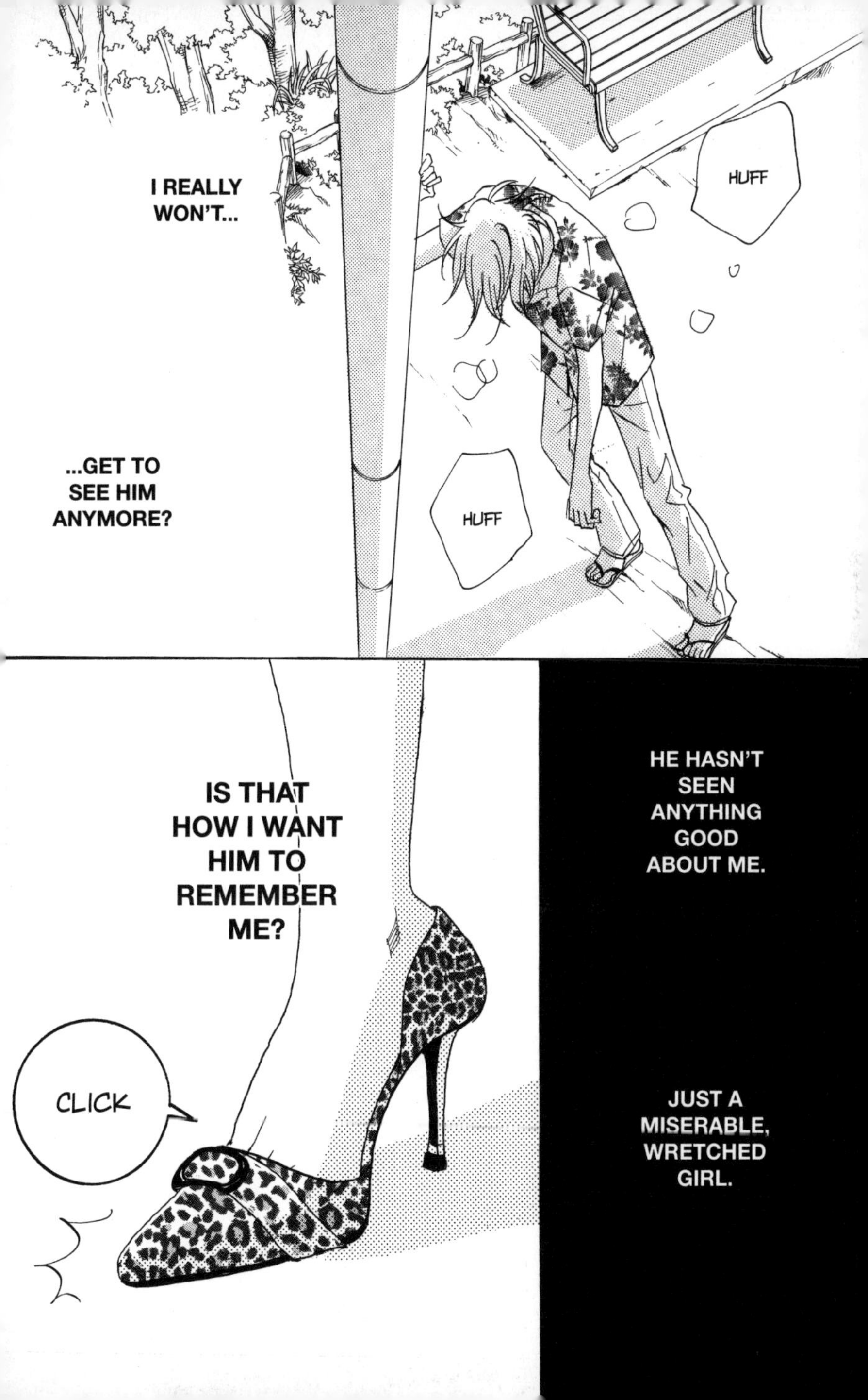
HUFF
I REALLY WON'T...
HUFF
...GET TO SEE HIM ANYMORE?
HE HASN'T SEEN ANYTHING GOOD ABOUT ME.
JUST A MISERABLE, WRETCHED GIRL.
IS THAT HOW I WANT HIM TO REMEMBER ME?
CLICK

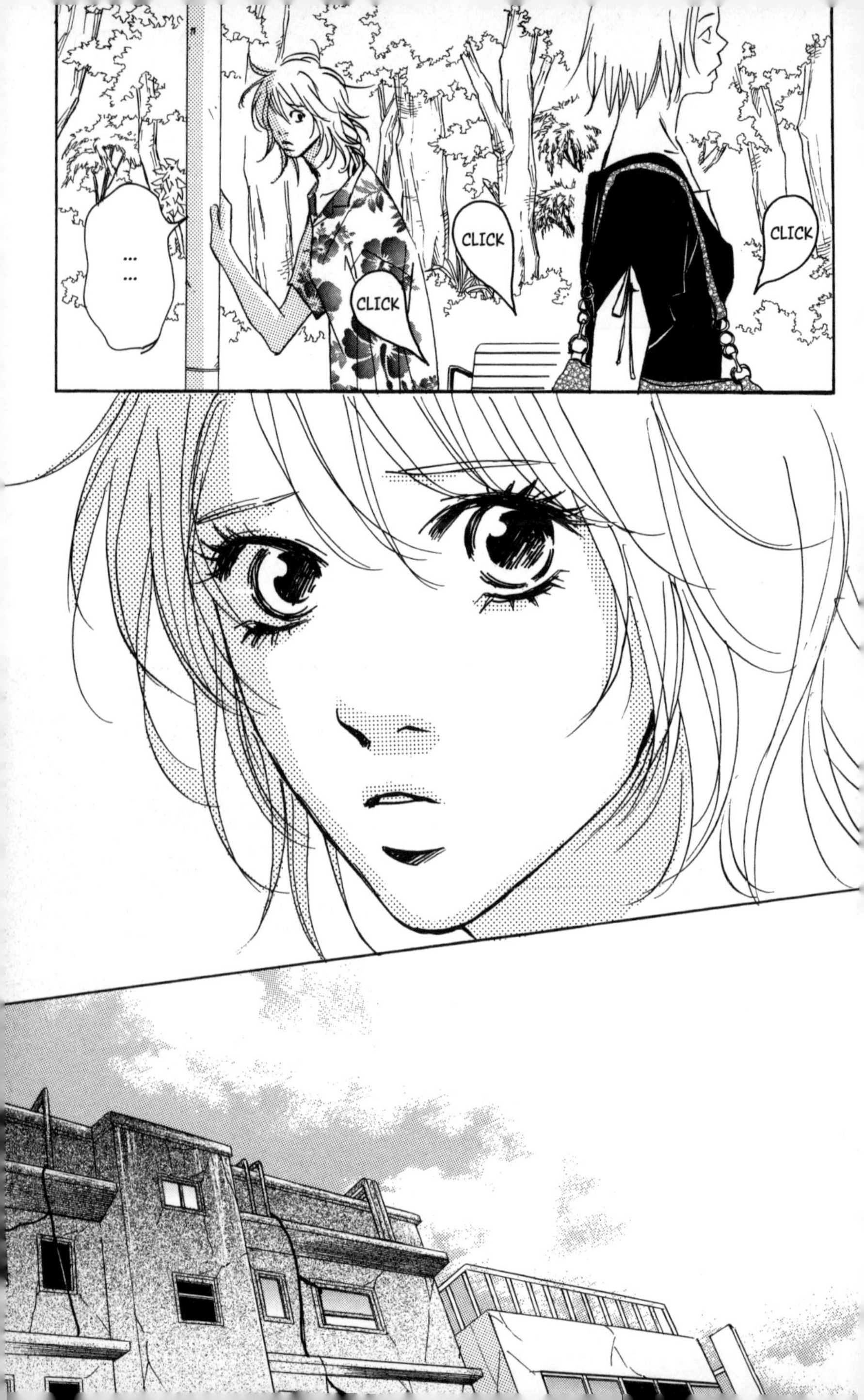
CLICK
CLICK
CLICK
... ...

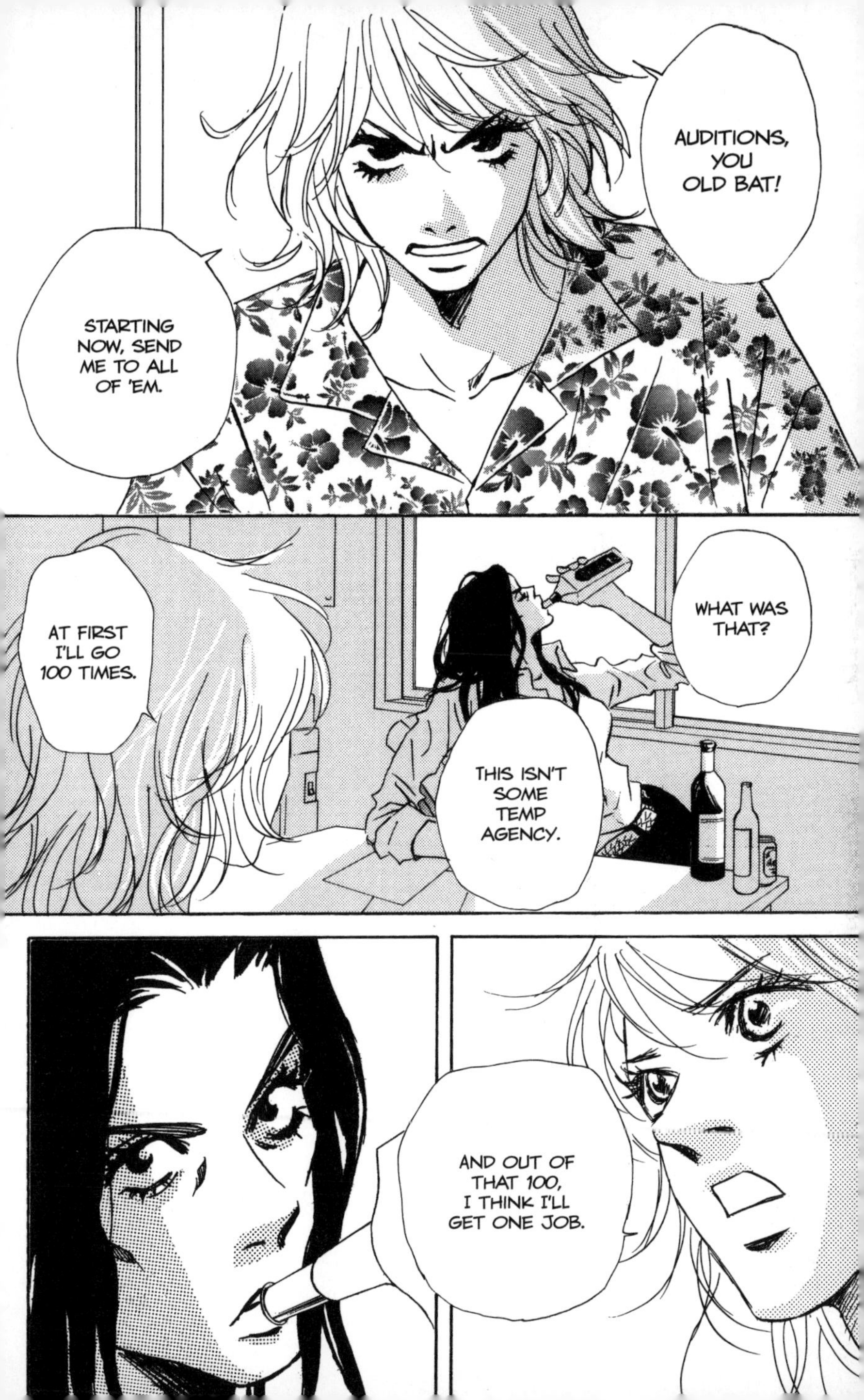
AUDITIONS, YOU OLD BAT!
STARTING NOW, SEND ME TO ALL OF 'EM.
WHAT WAS THAT?
THIS ISN'T SOME TEMP AGENCY.
AT FIRST I'LL GO 100 TIMES.
AND OUT OF THAT 100, I THINK I'LL GET ONE JOB.

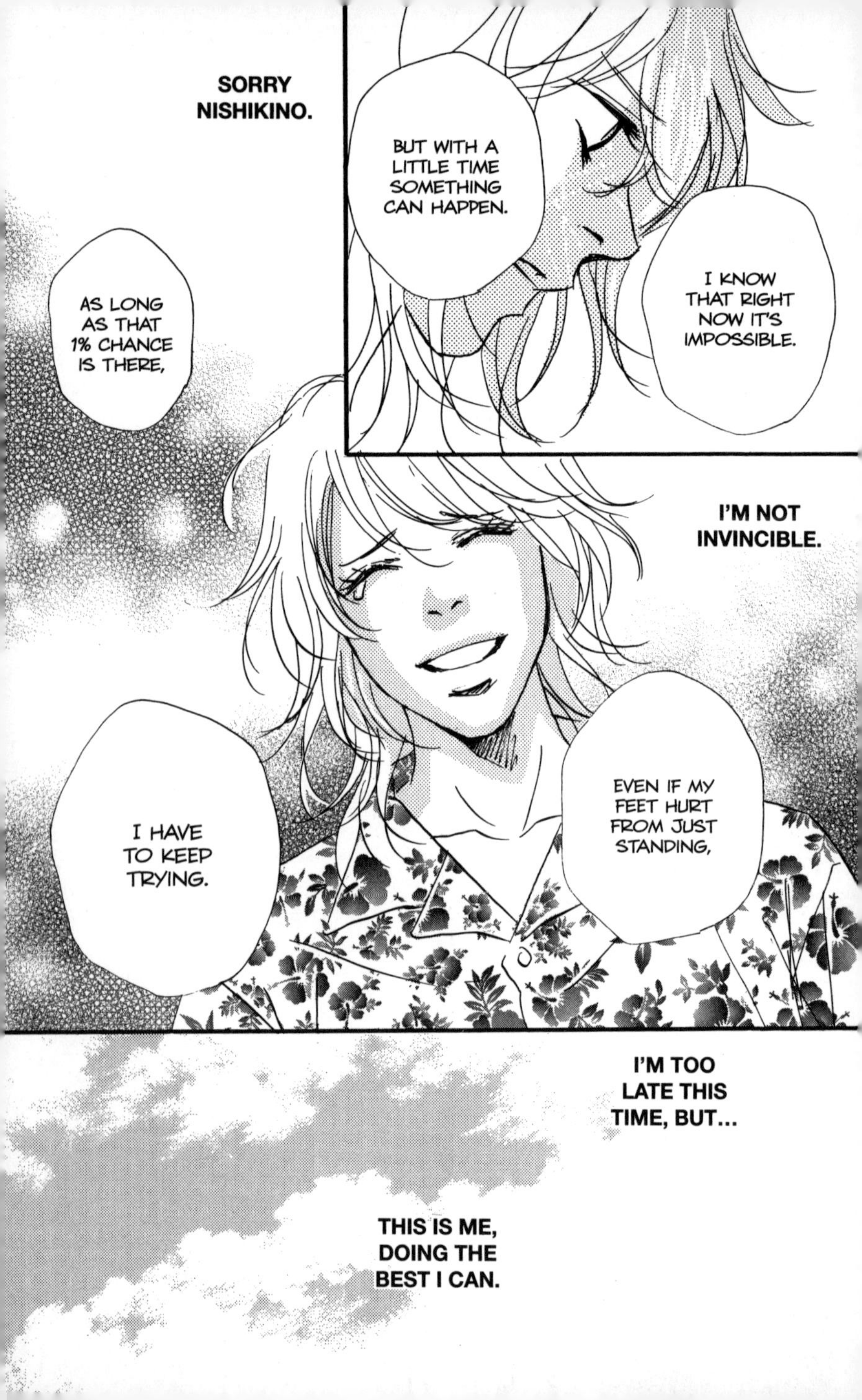
I KNOW THAT RIGHT NOW IT'S IMPOSSIBLE.
BUT WITH A LITTLE TIME SOMETHING CAN HAPPEN.
SORRY NISHIKINO.
AS LONG AS THAT 1% CHANCE IS THERE,
I'M NOT INVINCIBLE.
EVEN IF MY FEET HURT FROM JUST STANDING,
I HAVE TO KEEP TRYING.
I'M TOO LATE THIS TIME, BUT...
THIS IS ME, DOING THE BEST I CAN.

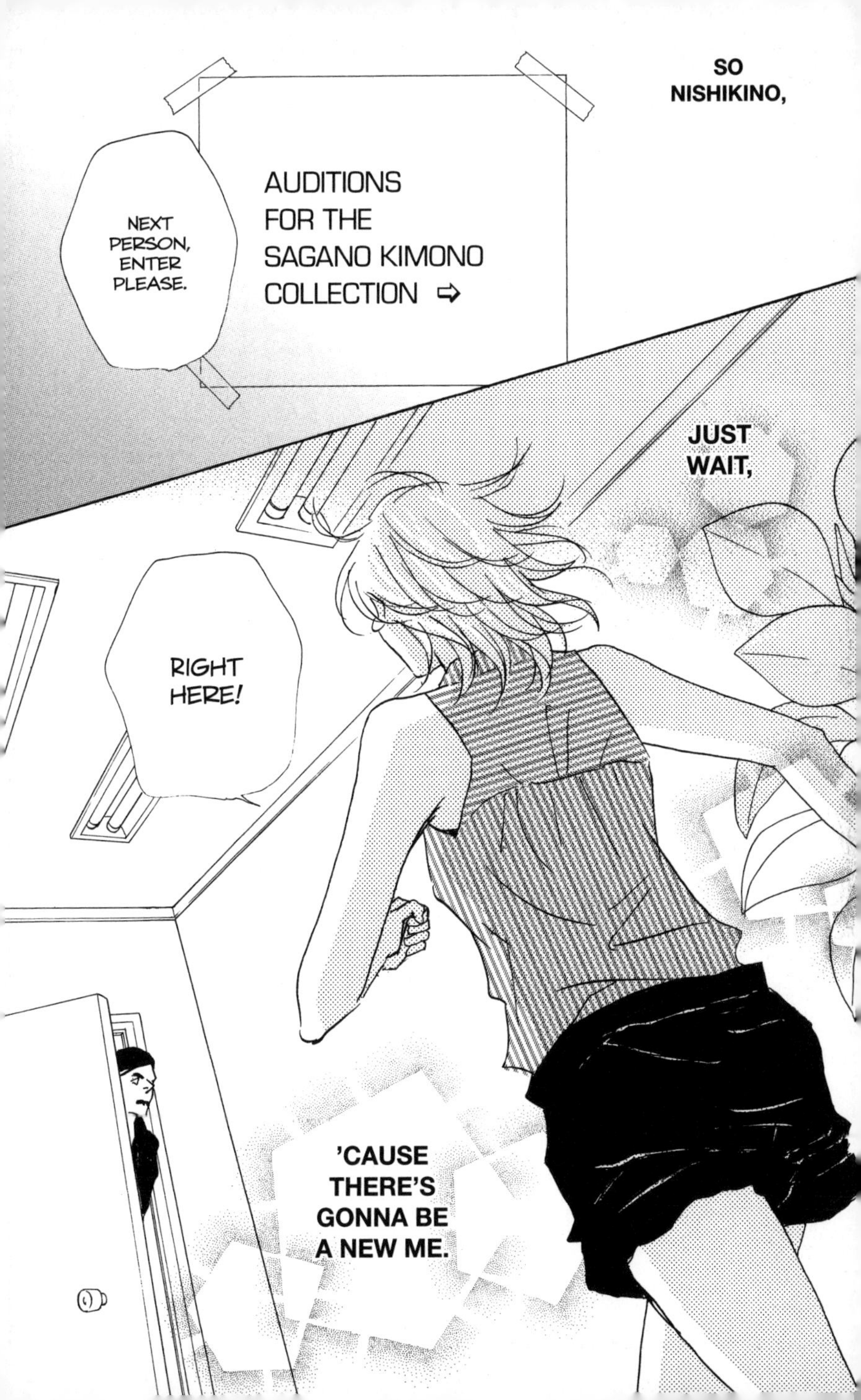
SO NISHIKINO,
AUDITIONS FOR THE SAGANO KIMONO COLLECTION ⇨
NEXT PERSON, ENTER PLEASE.
JUST WAIT,
RIGHT HERE!
'CAUSE THERE'S GONNA BE A NEW ME.

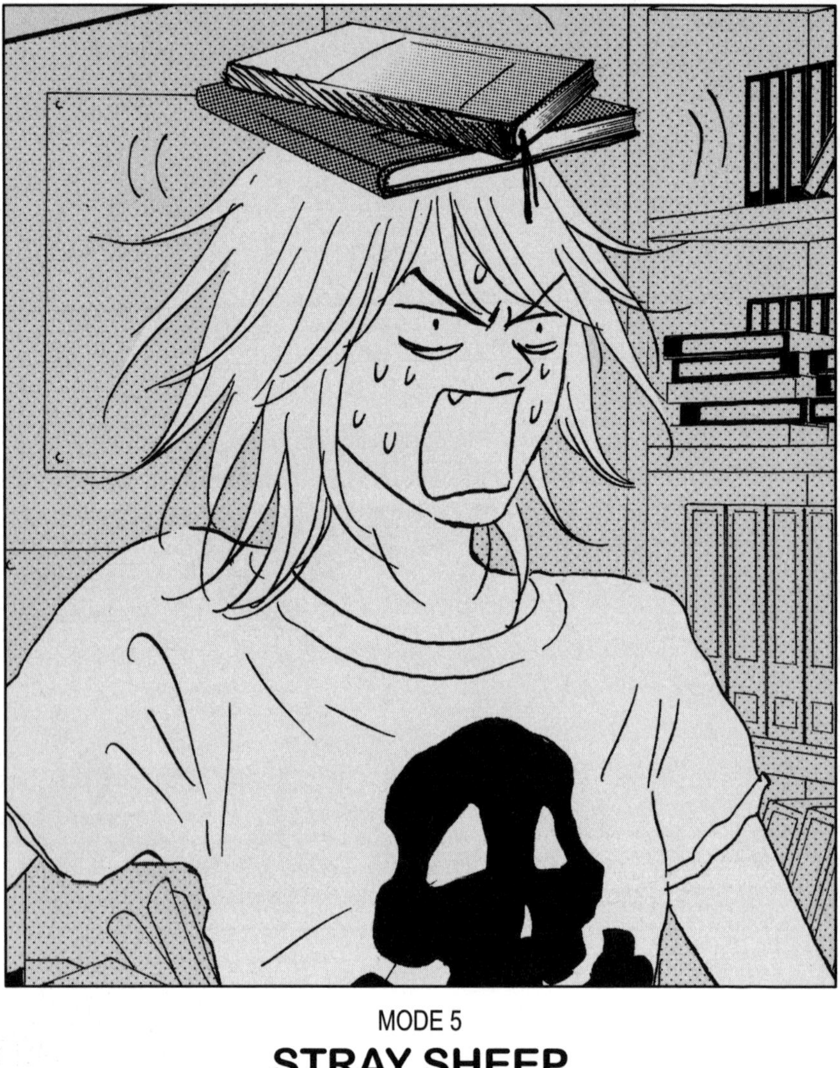

MODE 5

STRAY SHEEP

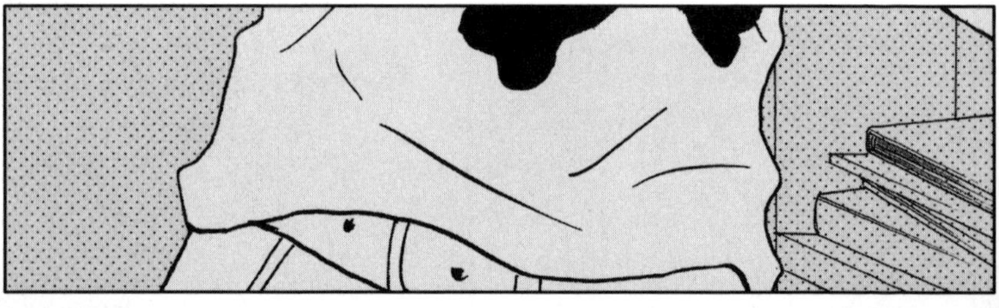

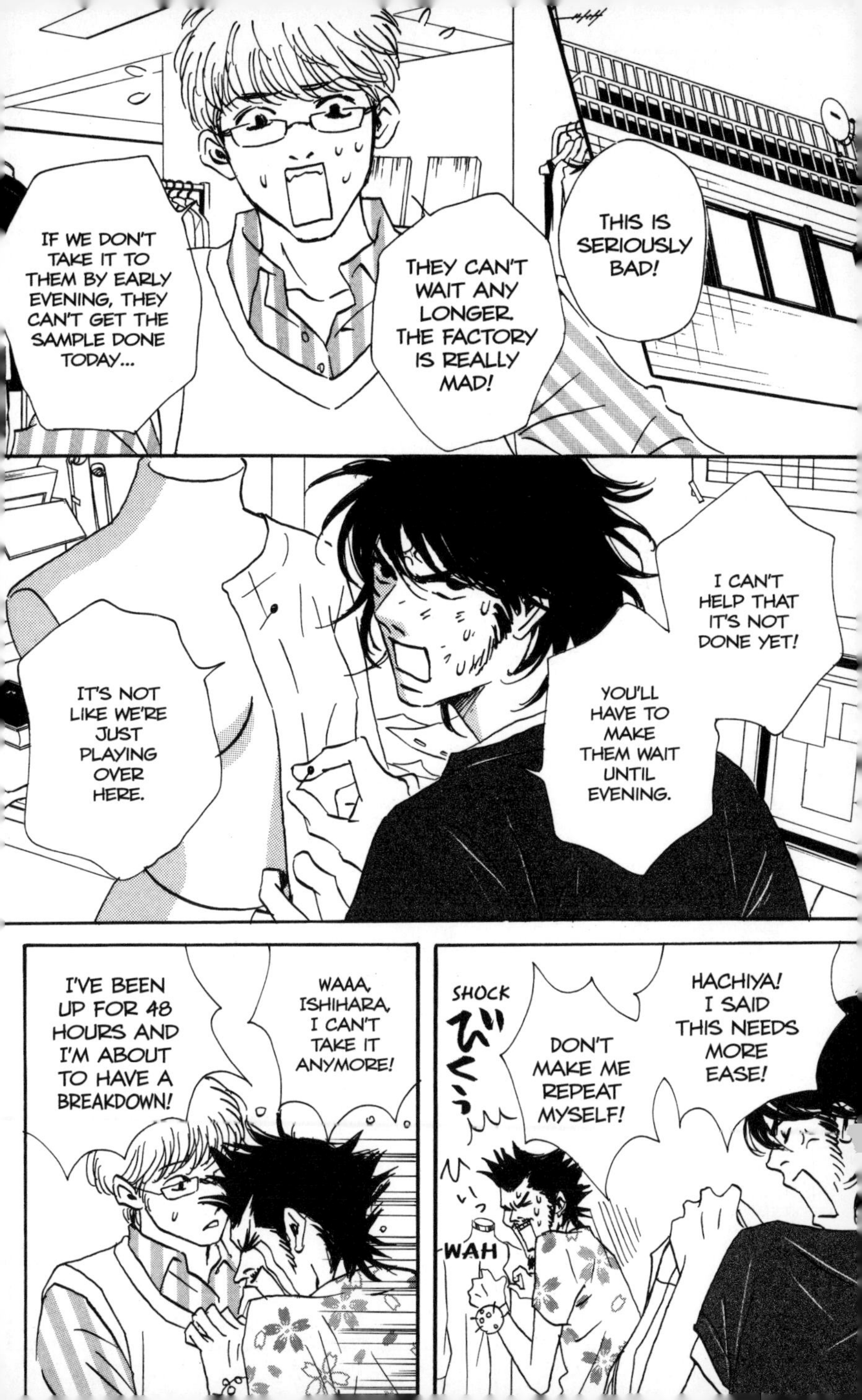
THIS IS SERIOUSLY BAD!
THEY CAN'T WAIT ANY LONGER THE FACTORY IS REALLY MAD!
IF WE DON'T TAKE IT TO THEM BY EARLY EVENING, THEY CAN'T GET THE SAMPLE DONE TODAY...
I CAN'T HELP THAT IT'S NOT DONE YET!
YOU'LL HAVE TO MAKE THEM WAIT UNTIL EVENING.
IT'S NOT LIKE WE'RE JUST PLAYING OVER HERE.
HACHIYA! I SAID THIS NEEDS MORE EASE!
DON'T MAKE ME REPEAT MYSELF!
SHOCK
びくっ
WAH
WAAA, ISHIHARA, I CAN'T TAKE IT ANYMORE!
I'VE BEEN UP FOR 48 HOURS AND I'M ABOUT TO HAVE A BREAKDOWN!

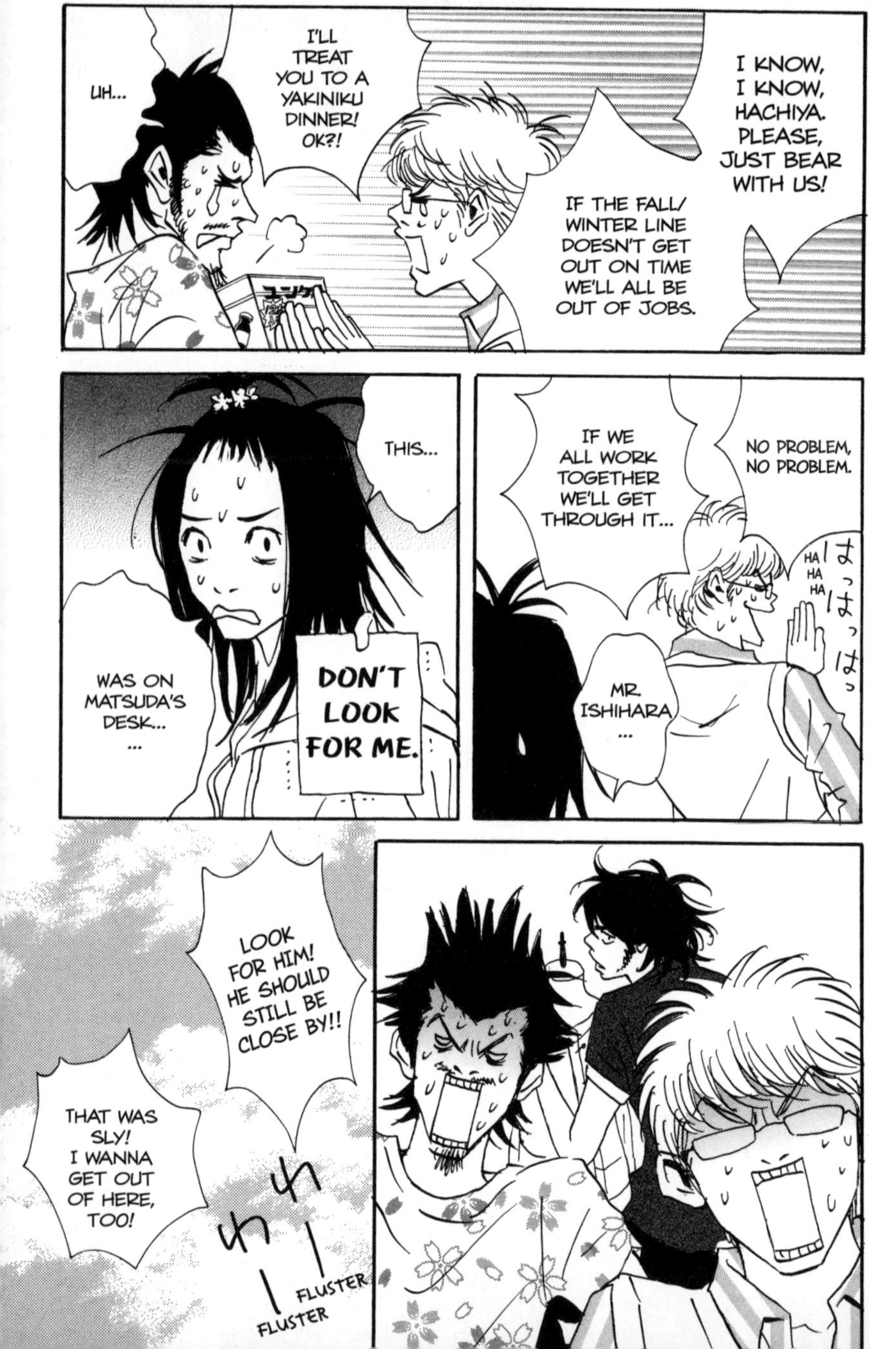
I KNOW, I KNOW, HACHIYA. PLEASE, JUST BEAR WITH US!
IF THE FALL/ WINTER LINE DOESN'T GET OUT ON TIME WE'LL ALL BE OUT OF JOBS.
I'LL TREAT YOU TO A YAKINIKU DINNER! OK?!
UH...
NO PROBLEM, NO PROBLEM.
IF WE ALL WORK TOGETHER WE'LL GET THROUGH IT...
はっはっはっ
HA HA HA
MR. ISHIHARA ...
THIS...
DON'T LOOK FOR ME.
WAS ON MATSUDA'S DESK... ...
LOOK FOR HIM! HE SHOULD STILL BE CLOSE BY!!
THAT WAS SLY! I WANNA GET OUT OF HERE, TOO!
わーわー
FLUSTER FLUSTER

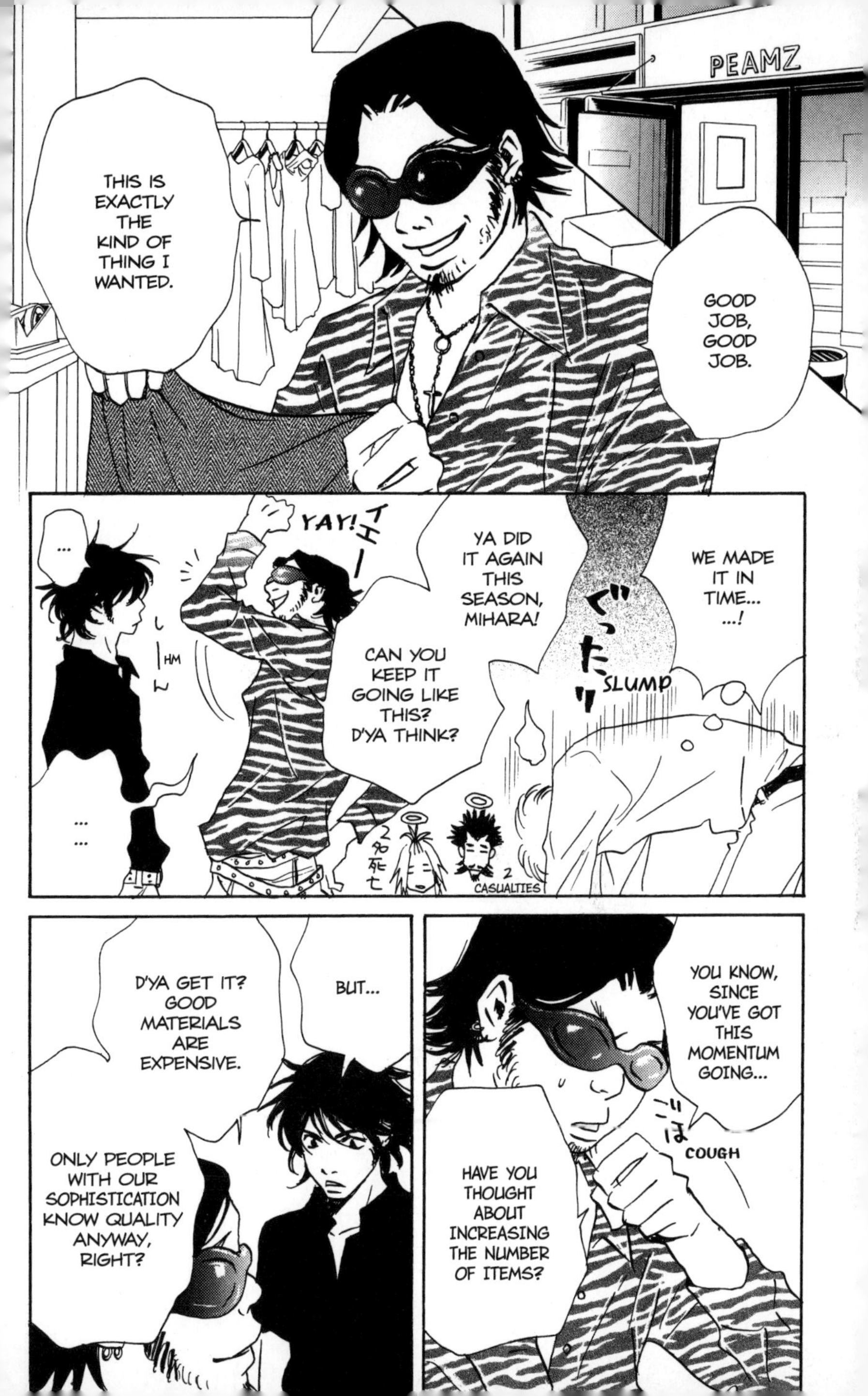
PEAMZ
THIS IS EXACTLY THE KIND OF THING I WANTED.
GOOD JOB, GOOD JOB.
WE MADE IT IN TIME... ...!
SLUMP
YA DID IT AGAIN THIS SEASON, MIHARA!
YAY!
CAN YOU KEEP IT GOING LIKE THIS? D'YA THINK?
...
HM
... ...
2 CASUALTIES
YOU KNOW, SINCE YOU'VE GOT THIS MOMENTUM GOING...
COUGH
HAVE YOU THOUGHT ABOUT INCREASING THE NUMBER OF ITEMS?
BUT...
D'YA GET IT? GOOD MATERIALS ARE EXPENSIVE.
ONLY PEOPLE WITH OUR SOPHISTICATION KNOW QUALITY ANYWAY, RIGHT?

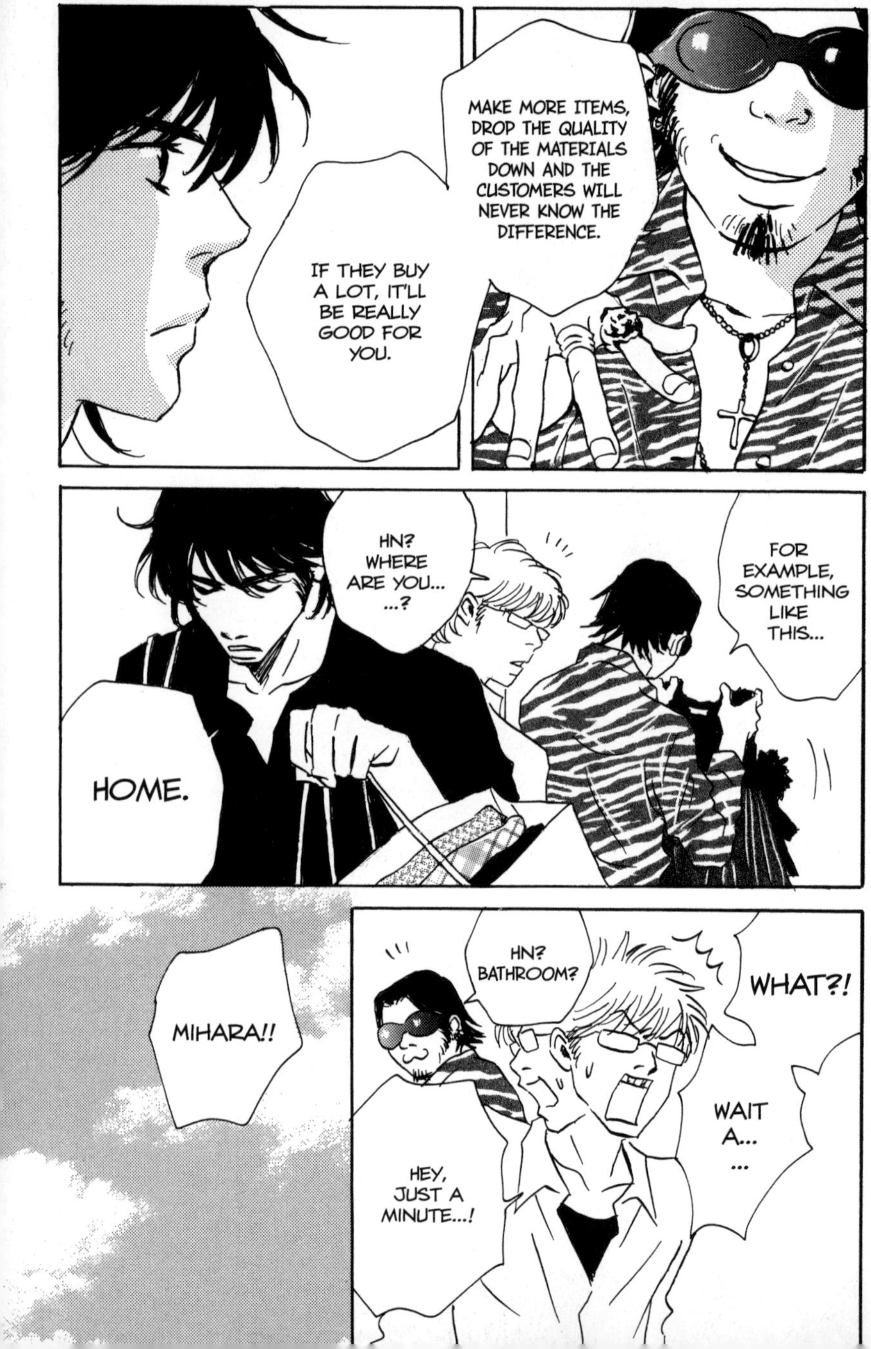
MAKE MORE ITEMS, DROP THE QUALITY OF THE MATERIALS DOWN AND THE CUSTOMERS WILL NEVER KNOW THE DIFFERENCE.
IF THEY BUY A LOT, IT'LL BE REALLY GOOD FOR YOU.
FOR EXAMPLE, SOMETHING LIKE THIS...
HN? WHERE ARE YOU... ...?
HOME.
WHAT?!
HN? BATHROOM?
WAIT A... ...
HEY, JUST A MINUTE...!
MIHARA!!

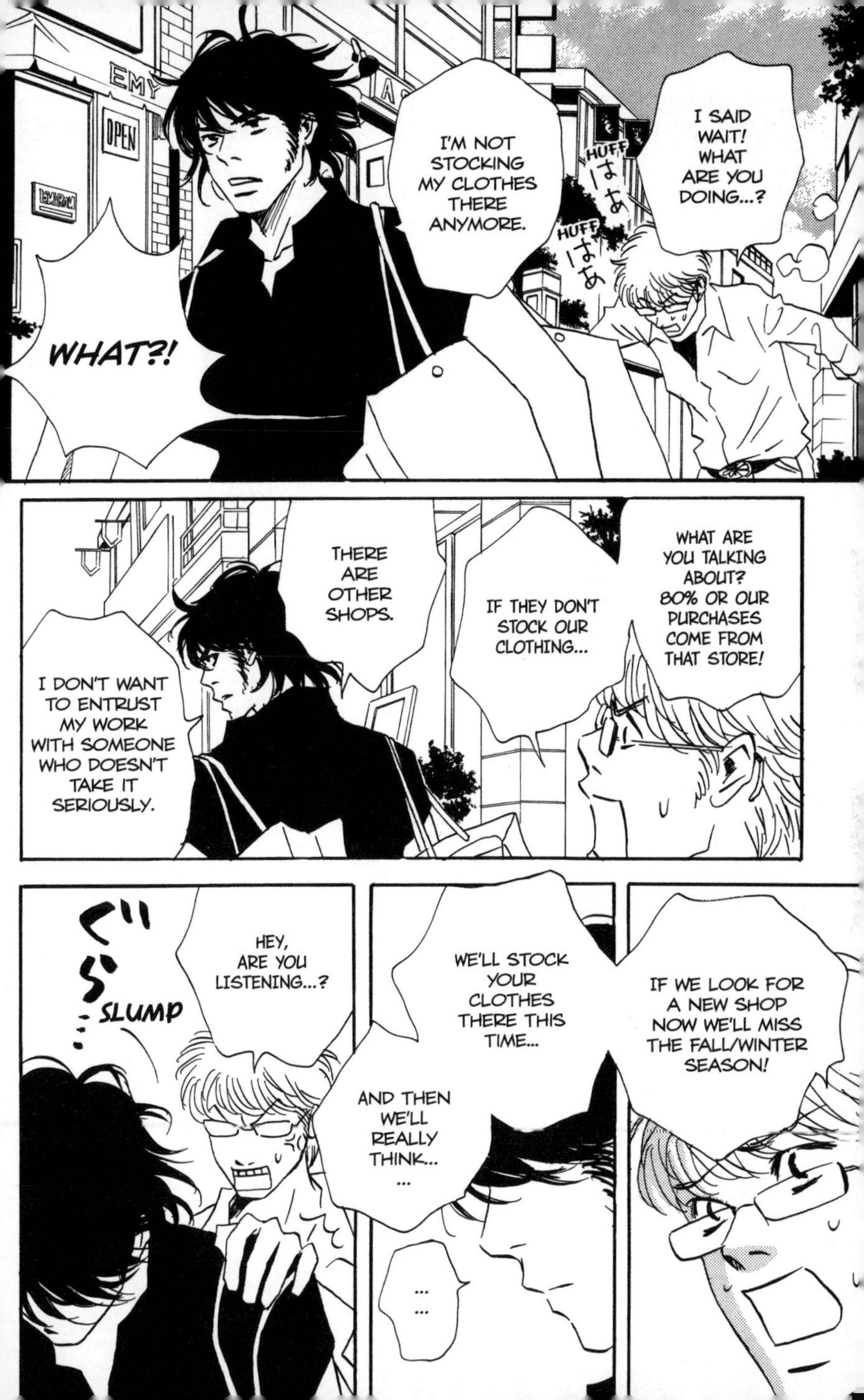
I SAID WAIT! WHAT ARE YOU DOING...?
HUFF はあ
HUFF はあ
I'M NOT STOCKING MY CLOTHES THERE ANYMORE.
WHAT?!
WHAT ARE YOU TALKING ABOUT? 80% OR OUR PURCHASES COME FROM THAT STORE!
IF THEY DON'T STOCK OUR CLOTHING...
THERE ARE OTHER SHOPS.
I DON'T WANT TO ENTRUST MY WORK WITH SOMEONE WHO DOESN'T TAKE IT SERIOUSLY.
IF WE LOOK FOR A NEW SHOP NOW WE'LL MISS THE FALL/WINTER SEASON!
WE'LL STOCK YOUR CLOTHES THERE THIS TIME...
AND THEN WE'LL REALLY THINK... ...
... ...
HEY, ARE YOU LISTENING...?
ぐら SLUMP

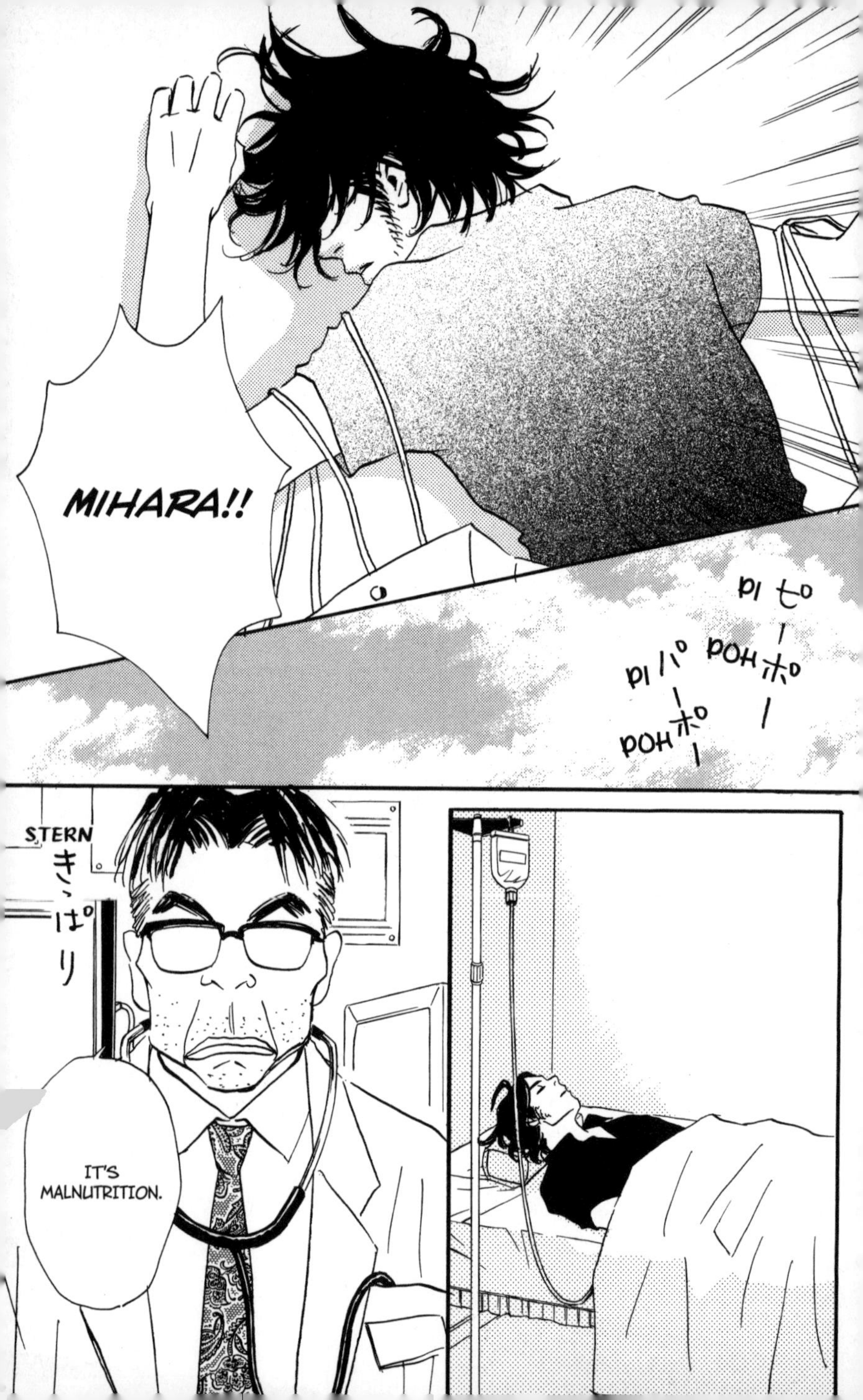
MIHARA!!
PI ピー POH ポー
PI パー POH ポー
STERN きっぱり
IT'S MALNUTRITION.

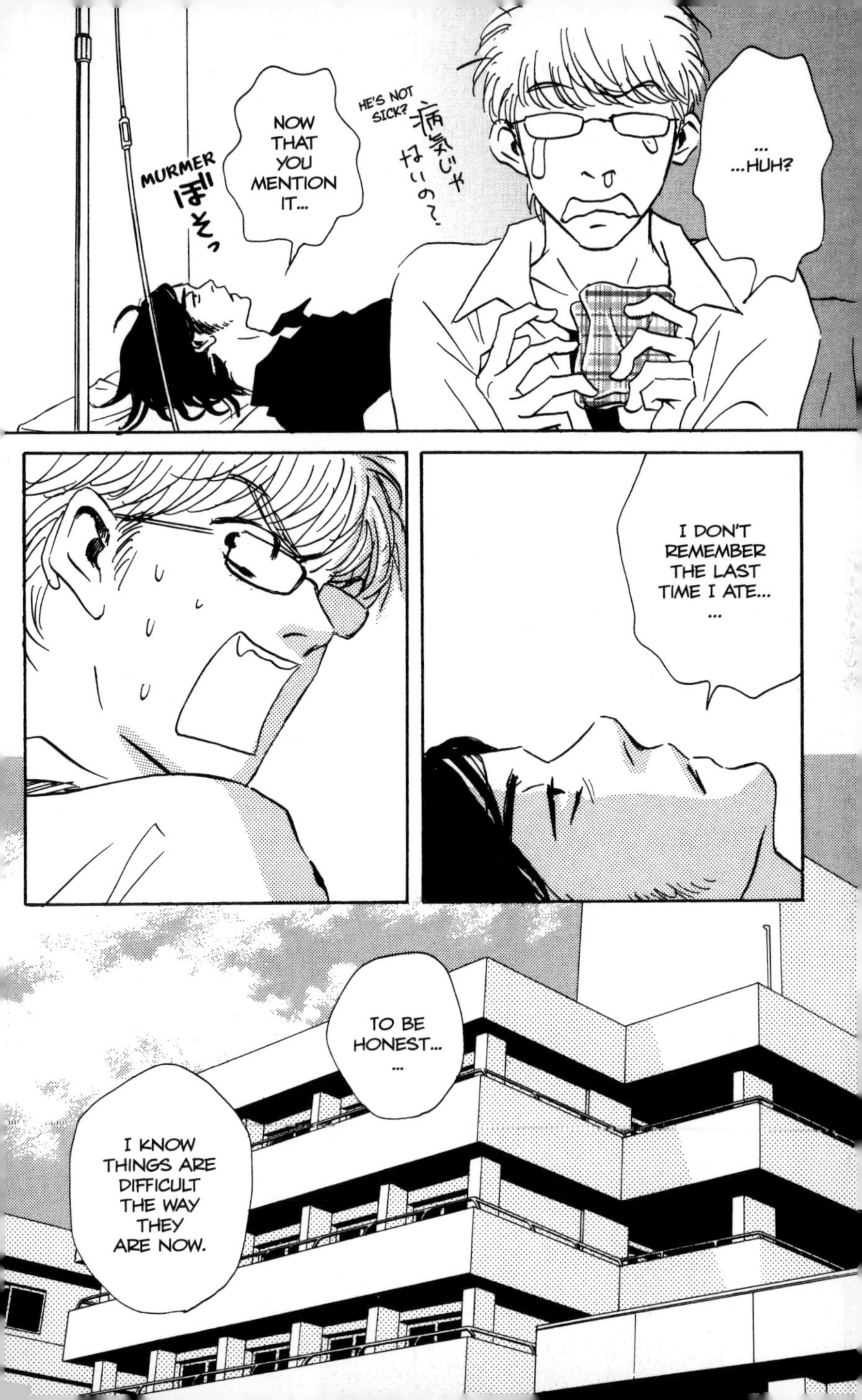
... ...HUH?
HE'S NOT SICK?
病気じゃないの？
NOW THAT YOU MENTION IT...
MURMER
ぼそっ
I DON'T REMEMBER THE LAST TIME I ATE... ...
TO BE HONEST... ...
I KNOW THINGS ARE DIFFICULT THE WAY THEY ARE NOW.

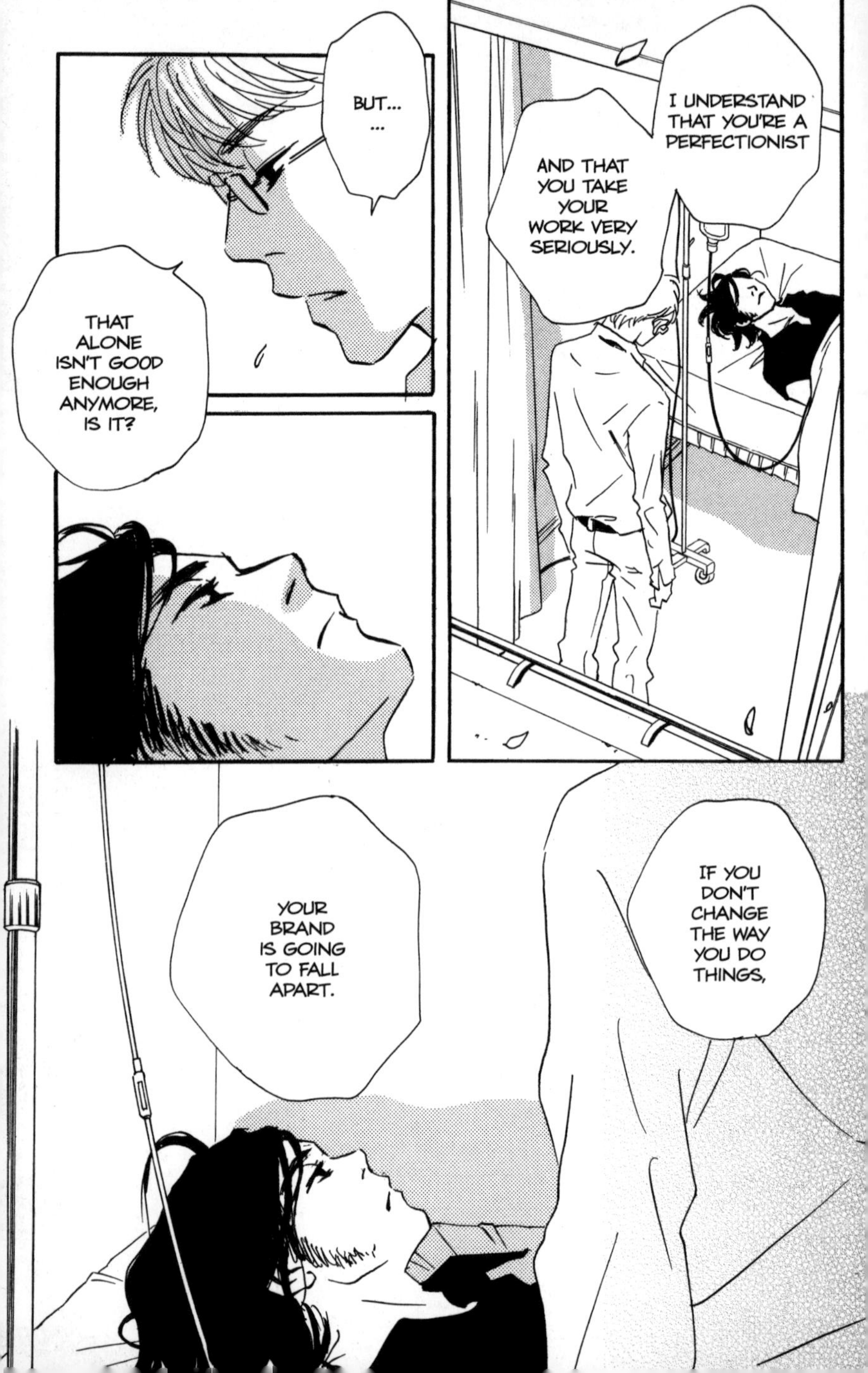
I UNDERSTAND THAT YOU'RE A PERFECTIONIST
AND THAT YOU TAKE YOUR WORK VERY SERIOUSLY.
BUT... ...
THAT ALONE ISN'T GOOD ENOUGH ANYMORE, IS IT?
IF YOU DON'T CHANGE THE WAY YOU DO THINGS,
YOUR BRAND IS GOING TO FALL APART.

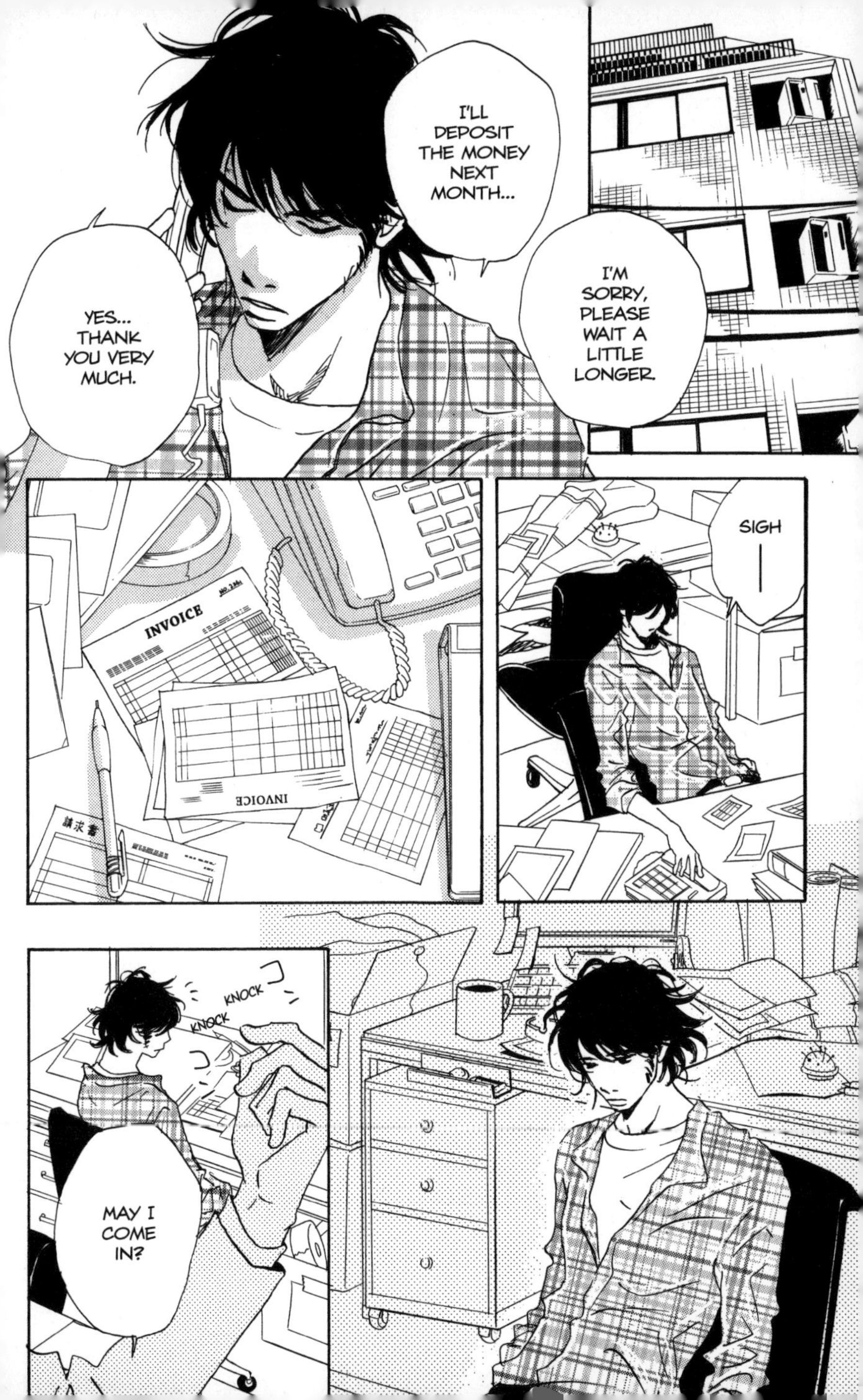
I'M SORRY, PLEASE WAIT A LITTLE LONGER.
I'LL DEPOSIT THE MONEY NEXT MONTH...
YES... THANK YOU VERY MUCH.
SIGH
INVOICE
INVOICE
請求書
KNOCK
KNOCK
MAY I COME IN?

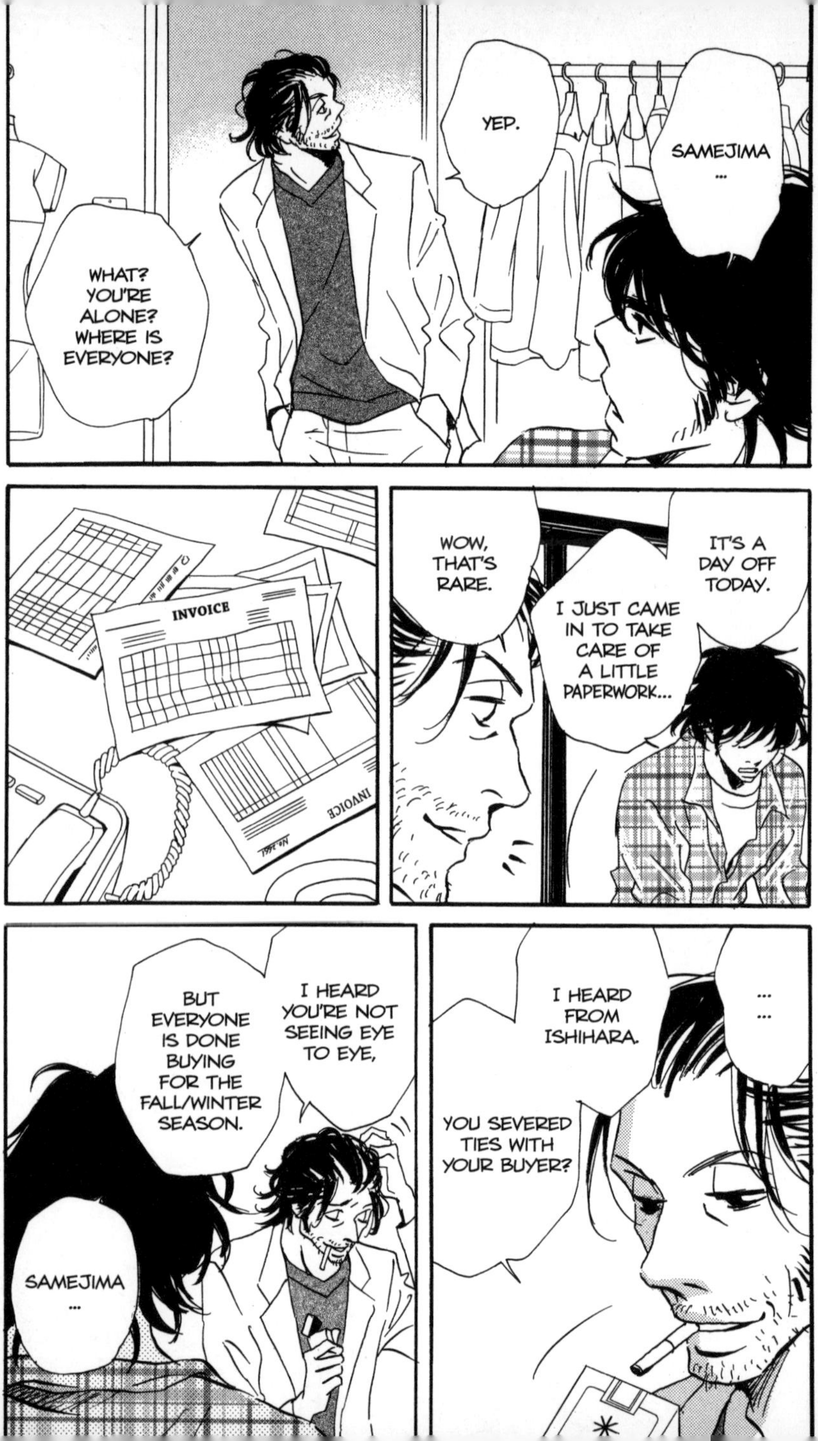
SAMEJIMA ...
YEP.
WHAT? YOU'RE ALONE? WHERE IS EVERYONE?
IT'S A DAY OFF TODAY.
I JUST CAME IN TO TAKE CARE OF A LITTLE PAPERWORK...
WOW, THAT'S RARE.
INVOICE
INVOICE
... ...
I HEARD FROM ISHIHARA.
YOU SEVERED TIES WITH YOUR BUYER?
I HEARD YOU'RE NOT SEEING EYE TO EYE,
BUT EVERYONE IS DONE BUYING FOR THE FALL/WINTER SEASON.
SAMEJIMA ...

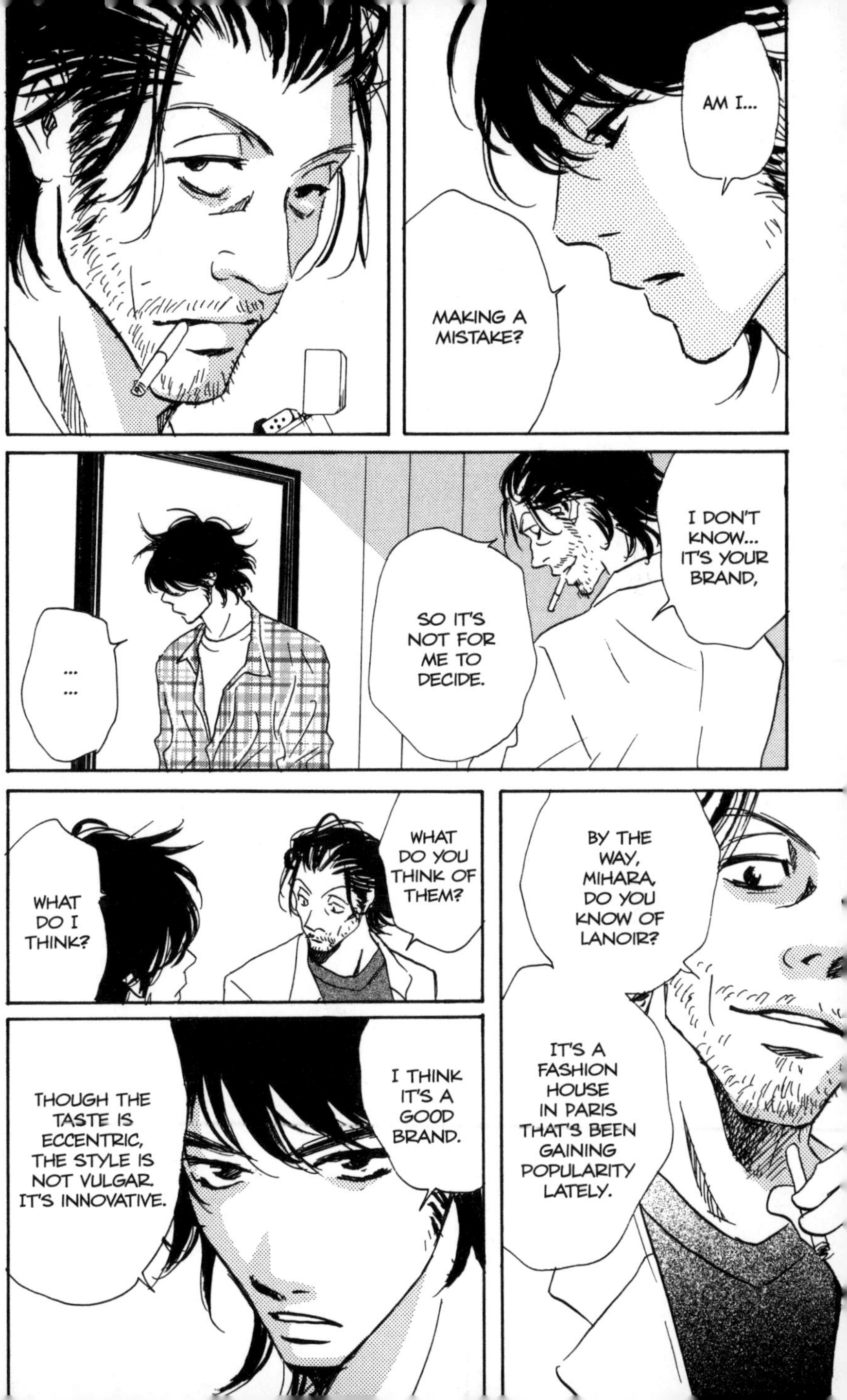
AM I...
MAKING A MISTAKE?
I DON'T KNOW... IT'S YOUR BRAND,
SO IT'S NOT FOR ME TO DECIDE.
... ...
BY THE WAY, MIHARA, DO YOU KNOW OF LANOIR?
IT'S A FASHION HOUSE IN PARIS THAT'S BEEN GAINING POPULARITY LATELY.
WHAT DO YOU THINK OF THEM?
WHAT DO I THINK?
I THINK IT'S A GOOD BRAND.
THOUGH THE TASTE IS ECCENTRIC, THE STYLE IS NOT VULGAR. IT'S INNOVATIVE.

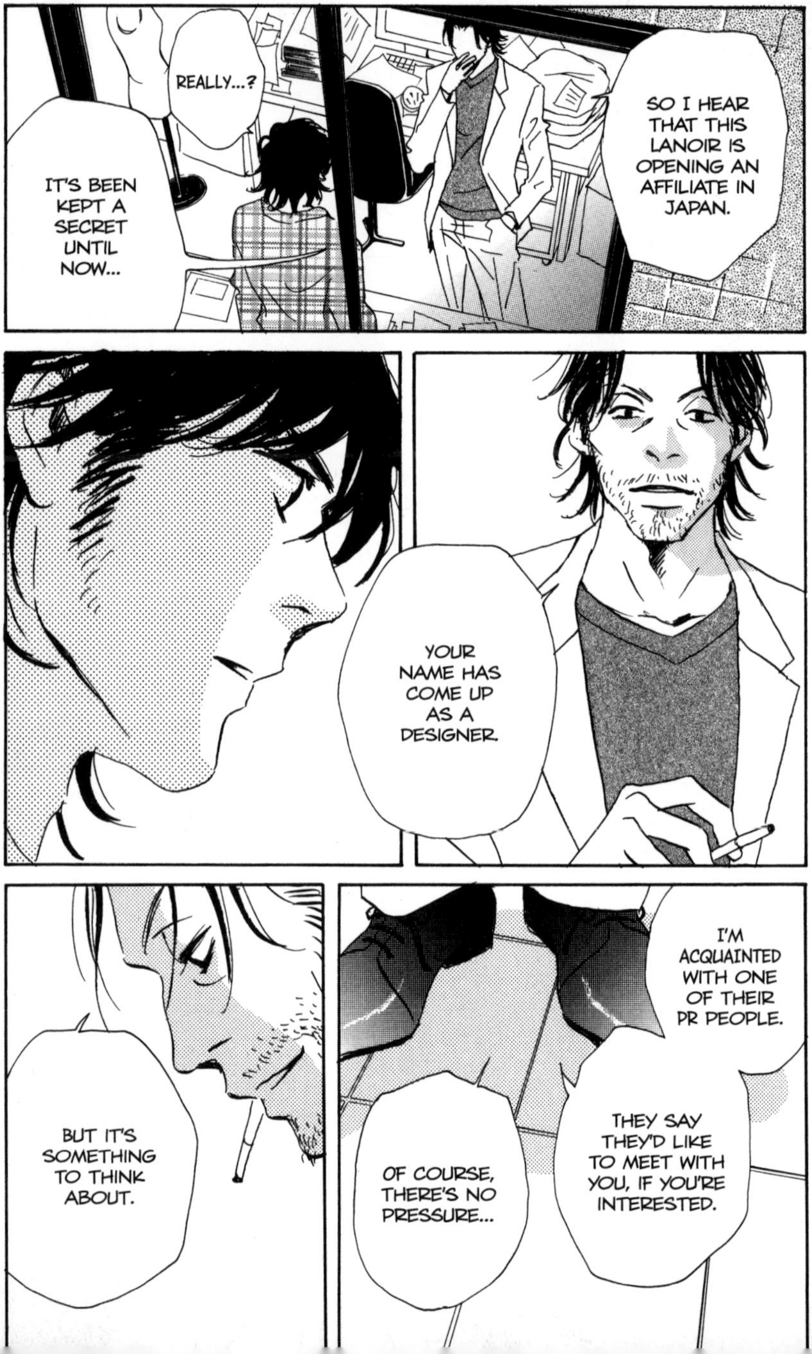
SO I HEAR THAT THIS LANOIR IS OPENING AN AFFILIATE IN JAPAN.
REALLY...?
IT'S BEEN KEPT A SECRET UNTIL NOW...
YOUR NAME HAS COME UP AS A DESIGNER.
I'M ACQUAINTED WITH ONE OF THEIR PR PEOPLE.
THEY SAY THEY'D LIKE TO MEET WITH YOU, IF YOU'RE INTERESTED.
OF COURSE, THERE'S NO PRESSURE...
BUT IT'S SOMETHING TO THINK ABOUT.

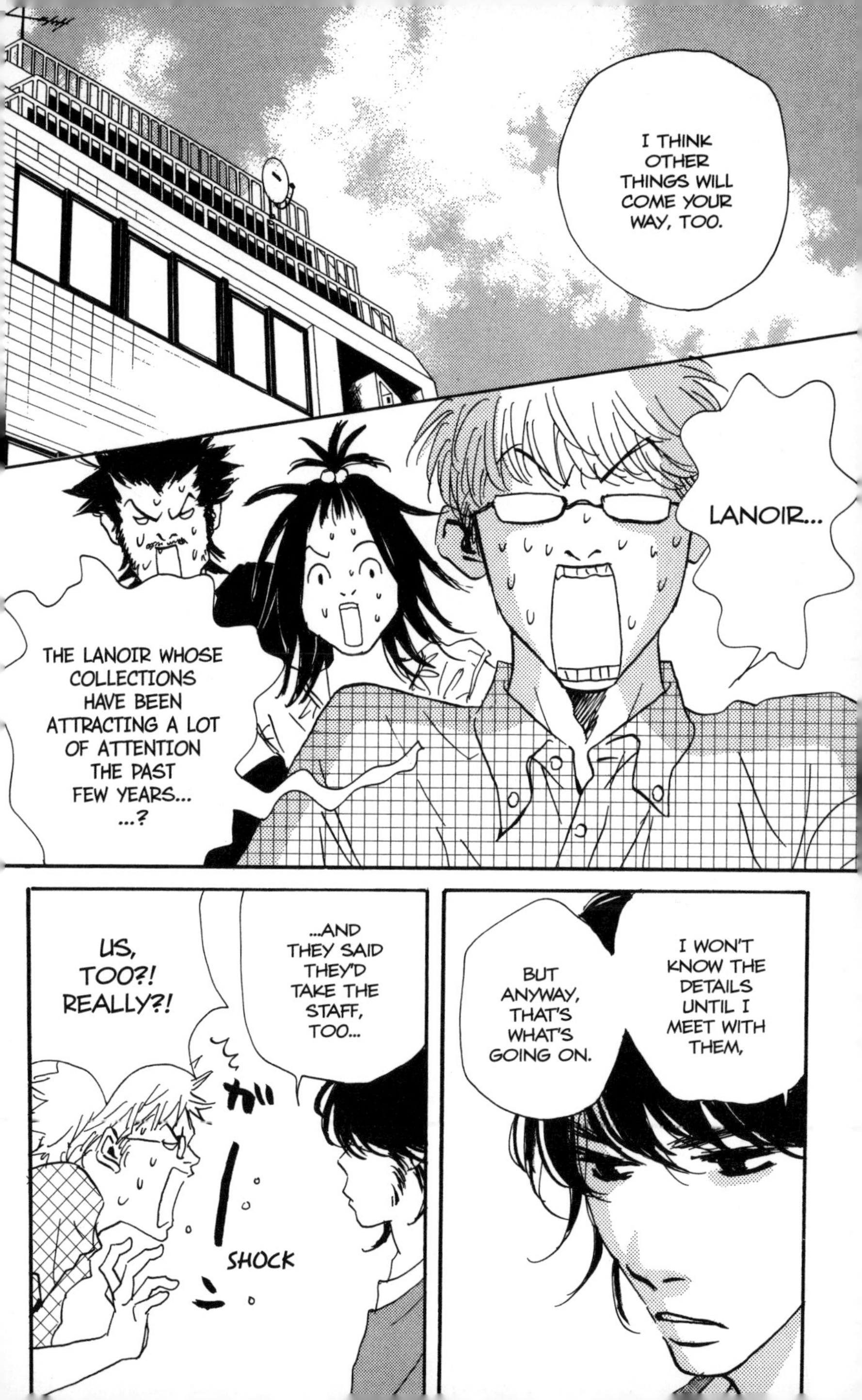
I THINK OTHER THINGS WILL COME YOUR WAY, TOO.
LANOIR...
THE LANOIR WHOSE COLLECTIONS HAVE BEEN ATTRACTING A LOT OF ATTENTION THE PAST FEW YEARS... ...?
I WON'T KNOW THE DETAILS UNTIL I MEET WITH THEM,
BUT ANYWAY, THAT'S WHAT'S GOING ON.
...AND THEY SAID THEY'D TAKE THE STAFF, TOO...
US, TOO?! REALLY?!
SHOCK

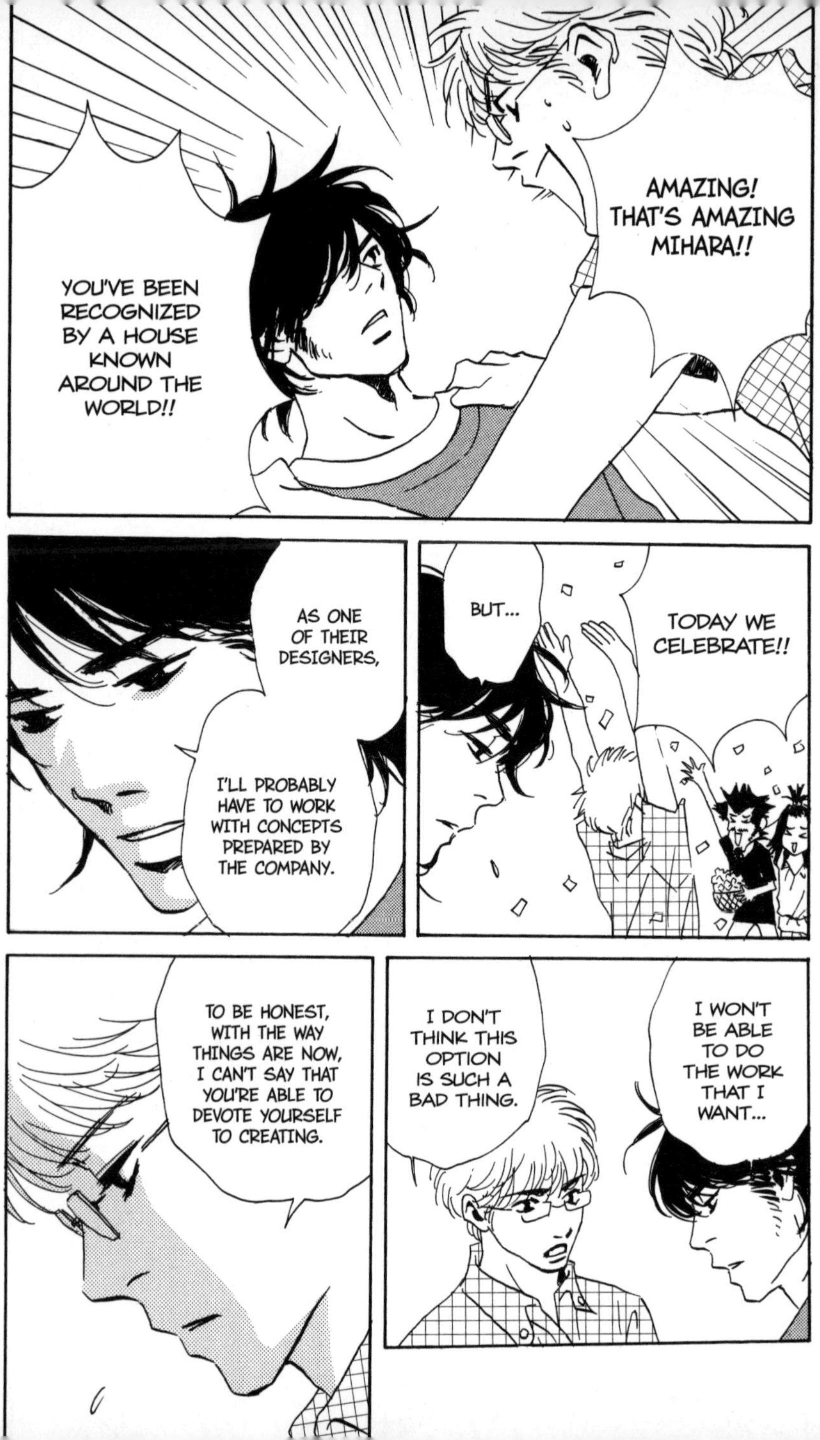
AMAZING! THAT'S AMAZING MIHARA!!
YOU'VE BEEN RECOGNIZED BY A HOUSE KNOWN AROUND THE WORLD!!
TODAY WE CELEBRATE!!
BUT...
AS ONE OF THEIR DESIGNERS,
I'LL PROBABLY HAVE TO WORK WITH CONCEPTS PREPARED BY THE COMPANY.
I WON'T BE ABLE TO DO THE WORK THAT I WANT...
I DON'T THINK THIS OPTION IS SUCH A BAD THING.
TO BE HONEST, WITH THE WAY THINGS ARE NOW, I CAN'T SAY THAT YOU'RE ABLE TO DEVOTE YOURSELF TO CREATING.

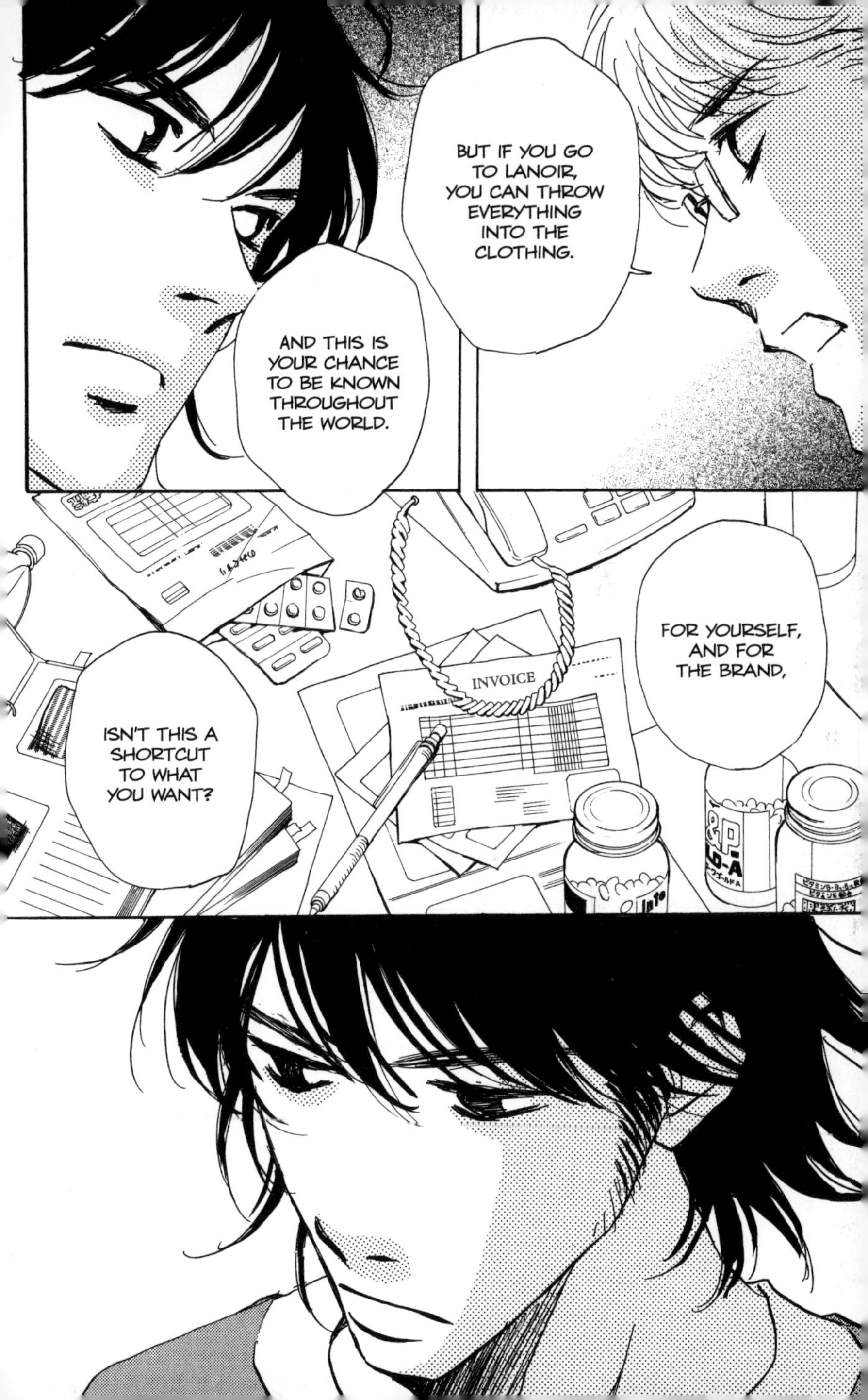
BUT IF YOU GO TO LANOIR, YOU CAN THROW EVERYTHING INTO THE CLOTHING.
AND THIS IS YOUR CHANCE TO BE KNOWN THROUGHOUT THE WORLD.
FOR YOURSELF, AND FOR THE BRAND,
INVOICE
ISN'T THIS A SHORTCUT TO WHAT YOU WANT?

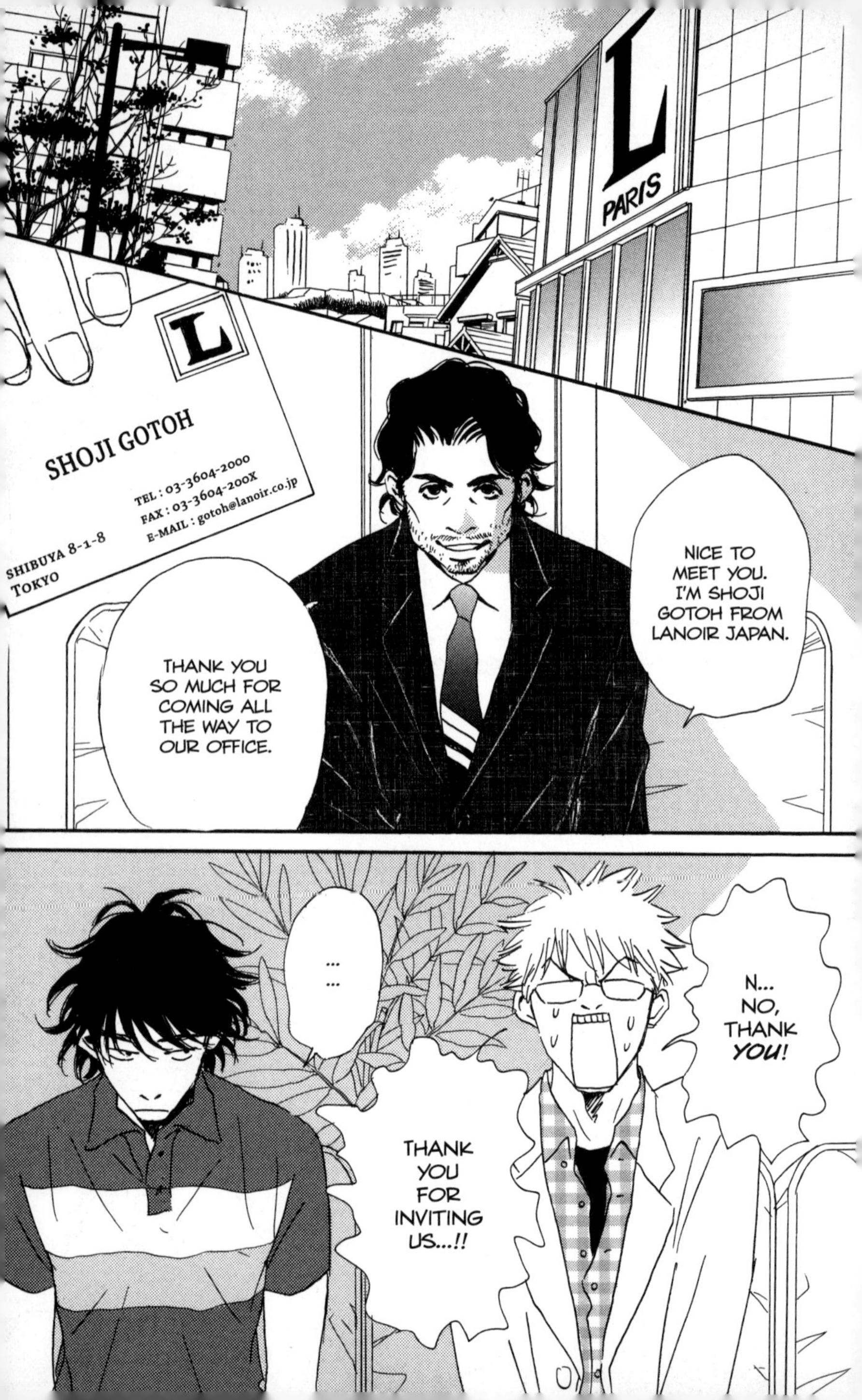
PARIS
NICE TO MEET YOU. I'M SHOJI GOTOH FROM LANOIR JAPAN.
SHOJI GOTOH
TEL : 03-3604-2000
FAX : 03-3604-200X
E-MAIL : gotoh@lanoir.co.jp
SHIBUYA 8-1-8
TOKYO
THANK YOU SO MUCH FOR COMING ALL THE WAY TO OUR OFFICE.
N... NO, THANK *YOU*!
THANK YOU FOR INVITING US...!!
... ...

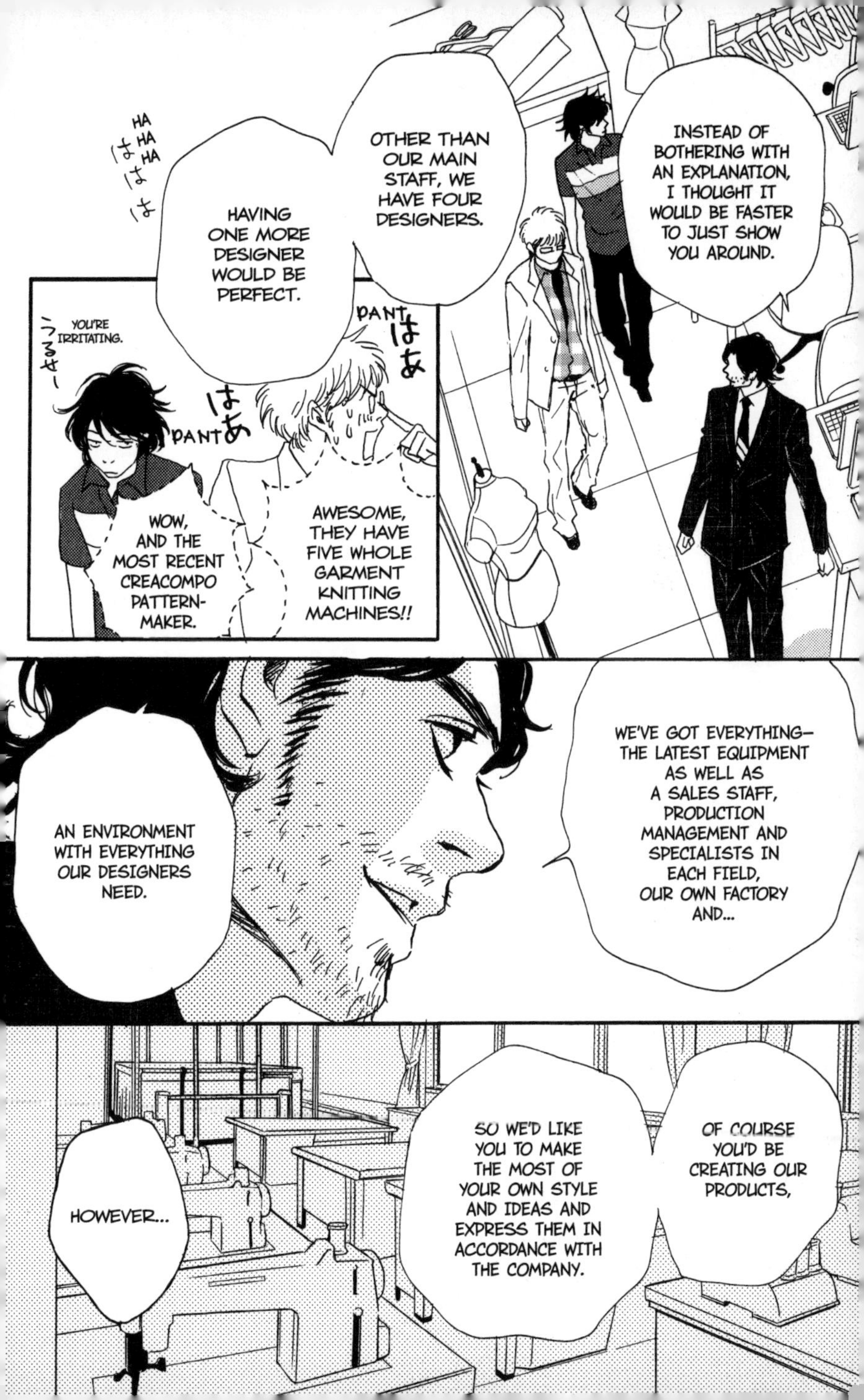

INSTEAD OF BOTHERING WITH AN EXPLANATION, I THOUGHT IT WOULD BE FASTER TO JUST SHOW YOU AROUND.
OTHER THAN OUR MAIN STAFF, WE HAVE FOUR DESIGNERS.
HAVING ONE MORE DESIGNER WOULD BE PERFECT.
HA HA HA ははは
PANT はあ
PANT はあ
AWESOME, THEY HAVE FIVE WHOLE GARMENT KNITTING MACHINES!!
WOW, AND THE MOST RECENT CREACOMPO PATTERN-MAKER.
YOU'RE IRRITATING. うるせー
WE'VE GOT EVERYTHING— THE LATEST EQUIPMENT AS WELL AS A SALES STAFF, PRODUCTION MANAGEMENT AND SPECIALISTS IN EACH FIELD, OUR OWN FACTORY AND...
AN ENVIRONMENT WITH EVERYTHING OUR DESIGNERS NEED.
OF COURSE YOU'D BE CREATING OUR PRODUCTS,
SO WE'D LIKE YOU TO MAKE THE MOST OF YOUR OWN STYLE AND IDEAS AND EXPRESS THEM IN ACCORDANCE WITH THE COMPANY.
HOWEVER...

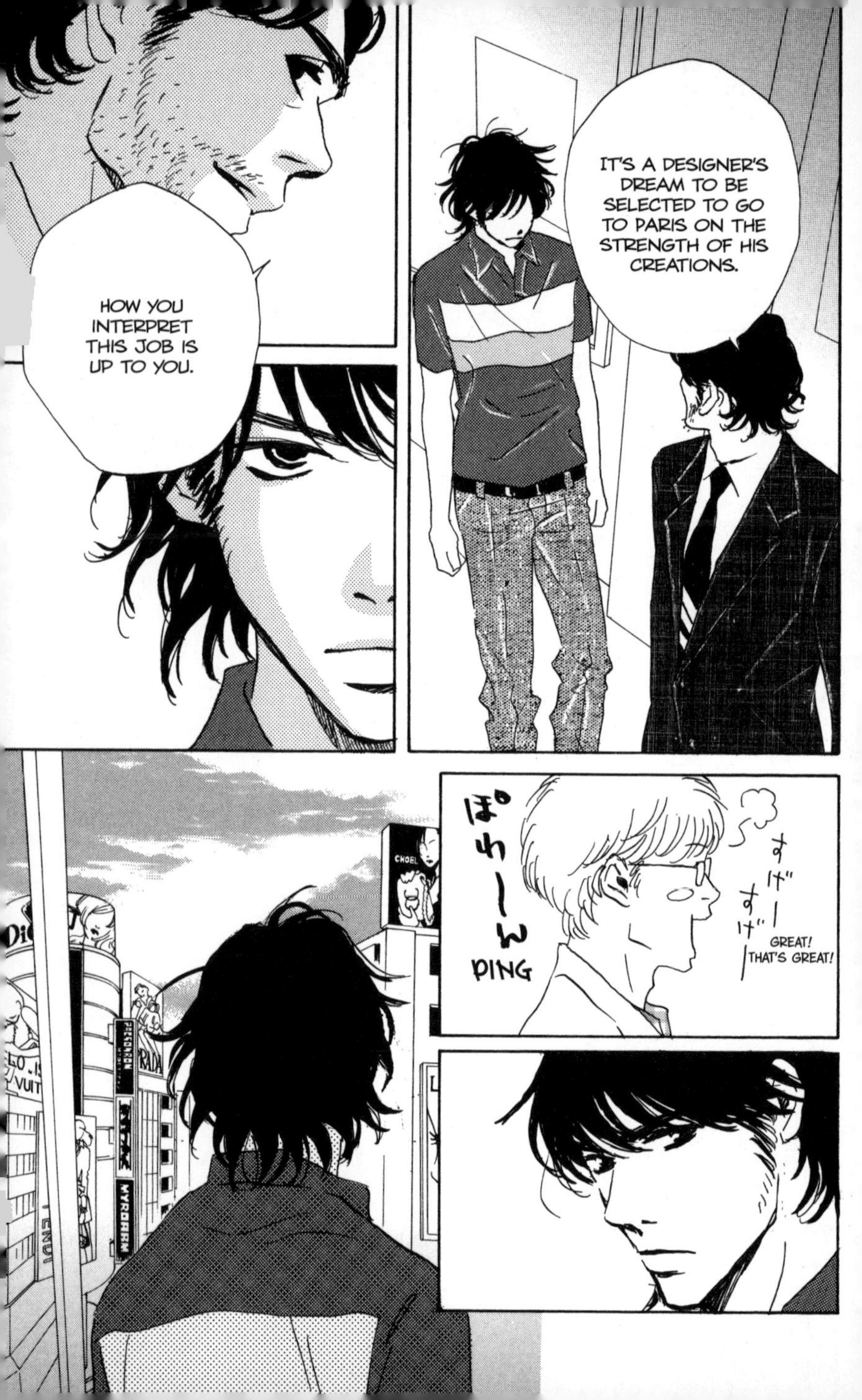
IT'S A DESIGNER'S DREAM TO BE SELECTED TO GO TO PARIS ON THE STRENGTH OF HIS CREATIONS.
HOW YOU INTERPRET THIS JOB IS UP TO YOU.
ぽわーん
PING
すげー すげー
GREAT! THAT'S GREAT!

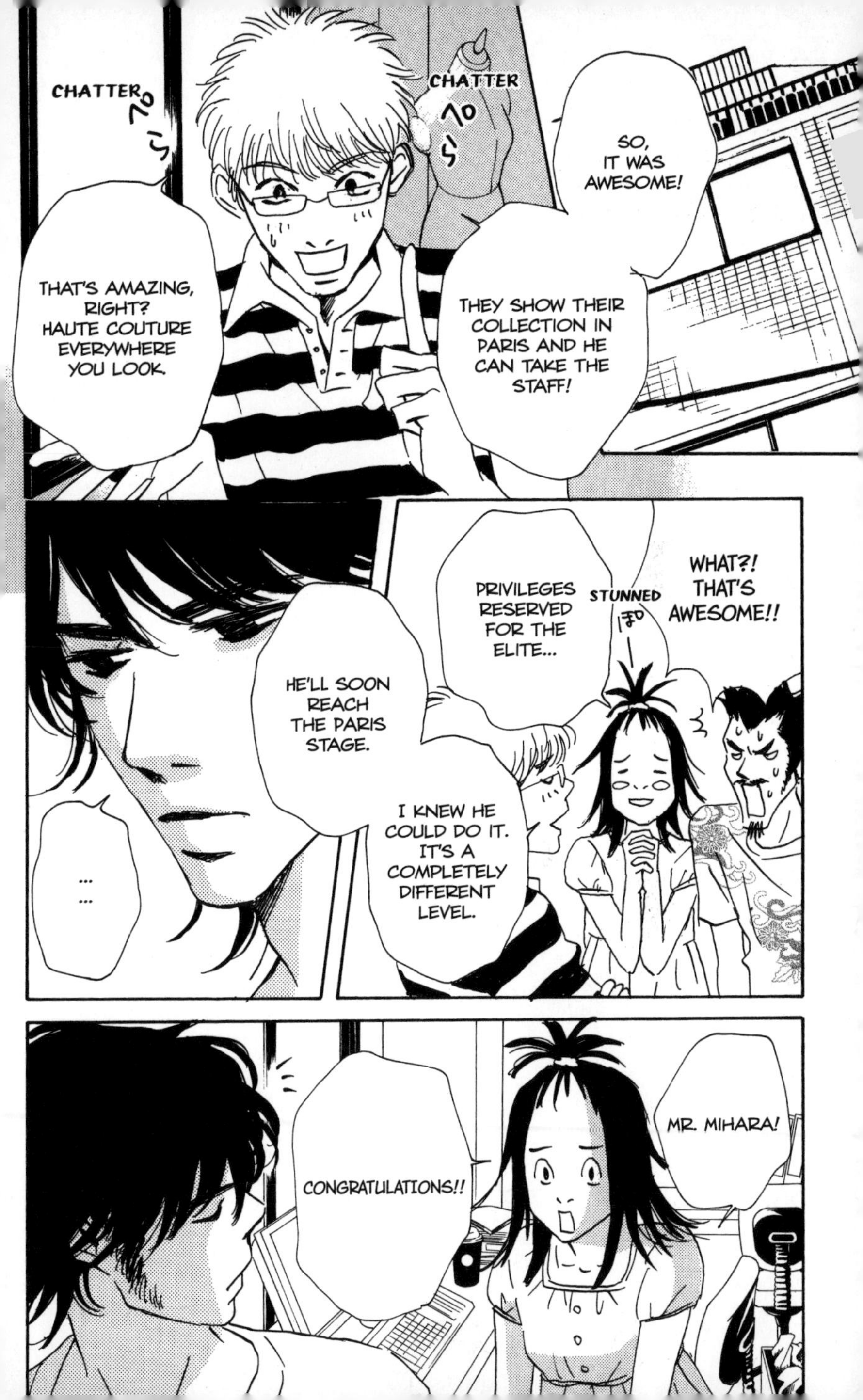
SO, IT WAS AWESOME!
THEY SHOW THEIR COLLECTION IN PARIS AND HE CAN TAKE THE STAFF!
CHATTER
CHATTER
THAT'S AMAZING, RIGHT? HAUTE COUTURE EVERYWHERE YOU LOOK.
WHAT?! THAT'S AWESOME!!
STUNNED
PRIVILEGES RESERVED FOR THE ELITE...
HE'LL SOON REACH THE PARIS STAGE.
I KNEW HE COULD DO IT. IT'S A COMPLETELY DIFFERENT LEVEL.
... ...
MR. MIHARA!
CONGRATULATIONS!!

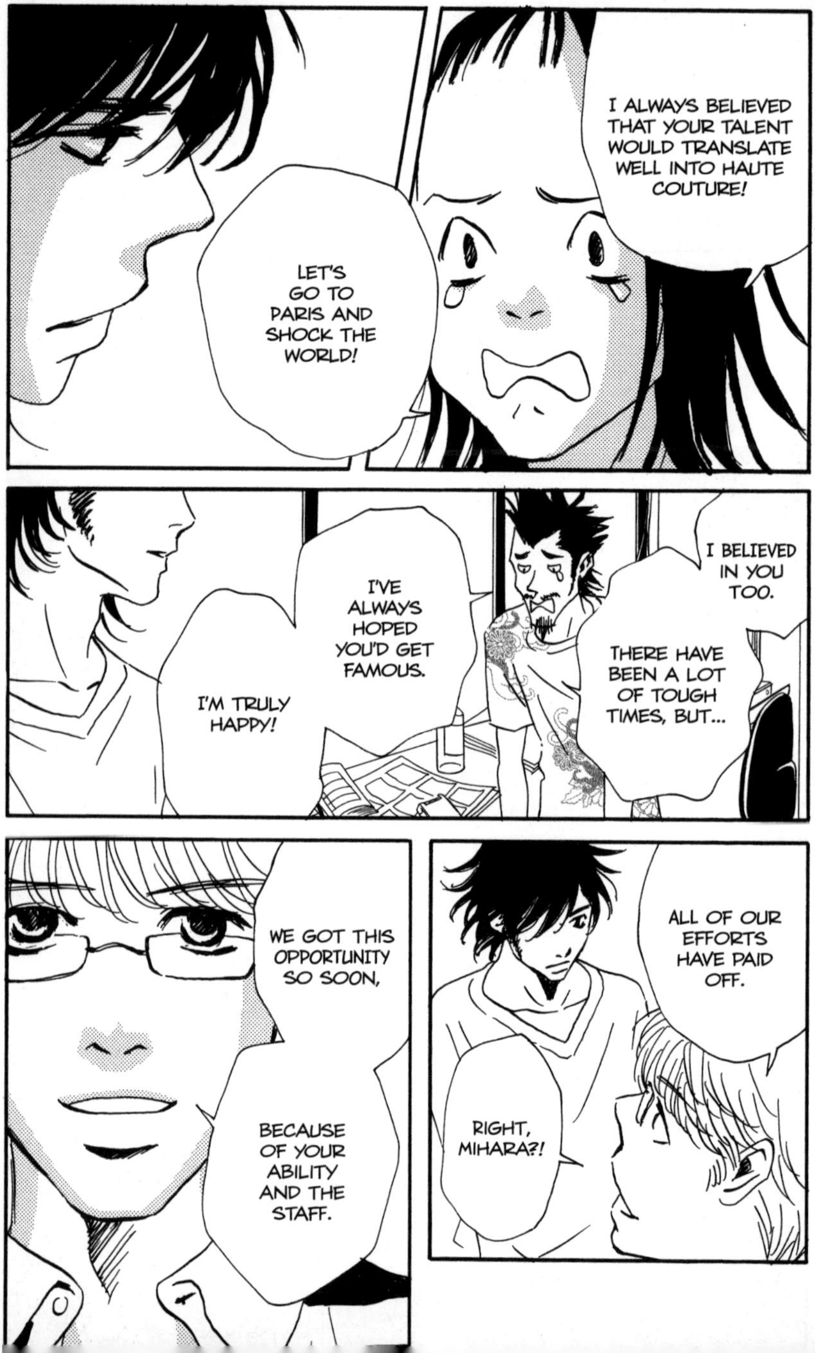
I ALWAYS BELIEVED THAT YOUR TALENT WOULD TRANSLATE WELL INTO HAUTE COUTURE!
LET'S GO TO PARIS AND SHOCK THE WORLD!
I BELIEVED IN YOU TOO.
THERE HAVE BEEN A LOT OF TOUGH TIMES, BUT...
I'VE ALWAYS HOPED YOU'D GET FAMOUS.
I'M TRULY HAPPY!
ALL OF OUR EFFORTS HAVE PAID OFF.
RIGHT, MIHARA?!
WE GOT THIS OPPORTUNITY SO SOON,
BECAUSE OF YOUR ABILITY AND THE STAFF.

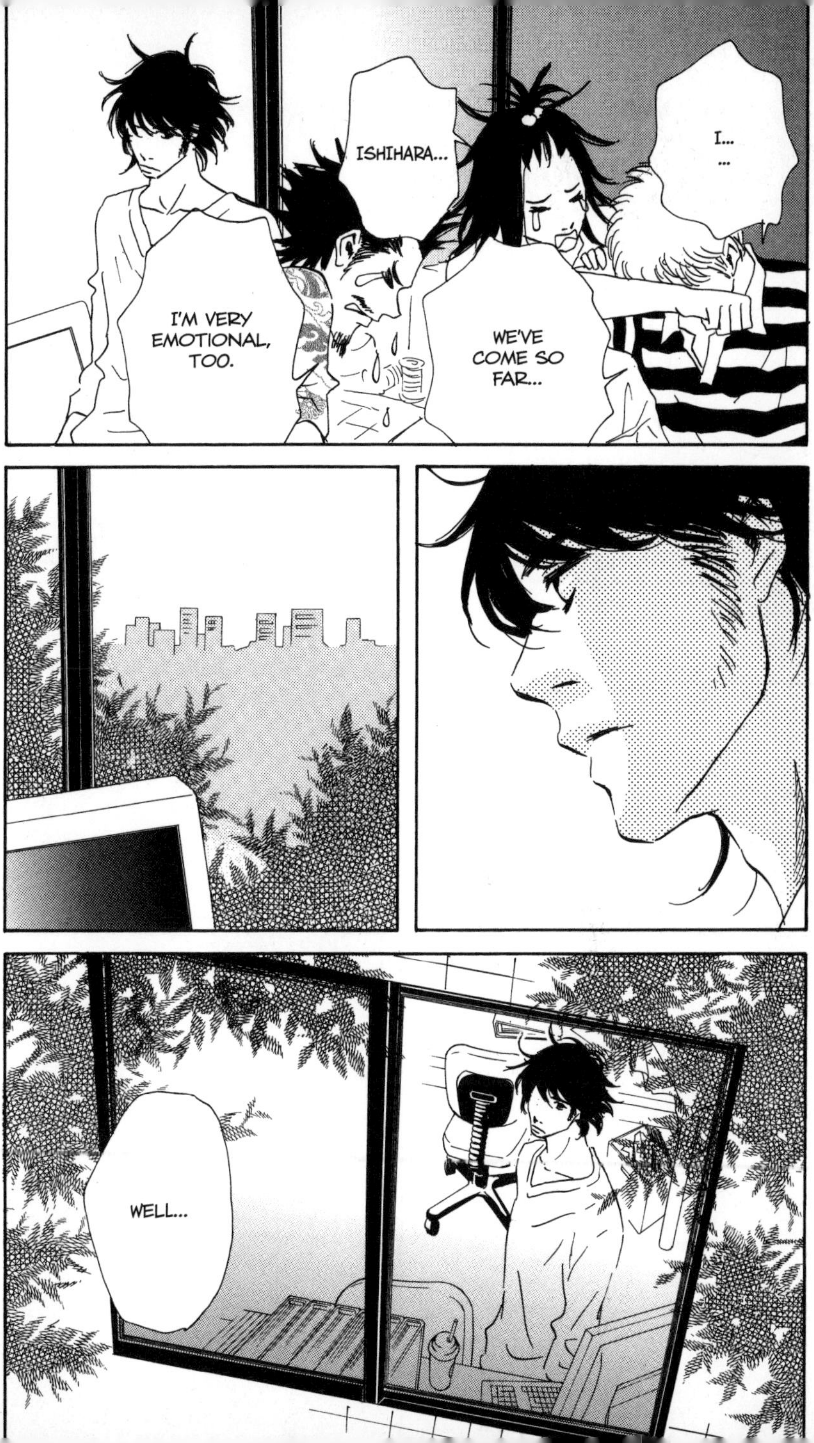
I...
...
ISHIHARA...
WE'VE COME SO FAR...
I'M VERY EMOTIONAL, TOO.
WELL...

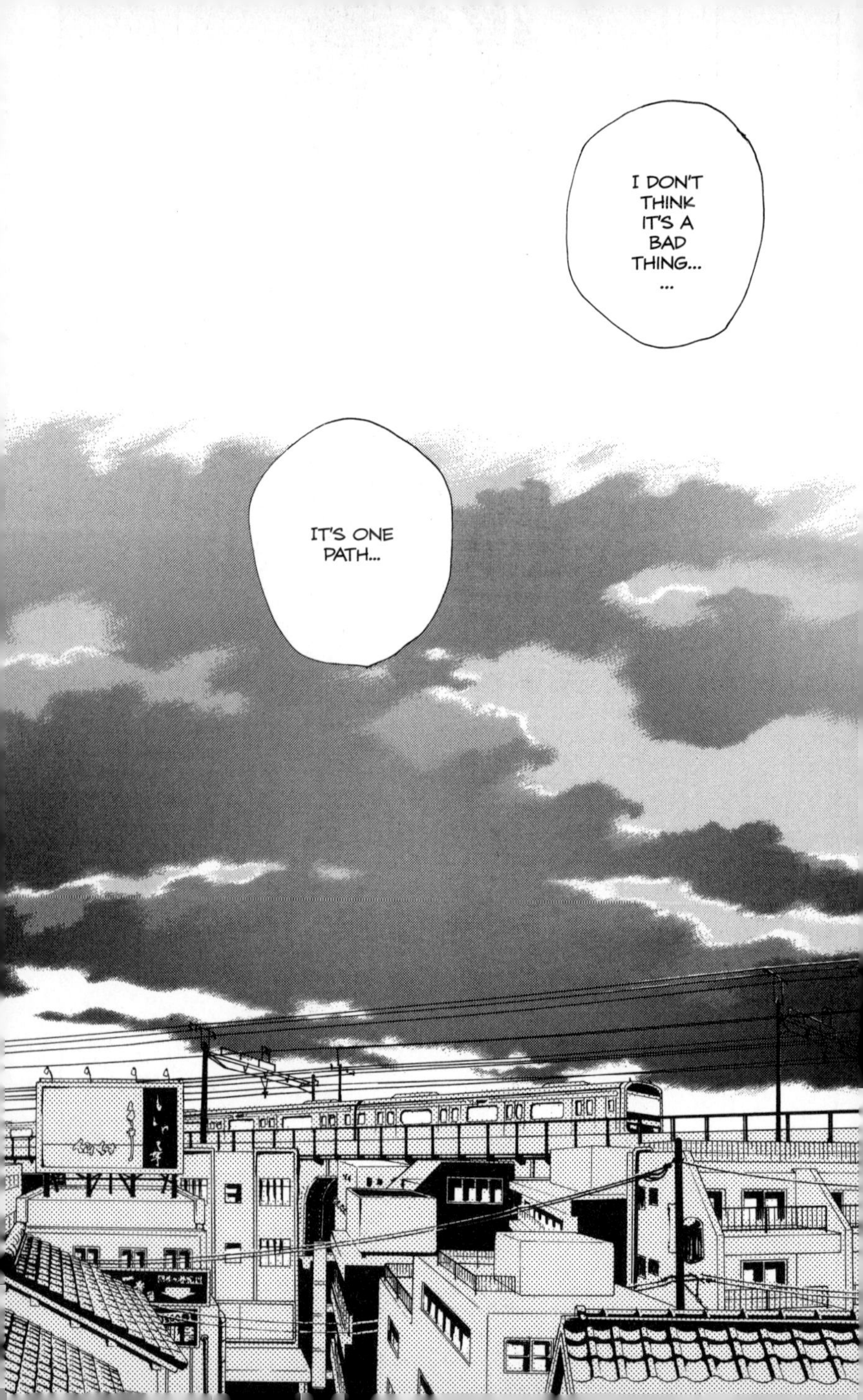
I DON'T THINK IT'S A BAD THING... ...
IT'S ONE PATH...

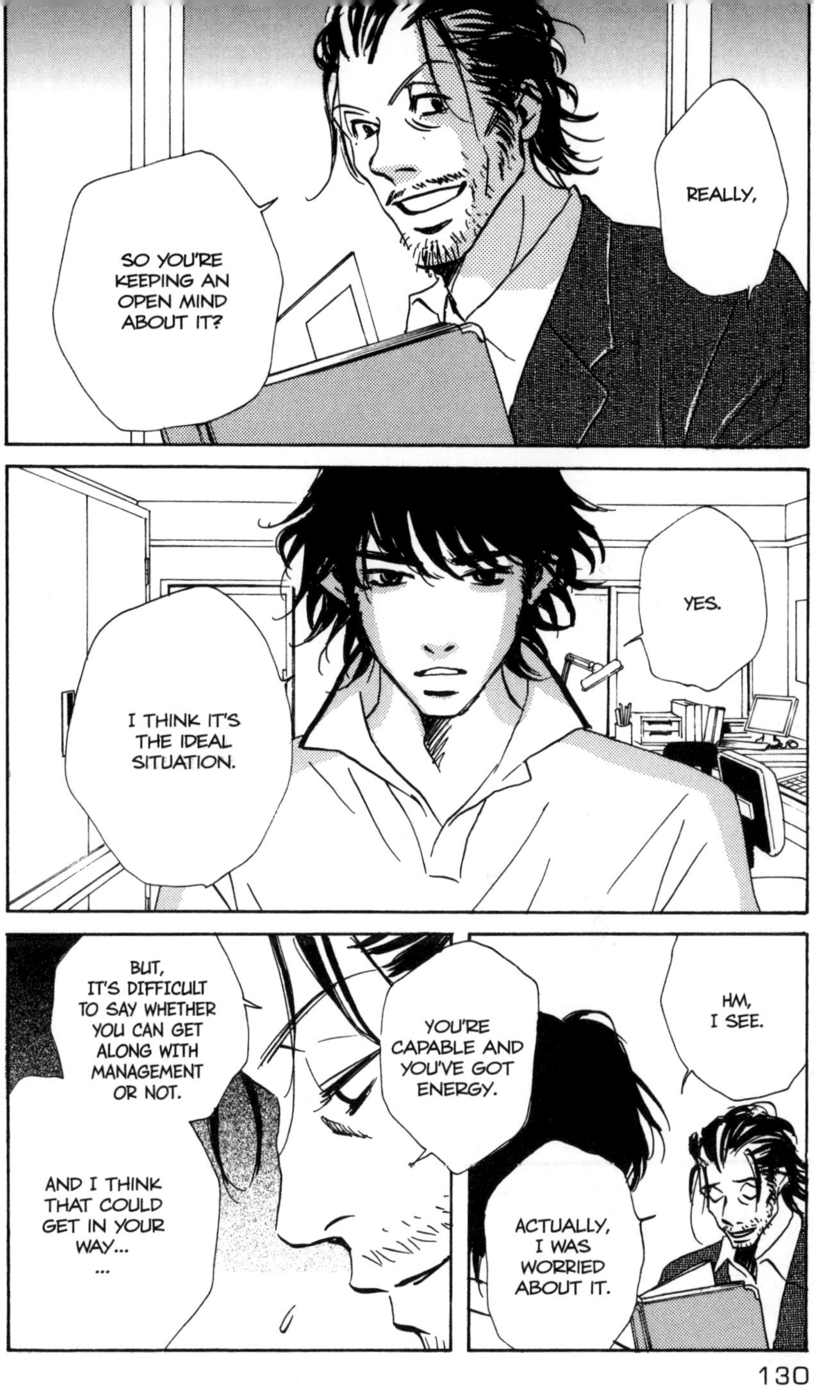

REALLY,
SO YOU'RE KEEPING AN OPEN MIND ABOUT IT?
YES.
I THINK IT'S THE IDEAL SITUATION.
HM, I SEE.
ACTUALLY, I WAS WORRIED ABOUT IT.
YOU'RE CAPABLE AND YOU'VE GOT ENERGY.
BUT, IT'S DIFFICULT TO SAY WHETHER YOU CAN GET ALONG WITH MANAGEMENT OR NOT.
AND I THINK THAT COULD GET IN YOUR WAY... ...

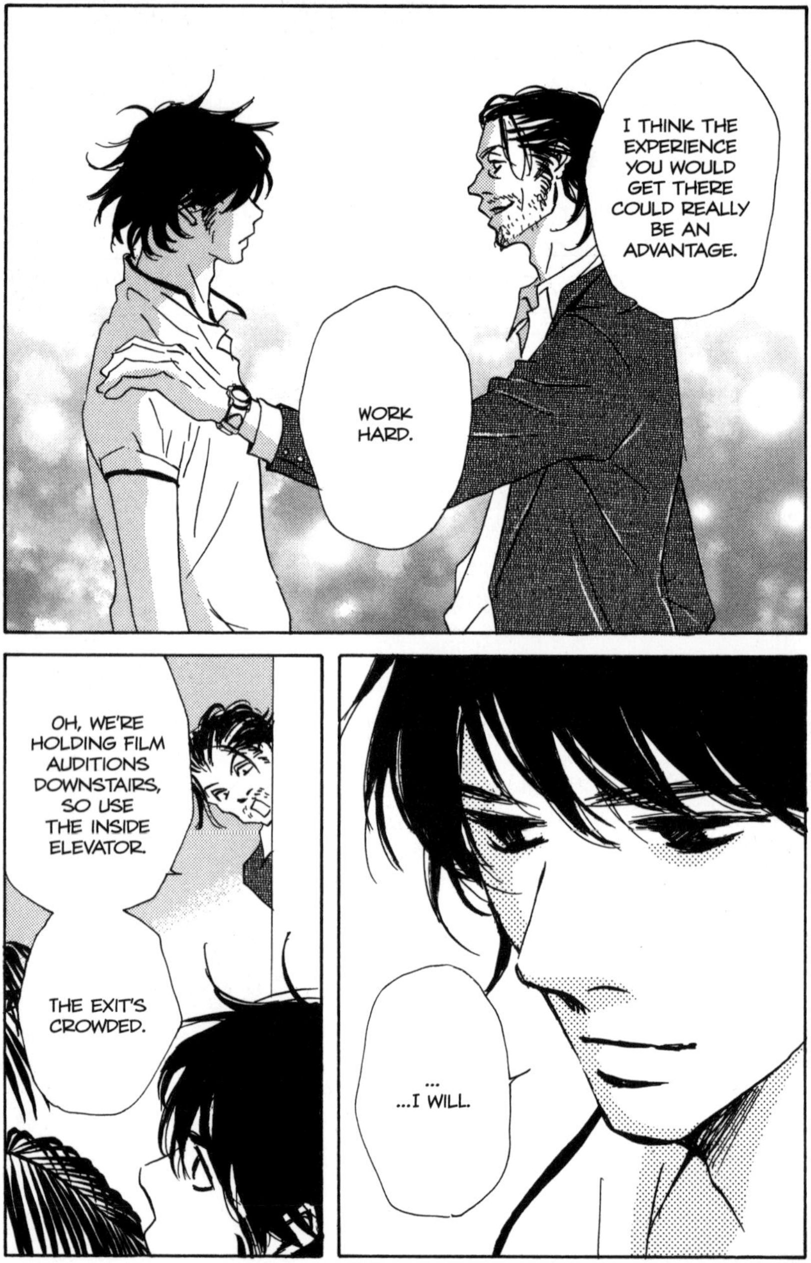
I THINK THE EXPERIENCE YOU WOULD GET THERE COULD REALLY BE AN ADVANTAGE.
WORK HARD.
... ...I WILL.
OH, WE'RE HOLDING FILM AUDITIONS DOWNSTAIRS, SO USE THE INSIDE ELEVATOR.
THE EXIT'S CROWDED.

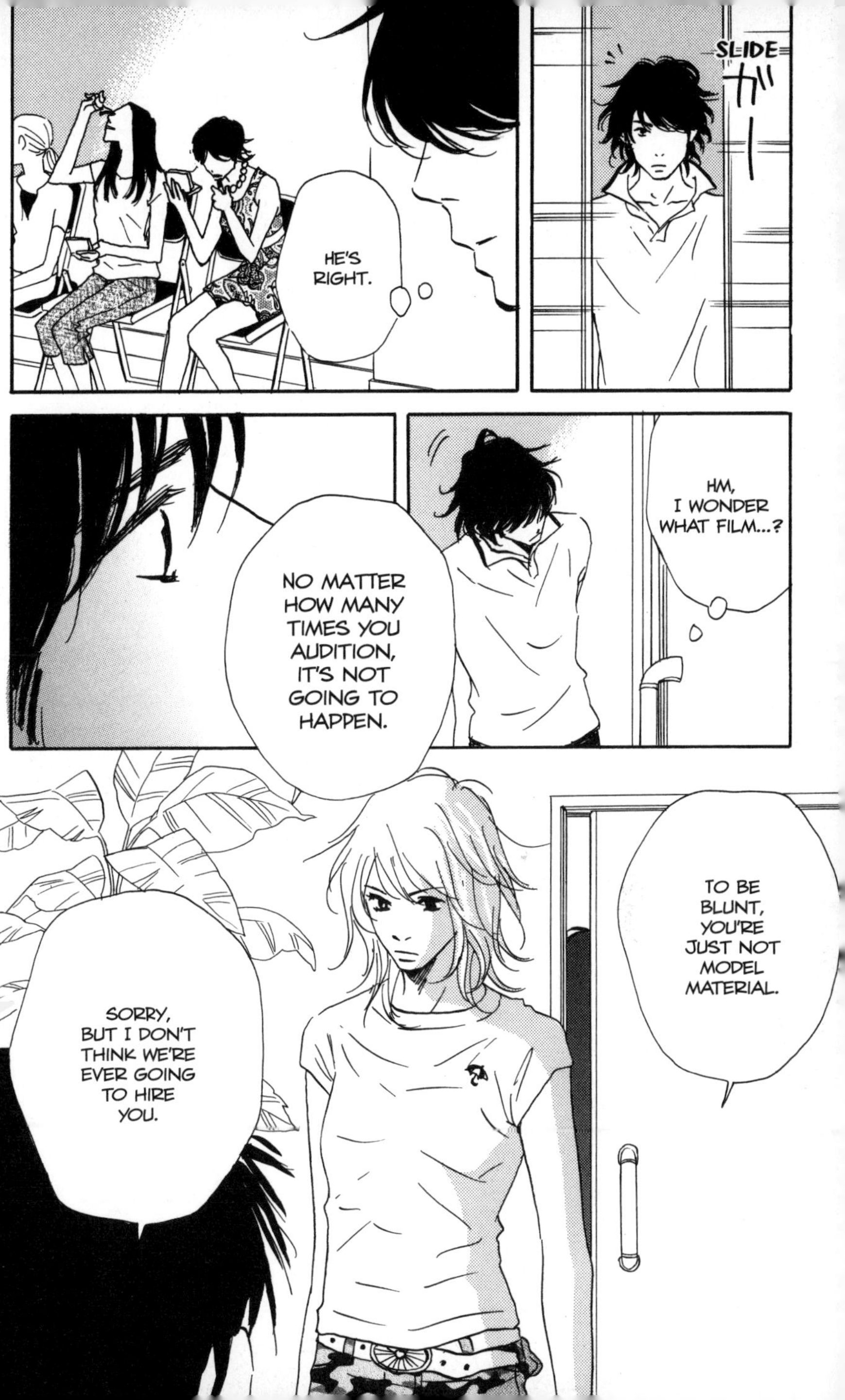
SLIDE
ガー
HE'S RIGHT.
HM, I WONDER WHAT FILM...?
NO MATTER HOW MANY TIMES YOU AUDITION, IT'S NOT GOING TO HAPPEN.
TO BE BLUNT, YOU'RE JUST NOT MODEL MATERIAL.
SORRY, BUT I DON'T THINK WE'RE EVER GOING TO HIRE YOU.

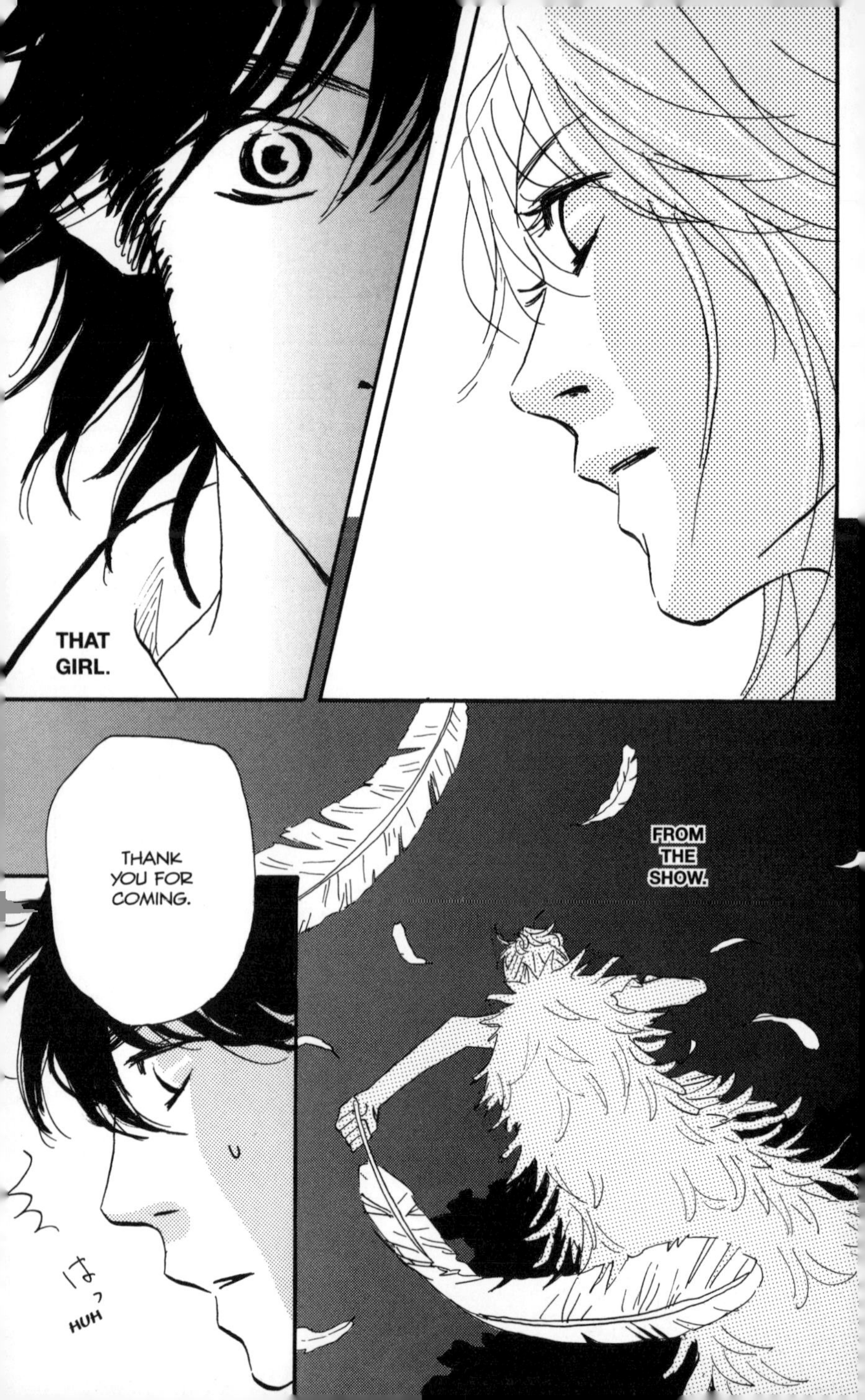
THAT GIRL.
FROM THE SHOW.
THANK YOU FOR COMING.
はっ
HUH

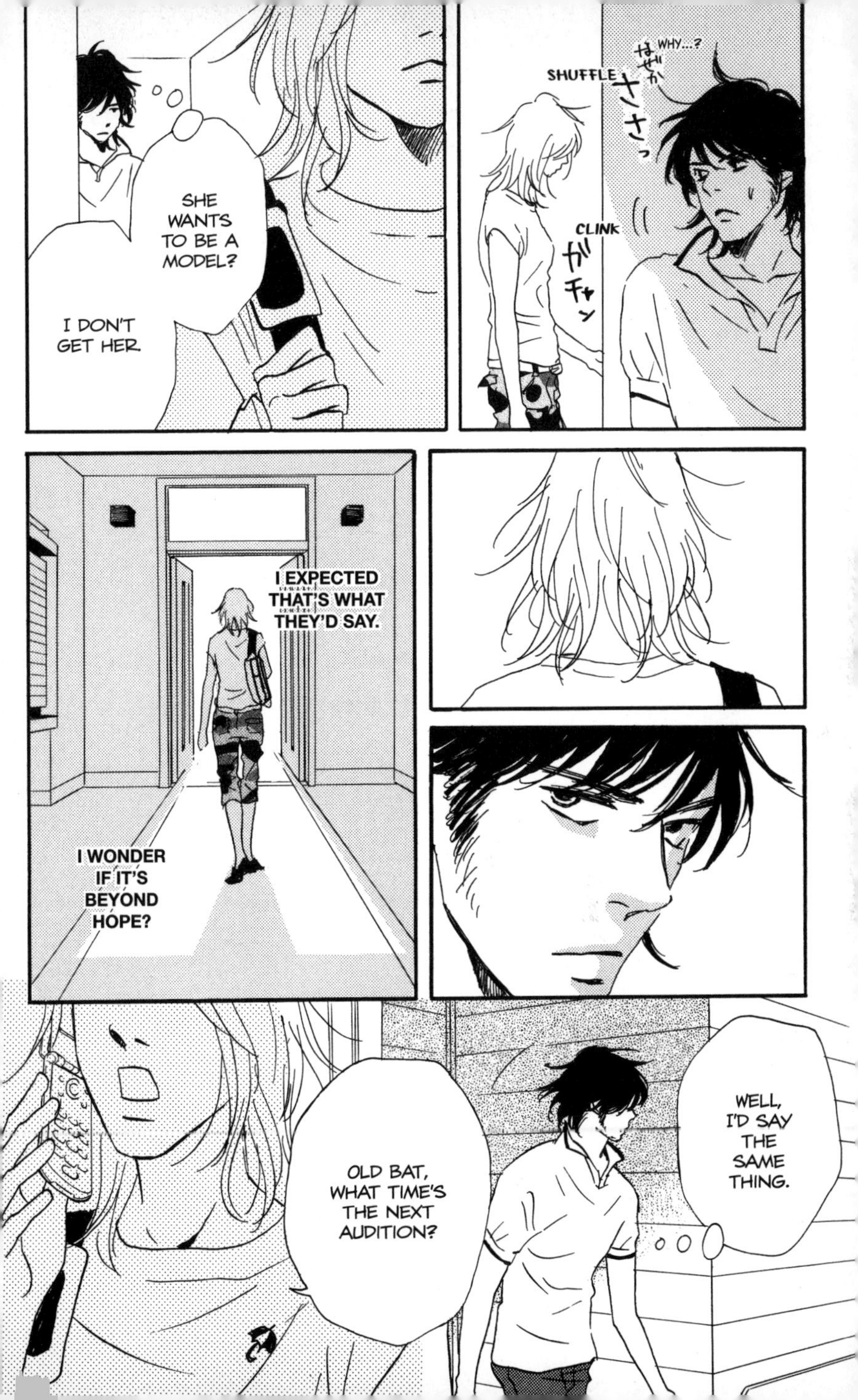
WHY...?
なぜか
SHUFFLE
ささっ
CLINK
ガチャン
SHE WANTS TO BE A MODEL?
I DON'T GET HER.
I EXPECTED THAT'S WHAT THEY'D SAY.
I WONDER IF IT'S BEYOND HOPE?
WELL, I'D SAY THE SAME THING.
OLD BAT, WHAT TIME'S THE NEXT AUDITION?

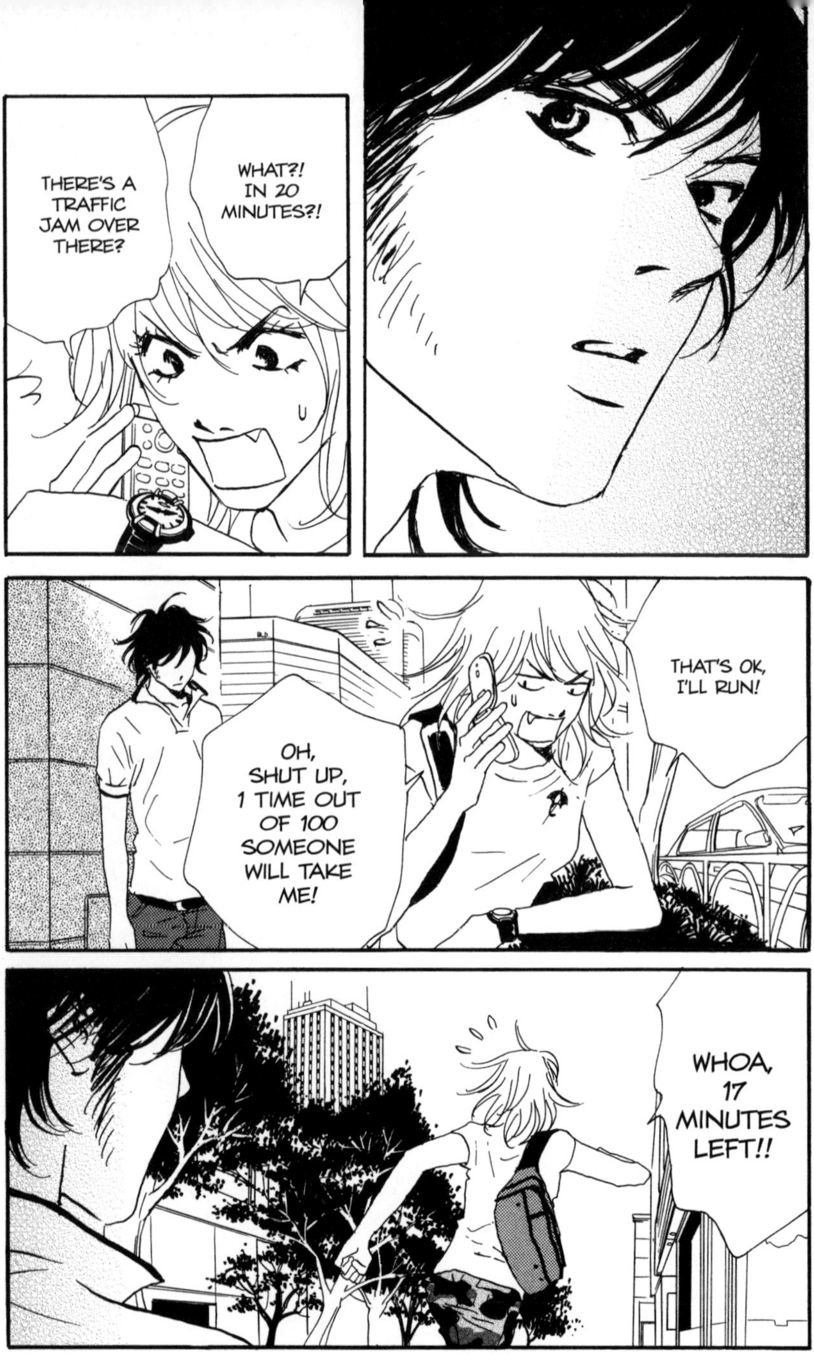
WHAT?! IN 20 MINUTES?!
THERE'S A TRAFFIC JAM OVER THERE?
THAT'S OK, I'LL RUN!
OH, SHUT UP, 1 TIME OUT OF 100 SOMEONE WILL TAKE ME!
WHOA, 17 MINUTES LEFT!!

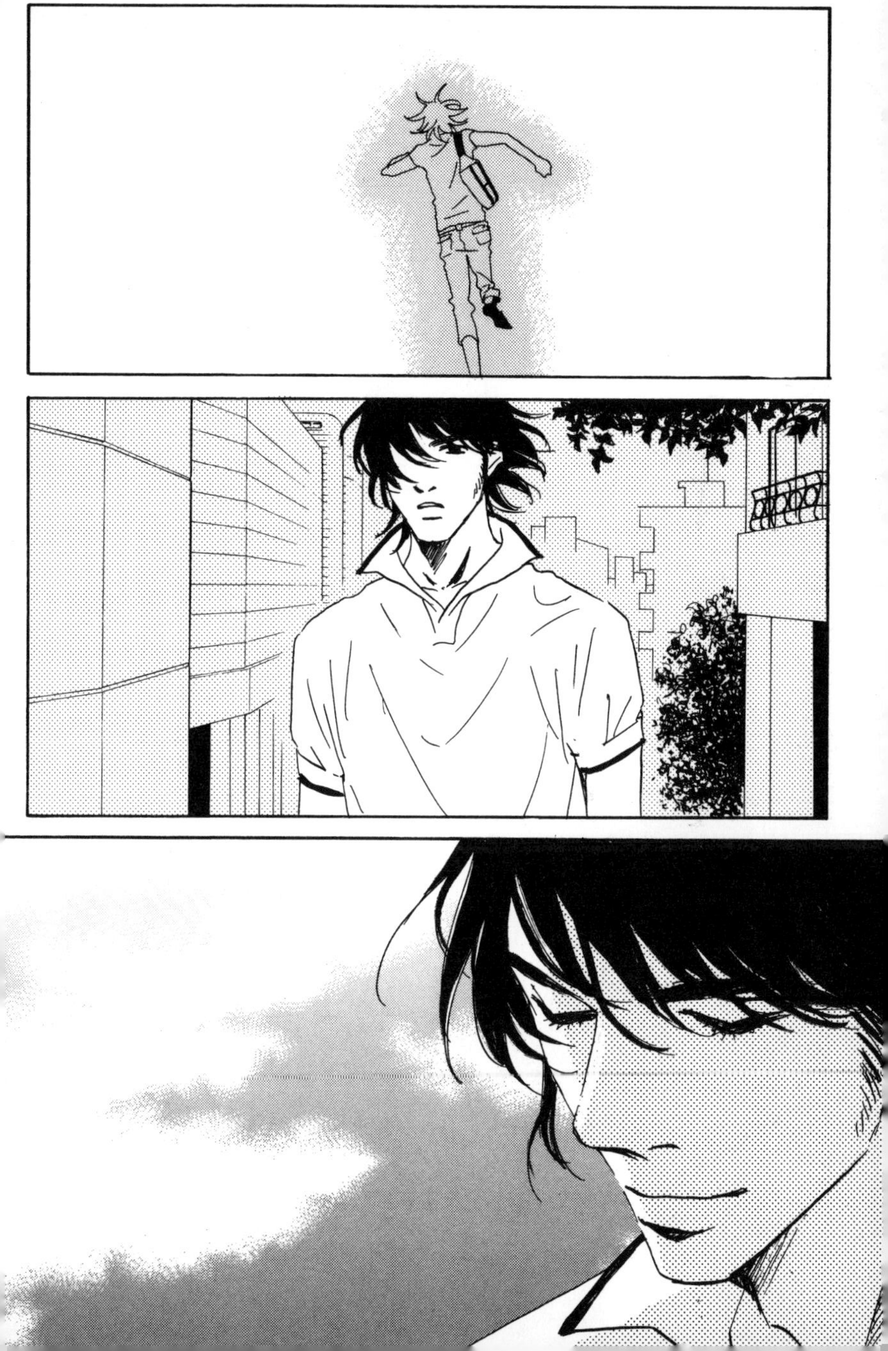

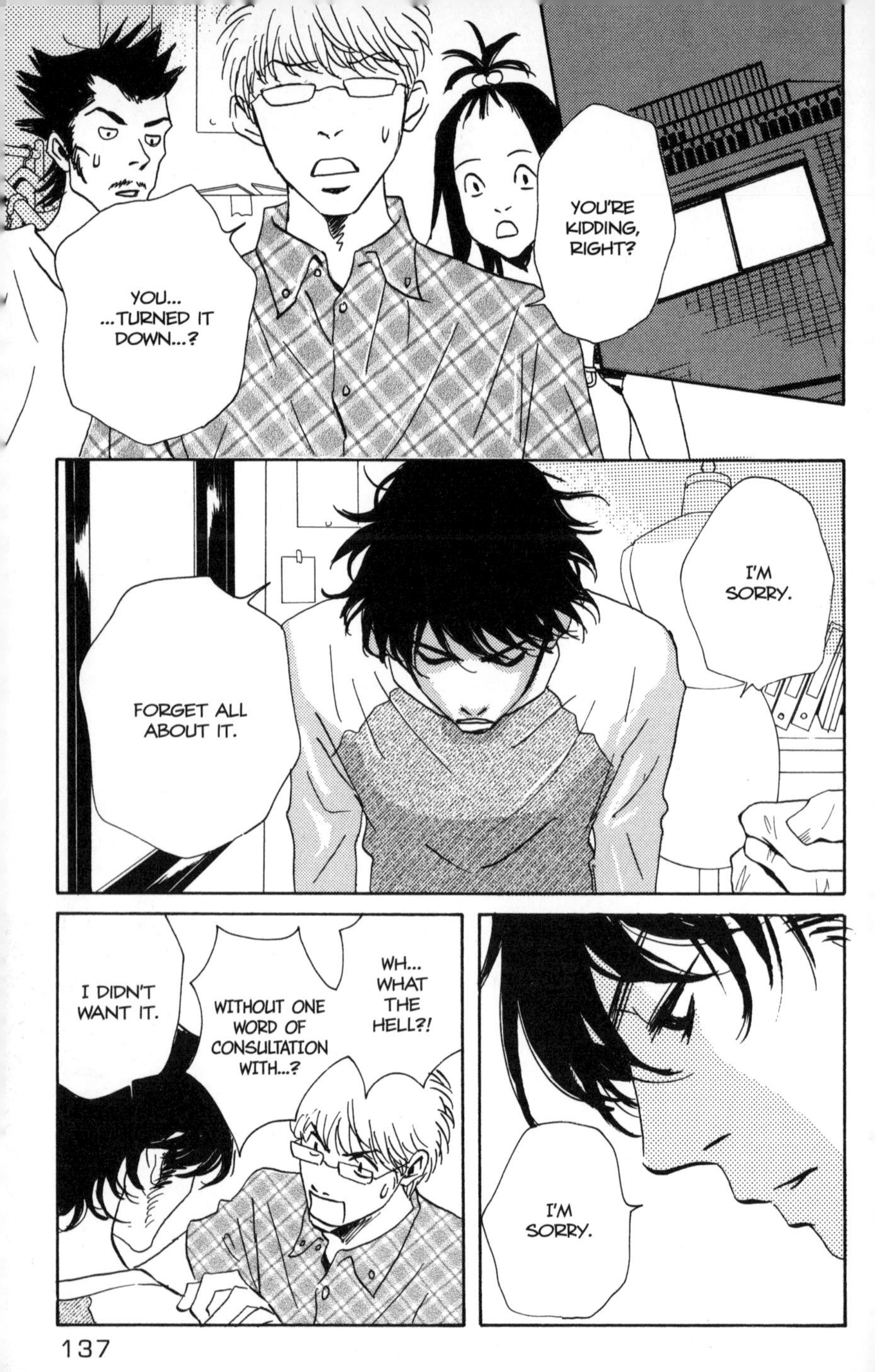
YOU'RE KIDDING, RIGHT?
YOU... ...TURNED IT DOWN...?
I'M SORRY.
FORGET ALL ABOUT IT.
I'M SORRY.
WH... WHAT THE HELL?!
WITHOUT ONE WORD OF CONSULTATION WITH...?
I DIDN'T WANT IT.

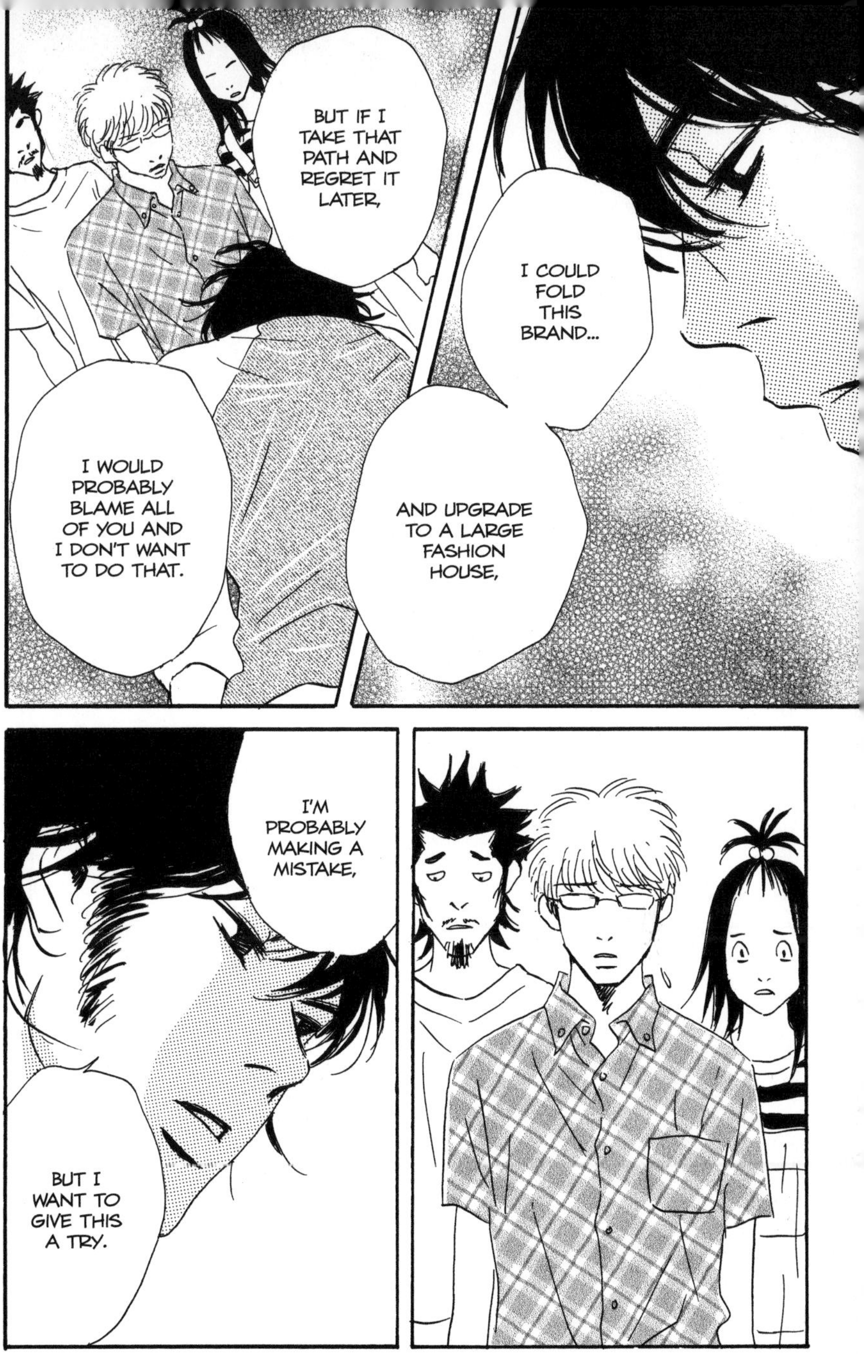
I COULD FOLD THIS BRAND...
AND UPGRADE TO A LARGE FASHION HOUSE,
BUT IF I TAKE THAT PATH AND REGRET IT LATER,
I WOULD PROBABLY BLAME ALL OF YOU AND I DON'T WANT TO DO THAT.
I'M PROBABLY MAKING A MISTAKE,
BUT I WANT TO GIVE THIS A TRY.

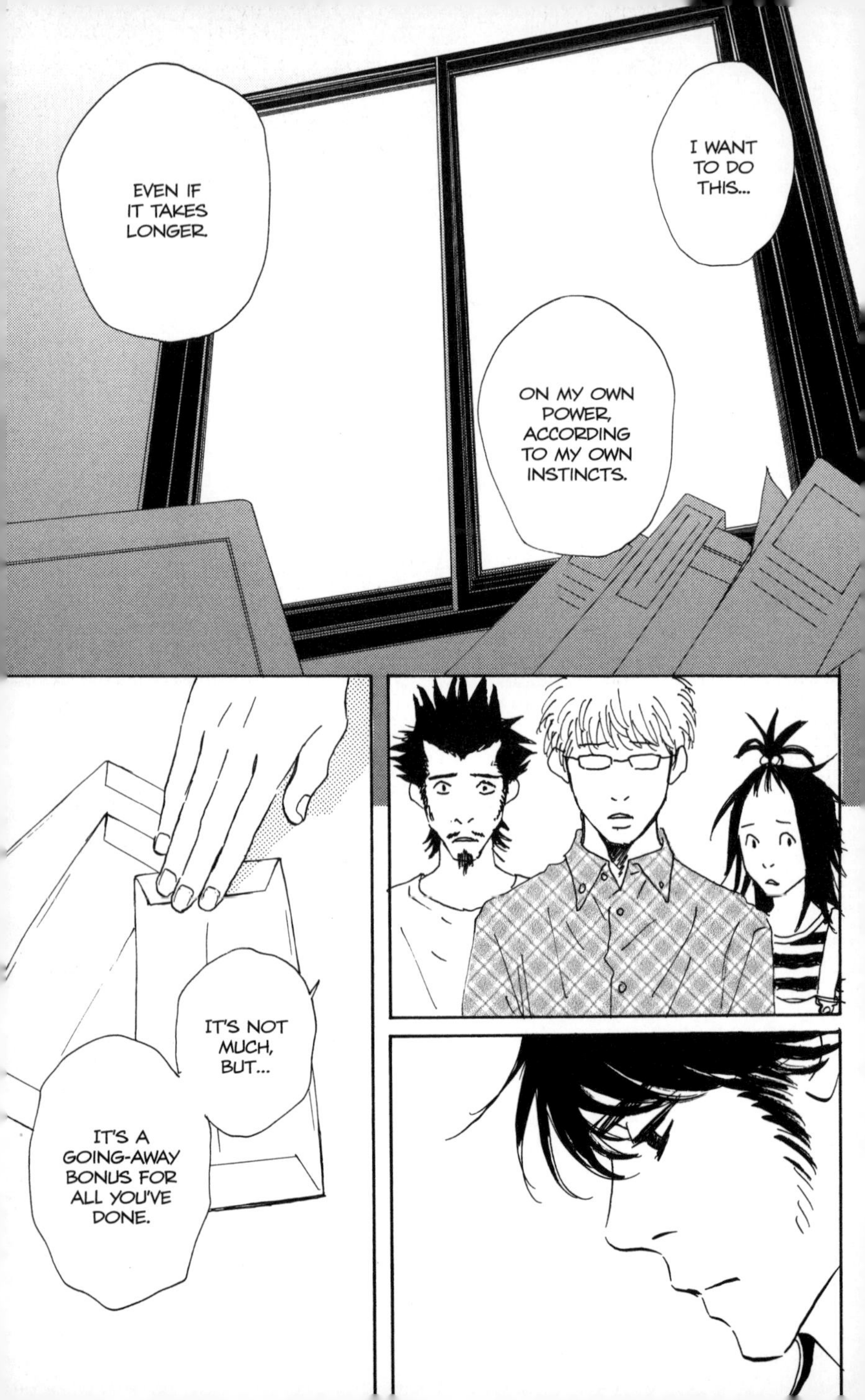
I WANT TO DO THIS...
ON MY OWN POWER, ACCORDING TO MY OWN INSTINCTS.
EVEN IF IT TAKES LONGER.
IT'S NOT MUCH, BUT...
IT'S A GOING-AWAY BONUS FOR ALL YOU'VE DONE.

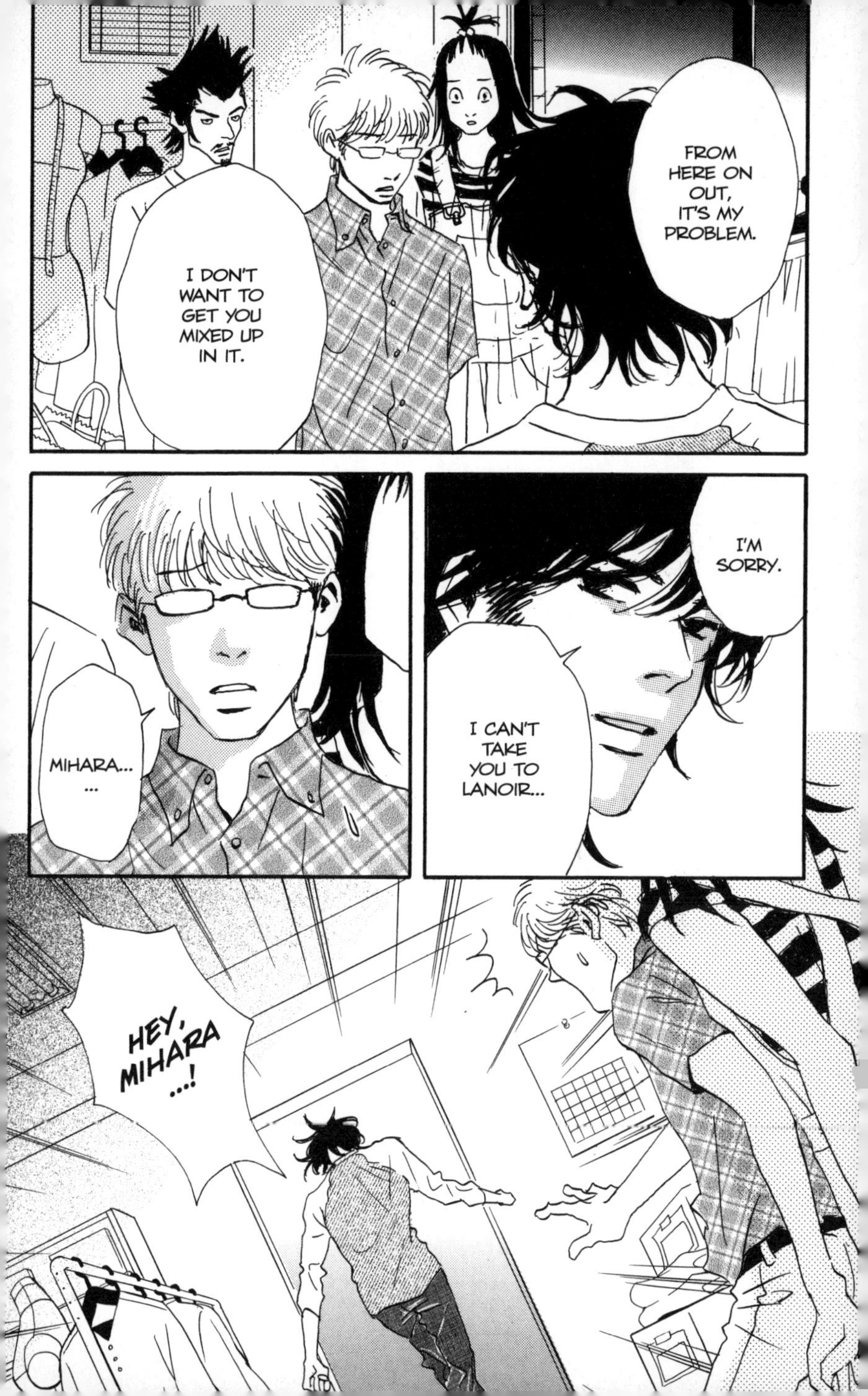
FROM HERE ON OUT, IT'S MY PROBLEM.
I DON'T WANT TO GET YOU MIXED UP IN IT.
I'M SORRY.
I CAN'T TAKE YOU TO LANOIR...
MIHARA... ...
HEY, MIHARA ...!

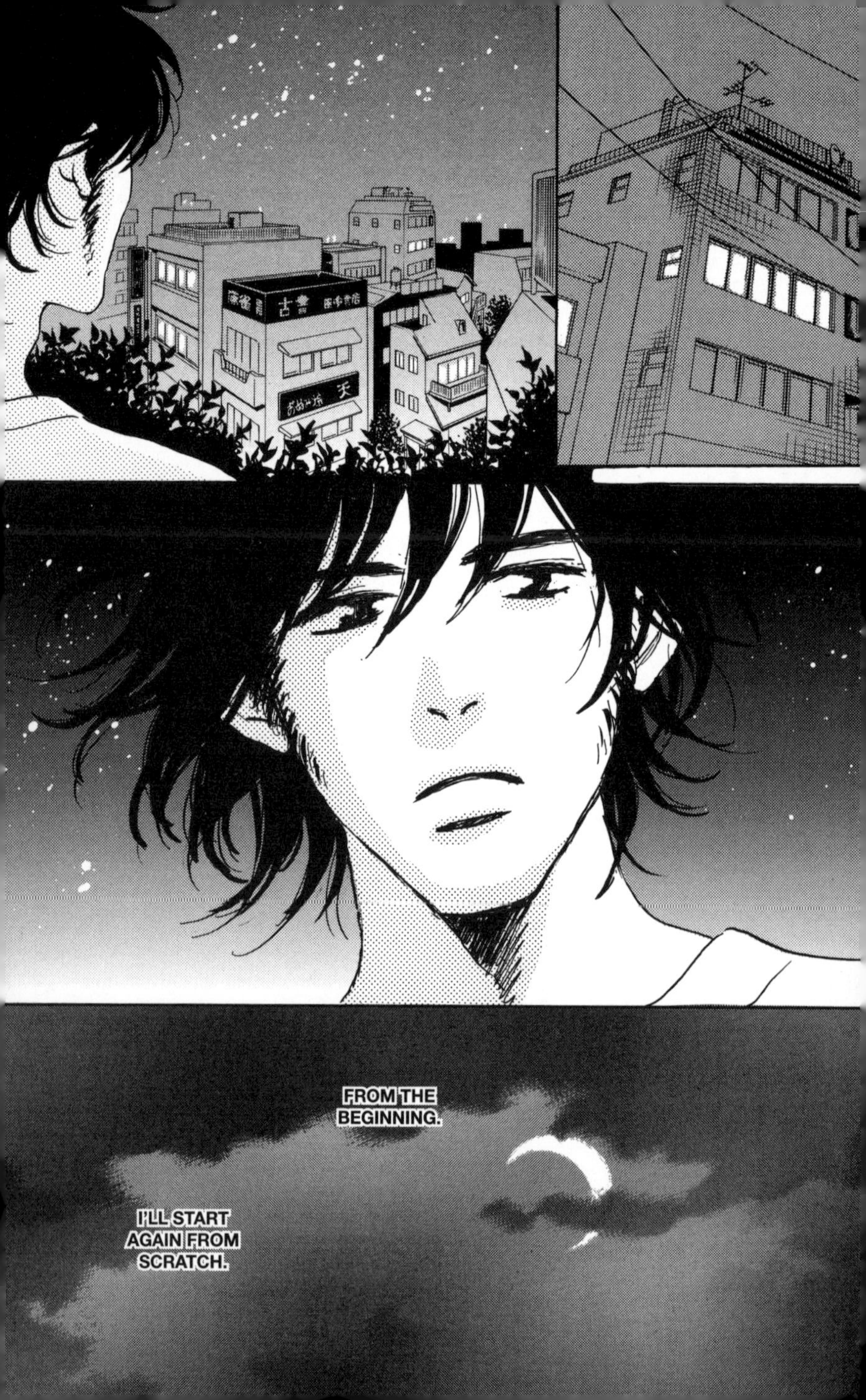
FROM THE BEGINNING.
I'LL START AGAIN FROM SCRATCH.

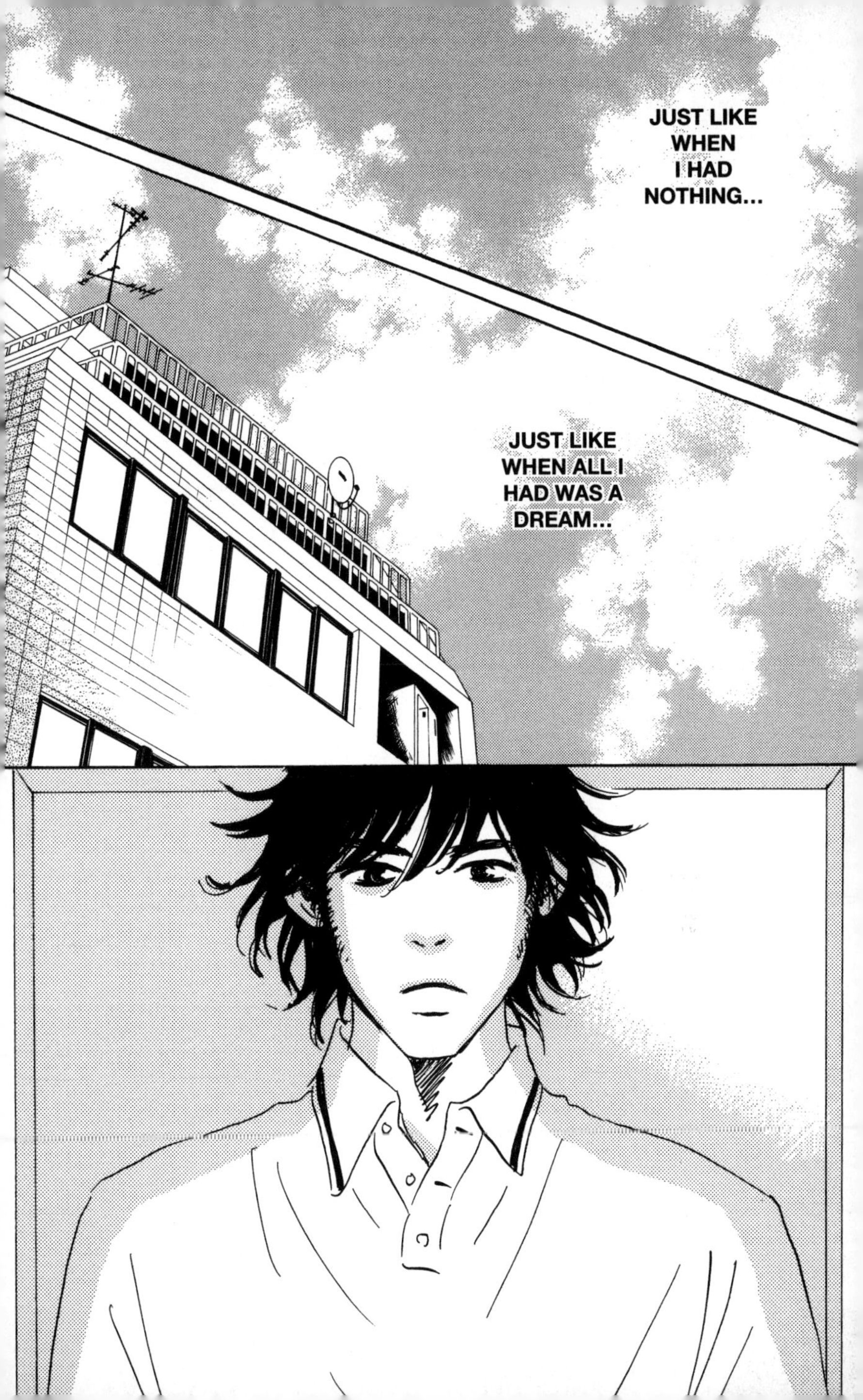
JUST LIKE WHEN I HAD NOTHING...
JUST LIKE WHEN ALL I HAD WAS A DREAM...

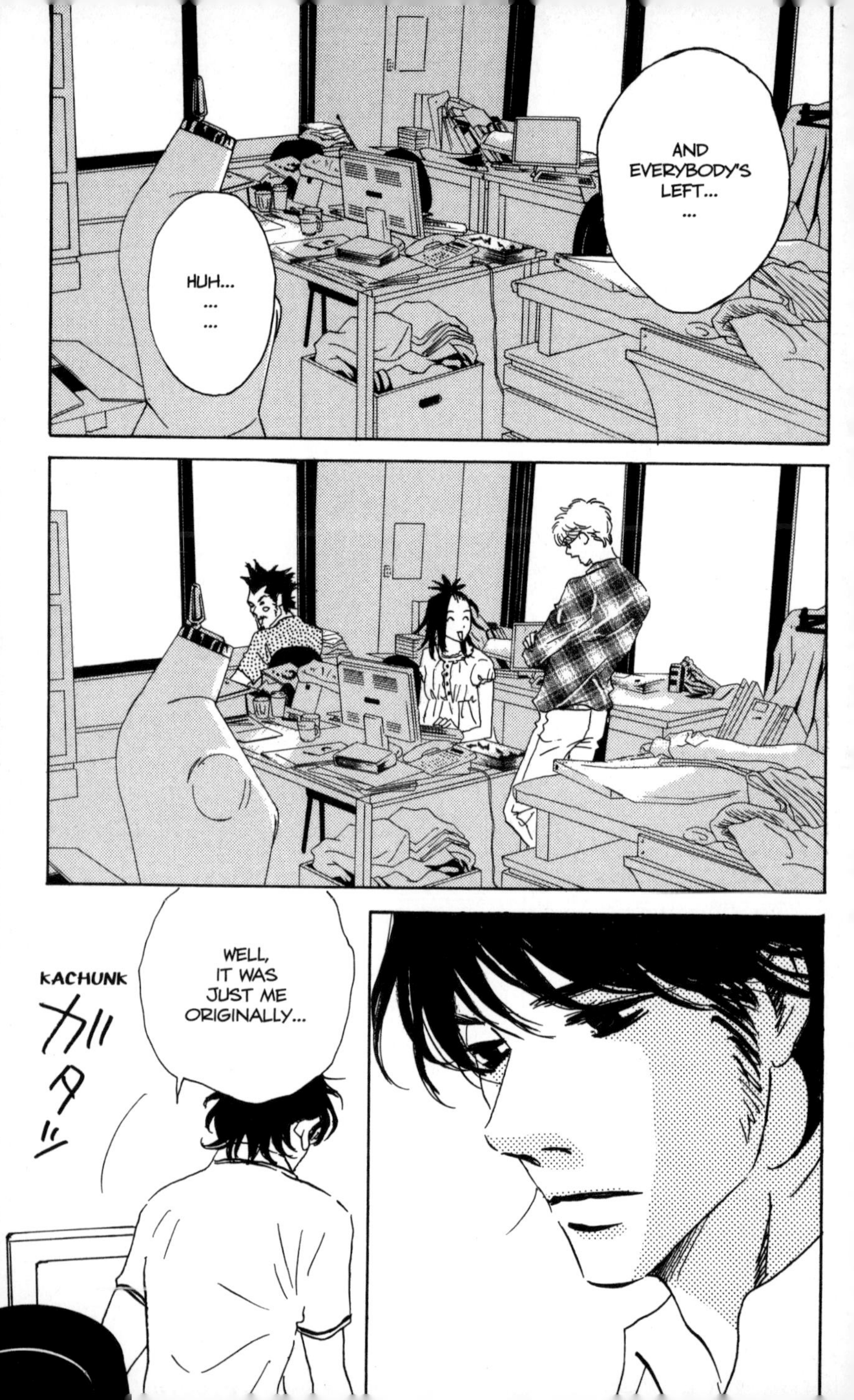
AND EVERYBODY'S LEFT... ...
HUH... ... ...
WELL, IT WAS JUST ME ORIGINALLY...
KACHUNK
ガタッ

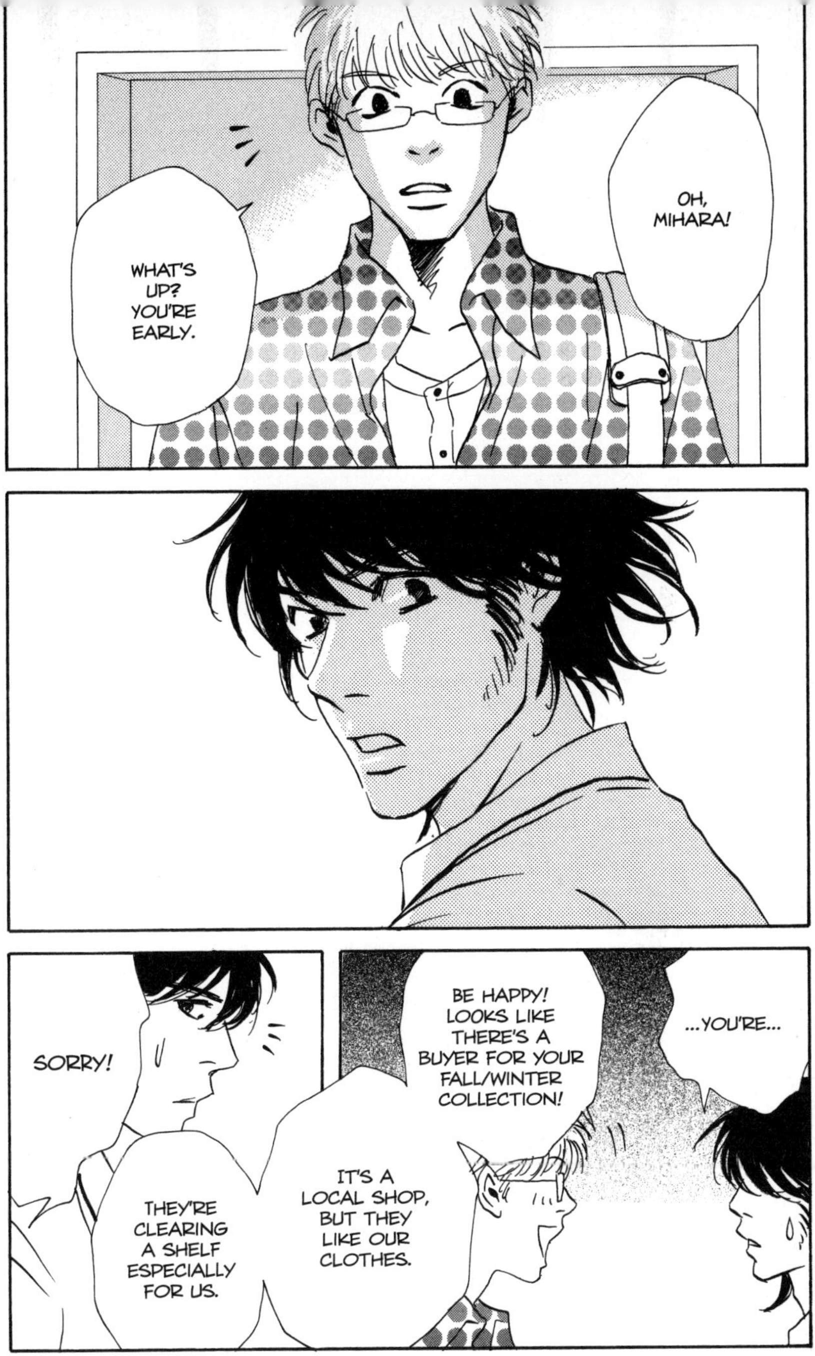
OH, MIHARA!
WHAT'S UP? YOU'RE EARLY.
...YOU'RE...
BE HAPPY! LOOKS LIKE THERE'S A BUYER FOR YOUR FALL/WINTER COLLECTION!
IT'S A LOCAL SHOP, BUT THEY LIKE OUR CLOTHES.
THEY'RE CLEARING A SHELF ESPECIALLY FOR US.
SORRY!

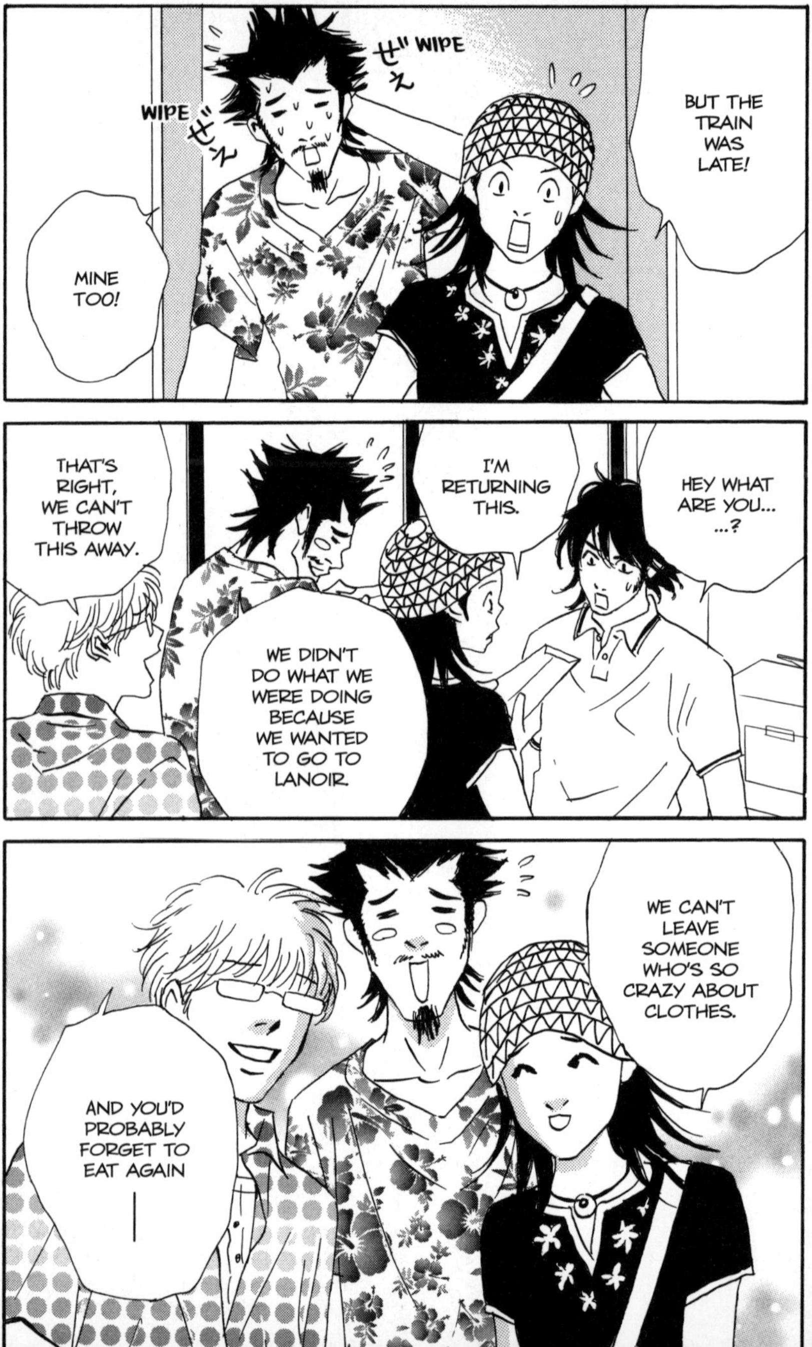
BUT THE TRAIN WAS LATE!
ぜぇ WIPE
WIPE ぜぇ
MINE TOO!
HEY WHAT ARE YOU... ...?
I'M RETURNING THIS.
THAT'S RIGHT, WE CAN'T THROW THIS AWAY.
WE DIDN'T DO WHAT WE WERE DOING BECAUSE WE WANTED TO GO TO LANOIR.
WE CAN'T LEAVE SOMEONE WHO'S SO CRAZY ABOUT CLOTHES.
AND YOU'D PROBABLY FORGET TO EAT AGAIN —

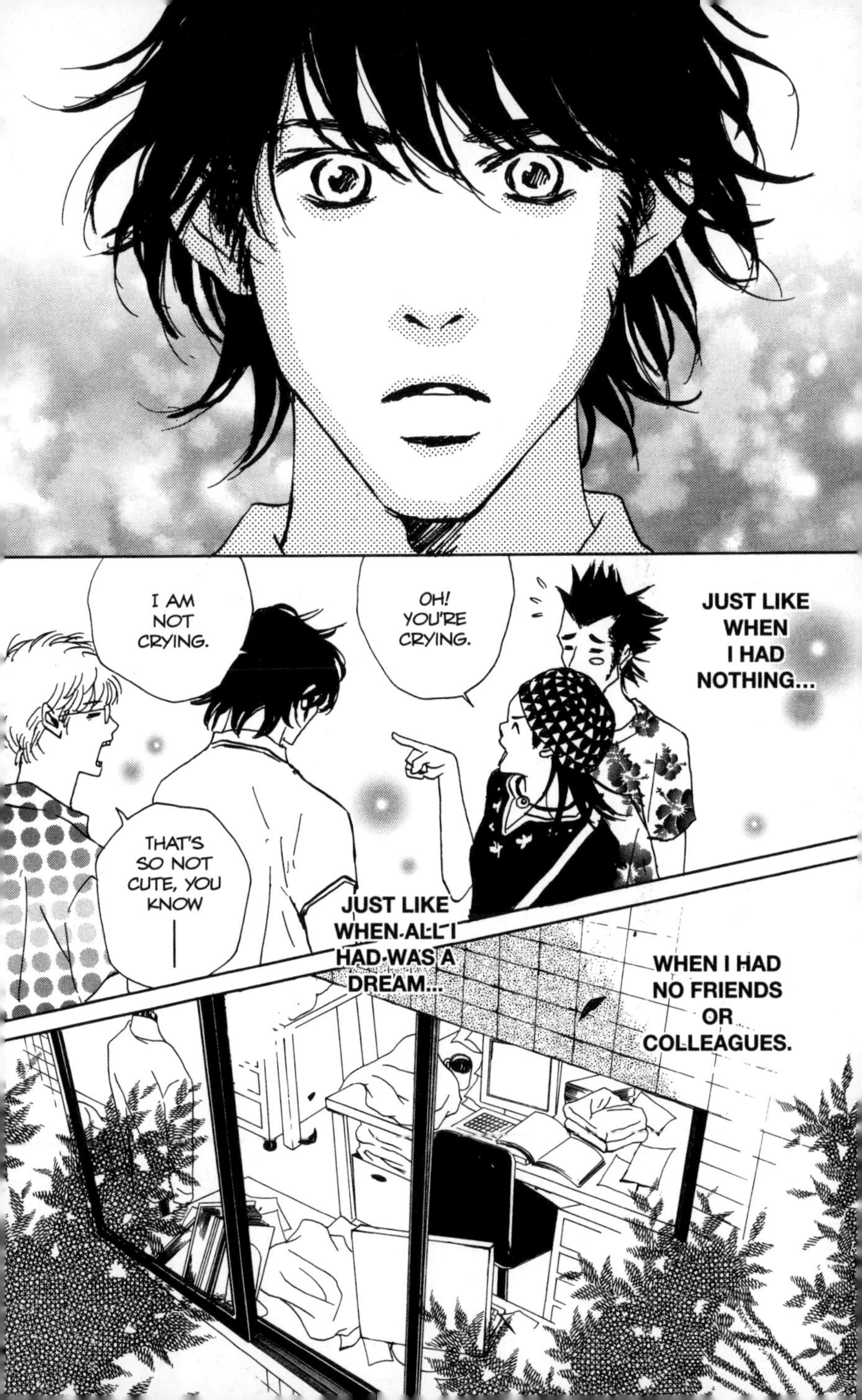
JUST LIKE WHEN I HAD NOTHING...
OH! YOU'RE CRYING.
I AM NOT CRYING.
THAT'S SO NOT CUTE, YOU KNOW —
JUST LIKE WHEN ALL I HAD WAS A DREAM...
WHEN I HAD NO FRIENDS OR COLLEAGUES.

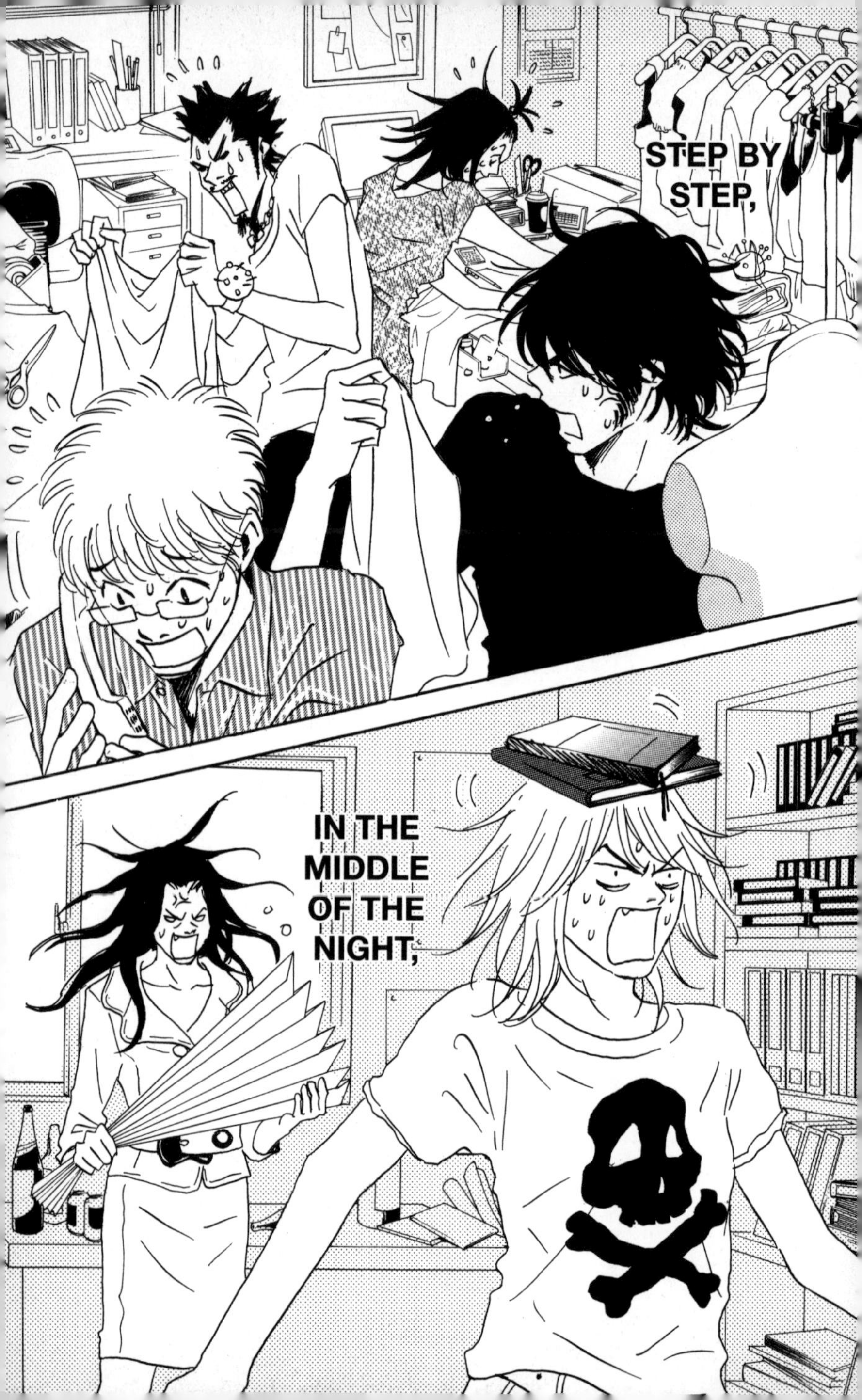
STEP BY STEP,
IN THE MIDDLE OF THE NIGHT,

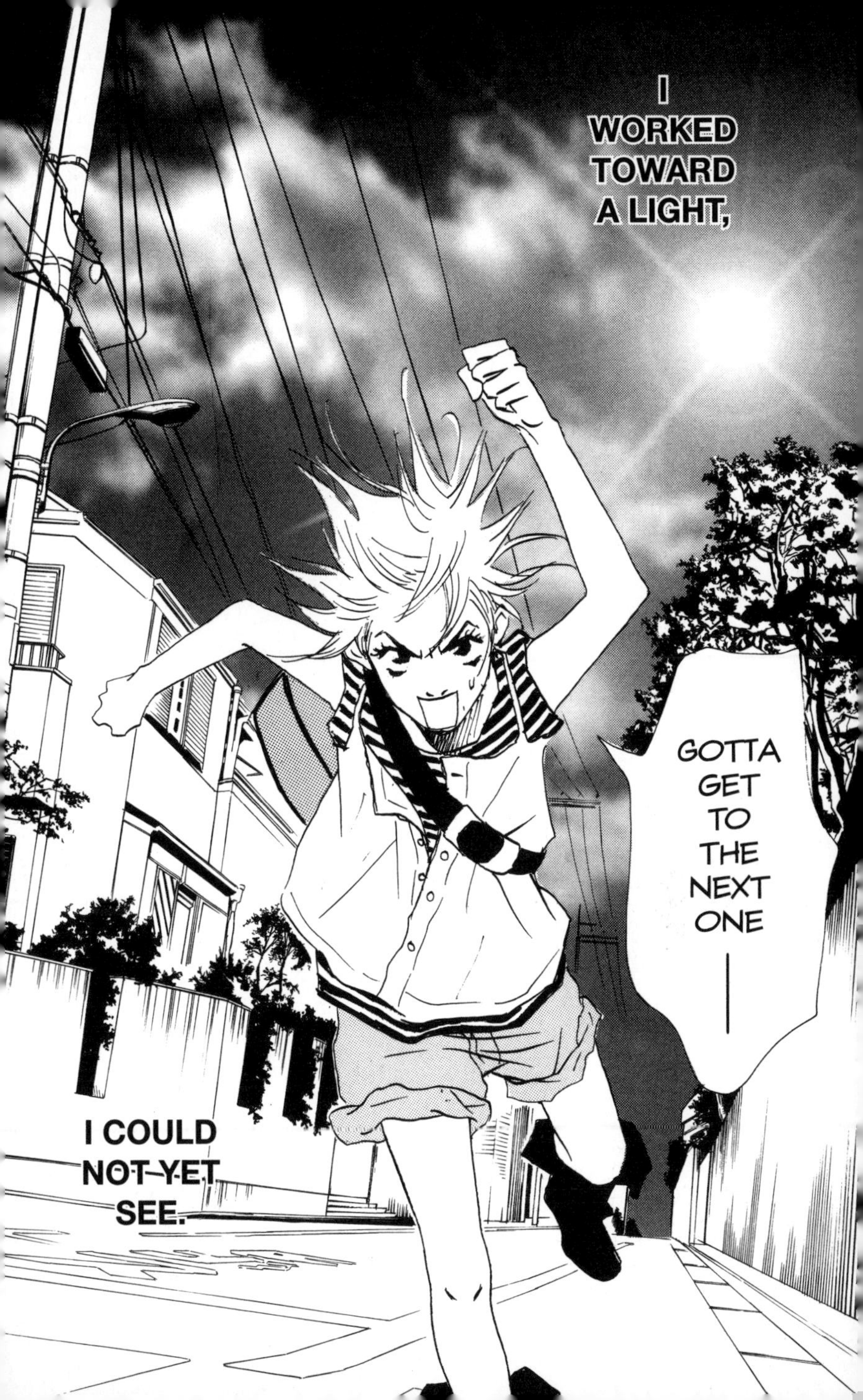
I WORKED TOWARD A LIGHT,
GOTTA GET TO THE NEXT ONE —
I COULD NOT YET SEE.

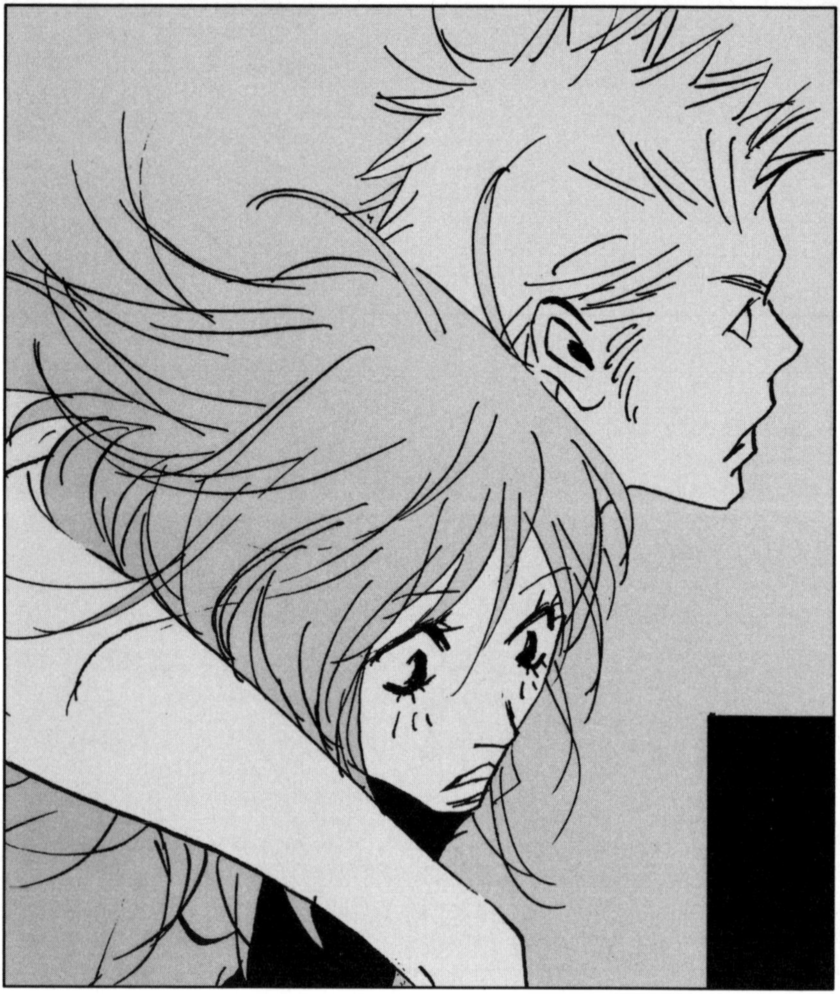

MODE 6

RELATIONSHIP

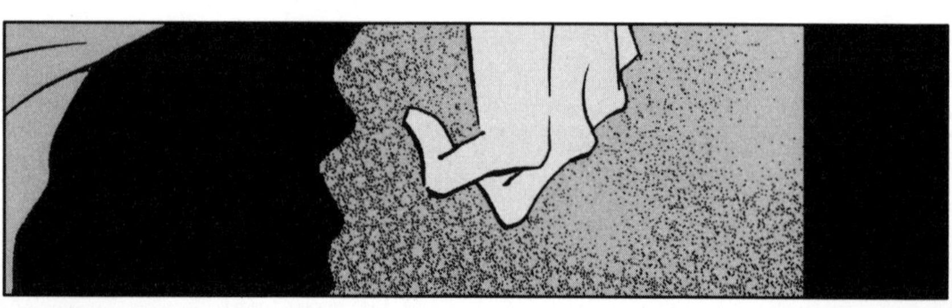

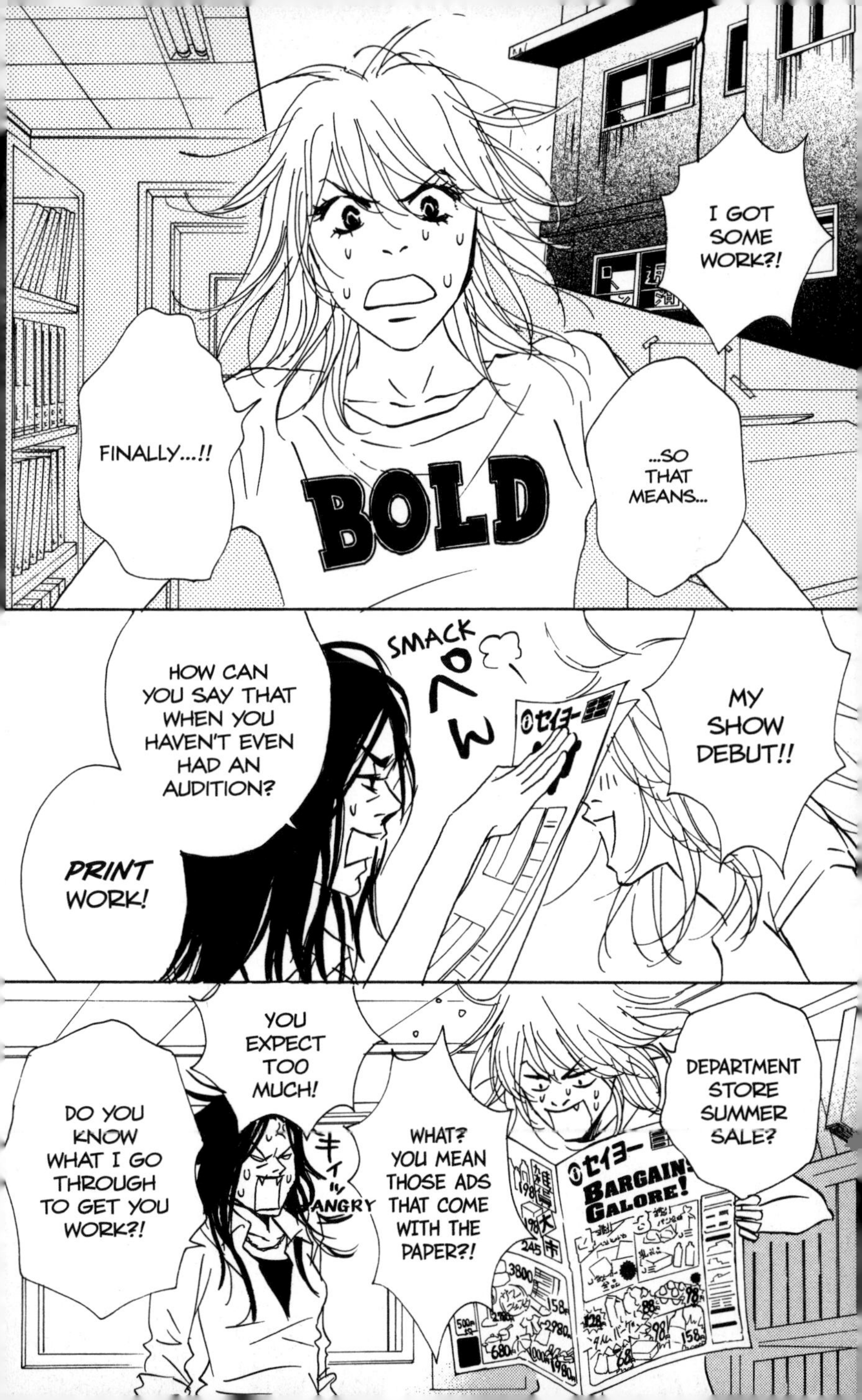
I GOT SOME WORK?!
...SO THAT MEANS...
BOLD
FINALLY...!!
MY SHOW DEBUT!!
SMACK
HOW CAN YOU SAY THAT WHEN YOU HAVEN'T EVEN HAD AN AUDITION?
PRINT WORK!
DEPARTMENT STORE SUMMER SALE?
BARGAINS GALORE!
WHAT? YOU MEAN THOSE ADS THAT COME WITH THE PAPER?!
YOU EXPECT TOO MUCH!
ANGRY
DO YOU KNOW WHAT I GO THROUGH TO GET YOU WORK?!

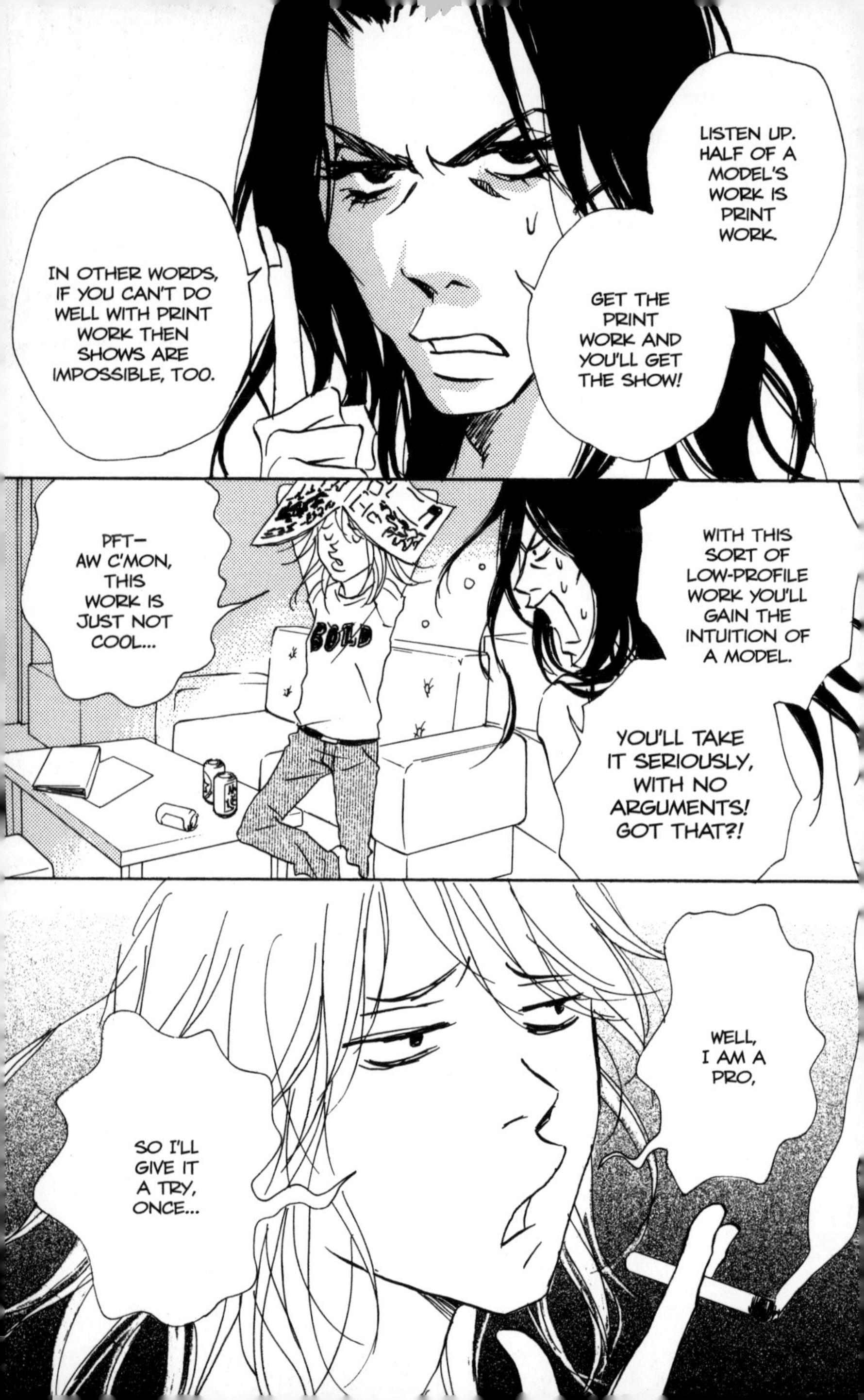
LISTEN UP. HALF OF A MODEL'S WORK IS PRINT WORK.
GET THE PRINT WORK AND YOU'LL GET THE SHOW!
IN OTHER WORDS, IF YOU CAN'T DO WELL WITH PRINT WORK THEN SHOWS ARE IMPOSSIBLE, TOO.
WITH THIS SORT OF LOW-PROFILE WORK YOU'LL GAIN THE INTUITION OF A MODEL.
YOU'LL TAKE IT SERIOUSLY, WITH NO ARGUMENTS! GOT THAT?!
BOLD
PFT— AW C'MON, THIS WORK IS JUST NOT COOL...
WELL, I AM A PRO,
SO I'LL GIVE IT A TRY, ONCE...

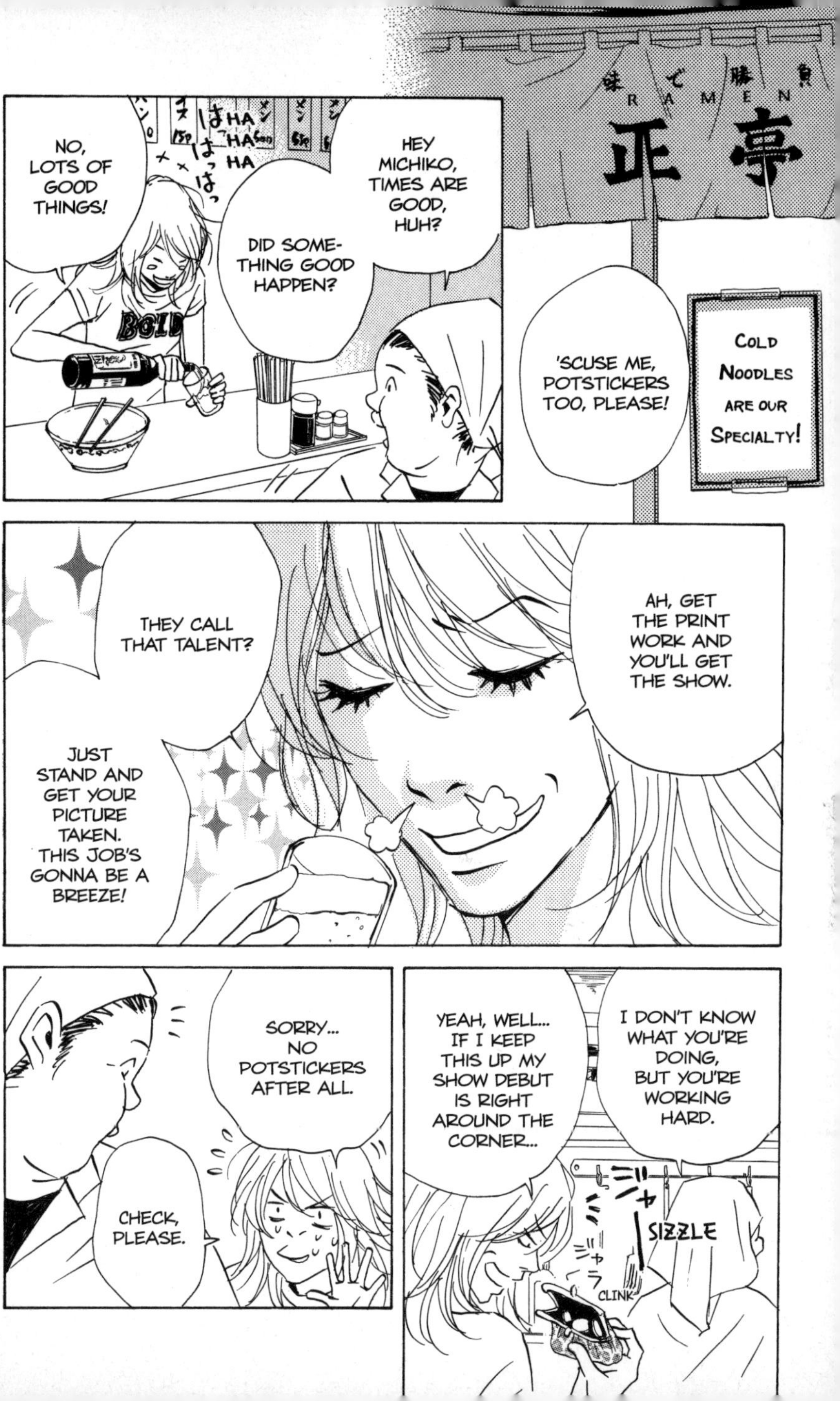
味で勝負
RAMEN
正亭
'SCUSE ME, POTSTICKERS TOO, PLEASE!
COLD NOODLES ARE OUR SPECIALTY!
HEY MICHIKO, TIMES ARE GOOD, HUH?
DID SOME-THING GOOD HAPPEN?
はははっ HA HA HA
NO, LOTS OF GOOD THINGS!
AH, GET THE PRINT WORK AND YOU'LL GET THE SHOW.
THEY CALL THAT TALENT?
JUST STAND AND GET YOUR PICTURE TAKEN. THIS JOB'S GONNA BE A BREEZE!
I DON'T KNOW WHAT YOU'RE DOING, BUT YOU'RE WORKING HARD.
YEAH, WELL... IF I KEEP THIS UP MY SHOW DEBUT IS RIGHT AROUND THE CORNER...
ジャ SIZZLE
ジャラ CLINK
SORRY... NO POTSTICKERS AFTER ALL.
CHECK, PLEASE.

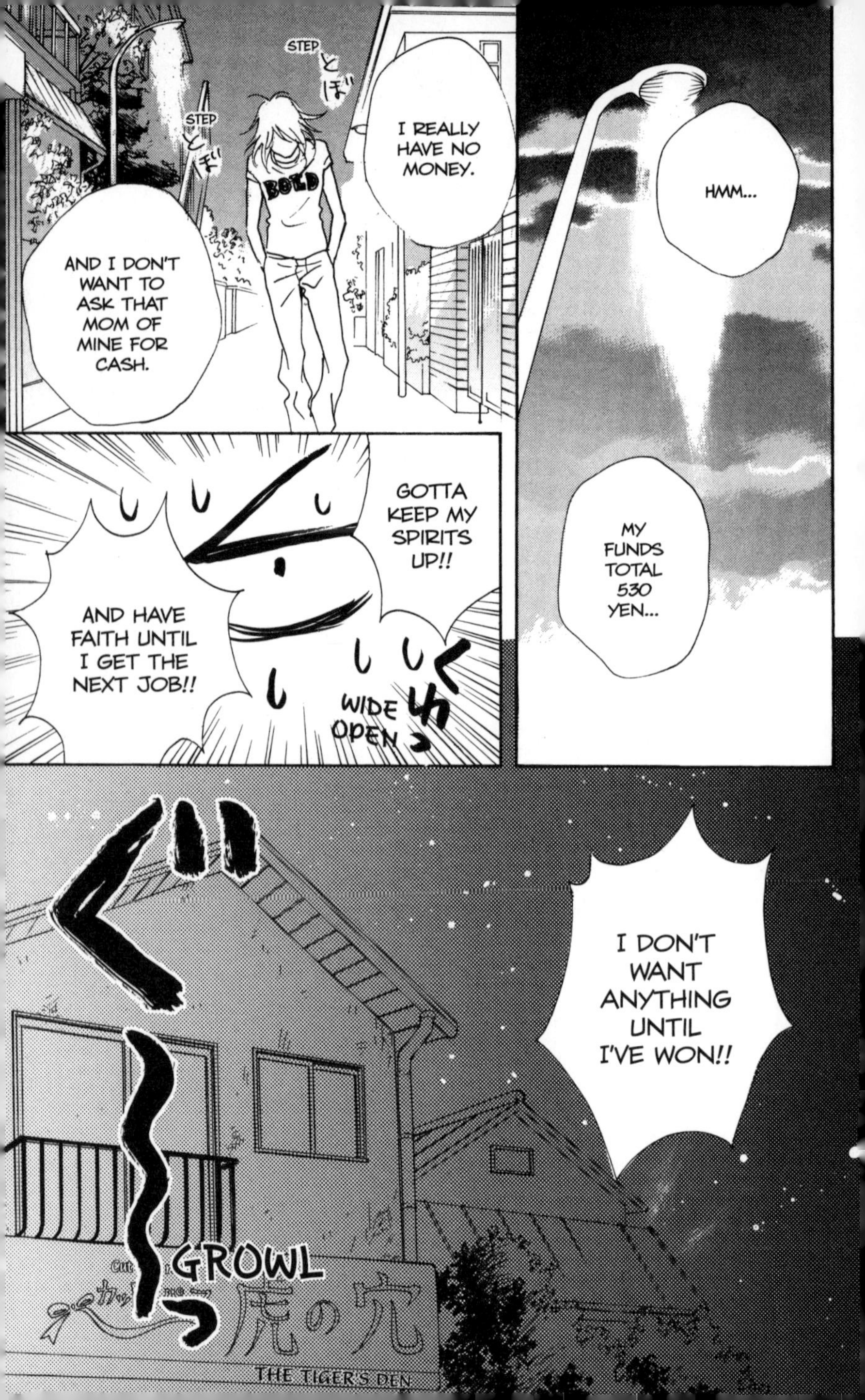
HMM...
MY FUNDS TOTAL 530 YEN...
STEP
STEP
I REALLY HAVE NO MONEY.
AND I DON'T WANT TO ASK THAT MOM OF MINE FOR CASH.
GOTTA KEEP MY SPIRITS UP!!
AND HAVE FAITH UNTIL I GET THE NEXT JOB!!
WIDE OPEN
I DON'T WANT ANYTHING UNTIL I'VE WON!!
GROWL
虎の穴
THE TIGER'S DEN

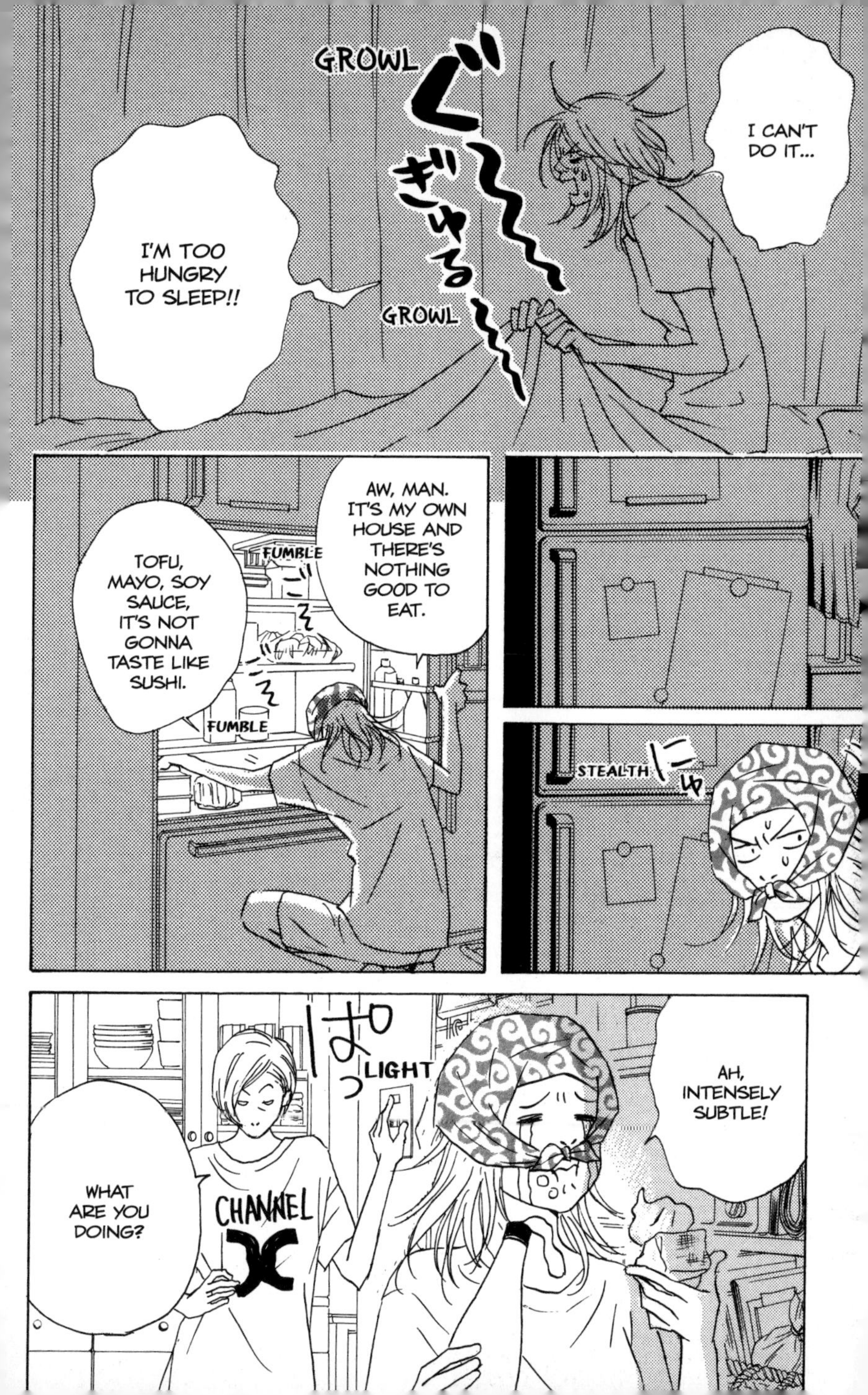
I CAN'T DO IT...
GROWL
ぐ〜〜〜
ぎゅる〜〜
GROWL
I'M TOO HUNGRY TO SLEEP!!
STEALTH
にゅ
AW, MAN. IT'S MY OWN HOUSE AND THERE'S NOTHING GOOD TO EAT.
FUMBLE
TOFU, MAYO, SOY SAUCE, IT'S NOT GONNA TASTE LIKE SUSHI.
FUMBLE
AH, INTENSELY SUBTLE!
ぱっ
LIGHT
WHAT ARE YOU DOING?
CHANNEL

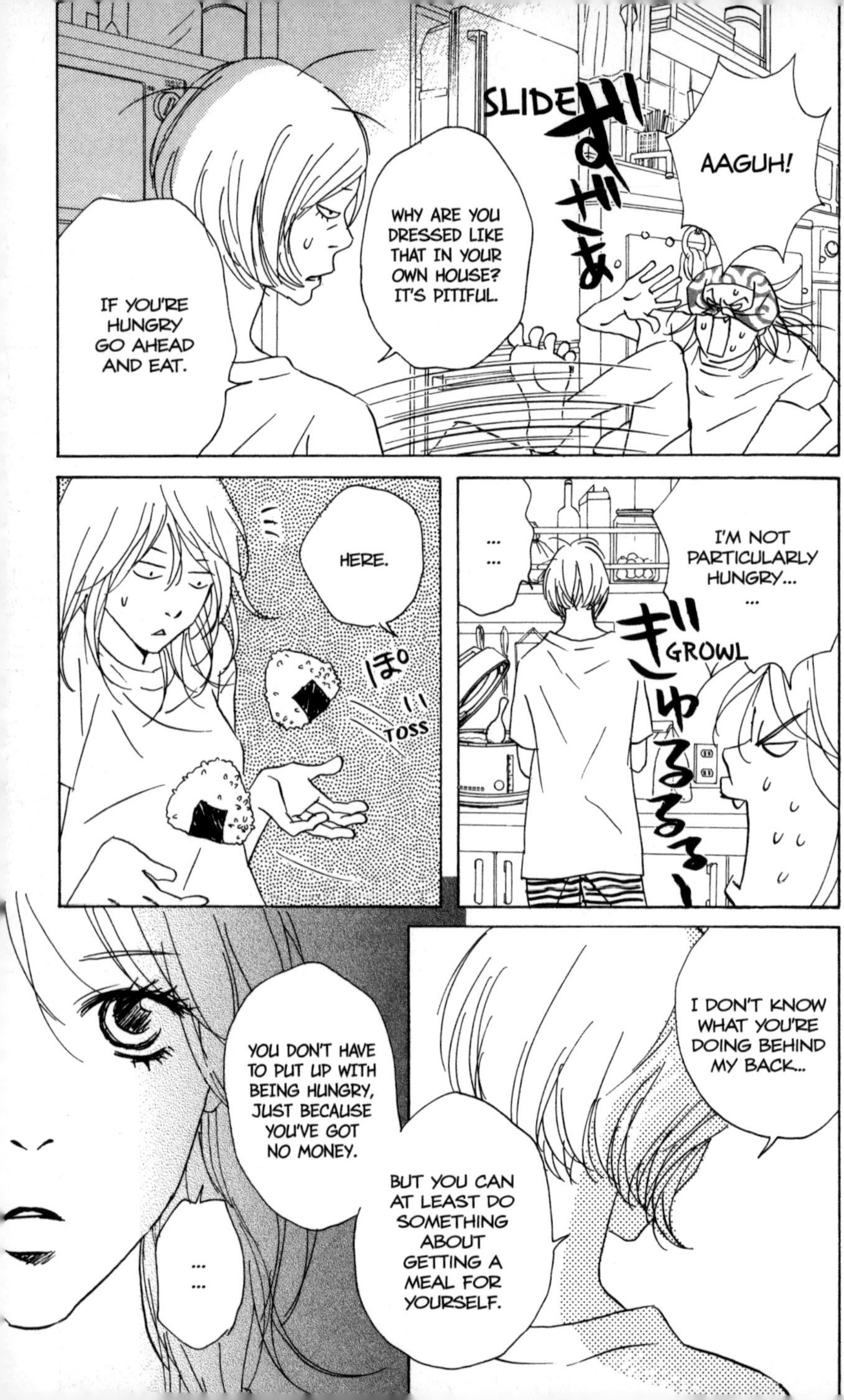

AAGUH!
SLIDE
WHY ARE YOU DRESSED LIKE THAT IN YOUR OWN HOUSE? IT'S PITIFUL.
IF YOU'RE HUNGRY GO AHEAD AND EAT.
I'M NOT PARTICULARLY HUNGRY... ...
GROWL
... ...
HERE.
TOSS
I DON'T KNOW WHAT YOU'RE DOING BEHIND MY BACK...
YOU DON'T HAVE TO PUT UP WITH BEING HUNGRY, JUST BECAUSE YOU'VE GOT NO MONEY.
BUT YOU CAN AT LEAST DO SOMETHING ABOUT GETTING A MEAL FOR YOURSELF.
... ...

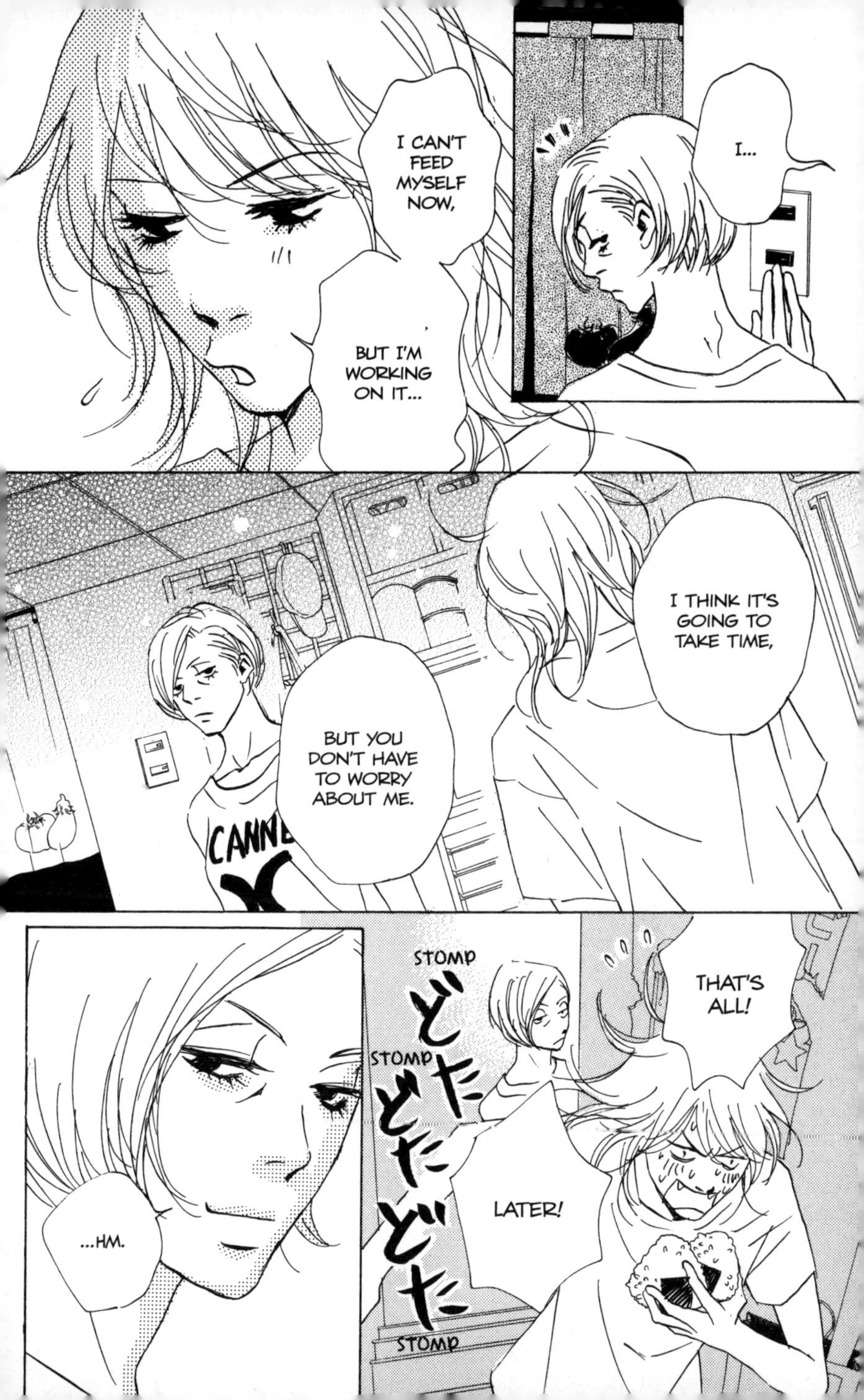
I...
I CAN'T FEED MYSELF NOW,
BUT I'M WORKING ON IT...
I THINK IT'S GOING TO TAKE TIME,
BUT YOU DON'T HAVE TO WORRY ABOUT ME.
THAT'S ALL!
STOMP
STOMP
どたどたどたどた
LATER!
STOMP
...HM.

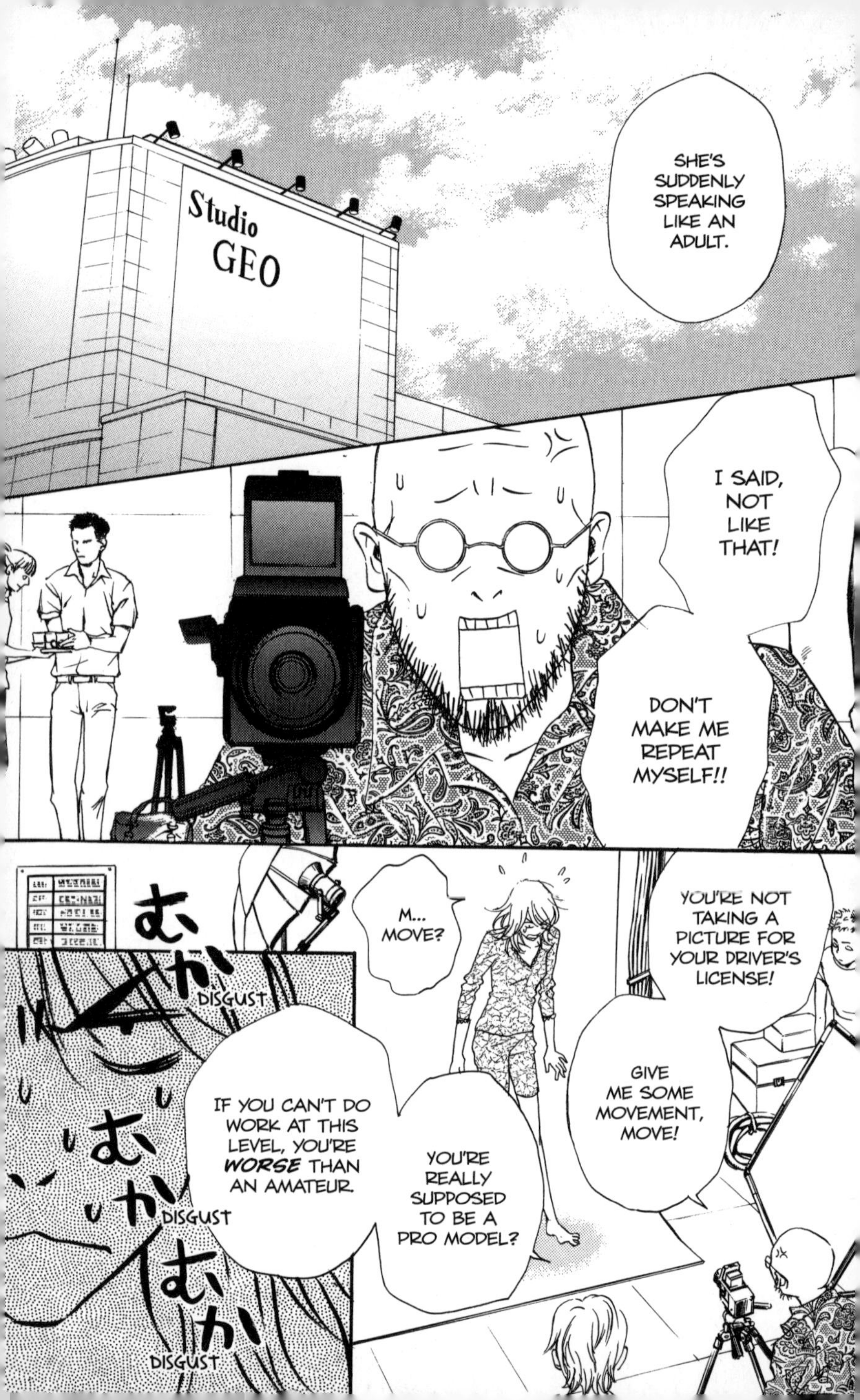
SHE'S SUDDENLY SPEAKING LIKE AN ADULT.
Studio GEO
I SAID, NOT LIKE THAT!
DON'T MAKE ME REPEAT MYSELF!!
YOU'RE NOT TAKING A PICTURE FOR YOUR DRIVER'S LICENSE!
GIVE ME SOME MOVEMENT, MOVE!
M... MOVE?
YOU'RE REALLY SUPPOSED TO BE A PRO MODEL?
IF YOU CAN'T DO WORK AT THIS LEVEL, YOU'RE ***WORSE*** THAN AN AMATEUR.
むか
DISGUST
むか
DISGUST
むか
DISGUST

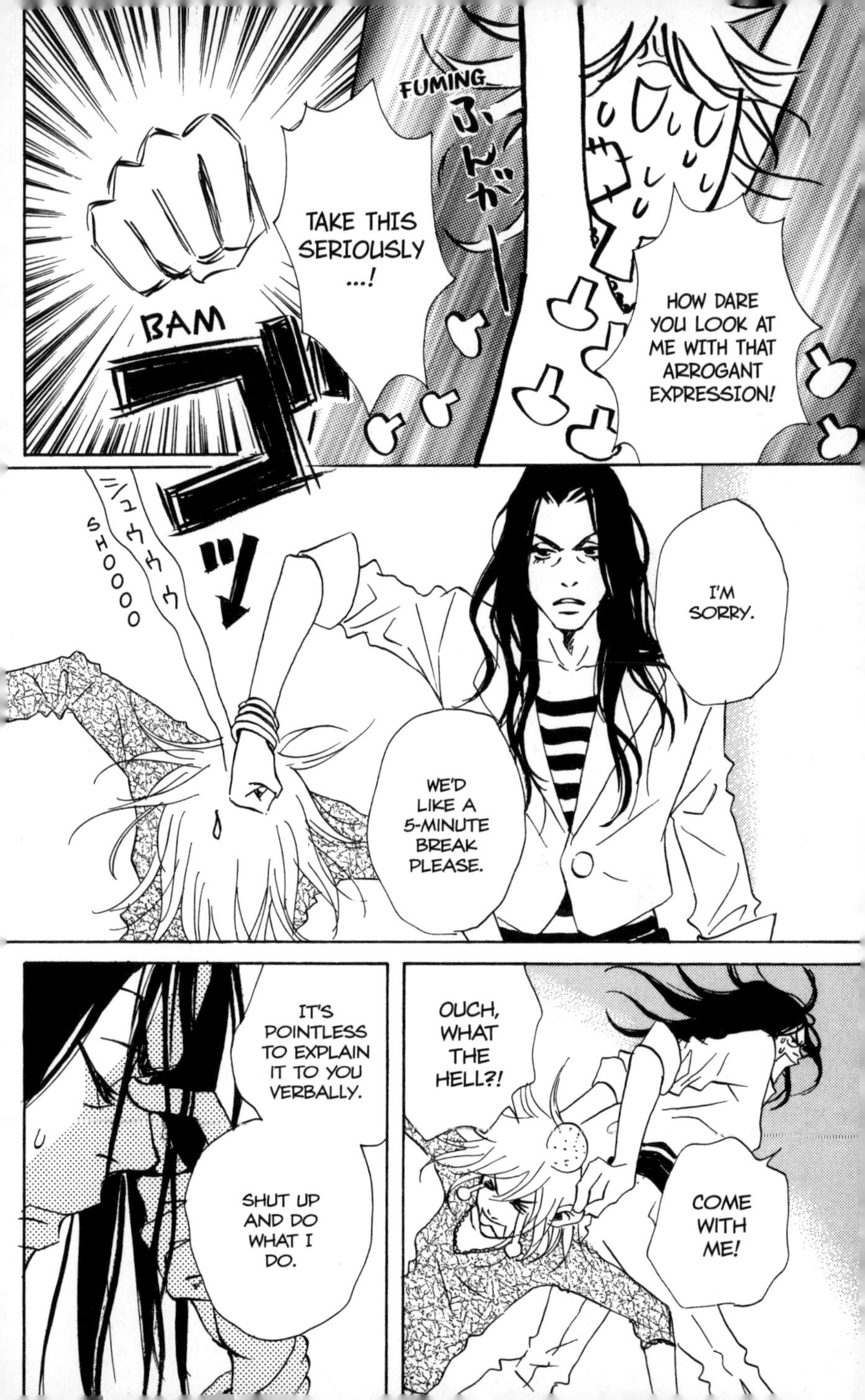
HOW DARE YOU LOOK AT ME WITH THAT ARROGANT EXPRESSION!
FUMING
ふんがー
TAKE THIS SERIOUSLY ...!
BAM
I'M SORRY.
WE'D LIKE A 5-MINUTE BREAK PLEASE.
SHOOOO
OUCH, WHAT THE HELL?!
COME WITH ME!
IT'S POINTLESS TO EXPLAIN IT TO YOU VERBALLY.
SHUT UP AND DO WHAT I DO.

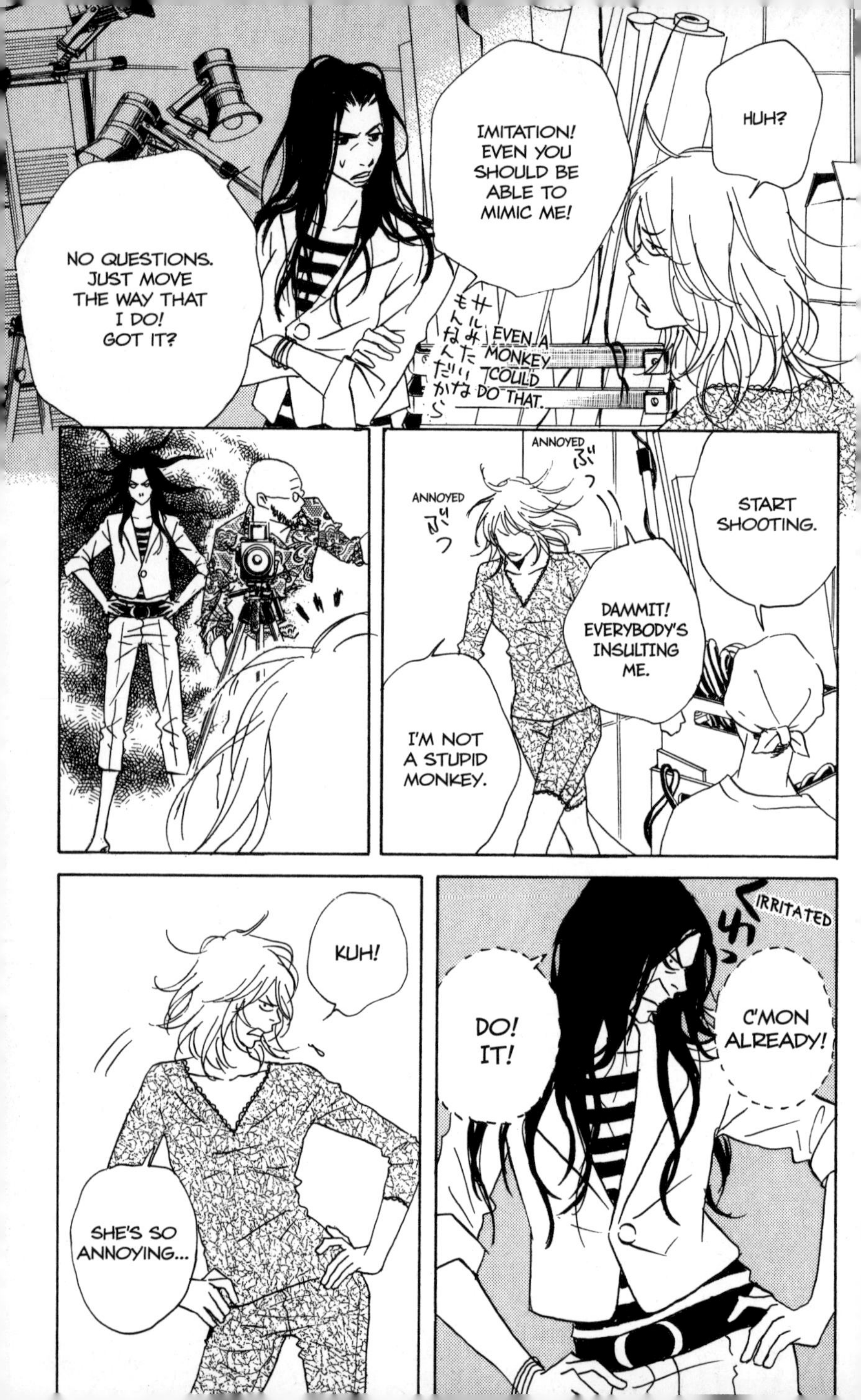
HUH?
IMITATION! EVEN YOU SHOULD BE ABLE TO MIMIC ME!
NO QUESTIONS. JUST MOVE THE WAY THAT I DO! GOT IT?
サルみたいなもんなんだから
EVEN A MONKEY COULD DO THAT.
START SHOOTING.
ANNOYED
ANNOYED
DAMMIT! EVERYBODY'S INSULTING ME.
I'M NOT A STUPID MONKEY.
IRRITATED
C'MON ALREADY!
DO! IT!
KUH!
SHE'S SO ANNOYING...

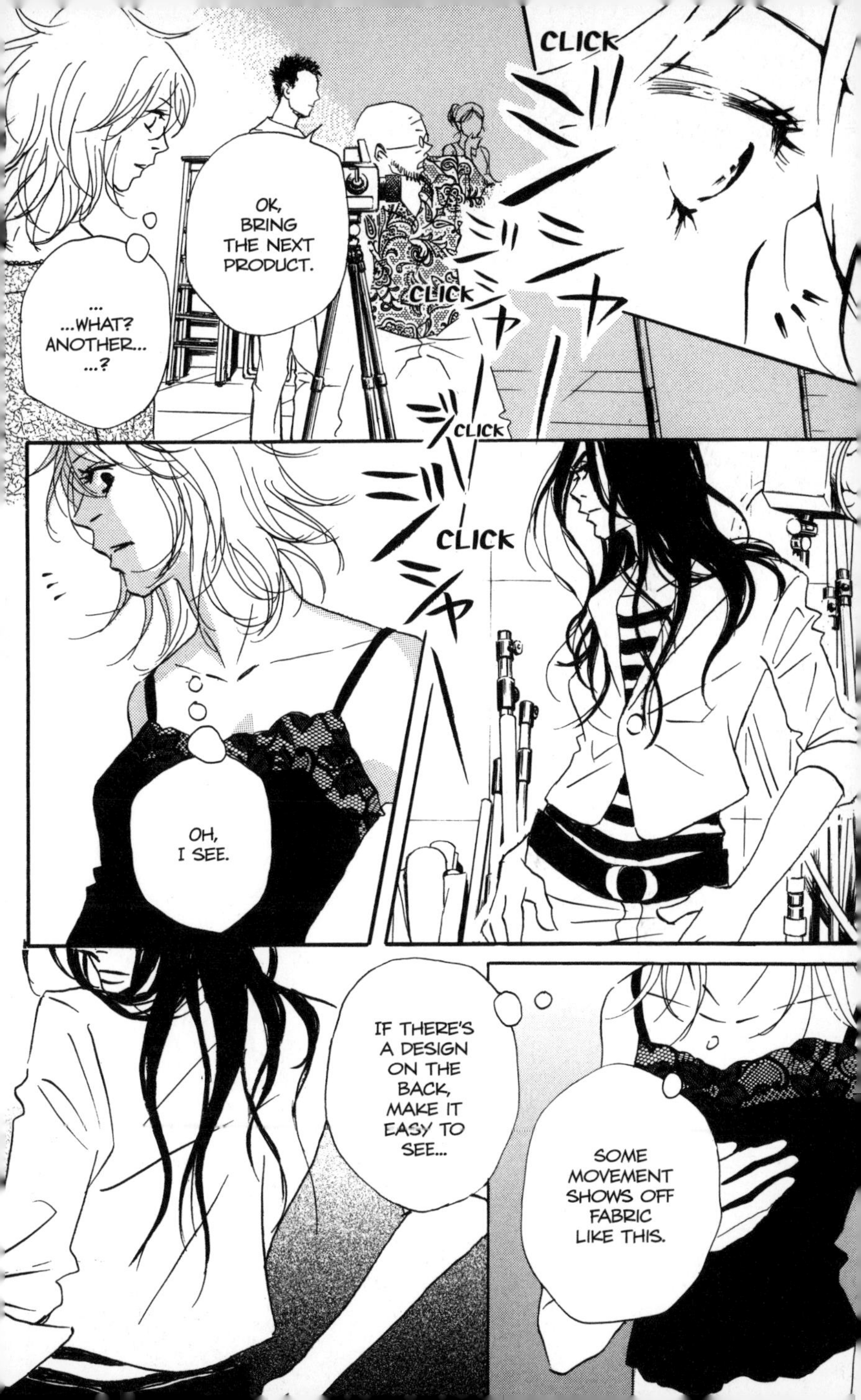
CLICK
OK, BRING THE NEXT PRODUCT.
CLICK
... ...WHAT? ANOTHER... ...?
CLICK
CLICK
OH, I SEE.
IF THERE'S A DESIGN ON THE BACK, MAKE IT EASY TO SEE...
SOME MOVEMENT SHOWS OFF FABRIC LIKE THIS.

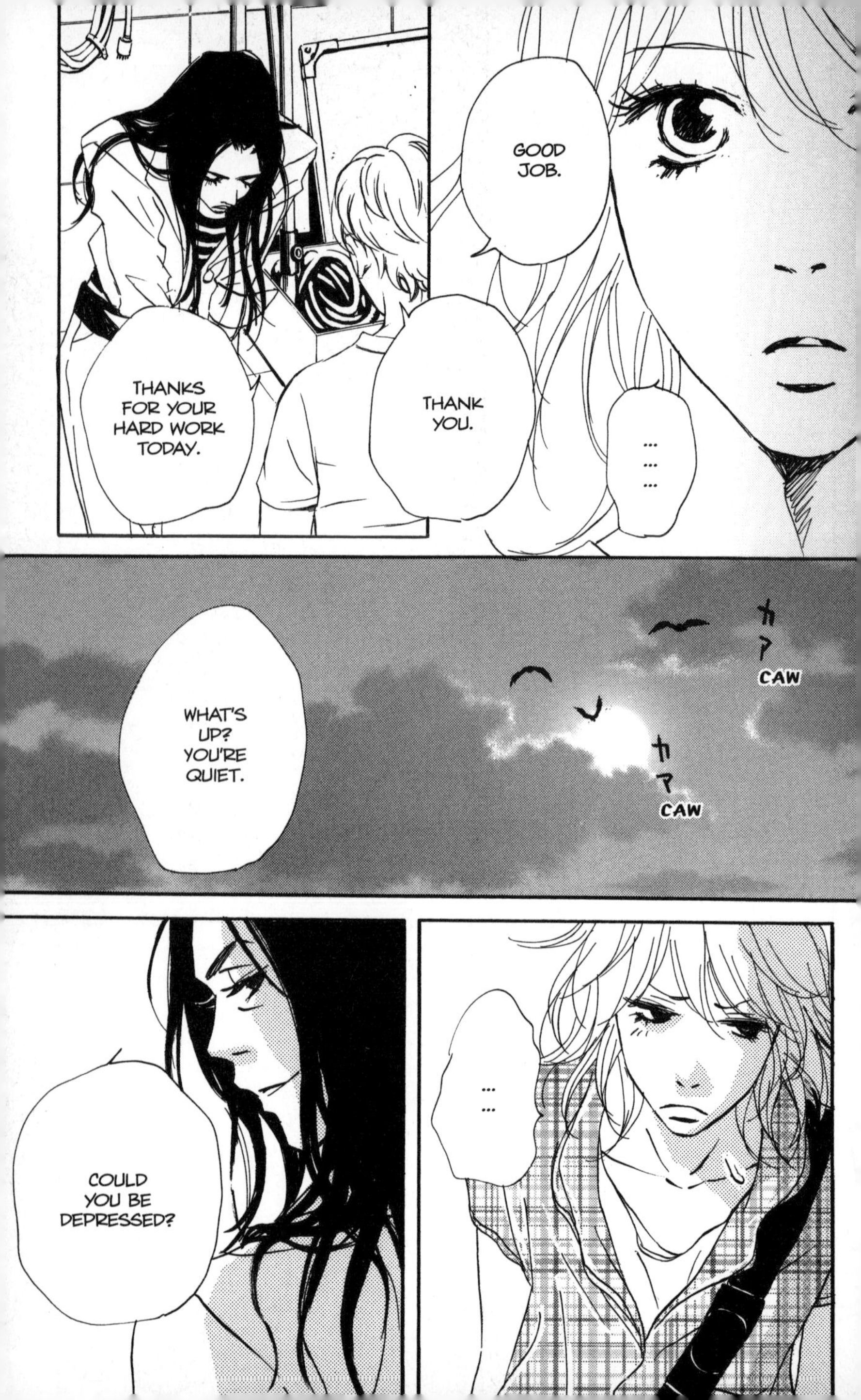
GOOD JOB.
......
THANK YOU.
THANKS FOR YOUR HARD WORK TODAY.
カア
CAW
カア
CAW
WHAT'S UP? YOU'RE QUIET.
......
COULD YOU BE DEPRESSED?

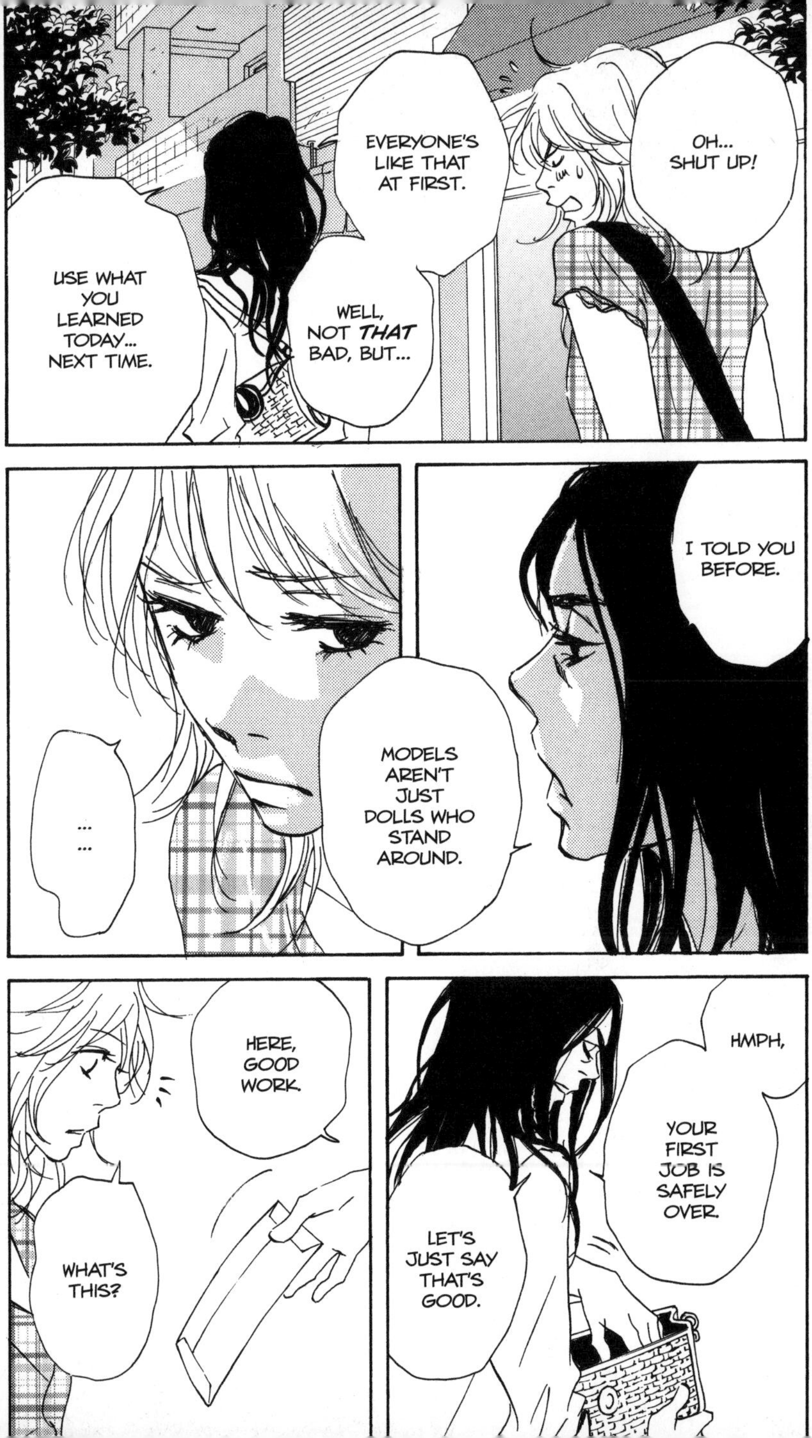
OH... SHUT UP!
EVERYONE'S LIKE THAT AT FIRST.
WELL, NOT *THAT* BAD, BUT...
USE WHAT YOU LEARNED TODAY... NEXT TIME.
I TOLD YOU BEFORE.
MODELS AREN'T JUST DOLLS WHO STAND AROUND.
... ...
HMPH,
YOUR FIRST JOB IS SAFELY OVER.
LET'S JUST SAY THAT'S GOOD.
HERE, GOOD WORK.
WHAT'S THIS?

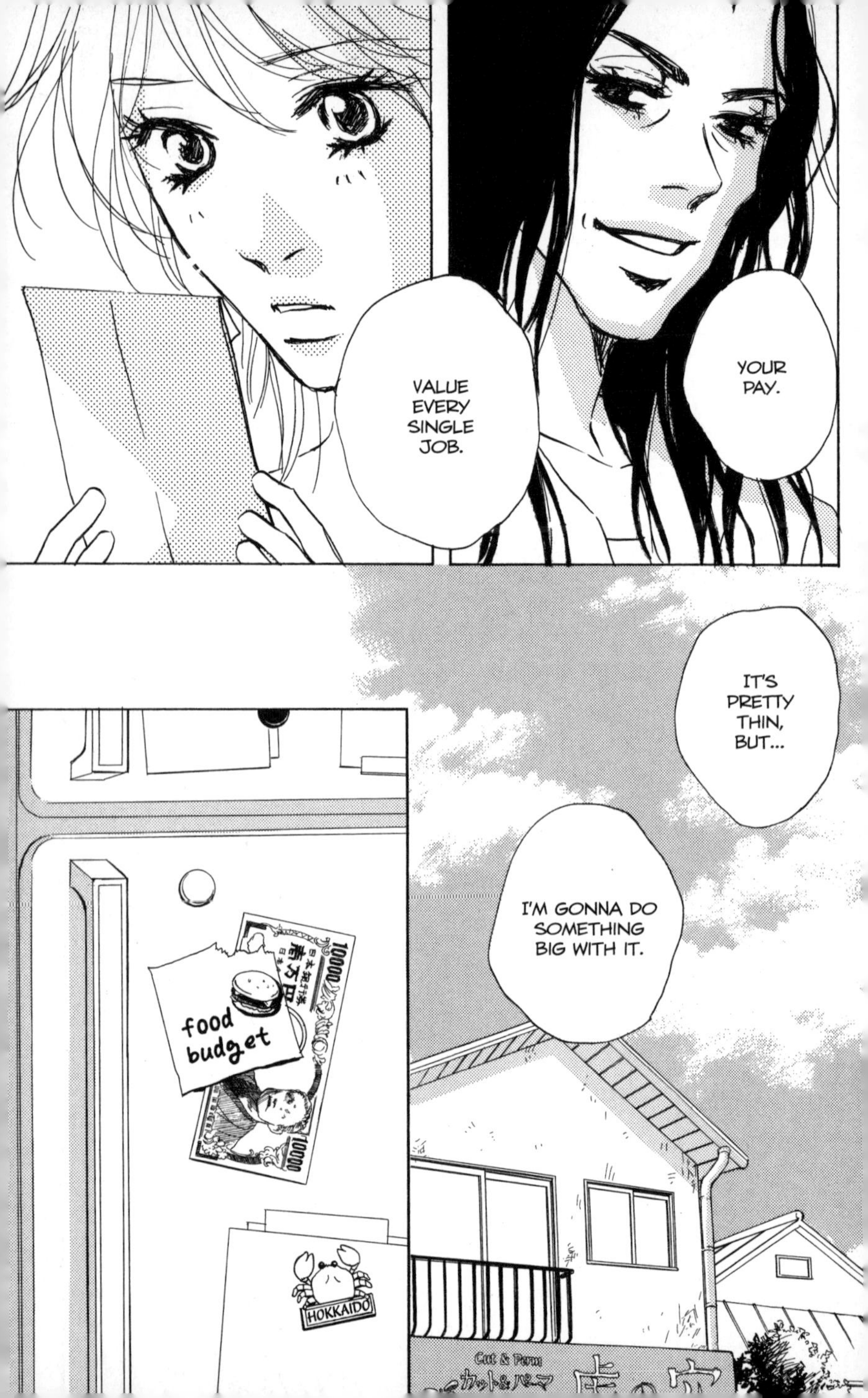

YOUR PAY.
VALUE EVERY SINGLE JOB.
IT'S PRETTY THIN, BUT...
I'M GONNA DO SOMETHING BIG WITH IT.
Cut & Perm
カット&パーマ
food budget
HOKKAIDO

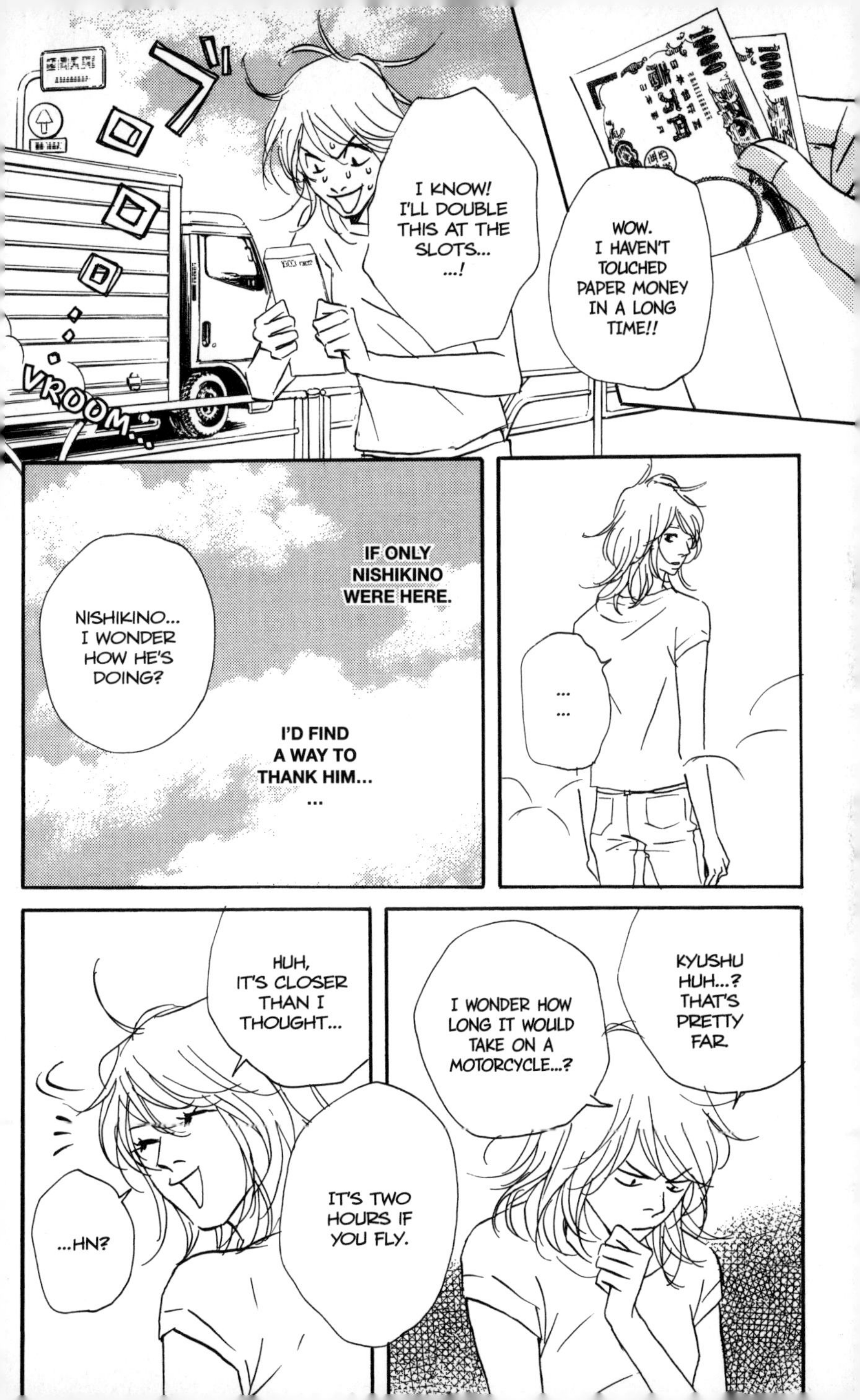
WOW. I HAVEN'T TOUCHED PAPER MONEY IN A LONG TIME!!
I KNOW! I'LL DOUBLE THIS AT THE SLOTS... ...!
VROOM...
... ...
IF ONLY NISHIKINO WERE HERE.
NISHIKINO... I WONDER HOW HE'S DOING?
I'D FIND A WAY TO THANK HIM... ...
KYUSHU HUH...? THAT'S PRETTY FAR.
I WONDER HOW LONG IT WOULD TAKE ON A MOTORCYCLE...?
HUH, IT'S CLOSER THAN I THOUGHT...
IT'S TWO HOURS IF YOU FLY.
...HN?

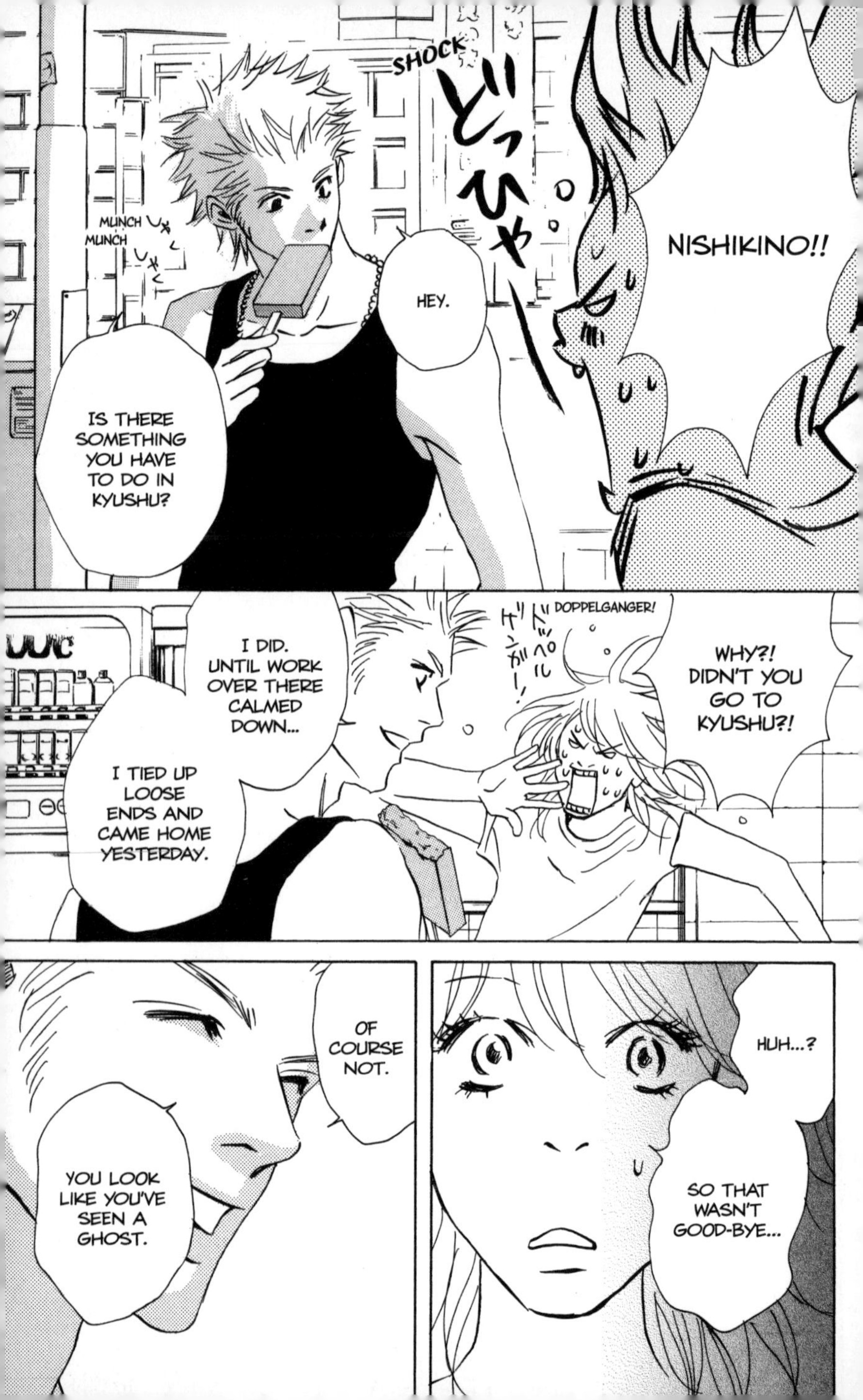
NISHIKINO!!
SHOCK
どっひゃ
HEY.
MUNCH MUNCH
IS THERE SOMETHING YOU HAVE TO DO IN KYUSHU?
WHY?! DIDN'T YOU GO TO KYUSHU?!
DOPPELGANGER!
I DID. UNTIL WORK OVER THERE CALMED DOWN...
I TIED UP LOOSE ENDS AND CAME HOME YESTERDAY.
HUH...?
SO THAT WASN'T GOOD-BYE...
OF COURSE NOT.
YOU LOOK LIKE YOU'VE SEEN A GHOST.

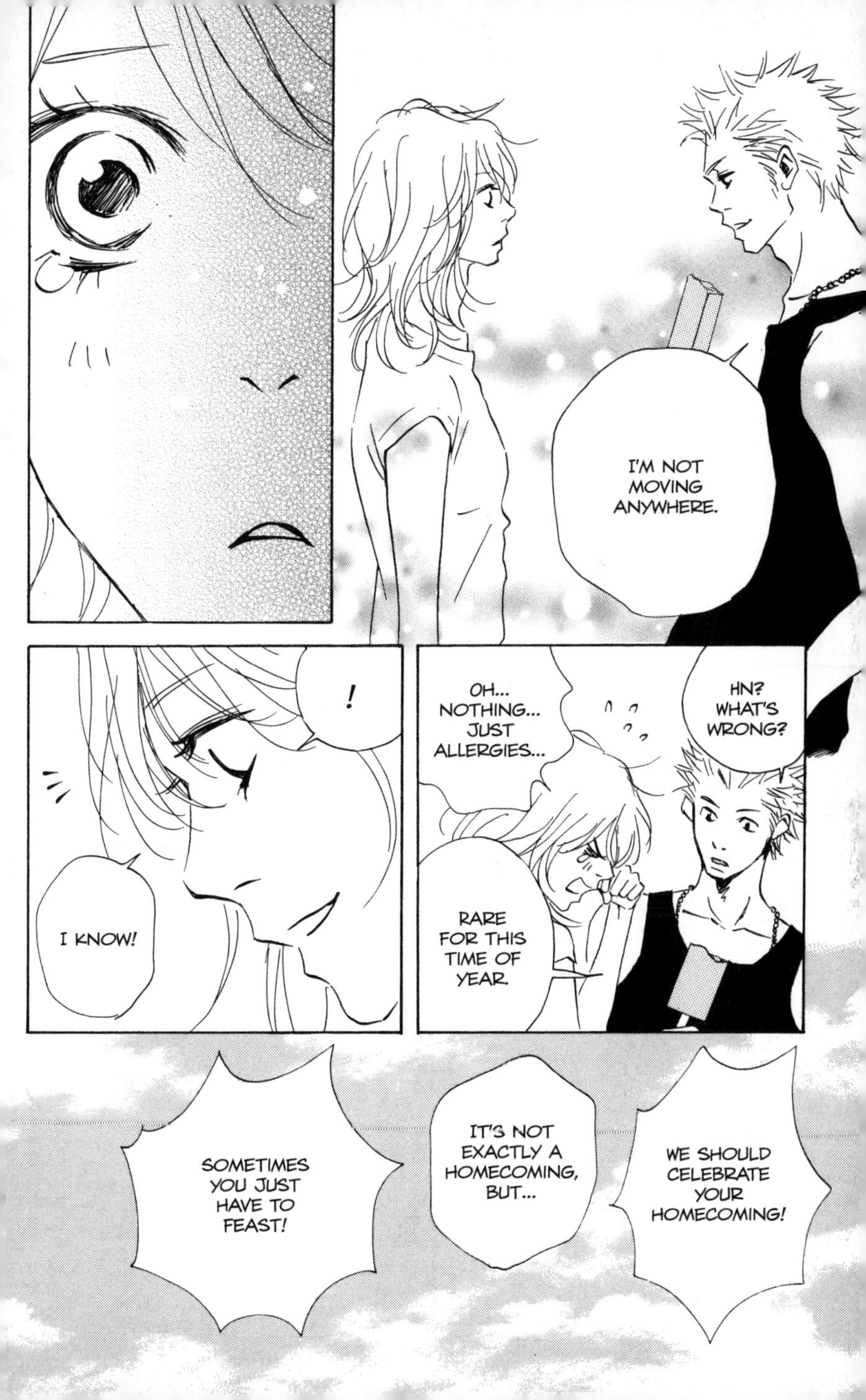
I'M NOT MOVING ANYWHERE.
HN? WHAT'S WRONG?
OH... NOTHING... JUST ALLERGIES...
RARE FOR THIS TIME OF YEAR.
!
I KNOW!
WE SHOULD CELEBRATE YOUR HOMECOMING!
IT'S NOT EXACTLY A HOMECOMING, BUT...
SOMETIMES YOU JUST HAVE TO FEAST!

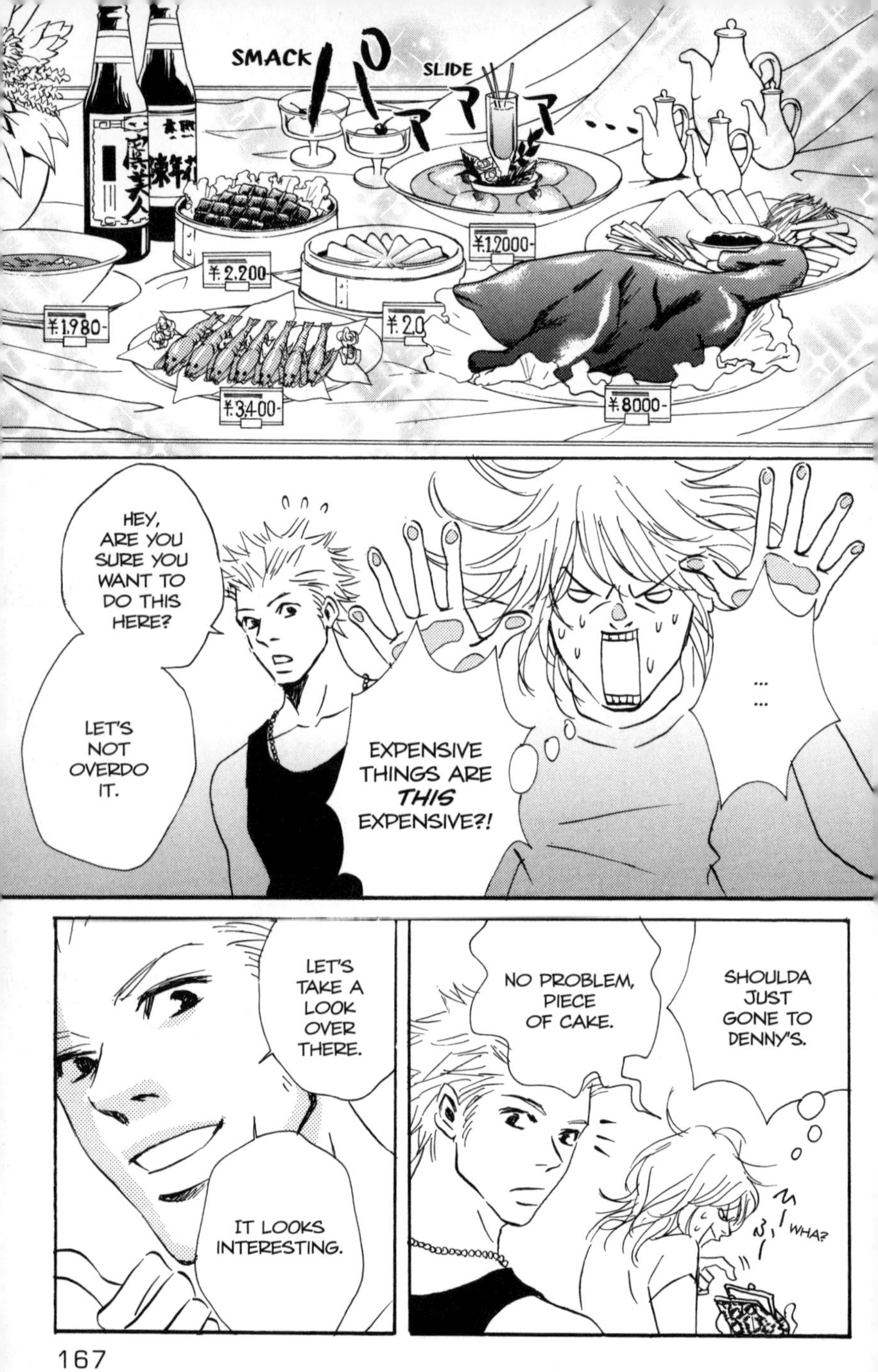
SLIDE
SMACK
¥12000-
¥8000-
¥2,0
¥2,200
¥3,400-
¥1,980-
……
EXPENSIVE THINGS ARE *THIS* EXPENSIVE?!
HEY, ARE YOU SURE YOU WANT TO DO THIS HERE?
LET'S NOT OVERDO IT.
SHOULDA JUST GONE TO DENNY'S.
NO PROBLEM, PIECE OF CAKE.
WHA?
LET'S TAKE A LOOK OVER THERE.
IT LOOKS INTERESTING.

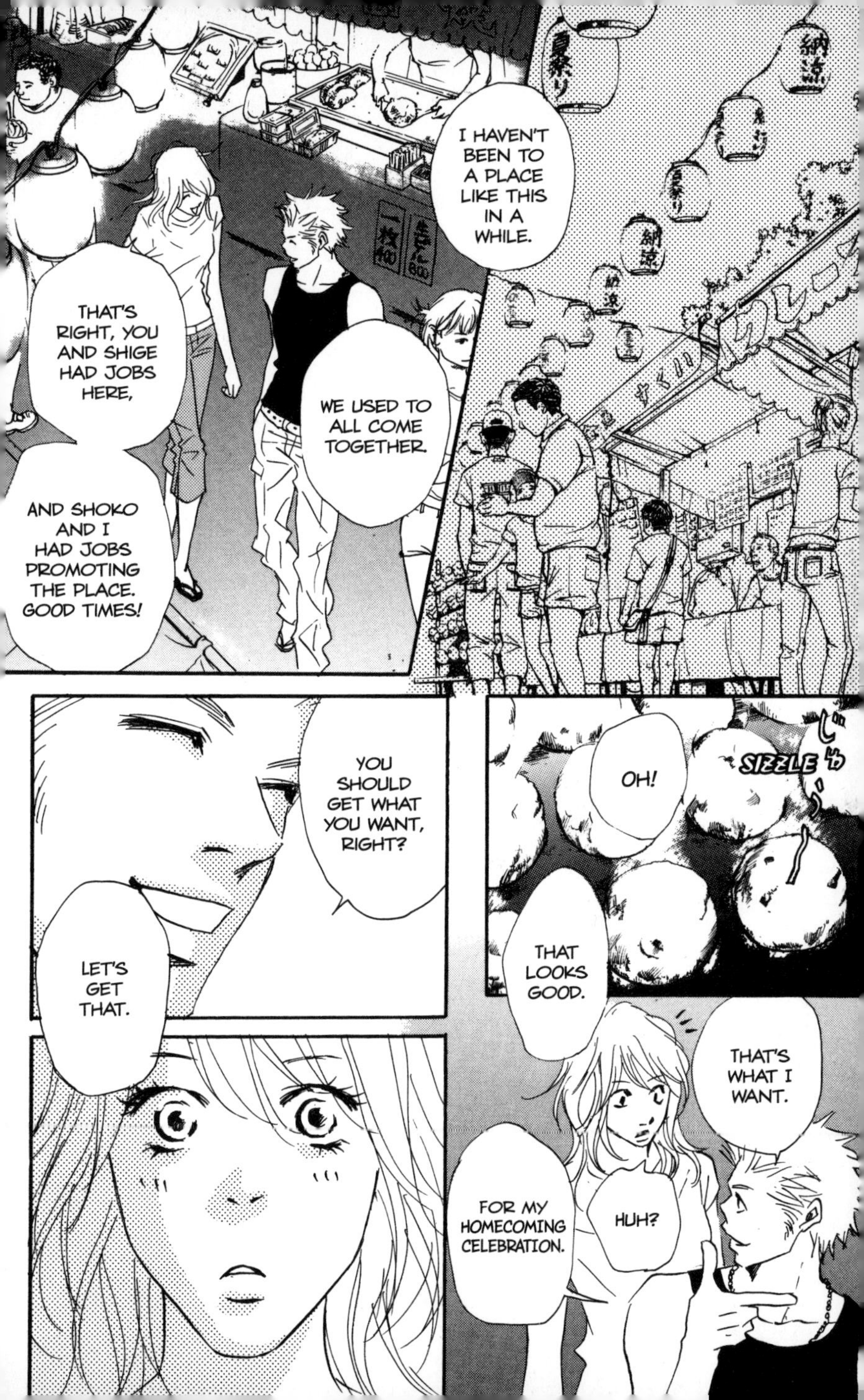
I HAVEN'T BEEN TO A PLACE LIKE THIS IN A WHILE.
WE USED TO ALL COME TOGETHER.
THAT'S RIGHT, YOU AND SHIGE HAD JOBS HERE,
AND SHOKO AND I HAD JOBS PROMOTING THE PLACE. GOOD TIMES!
SIZZLE
OH!
THAT LOOKS GOOD.
YOU SHOULD GET WHAT YOU WANT, RIGHT?
LET'S GET THAT.
THAT'S WHAT I WANT.
FOR MY HOMECOMING CELEBRATION.
HUH?

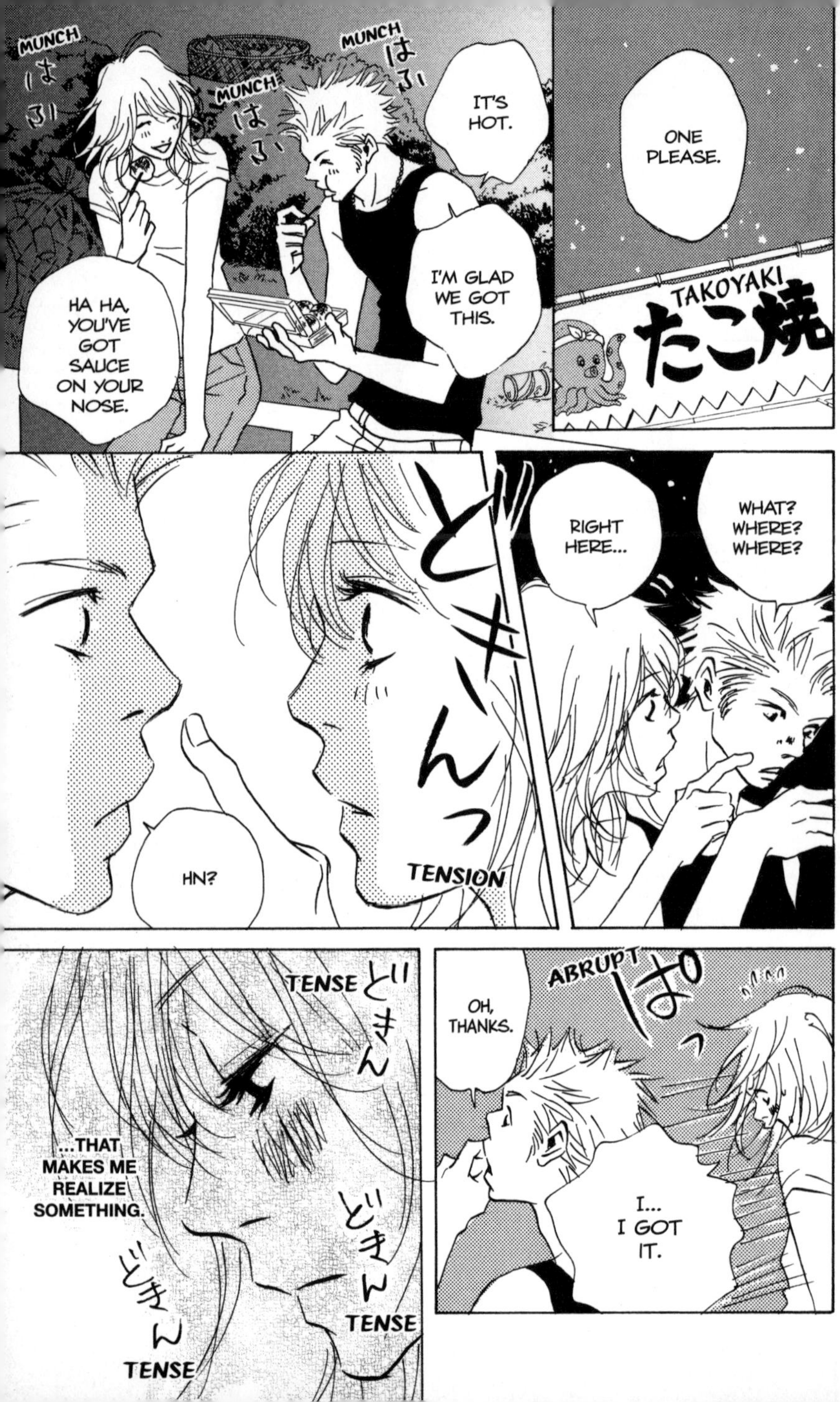
ONE PLEASE.
TAKOYAKI
たこ焼
MUNCH はふ
MUNCH はふ
MUNCH はふ
IT'S HOT.
I'M GLAD WE GOT THIS.
HA HA, YOU'VE GOT SAUCE ON YOUR NOSE.
WHAT? WHERE? WHERE?
RIGHT HERE...
どきんっ
TENSION
HN?
ABRUPT ぱっ
OH, THANKS.
I... I GOT IT.
TENSE どきん
TENSE どきん
TENSE どきん
...THAT MAKES ME REALIZE SOMETHING.

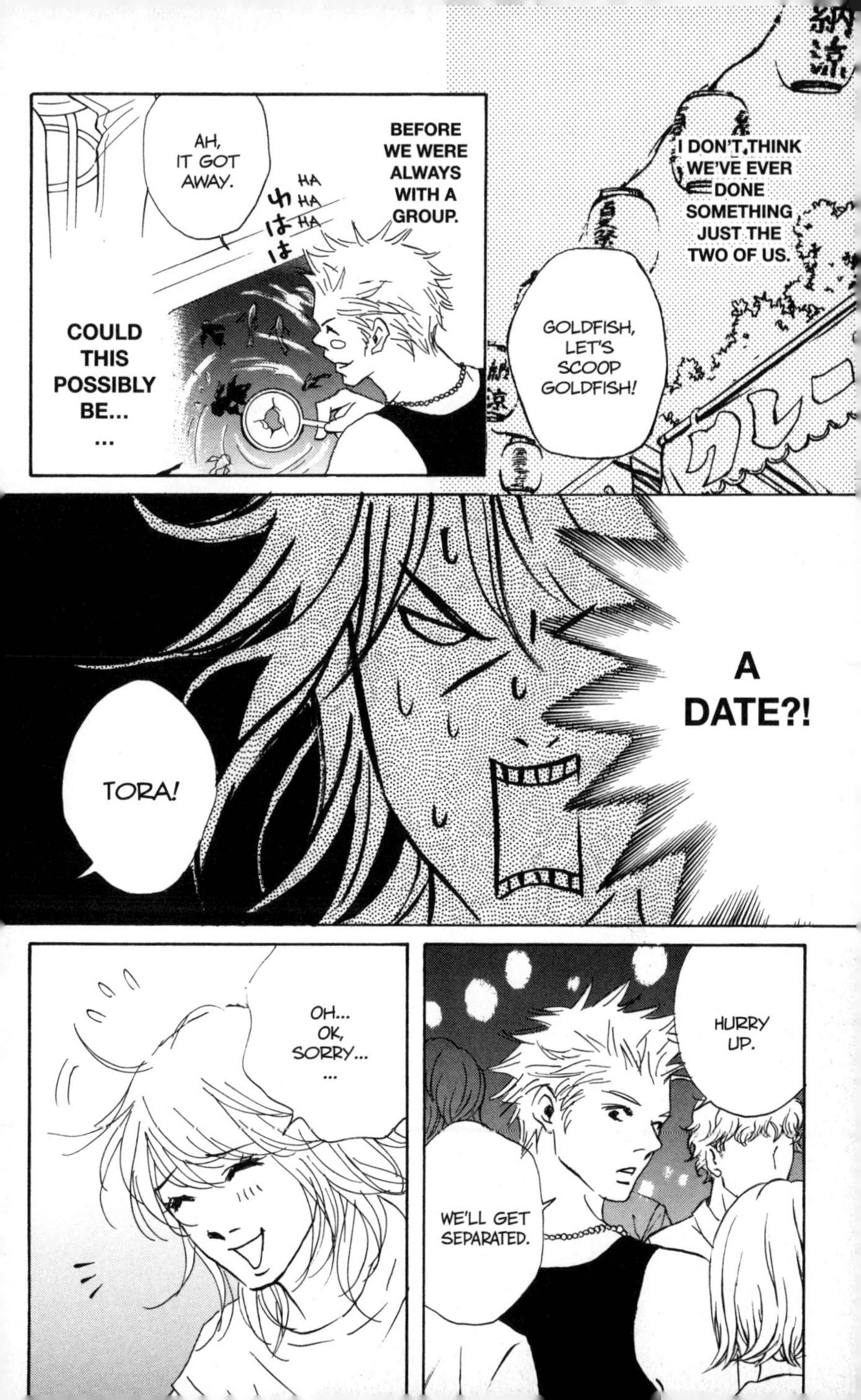
I DON'T THINK WE'VE EVER DONE SOMETHING JUST THE TWO OF US.
GOLDFISH, LET'S SCOOP GOLDFISH!
BEFORE WE WERE ALWAYS WITH A GROUP.
AH, IT GOT AWAY.
わはは HA HA HA
COULD THIS POSSIBLY BE... ...
A DATE?!
TORA!
HURRY UP.
WE'LL GET SEPARATED.
OH... OK, SORRY... ...

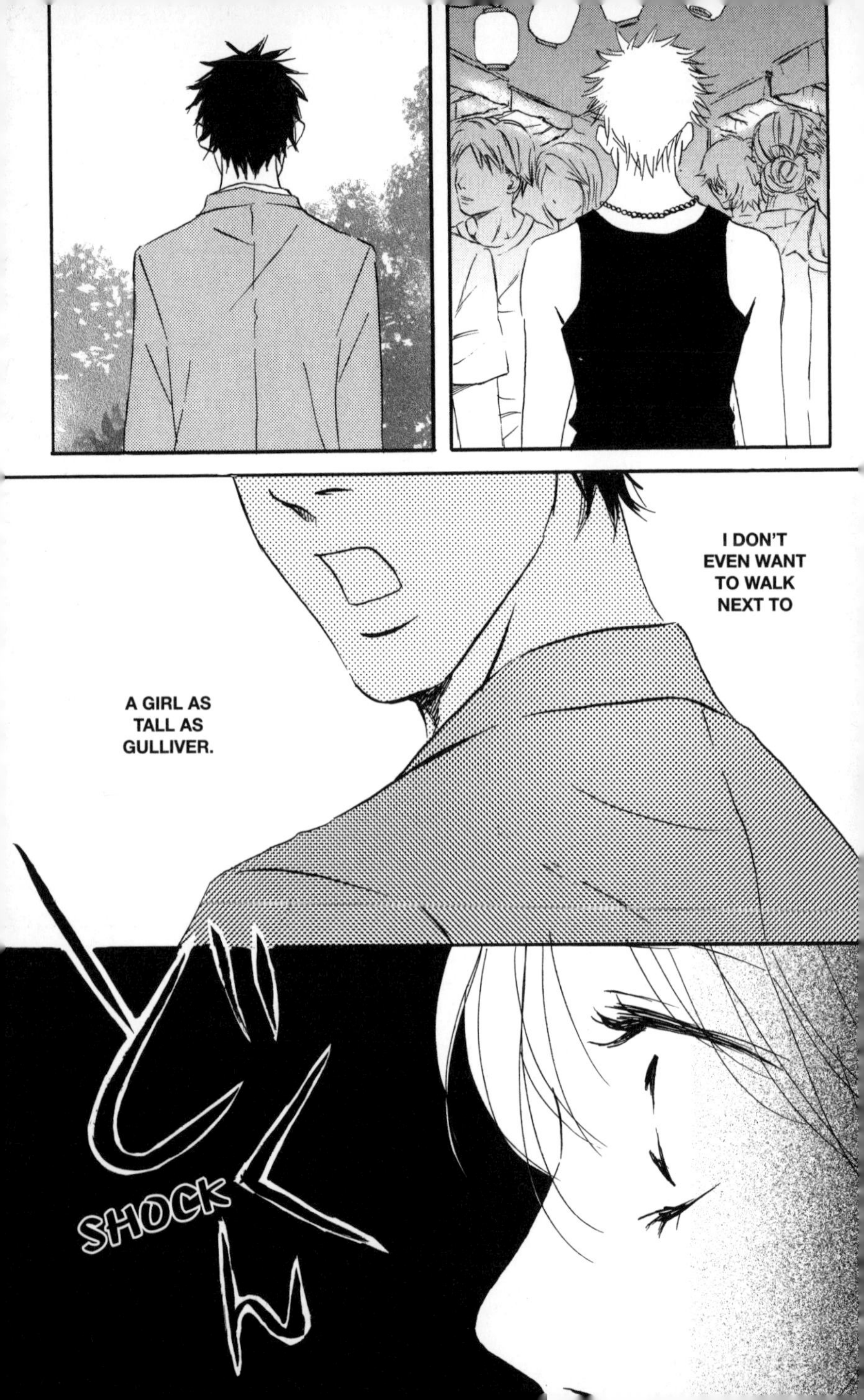
I DON'T EVEN WANT TO WALK NEXT TO
A GIRL AS TALL AS GULLIVER.
SHOCK

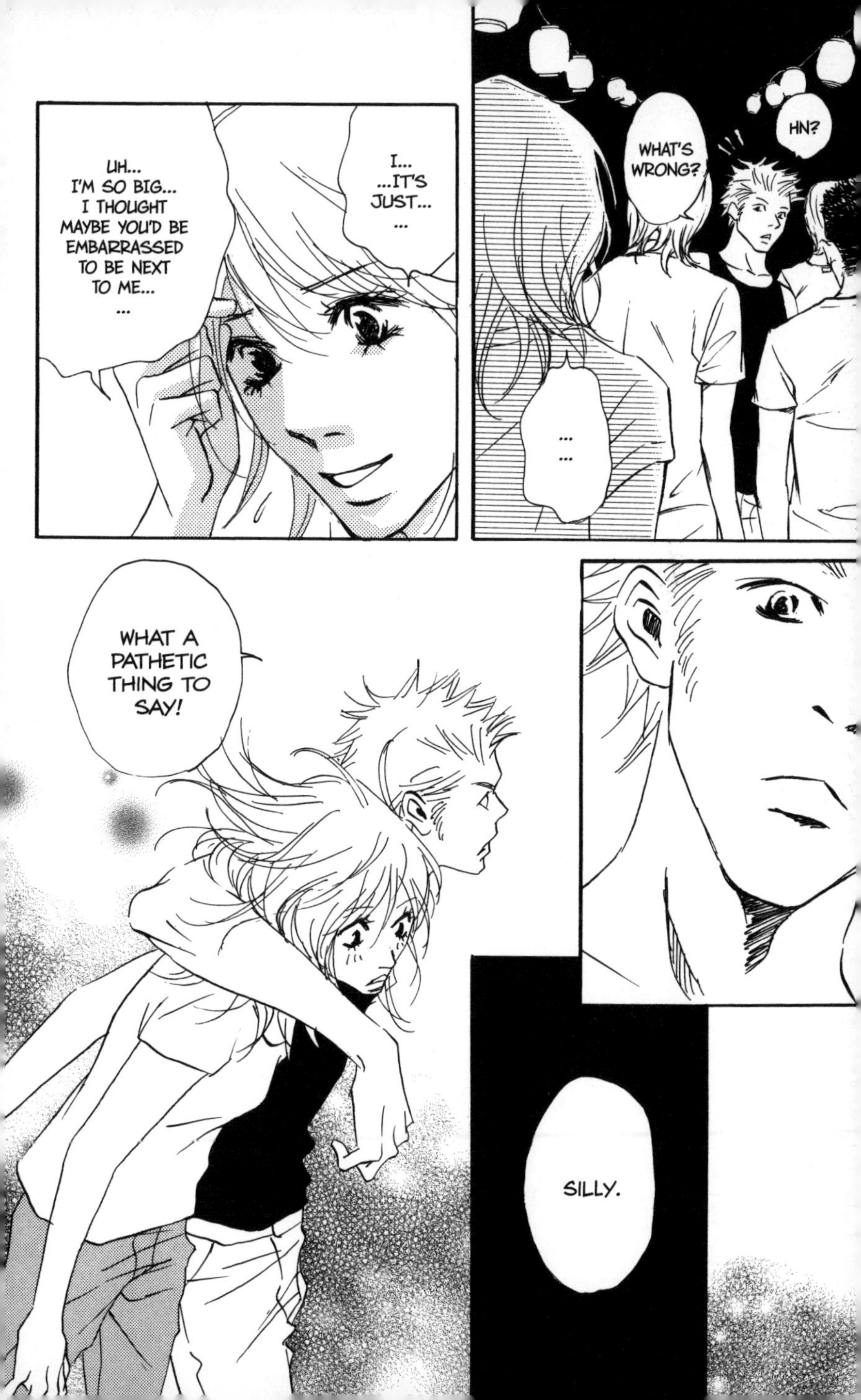
WHAT'S WRONG?
HN?
... ...
I... ...IT'S JUST... ...
UH... I'M SO BIG... I THOUGHT MAYBE YOU'D BE EMBARRASSED TO BE NEXT TO ME... ...
SILLY.
WHAT A PATHETIC THING TO SAY!

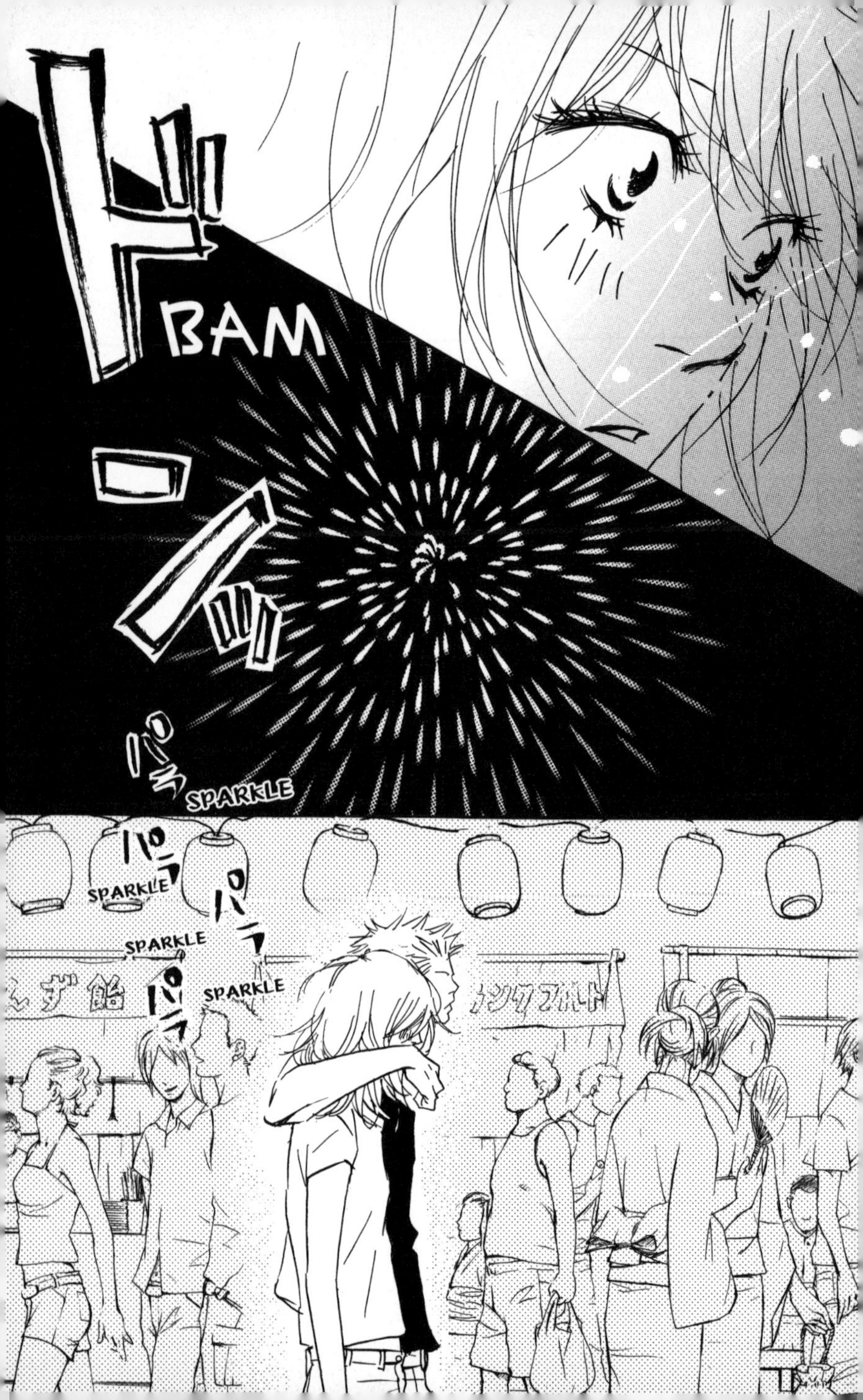
ドーン
BAM
パラ
SPARKLE
パラ
SPARKLE
パラ
SPARKLE
パラ
SPARKLE

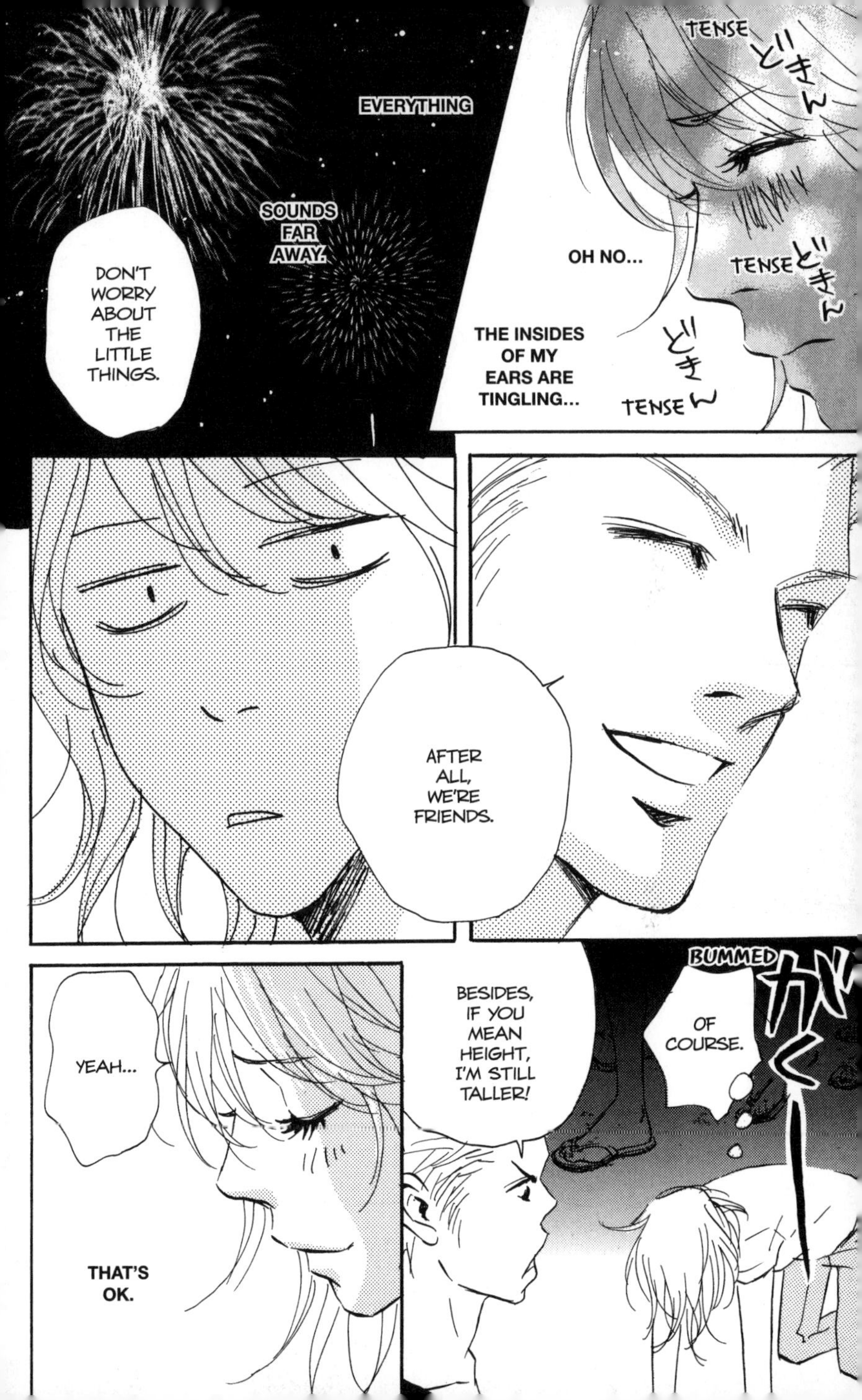
TENSE どきん
TENSE どきん
TENSE どきん
OH NO...
THE INSIDES OF MY EARS ARE TINGLING...
EVERYTHING
SOUNDS FAR AWAY.
DON'T WORRY ABOUT THE LITTLE THINGS.
AFTER ALL, WE'RE FRIENDS.
BUMMED がくー
OF COURSE.
BESIDES, IF YOU MEAN HEIGHT, I'M STILL TALLER!
YEAH...
THAT'S OK.

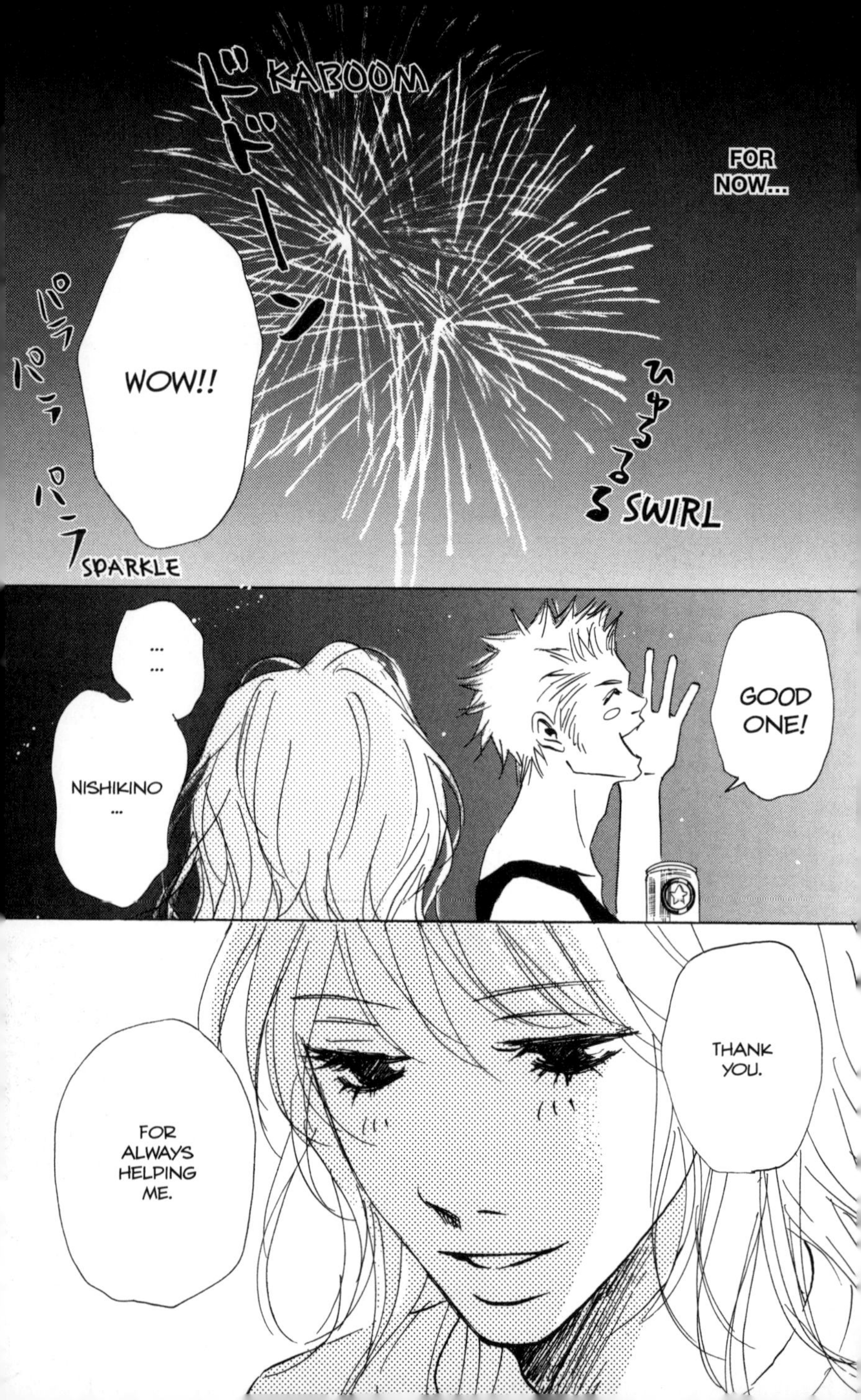
FOR NOW...
ひゅるるる SWIRL
ドドーン KABOOM
WOW!!
パラパラパーラ SPARKLE
GOOD ONE!
......
NISHIKINO...
THANK YOU.
FOR ALWAYS HELPING ME.

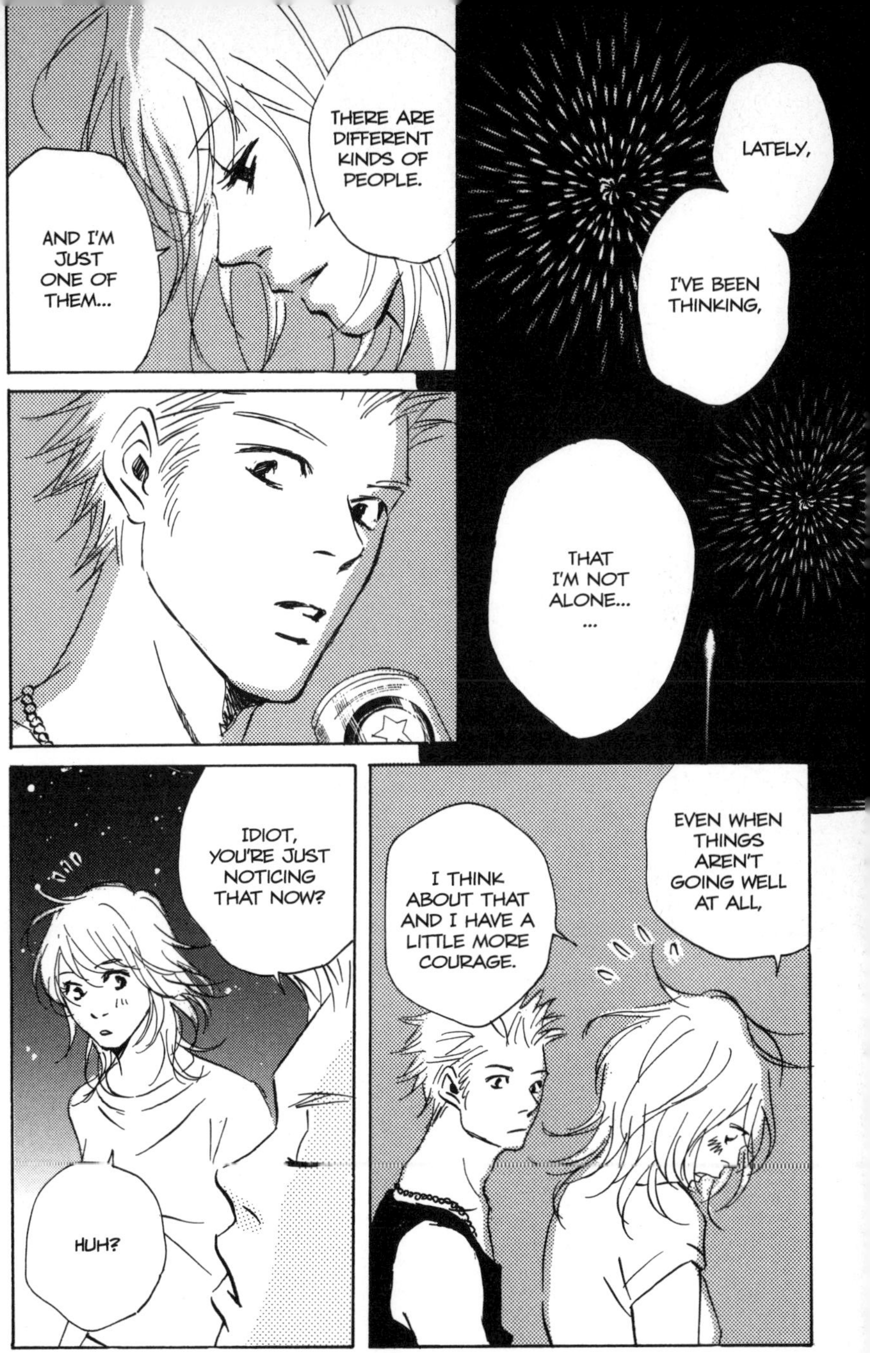
LATELY,
I'VE BEEN THINKING,
THAT I'M NOT ALONE... ...
THERE ARE DIFFERENT KINDS OF PEOPLE.
AND I'M JUST ONE OF THEM...
EVEN WHEN THINGS AREN'T GOING WELL AT ALL,
I THINK ABOUT THAT AND I HAVE A LITTLE MORE COURAGE.
IDIOT, YOU'RE JUST NOTICING THAT NOW?
HUH?

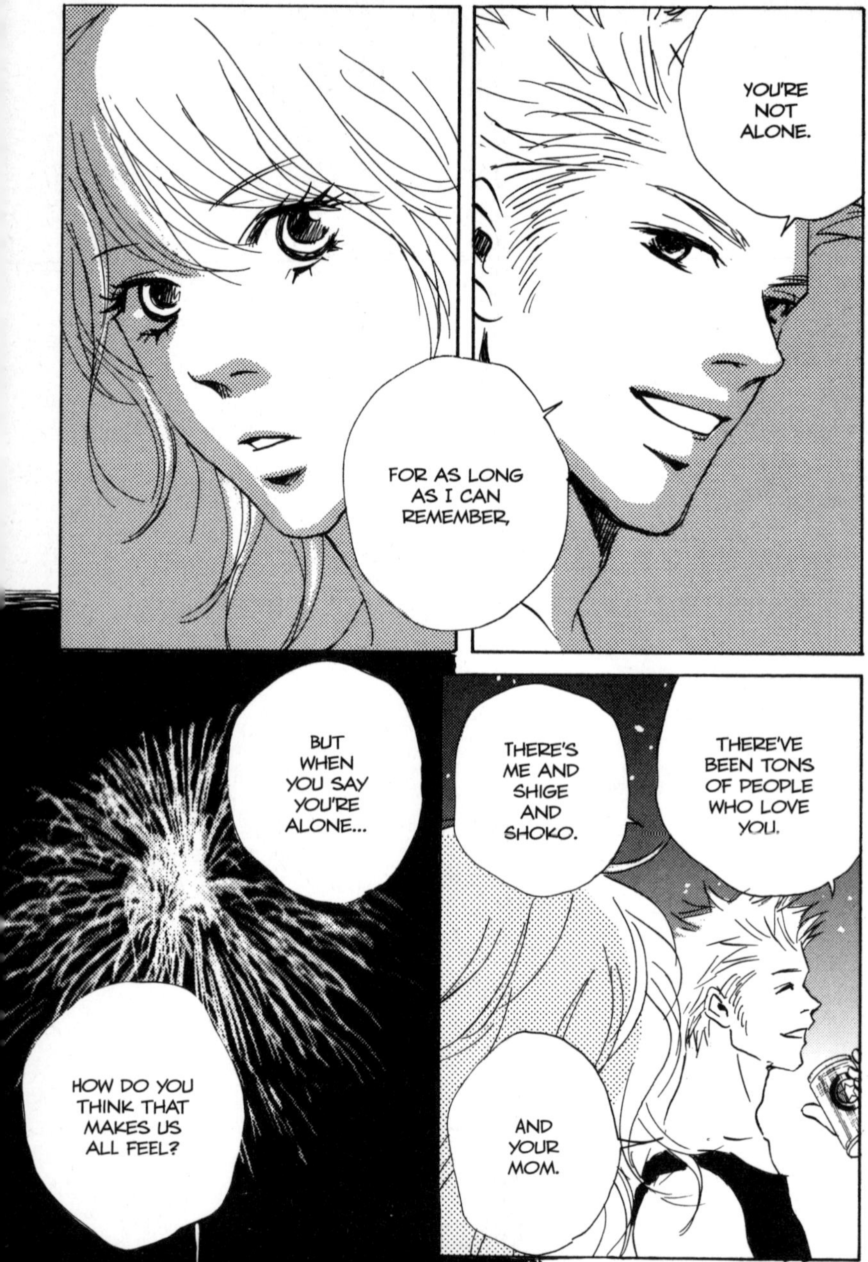
YOU'RE NOT ALONE.
FOR AS LONG AS I CAN REMEMBER,
THERE'VE BEEN TONS OF PEOPLE WHO LOVE YOU.
THERE'S ME AND SHIGE AND SHOKO.
AND YOUR MOM.
BUT WHEN YOU SAY YOU'RE ALONE...
HOW DO YOU THINK THAT MAKES US ALL FEEL?

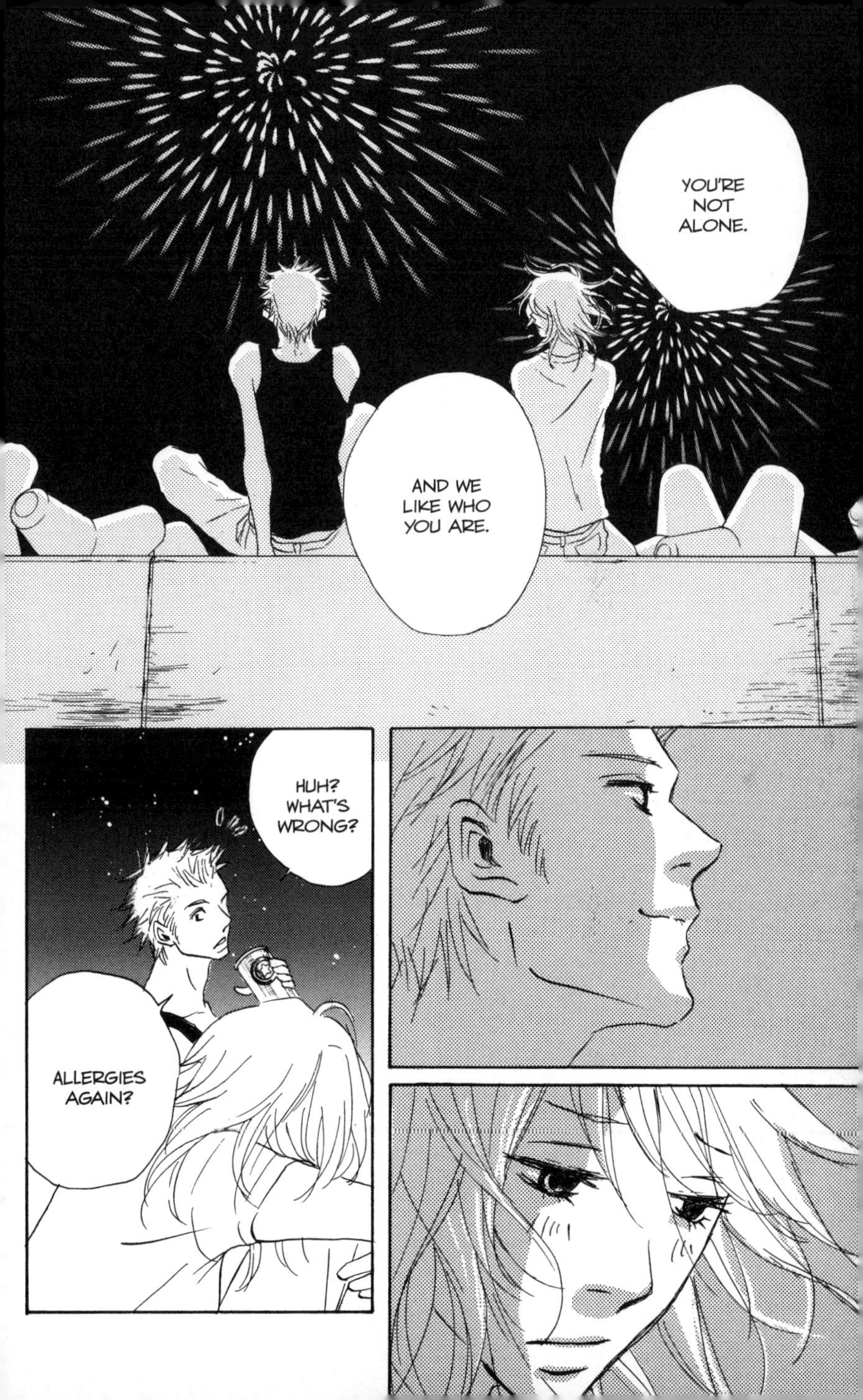
YOU'RE NOT ALONE.
AND WE LIKE WHO YOU ARE.
HUH? WHAT'S WRONG?
ALLERGIES AGAIN?

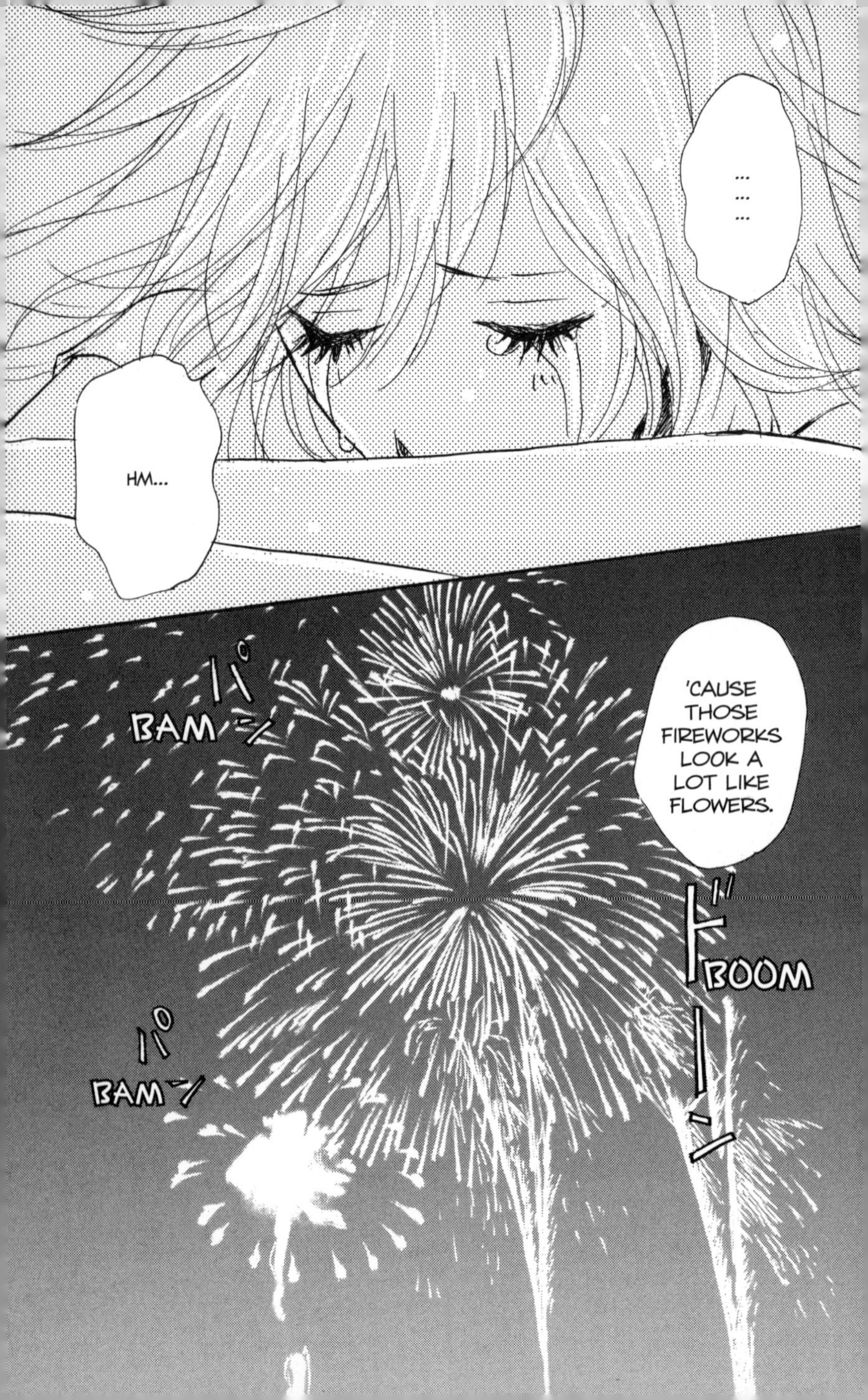
……
HM...
'CAUSE THOSE FIREWORKS LOOK A LOT LIKE FLOWERS.
BAM
BOOM
BAM

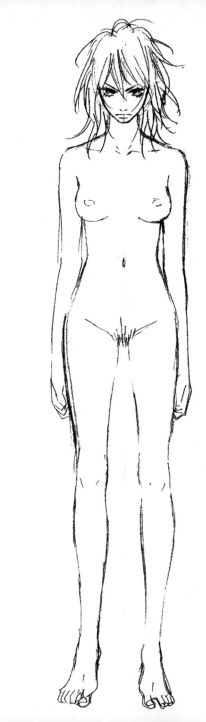

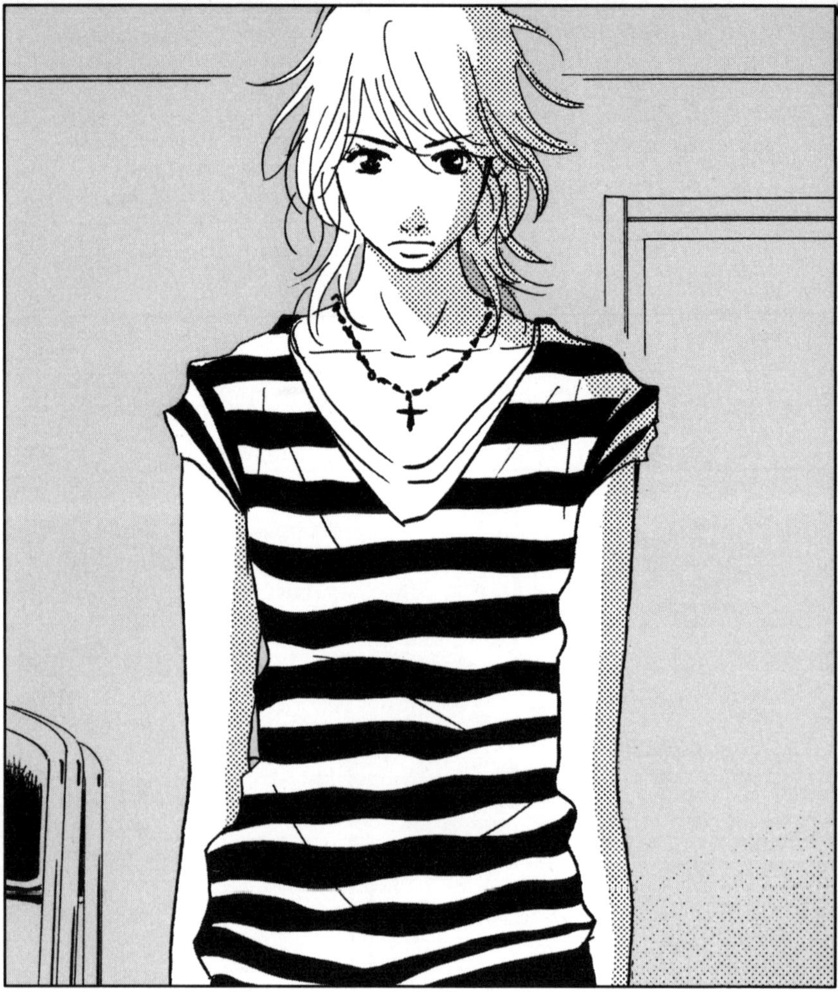

MODE 7

WALL

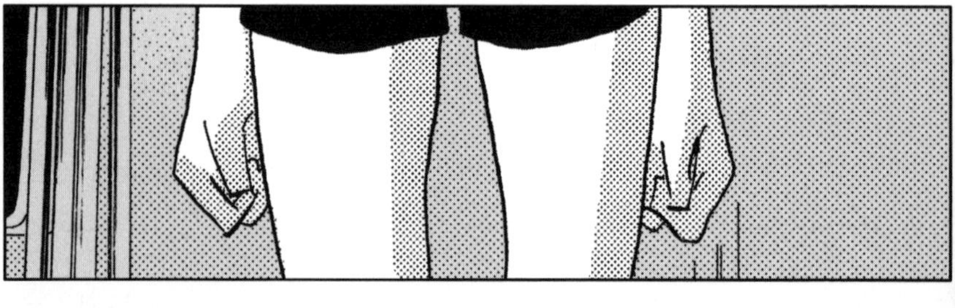

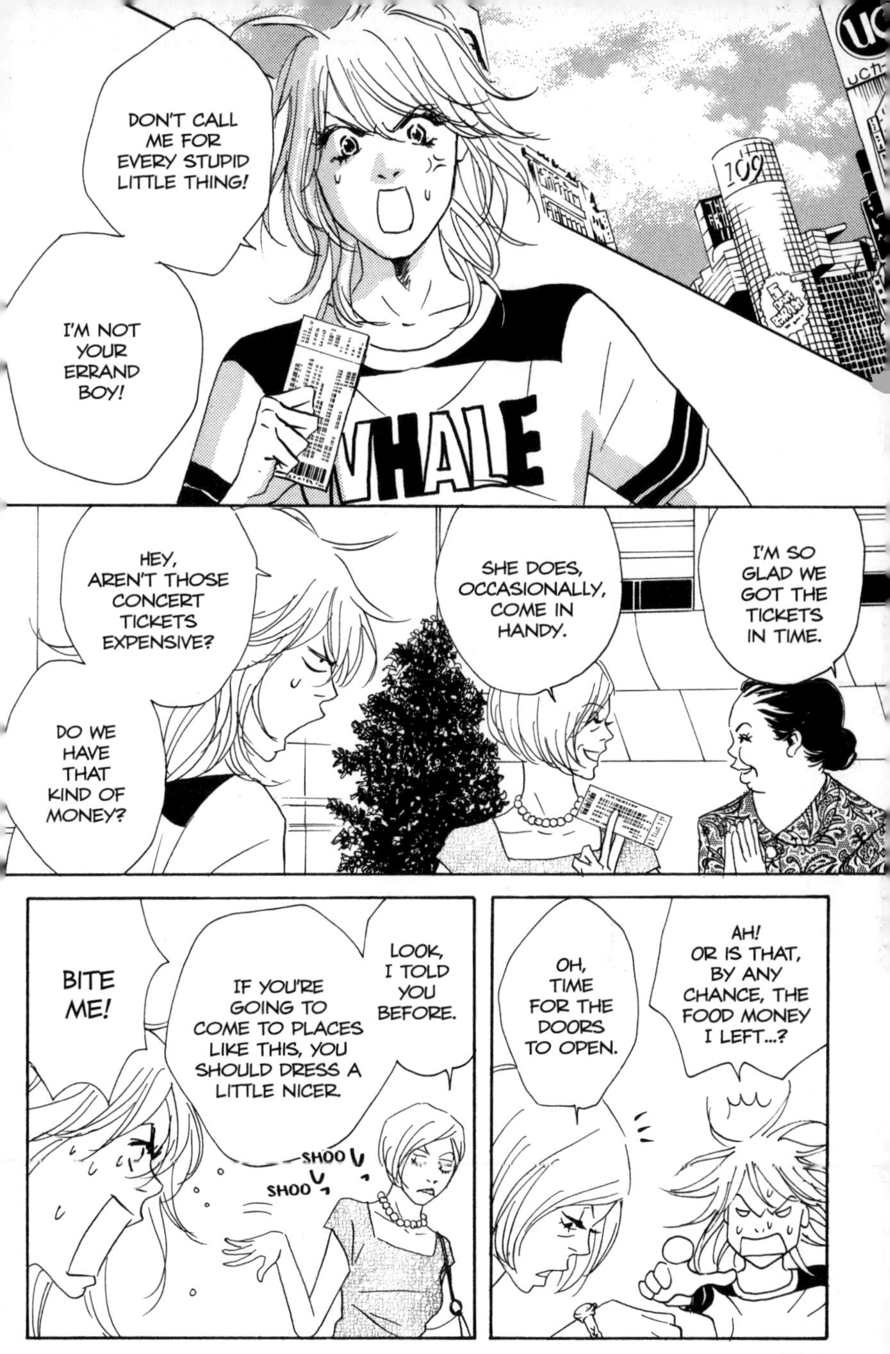

DON'T CALL ME FOR EVERY STUPID LITTLE THING!
I'M NOT YOUR ERRAND BOY!
I'M SO GLAD WE GOT THE TICKETS IN TIME.
SHE DOES, OCCASIONALLY, COME IN HANDY.
HEY, AREN'T THOSE CONCERT TICKETS EXPENSIVE?
DO WE HAVE THAT KIND OF MONEY?
AH! OR IS THAT, BY ANY CHANCE, THE FOOD MONEY I LEFT...?
OH, TIME FOR THE DOORS TO OPEN.
LOOK, I TOLD YOU BEFORE.
IF YOU'RE GOING TO COME TO PLACES LIKE THIS, YOU SHOULD DRESS A LITTLE NICER.
SHOO
SHOO
BITE ME!

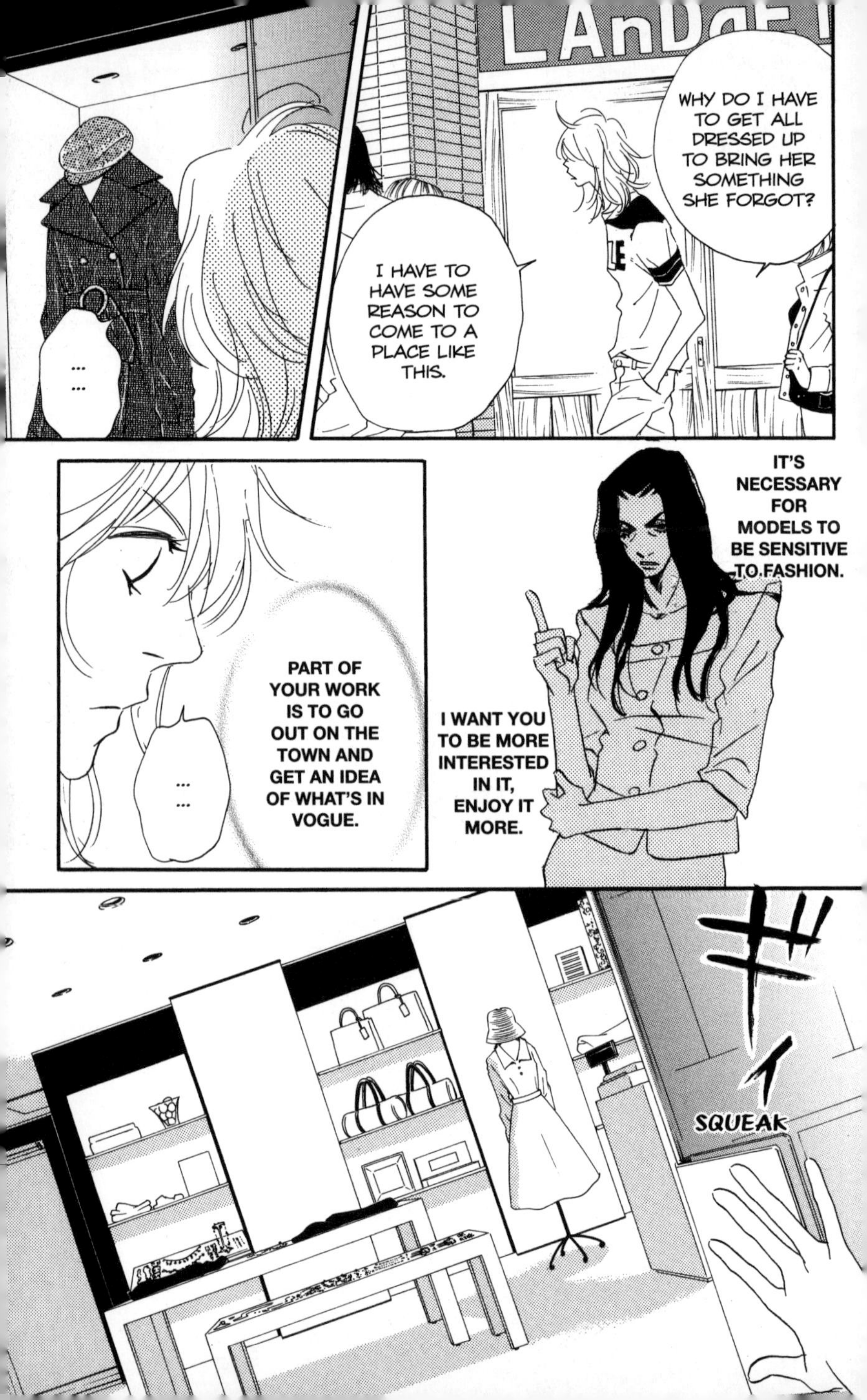
WHY DO I HAVE TO GET ALL DRESSED UP TO BRING HER SOMETHING SHE FORGOT?
I HAVE TO HAVE SOME REASON TO COME TO A PLACE LIKE THIS.
......
IT'S NECESSARY FOR MODELS TO BE SENSITIVE TO FASHION.
I WANT YOU TO BE MORE INTERESTED IN IT, ENJOY IT MORE.
PART OF YOUR WORK IS TO GO OUT ON THE TOWN AND GET AN IDEA OF WHAT'S IN VOGUE.
......
SQUEAK

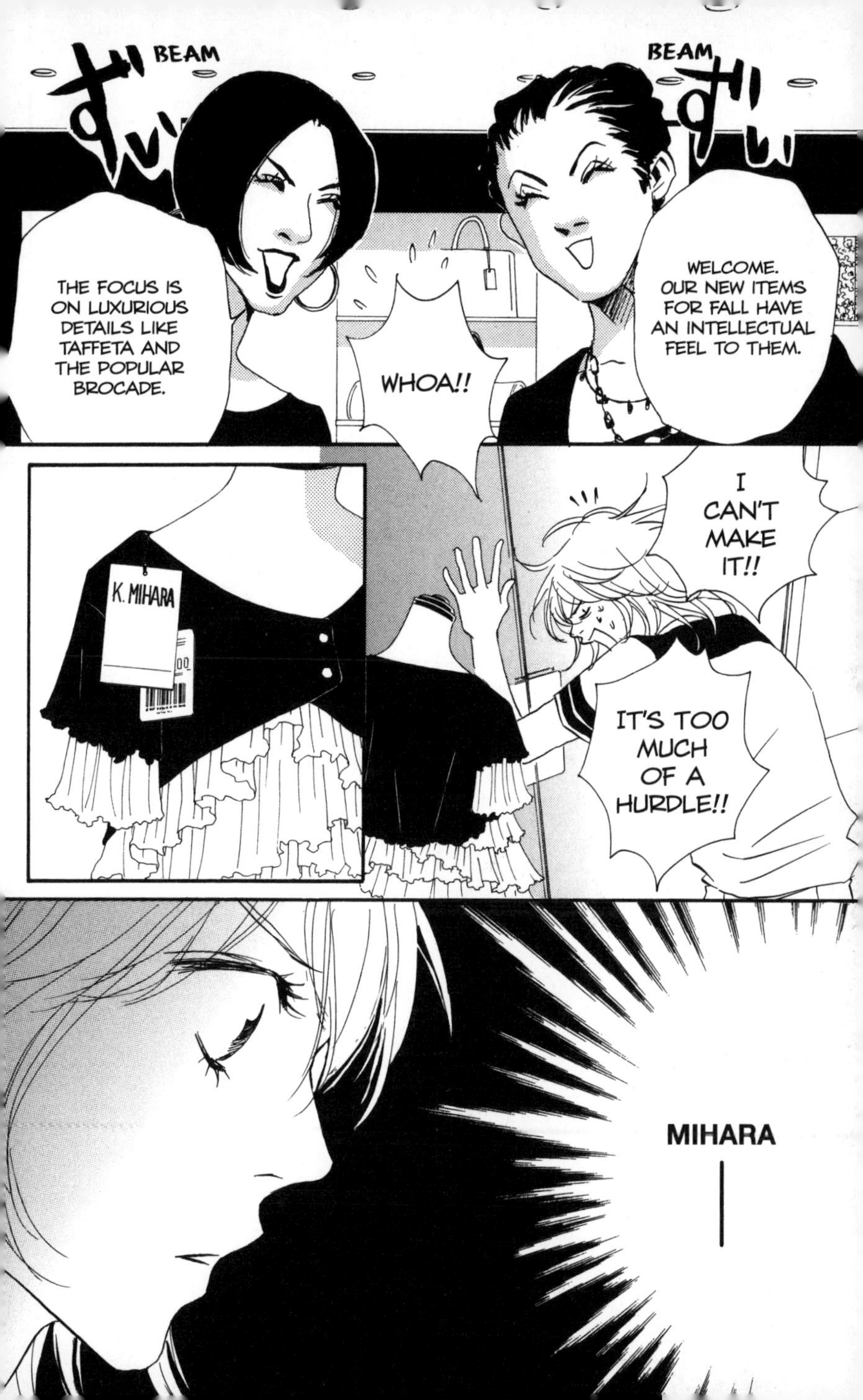
BEAM
WELCOME. OUR NEW ITEMS FOR FALL HAVE AN INTELLECTUAL FEEL TO THEM.
BEAM
THE FOCUS IS ON LUXURIOUS DETAILS LIKE TAFFETA AND THE POPULAR BROCADE.
WHOA!!
I CAN'T MAKE IT!!
IT'S TOO MUCH OF A HURDLE!!
K. MIHARA
MIHARA

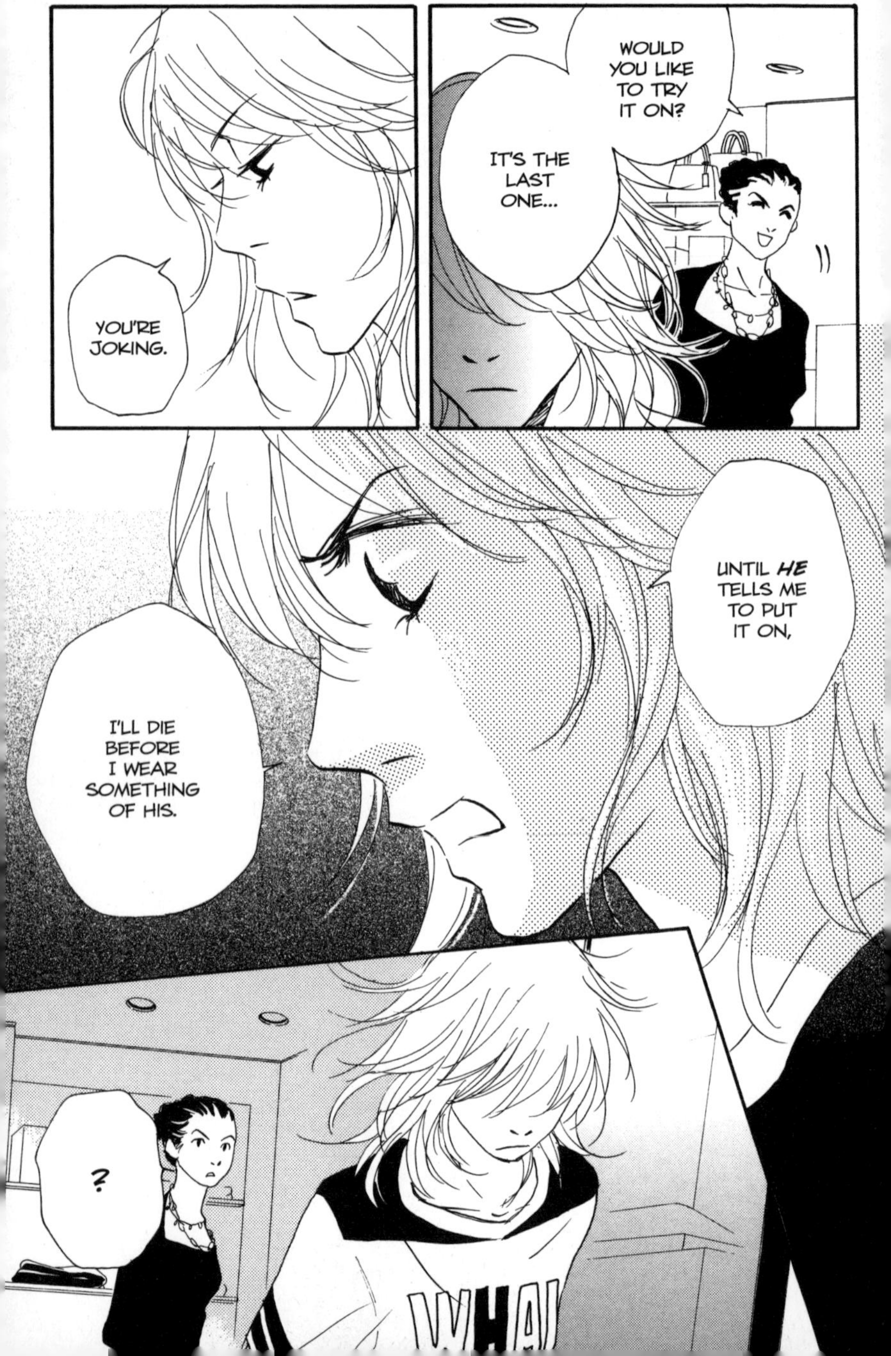
WOULD YOU LIKE TO TRY IT ON?
IT'S THE LAST ONE...
YOU'RE JOKING.
UNTIL *HE* TELLS ME TO PUT IT ON,
I'LL DIE BEFORE I WEAR SOMETHING OF HIS.
?

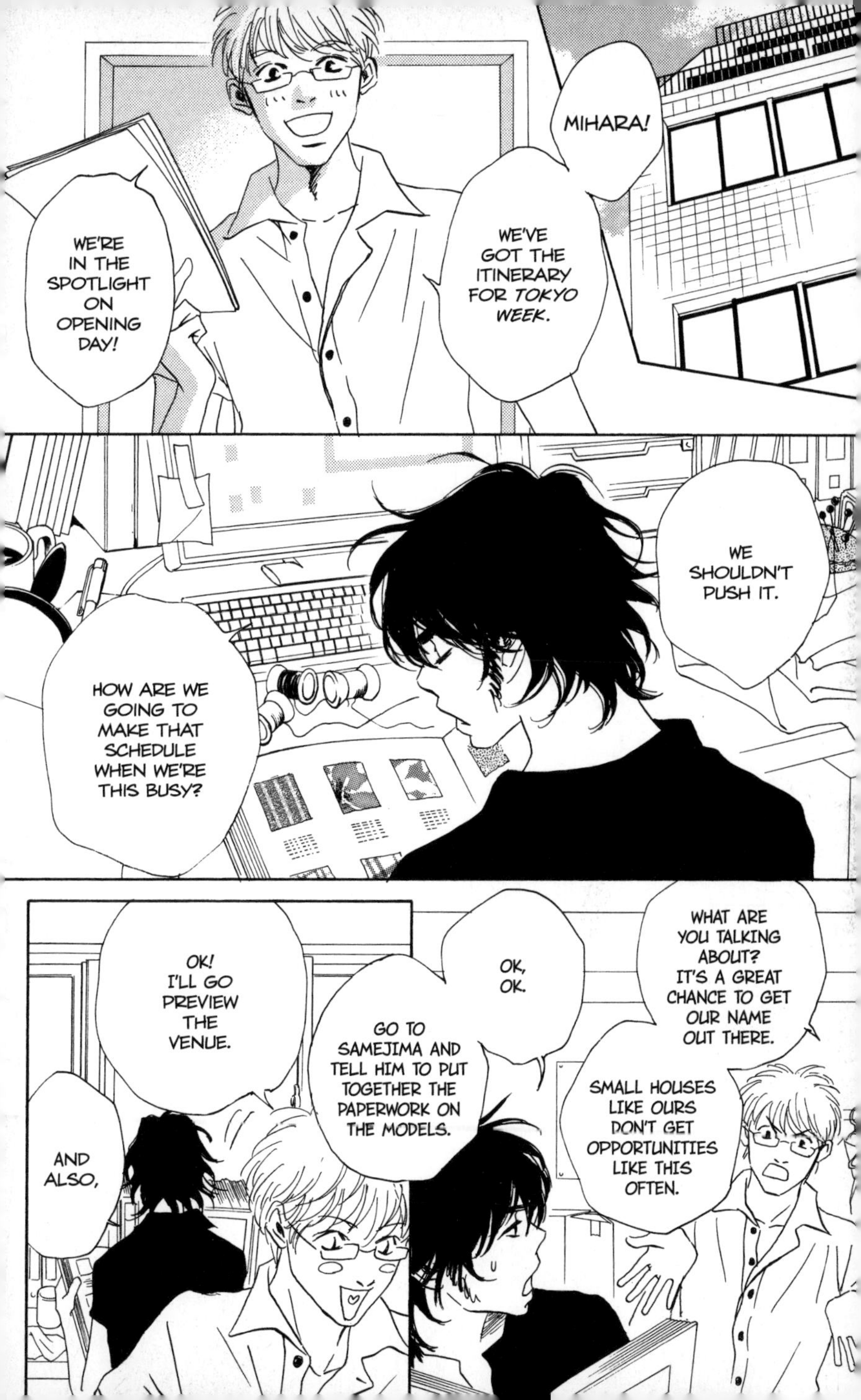
MIHARA!
WE'VE GOT THE ITINERARY FOR TOKYO WEEK.
WE'RE IN THE SPOTLIGHT ON OPENING DAY!
WE SHOULDN'T PUSH IT.
HOW ARE WE GOING TO MAKE THAT SCHEDULE WHEN WE'RE THIS BUSY?
WHAT ARE YOU TALKING ABOUT? IT'S A GREAT CHANCE TO GET OUR NAME OUT THERE.
SMALL HOUSES LIKE OURS DON'T GET OPPORTUNITIES LIKE THIS OFTEN.
OK, OK.
GO TO SAMEJIMA AND TELL HIM TO PUT TOGETHER THE PAPERWORK ON THE MODELS.
OK! I'LL GO PREVIEW THE VENUE.
AND ALSO,

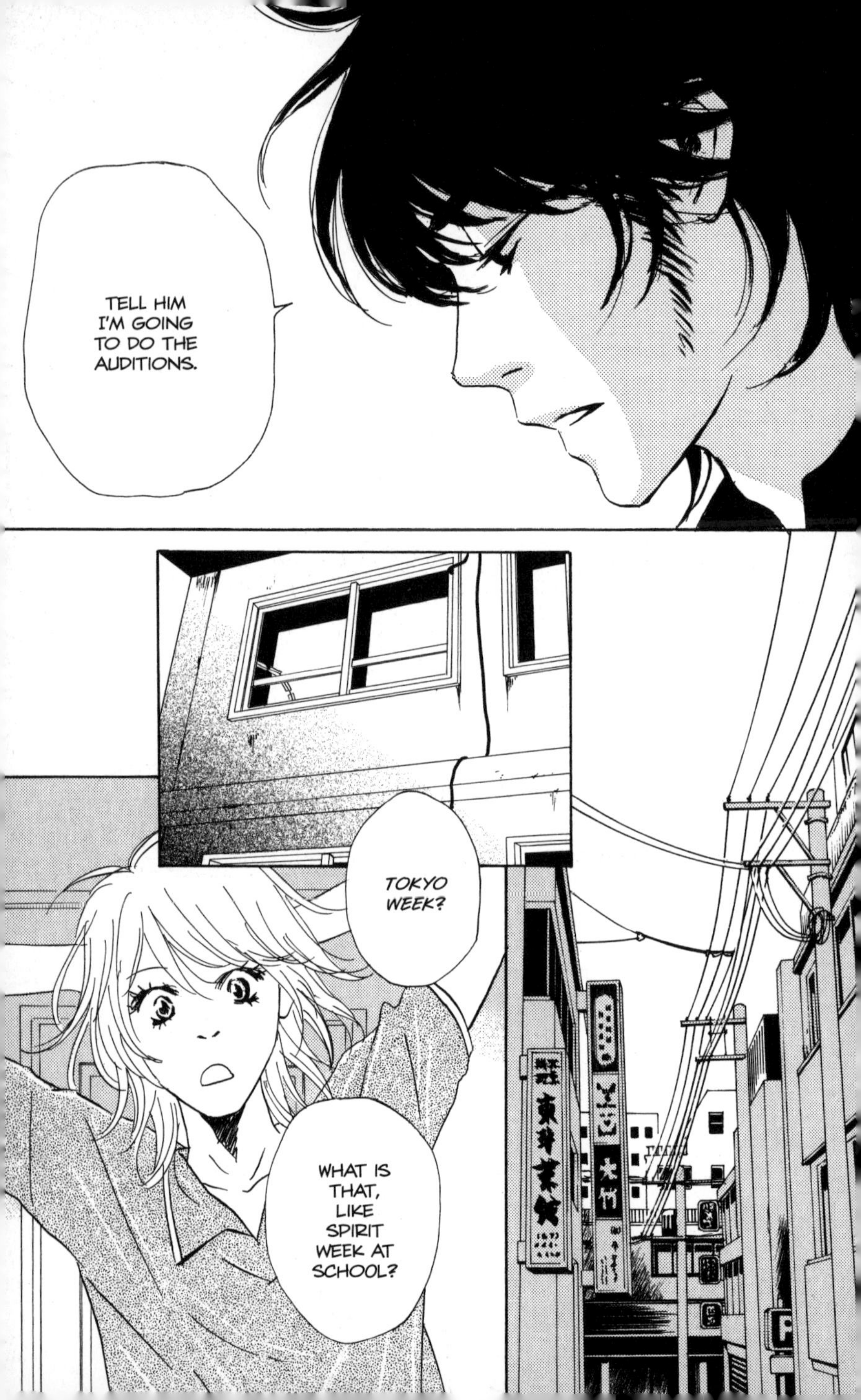
TELL HIM I'M GOING TO DO THE AUDITIONS.
TOKYO WEEK?
WHAT IS THAT, LIKE SPIRIT WEEK AT SCHOOL?

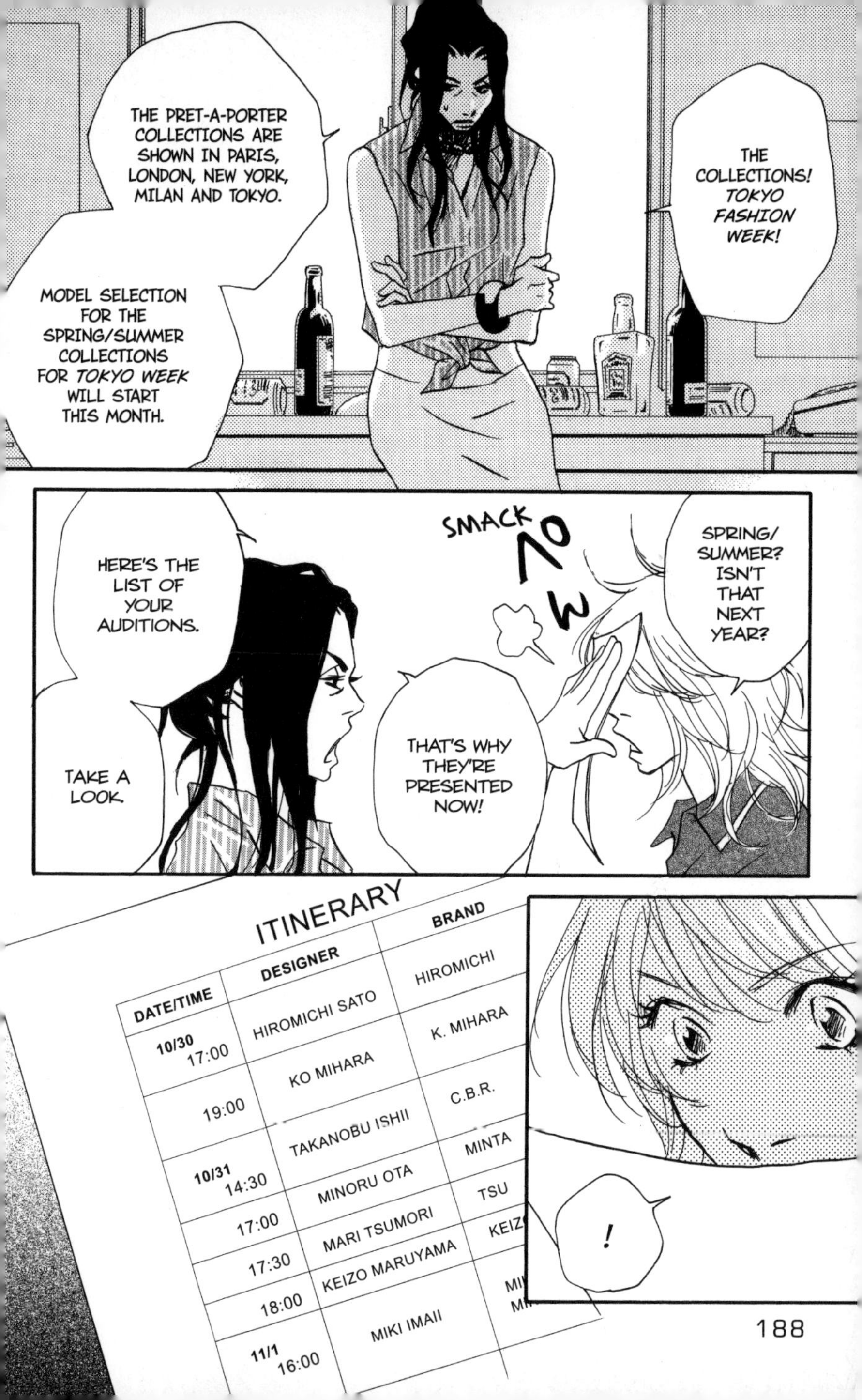
THE COLLECTIONS! *TOKYO FASHION WEEK!*
THE PRET-A-PORTER COLLECTIONS ARE SHOWN IN PARIS, LONDON, NEW YORK, MILAN AND TOKYO.
MODEL SELECTION FOR THE SPRING/SUMMER COLLECTIONS FOR *TOKYO WEEK* WILL START THIS MONTH.
SPRING/ SUMMER? ISN'T THAT NEXT YEAR?
SMACK
THAT'S WHY THEY'RE PRESENTED NOW!
HERE'S THE LIST OF YOUR AUDITIONS.
TAKE A LOOK.
!
ITINERARY

DATE/TIME	DESIGNER	BRAND
10/30 17:00	HIROMICHI SATO	HIROMICHI
19:00	KO MIHARA	K. MIHARA
	TAKANOBU ISHII	C.B.R.
10/31 14:30	MINORU OTA	MINTA
17:00	MARI TSUMORI	TSU
17:30	KEIZO MARUYAMA	KEIZ
18:00	MIKI IMAII	MI MI
11/1 16:00		

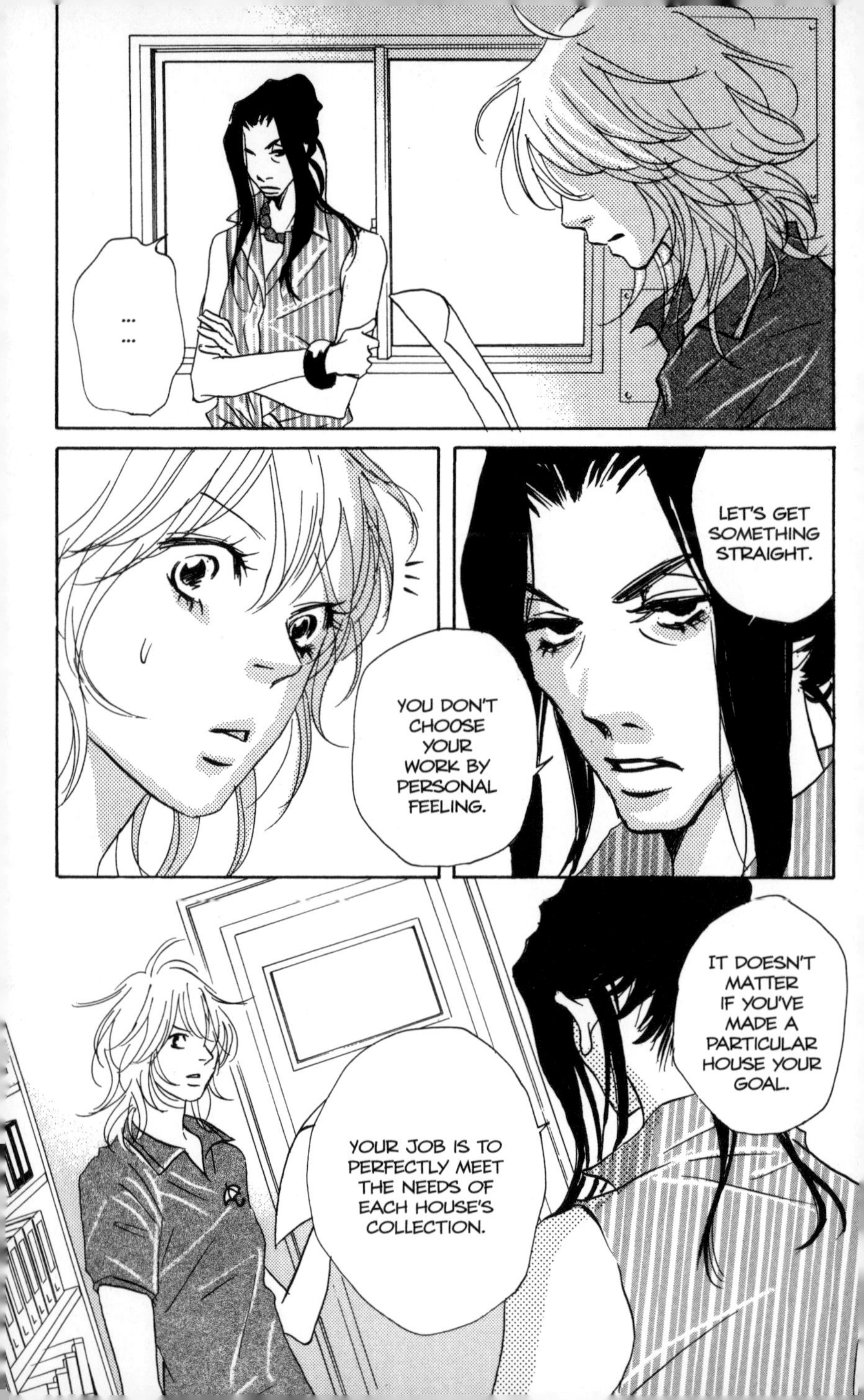

......
LET'S GET SOMETHING STRAIGHT.
YOU DON'T CHOOSE YOUR WORK BY PERSONAL FEELING.
IT DOESN'T MATTER IF YOU'VE MADE A PARTICULAR HOUSE YOUR GOAL.
YOUR JOB IS TO PERFECTLY MEET THE NEEDS OF EACH HOUSE'S COLLECTION.

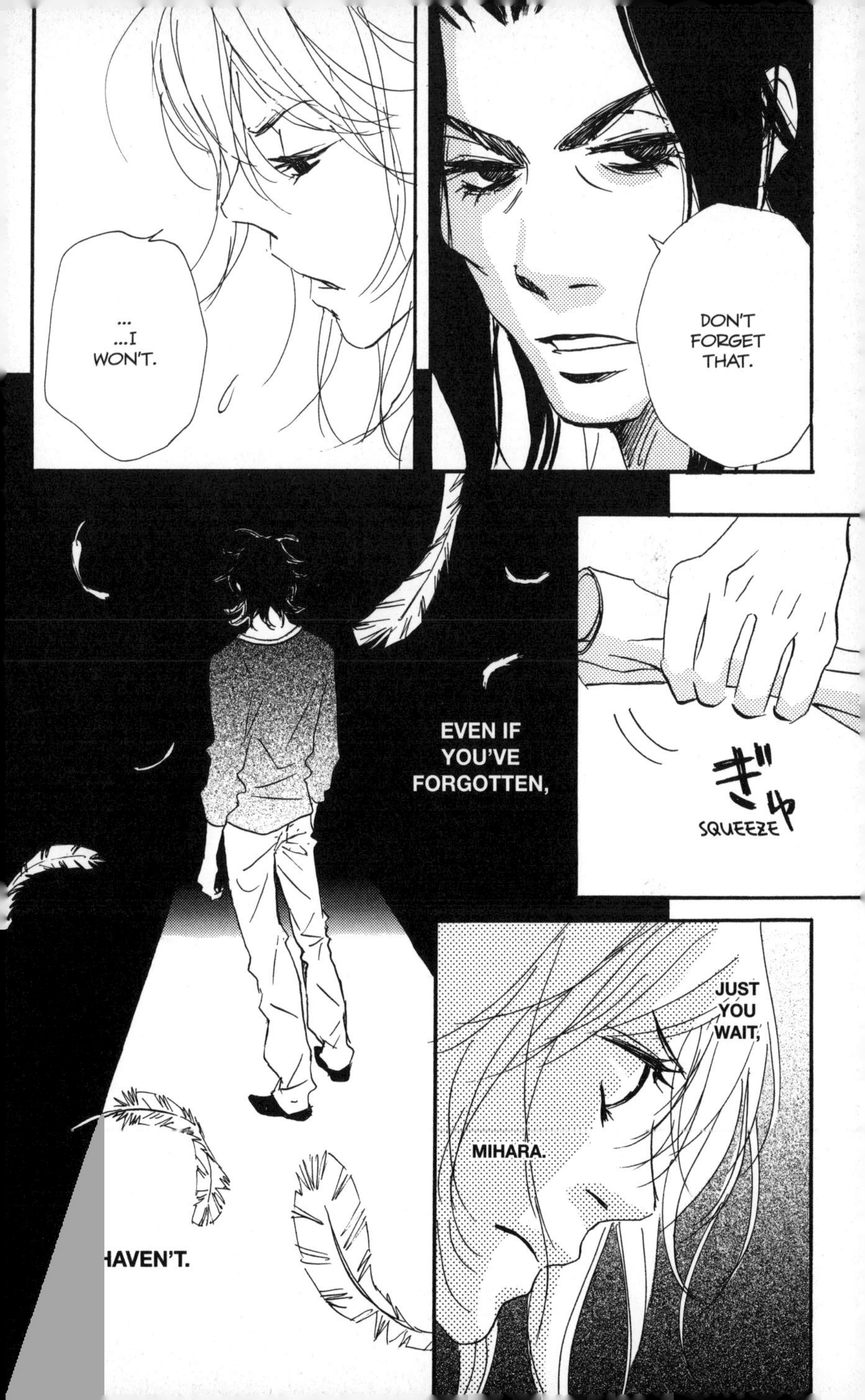
DON'T FORGET THAT.
...
...I WON'T.
ぎゅ
SQUEEZE
JUST YOU WAIT,
MIHARA.
EVEN IF YOU'VE FORGOTTEN,
HAVEN'T.

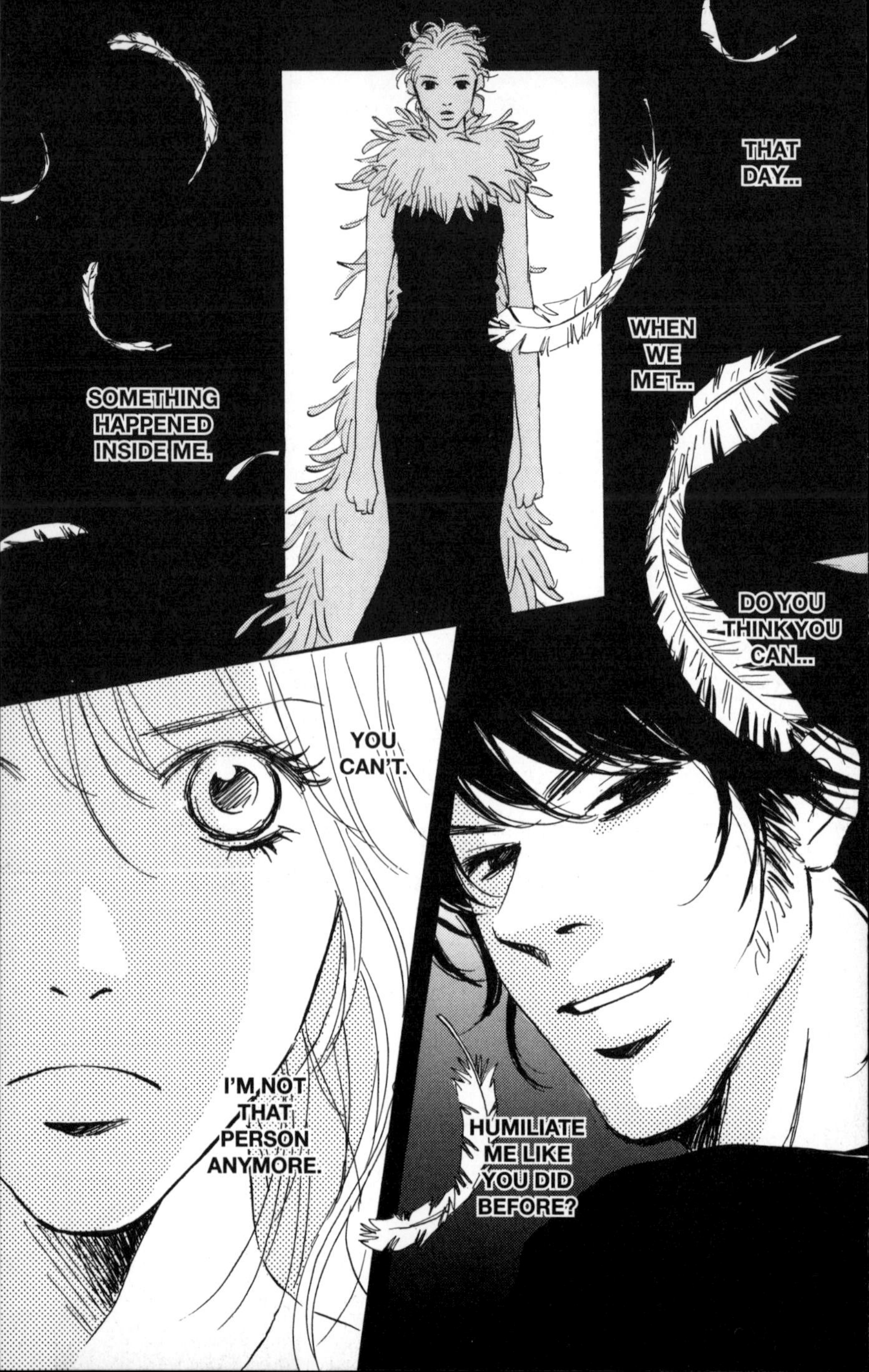
THAT DAY...
WHEN WE MET...
SOMETHING HAPPENED INSIDE ME.
DO YOU THINK YOU CAN...
HUMILIATE ME LIKE YOU DID BEFORE?
YOU CAN'T.
I'M NOT THAT PERSON ANYMORE.

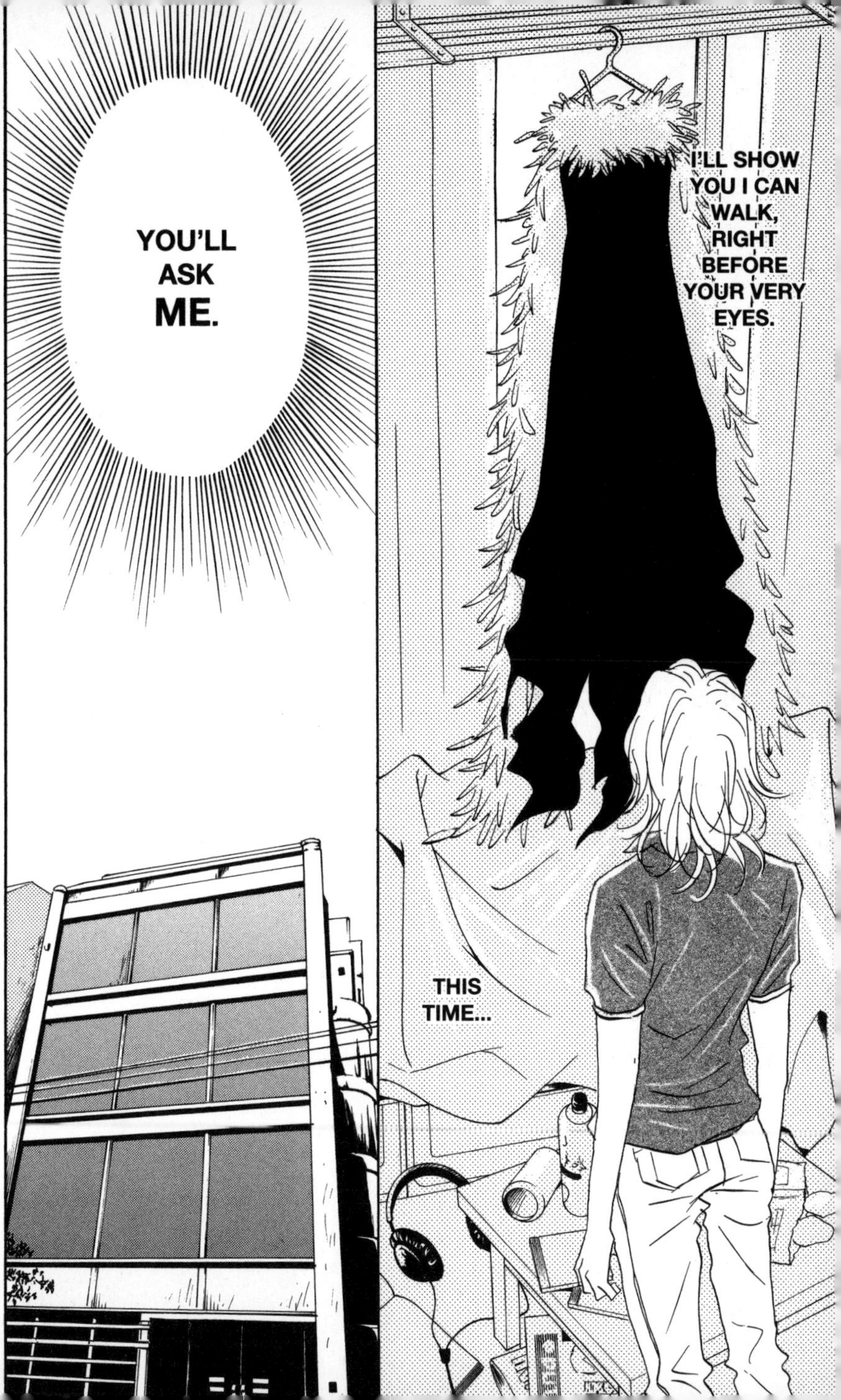
I'LL SHOW YOU I CAN WALK, RIGHT BEFORE YOUR VERY EYES.
THIS TIME...
YOU'LL ASK ME.

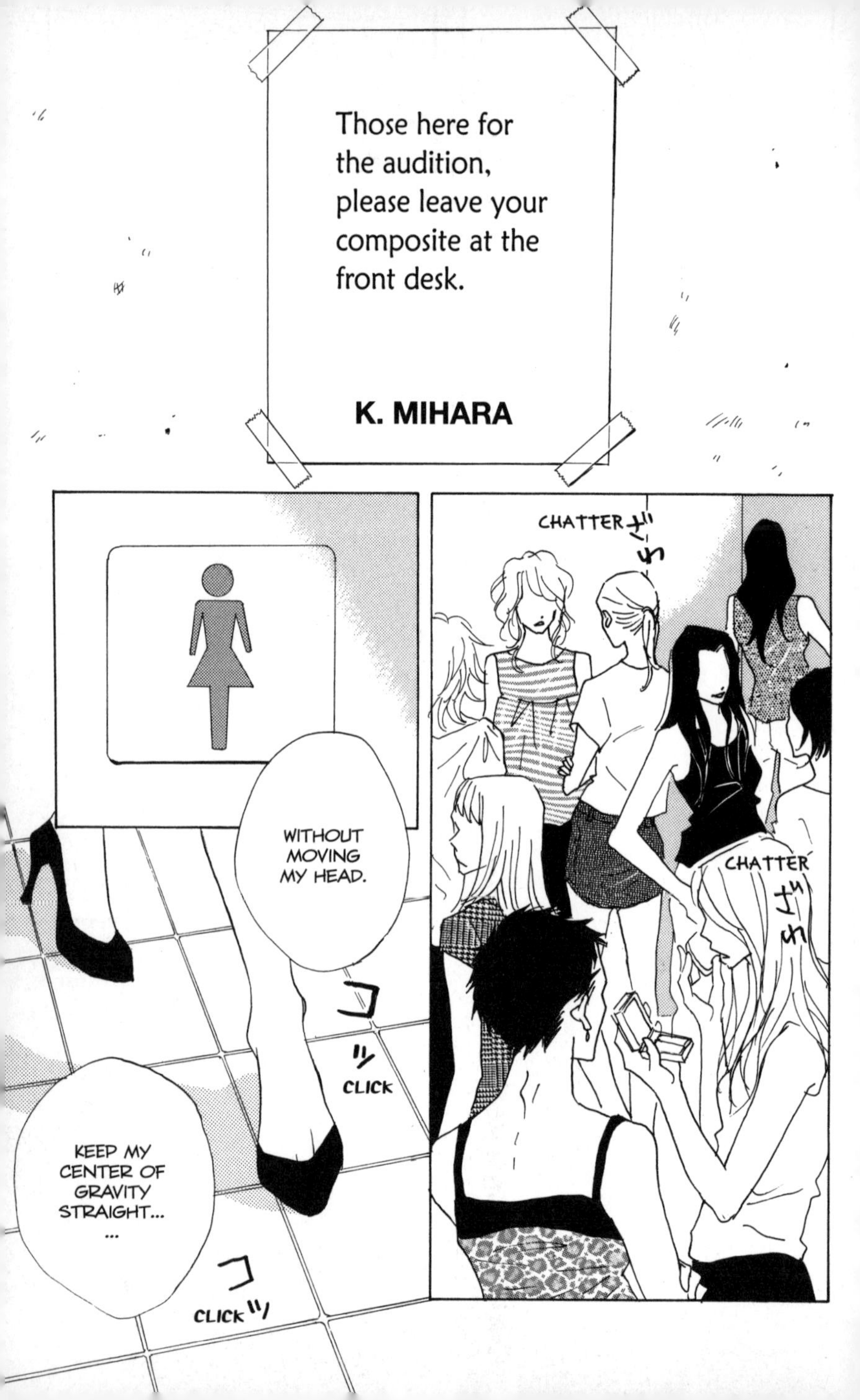
Those here for the audition, please leave your composite at the front desk.
K. MIHARA
CHATTER ざわ
CHATTER ざわ
WITHOUT MOVING MY HEAD.
コツ CLICK
KEEP MY CENTER OF GRAVITY STRAIGHT... ...
コツ CLICK

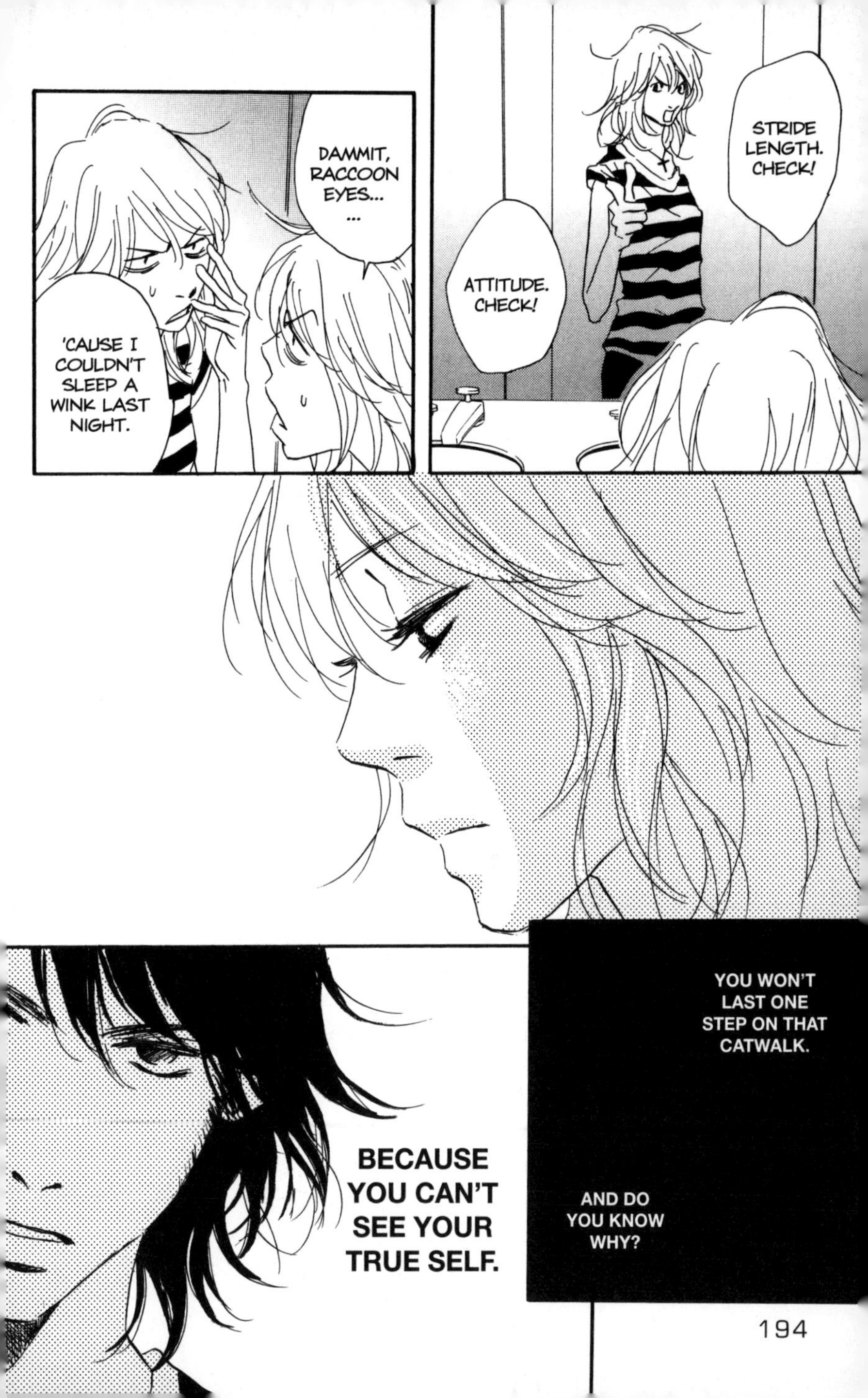
STRIDE LENGTH. CHECK!
ATTITUDE. CHECK!
DAMMIT, RACCOON EYES... ...
'CAUSE I COULDN'T SLEEP A WINK LAST NIGHT.
YOU WON'T LAST ONE STEP ON THAT CATWALK.
AND DO YOU KNOW WHY?
BECAUSE YOU CAN'T SEE YOUR TRUE SELF.

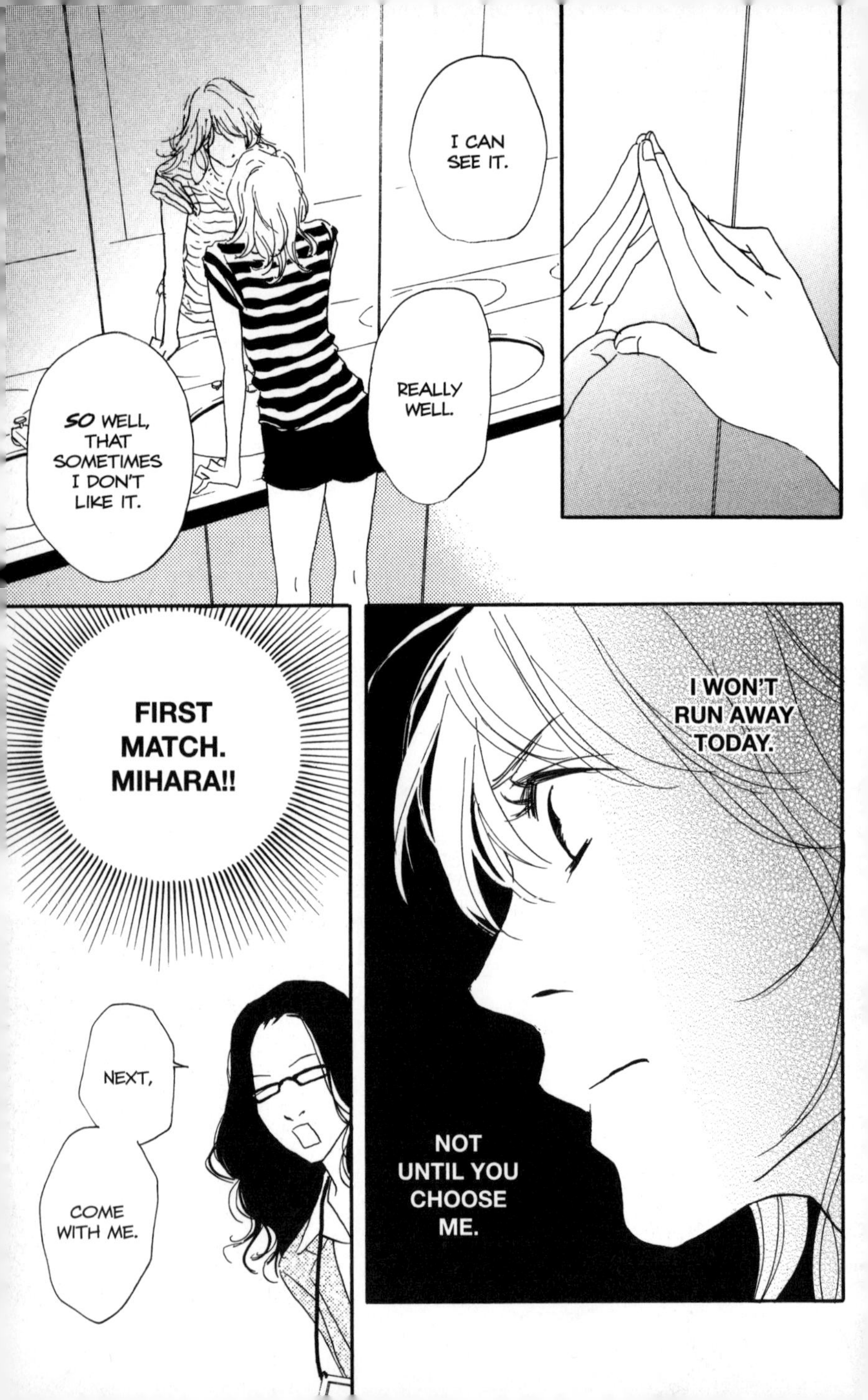
I CAN SEE IT.
REALLY WELL.
SO WELL, THAT SOMETIMES I DON'T LIKE IT.
I WON'T RUN AWAY TODAY.
NOT UNTIL YOU CHOOSE ME.
FIRST MATCH. MIHARA!!
NEXT,
COME WITH ME.

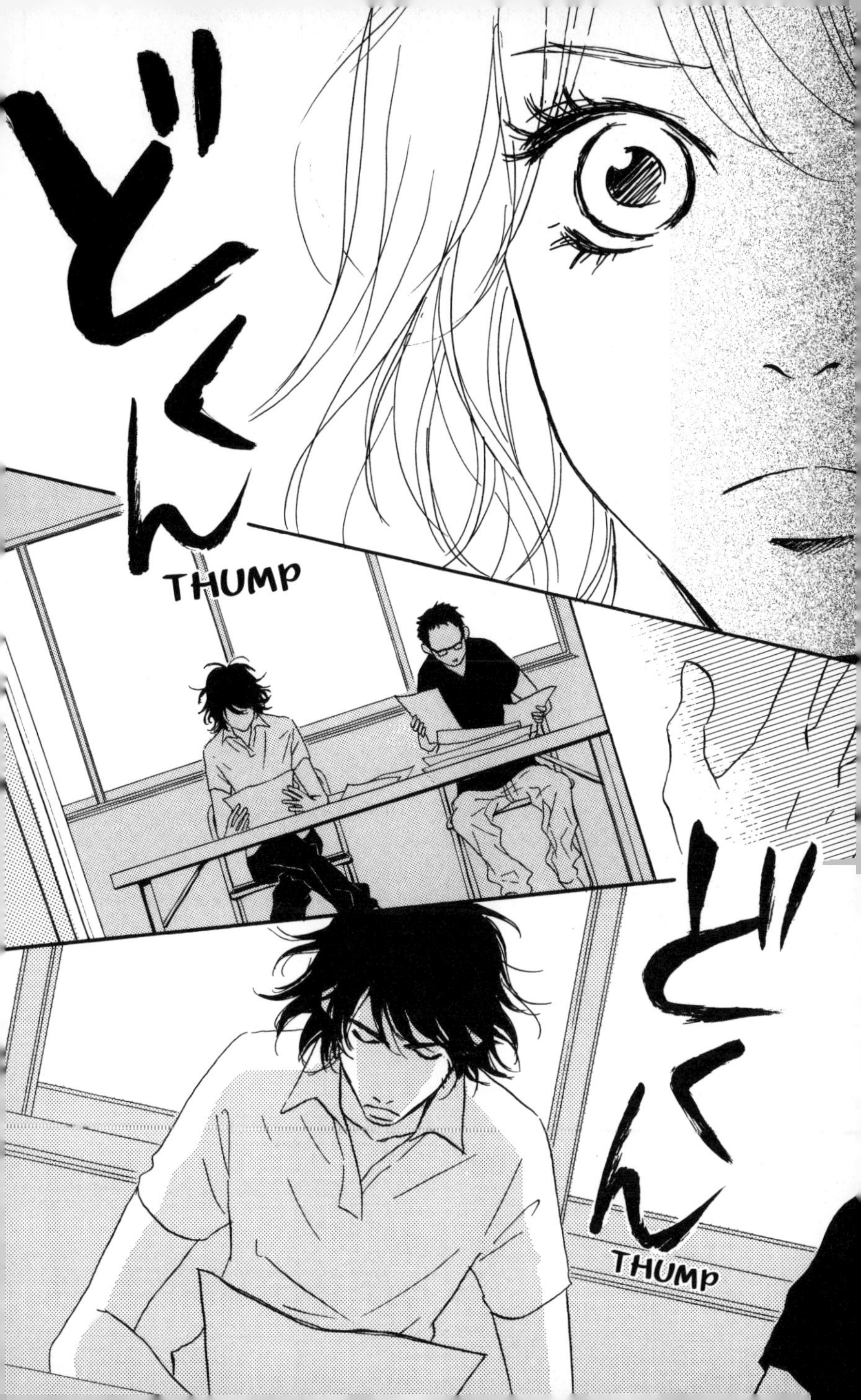
どくん
THUMP
どくん
THUMP

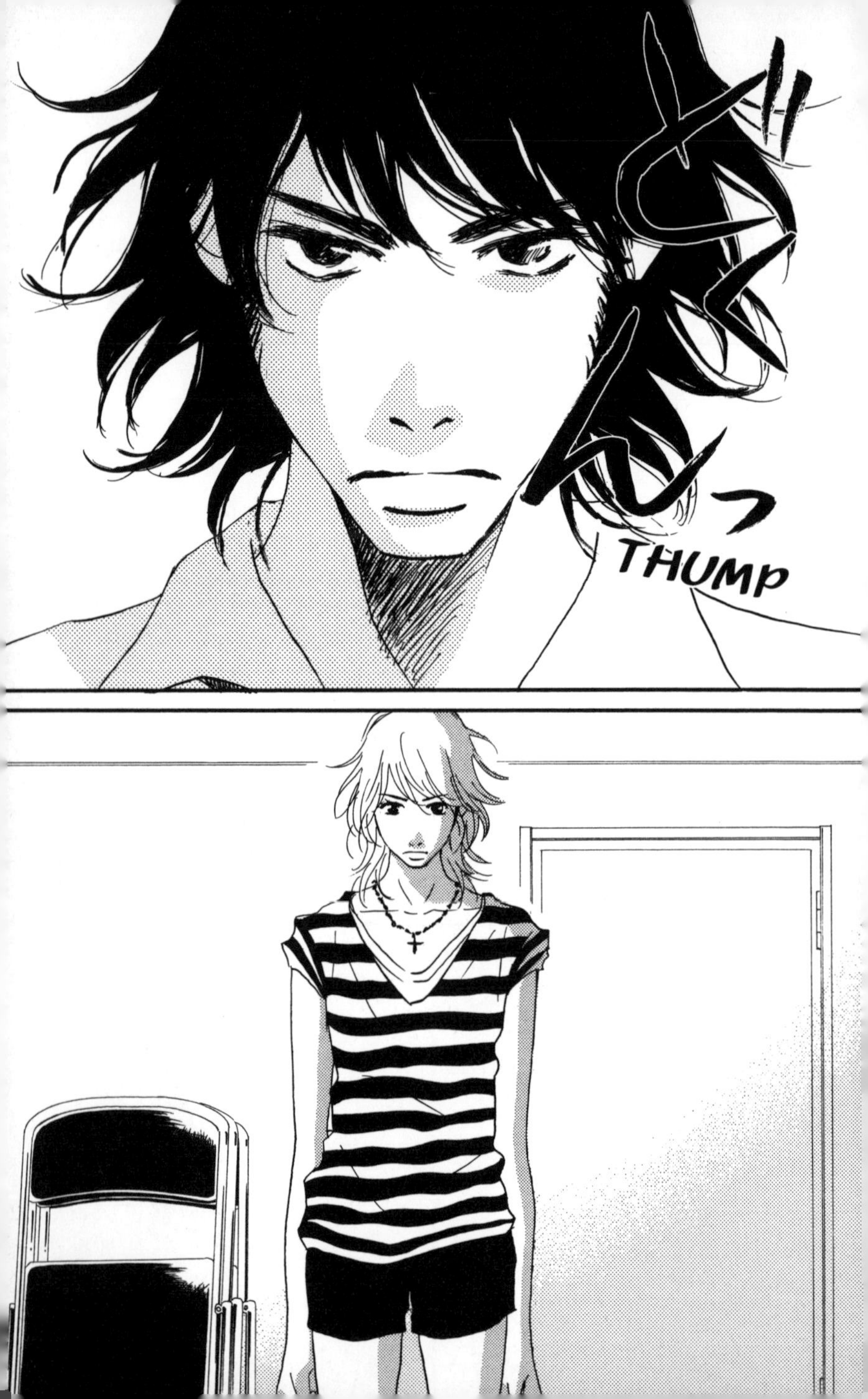
どんっ
THUMP

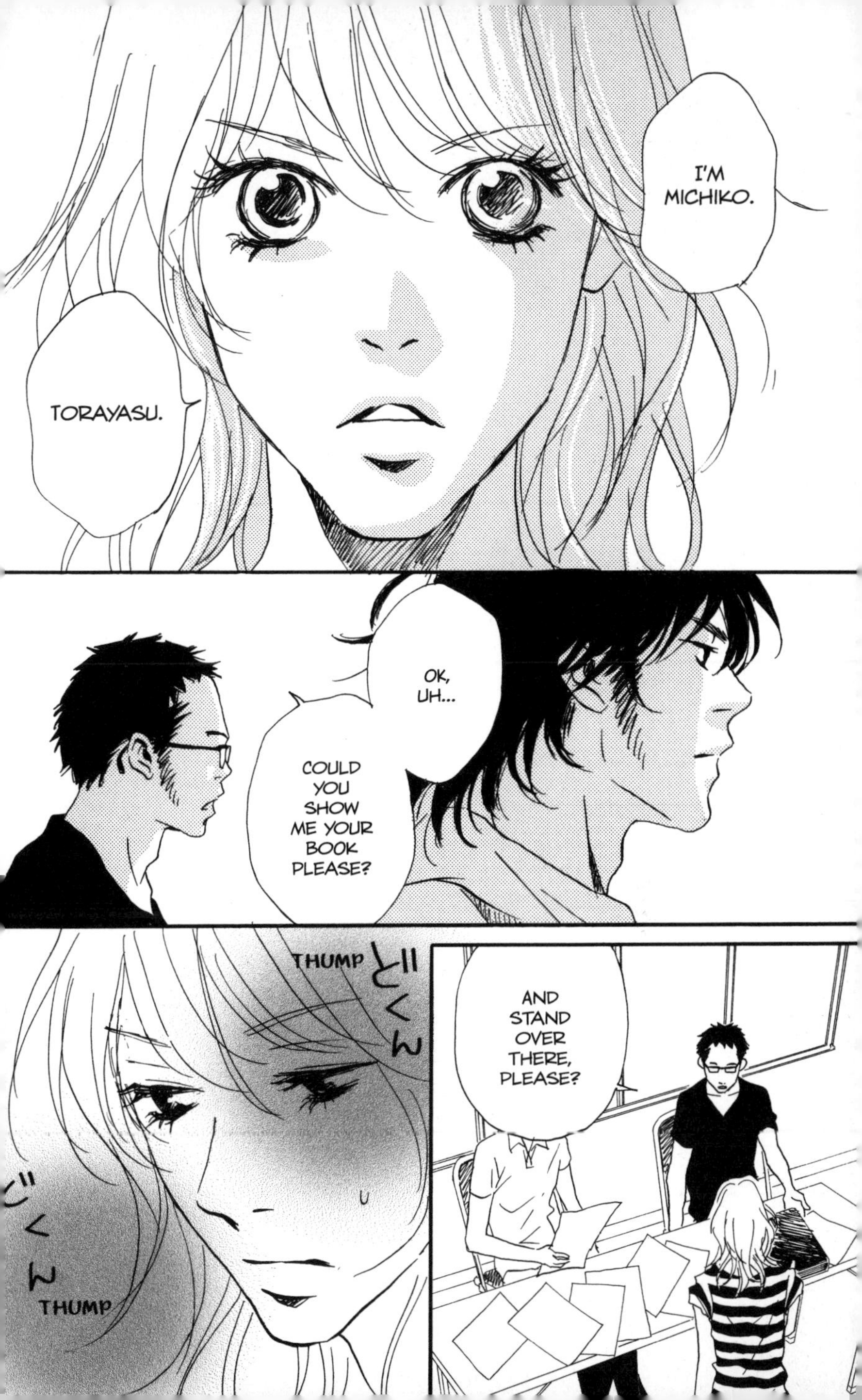
I'M MICHIKO.
TORAYASU.
OK, UH...
COULD YOU SHOW ME YOUR BOOK PLEASE?
AND STAND OVER THERE, PLEASE?
THUMP
THUMP

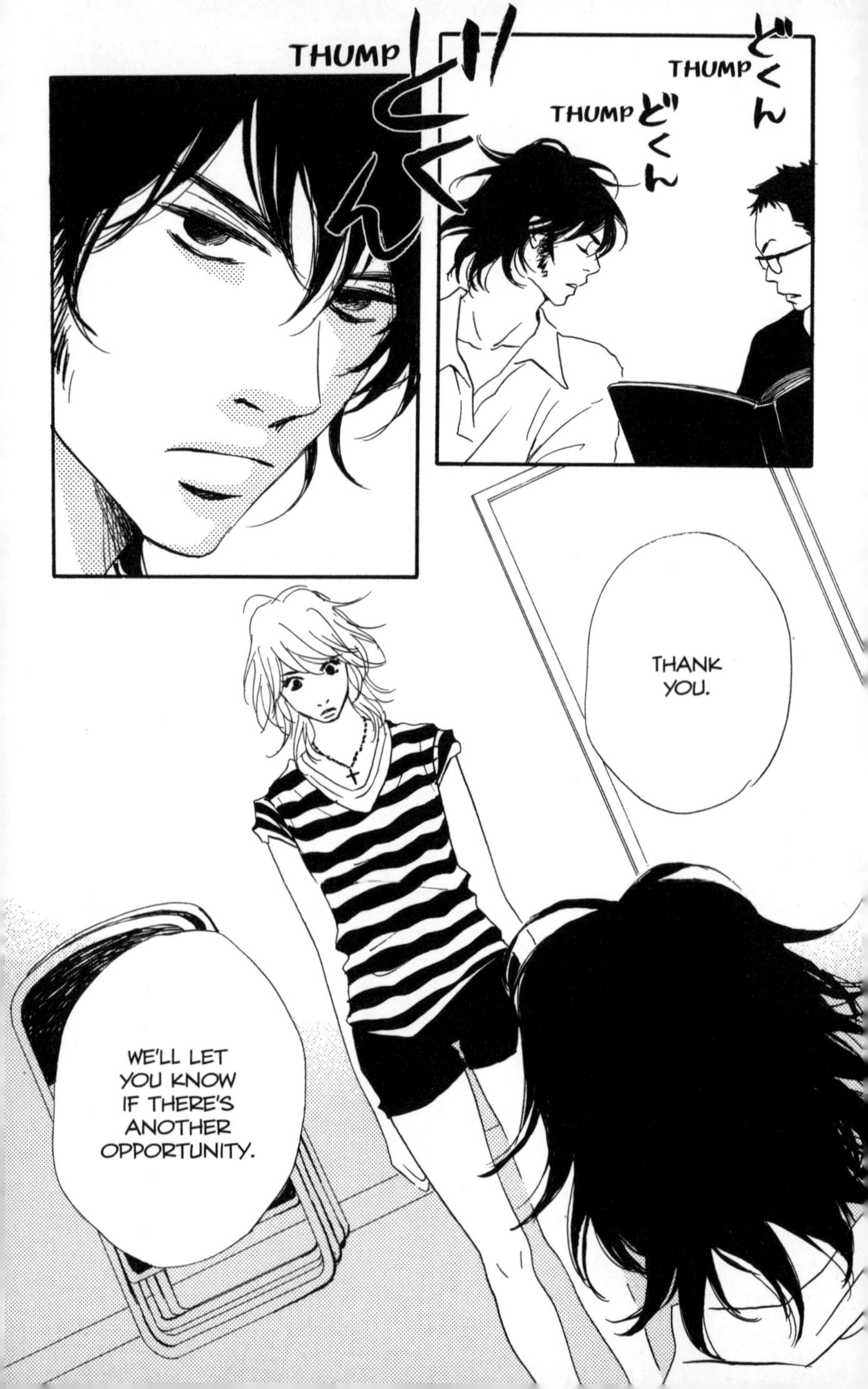
THUMP どくん
THUMP どくん
THUMP どくん
THANK YOU.
WE'LL LET YOU KNOW IF THERE'S ANOTHER OPPORTUNITY.

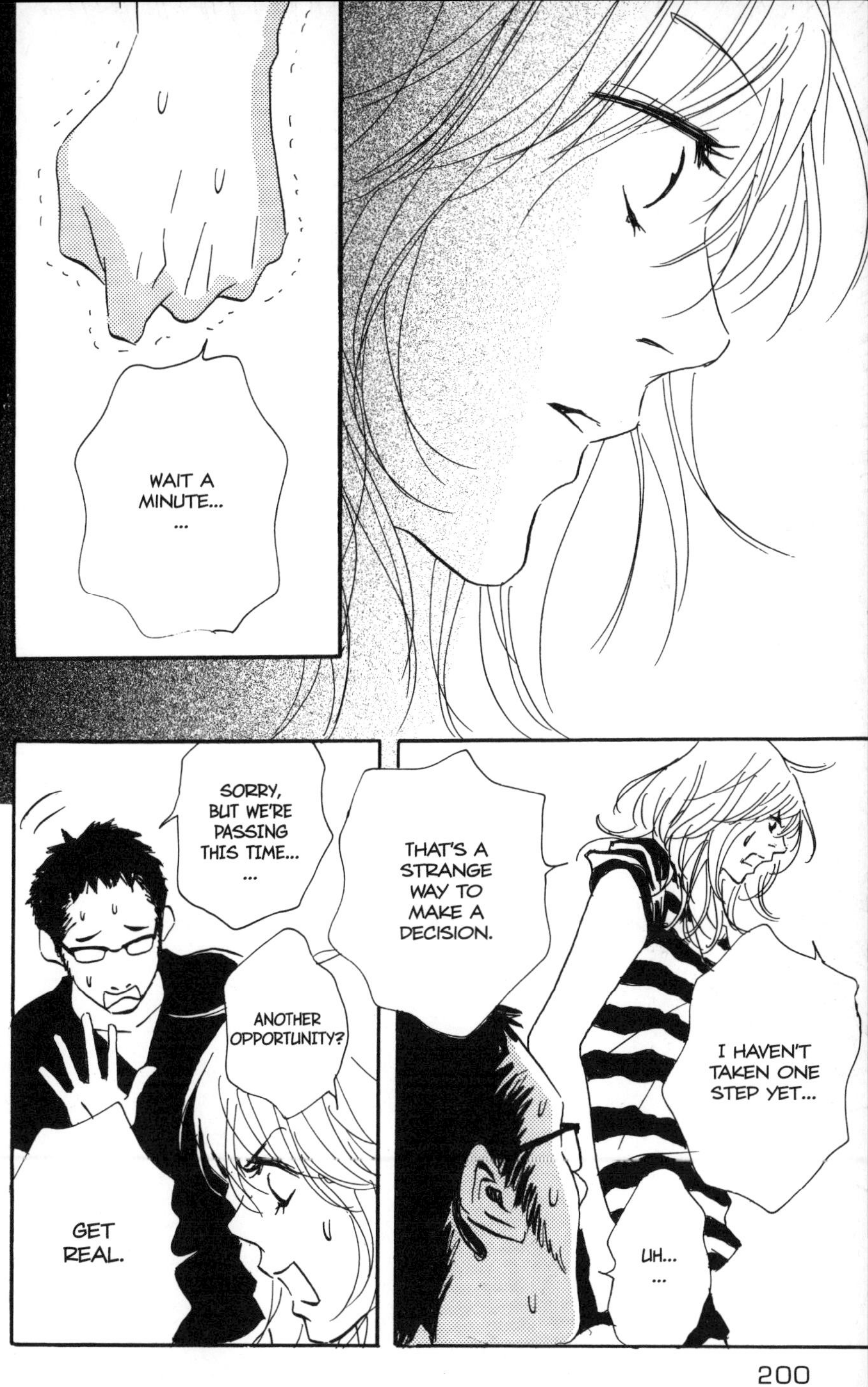
WAIT A MINUTE... ...
THAT'S A STRANGE WAY TO MAKE A DECISION.
I HAVEN'T TAKEN ONE STEP YET...
UH... ...
SORRY, BUT WE'RE PASSING THIS TIME... ...
ANOTHER OPPORTUNITY?
GET REAL.

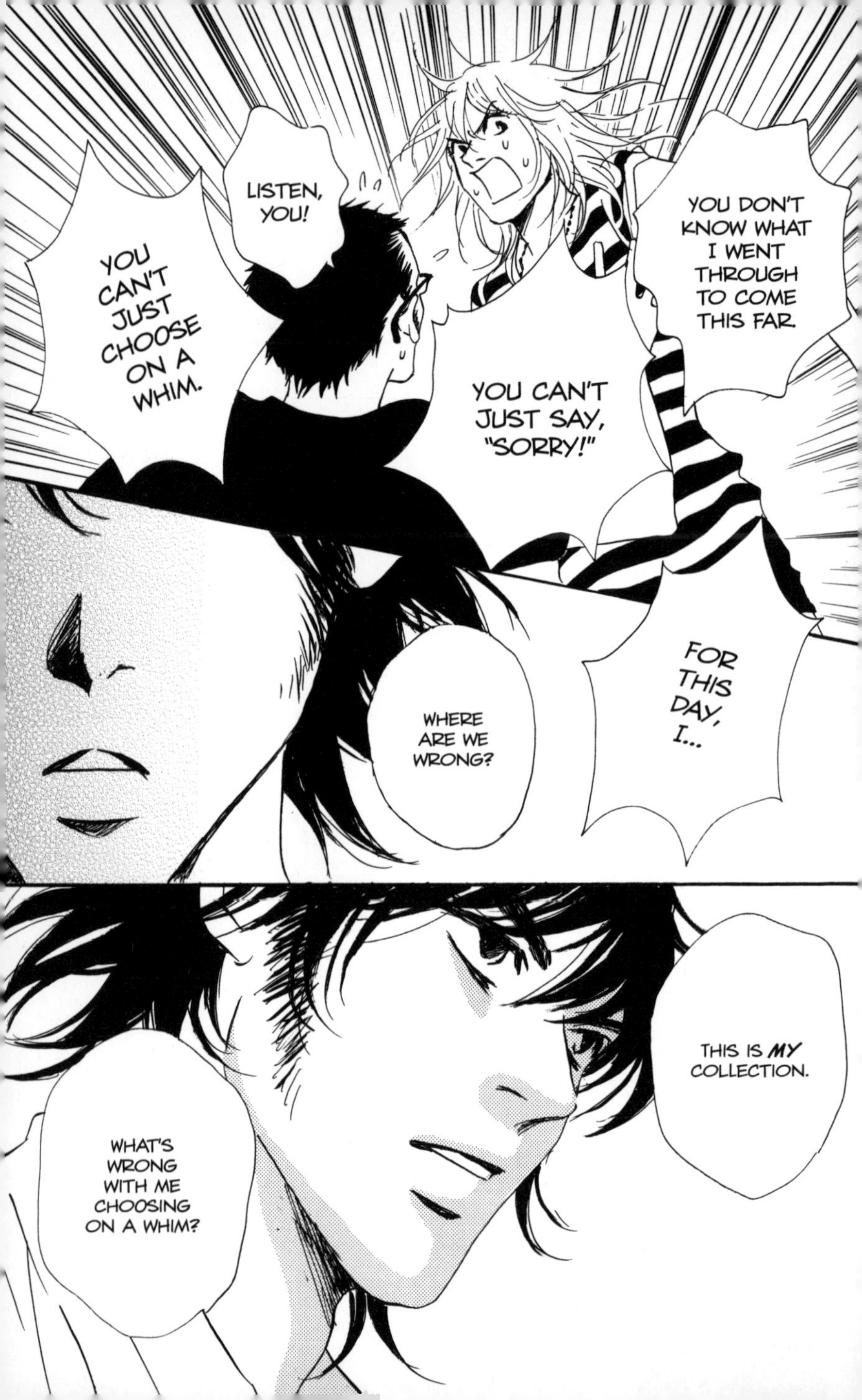
YOU DON'T KNOW WHAT I WENT THROUGH TO COME THIS FAR.
LISTEN, YOU!
YOU CAN'T JUST CHOOSE ON A WHIM.
YOU CAN'T JUST SAY, "SORRY!"
FOR THIS DAY, I...
WHERE ARE WE WRONG?
THIS IS *MY* COLLECTION.
WHAT'S WRONG WITH ME CHOOSING ON A WHIM?

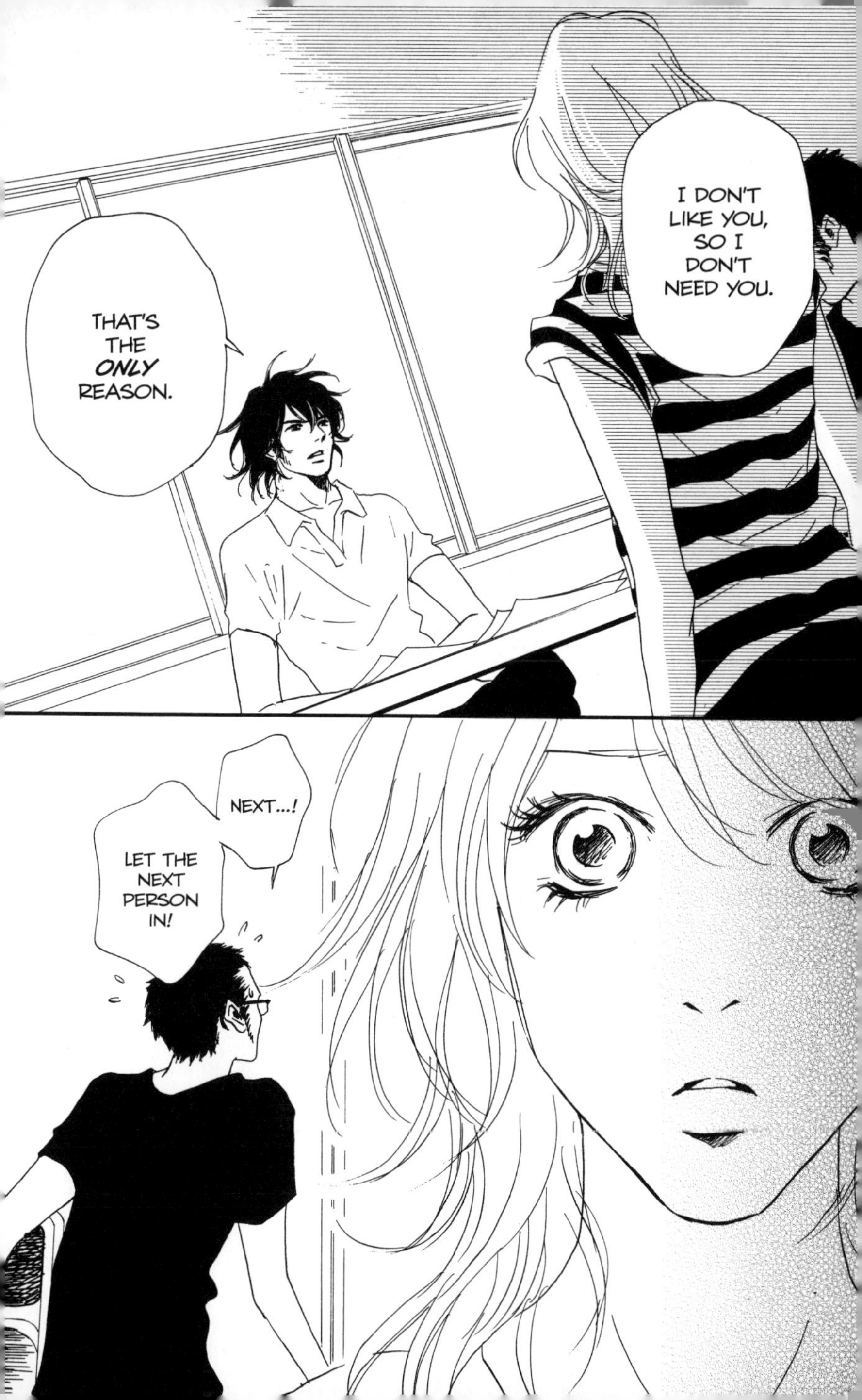
I DON'T LIKE YOU, SO I DON'T NEED YOU.
THAT'S THE ONLY REASON.
NEXT...!
LET THE NEXT PERSON IN!

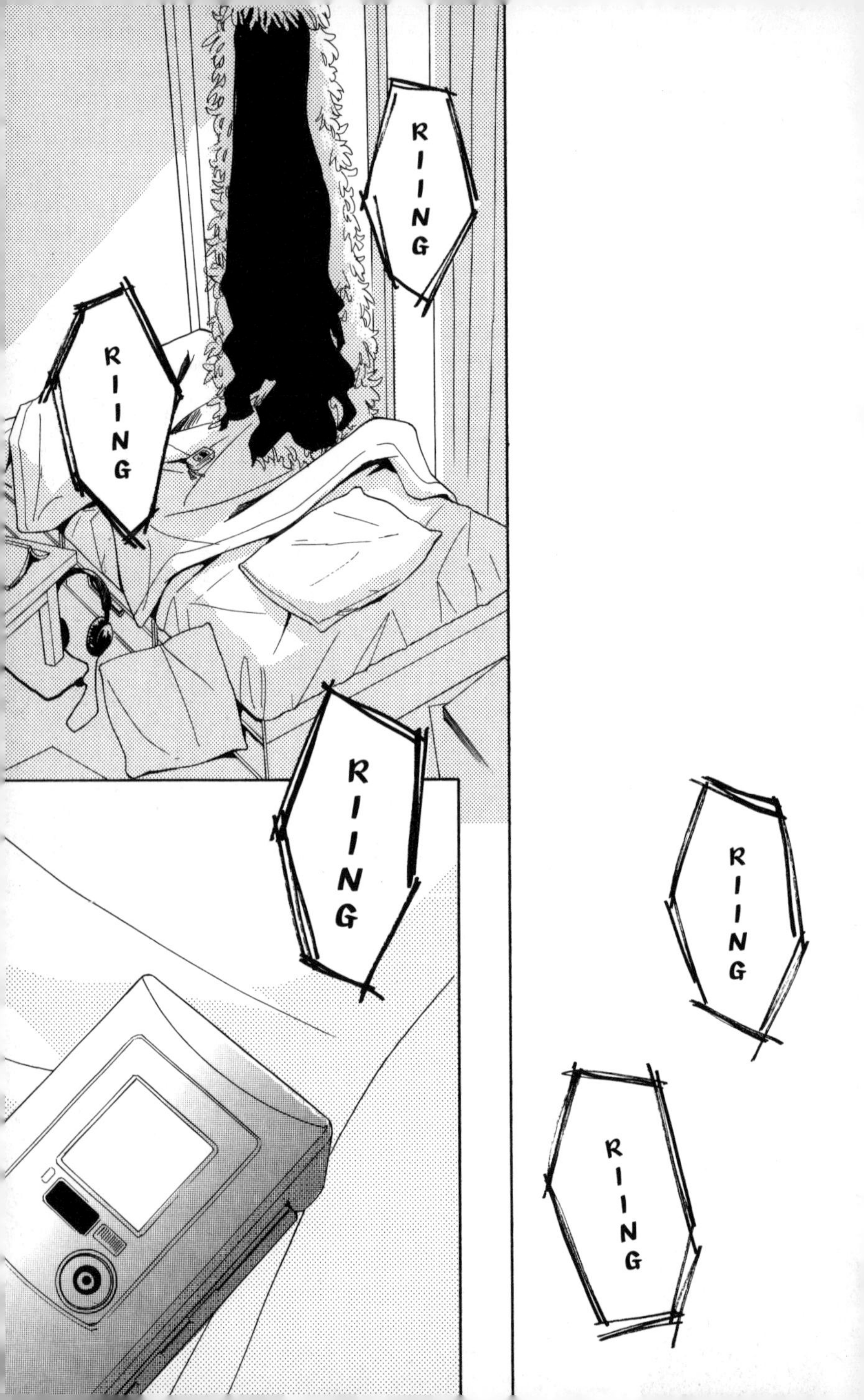
RIIING
RIIING
RIIING
RIIING
RIIING

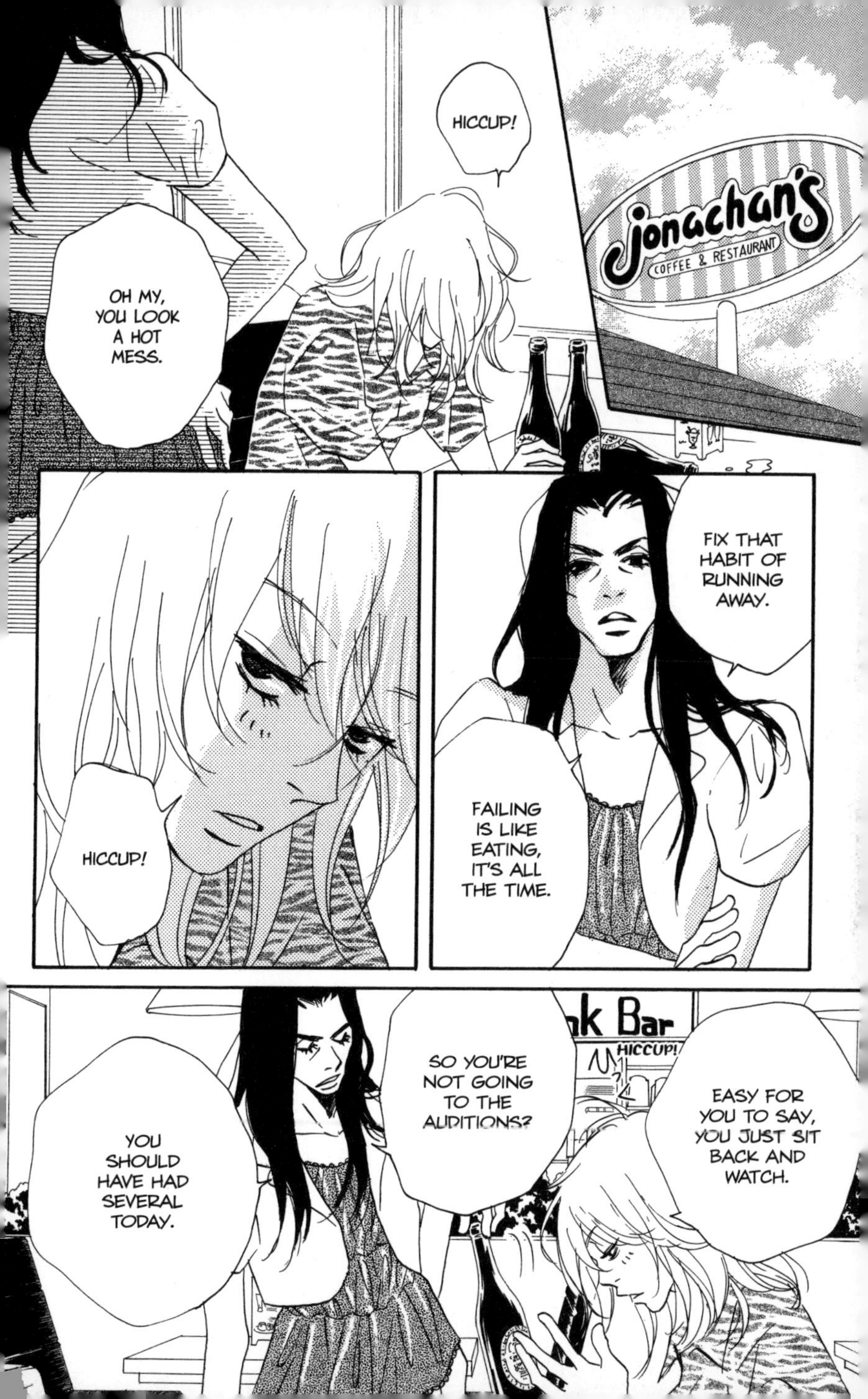
jonachan's
COFFEE & RESTAURANT
HICCUP!
OH MY, YOU LOOK A HOT MESS.
FIX THAT HABIT OF RUNNING AWAY.
FAILING IS LIKE EATING, IT'S ALL THE TIME.
HICCUP!
HICCUP!
EASY FOR YOU TO SAY, YOU JUST SIT BACK AND WATCH.
SO YOU'RE NOT GOING TO THE AUDITIONS?
YOU SHOULD HAVE HAD SEVERAL TODAY.

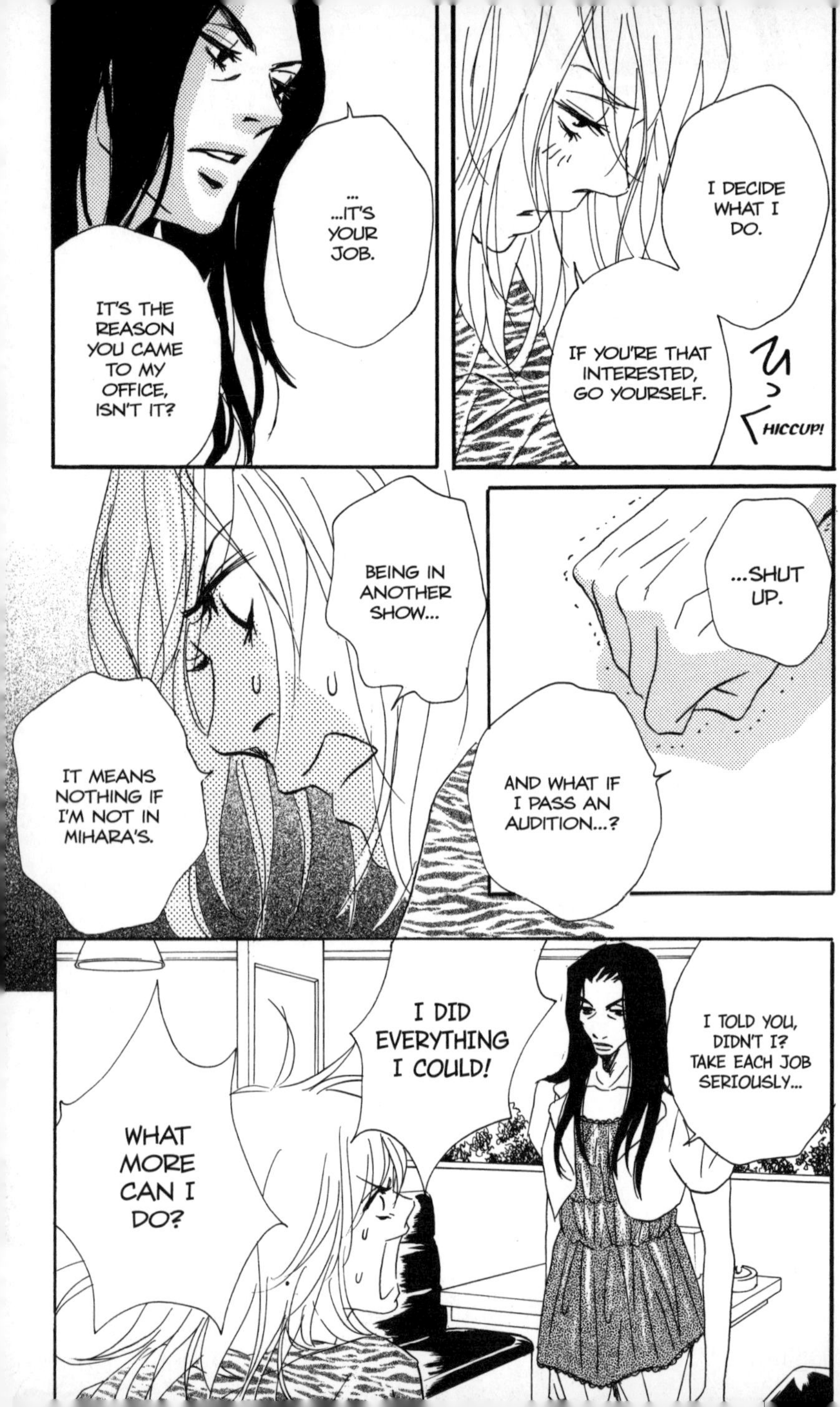
I DECIDE WHAT I DO.
IF YOU'RE THAT INTERESTED, GO YOURSELF.
HICCUP!
... ...IT'S YOUR JOB.
IT'S THE REASON YOU CAME TO MY OFFICE, ISN'T IT?
...SHUT UP.
AND WHAT IF I PASS AN AUDITION...?
BEING IN ANOTHER SHOW...
IT MEANS NOTHING IF I'M NOT IN MIHARA'S.
I TOLD YOU, DIDN'T I? TAKE EACH JOB SERIOUSLY...
I DID EVERYTHING I COULD!
WHAT MORE CAN I DO?

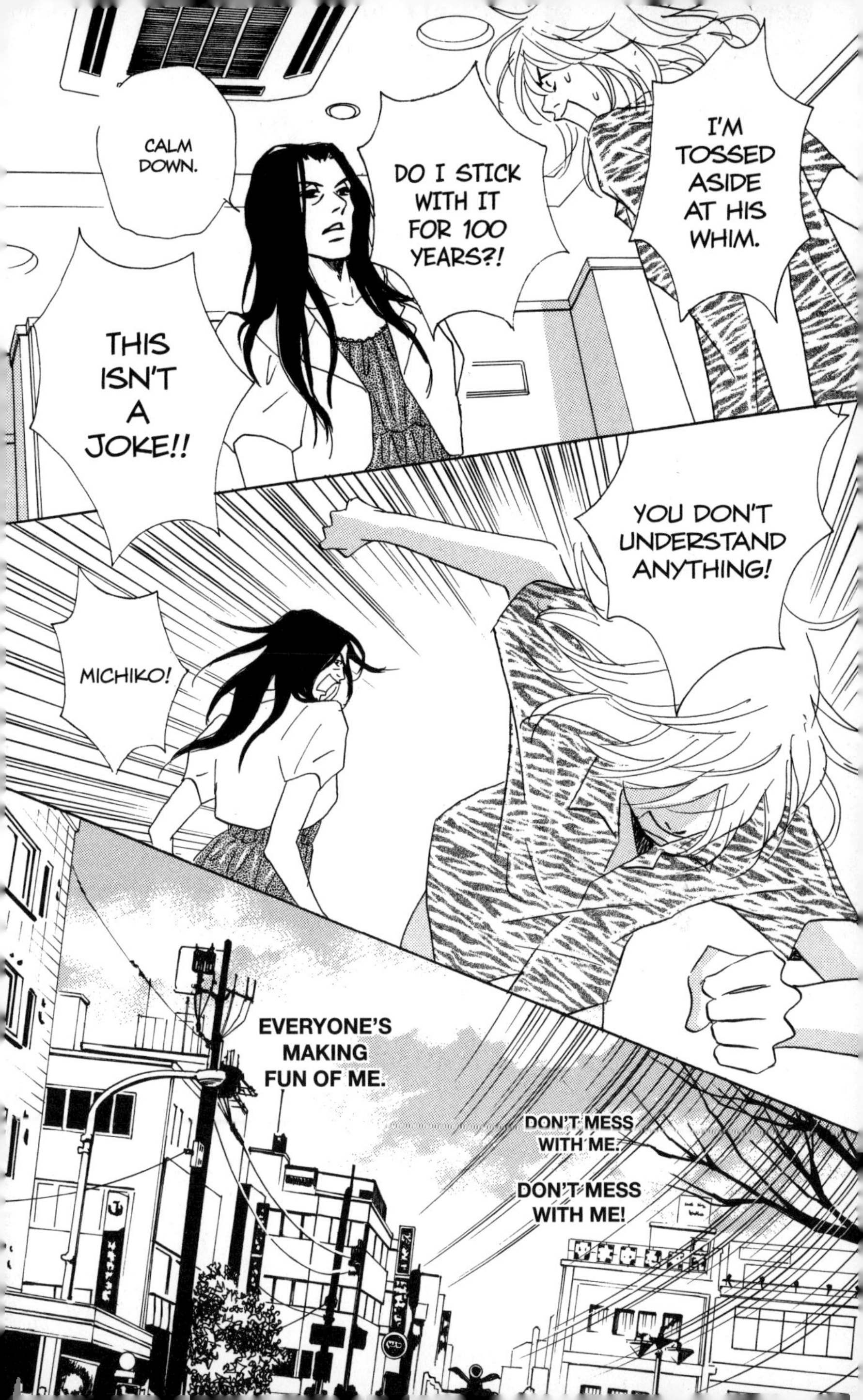
I'M TOSSED ASIDE AT HIS WHIM.
DO I STICK WITH IT FOR 100 YEARS?!
CALM DOWN.
THIS ISN'T A JOKE!!
YOU DON'T UNDERSTAND ANYTHING!
MICHIKO!
DON'T MESS WITH ME.
DON'T MESS WITH ME!
EVERYONE'S MAKING FUN OF ME.

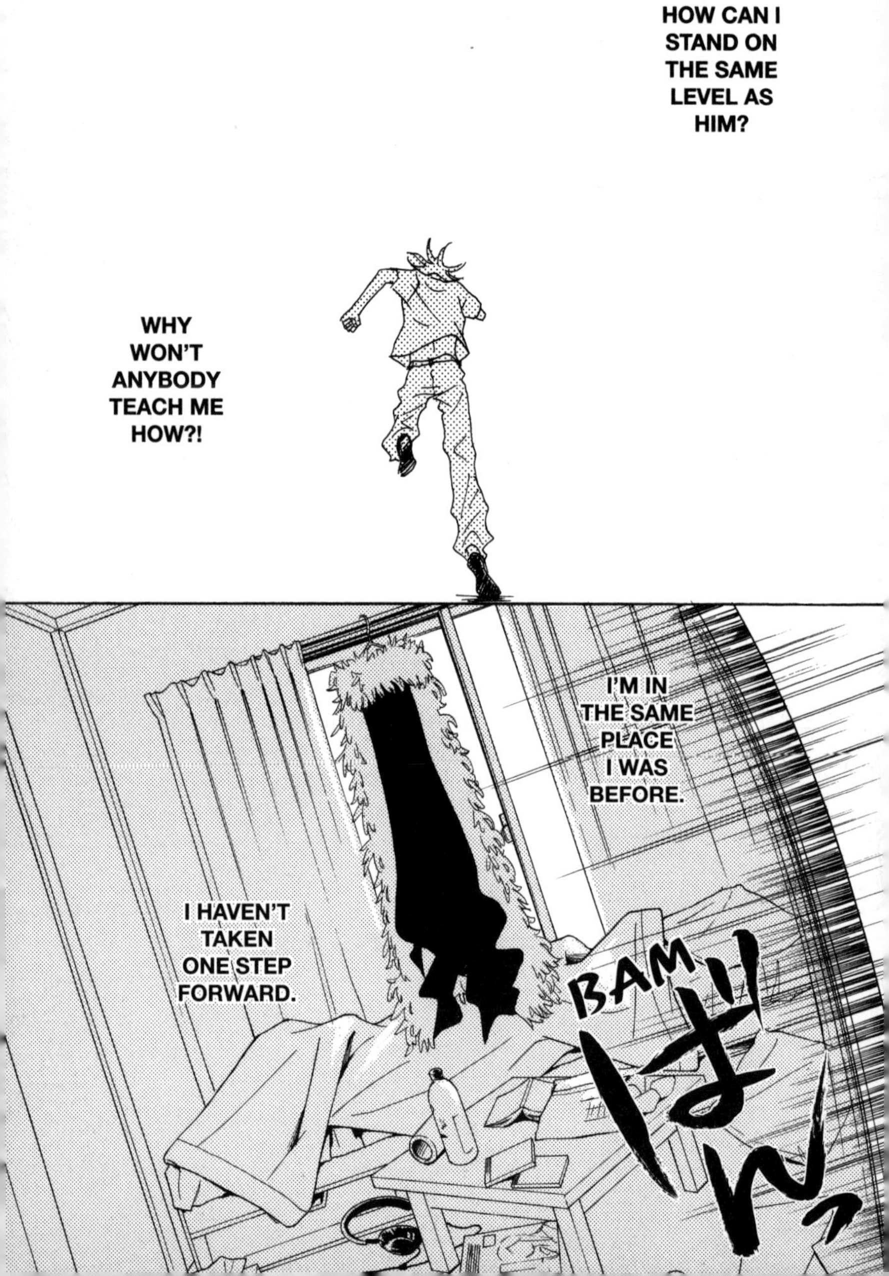
HOW CAN I STAND ON THE SAME LEVEL AS HIM?
WHY WON'T ANYBODY TEACH ME HOW?!
I'M IN THE SAME PLACE I WAS BEFORE.
I HAVEN'T TAKEN ONE STEP FORWARD.
BAM
ばん

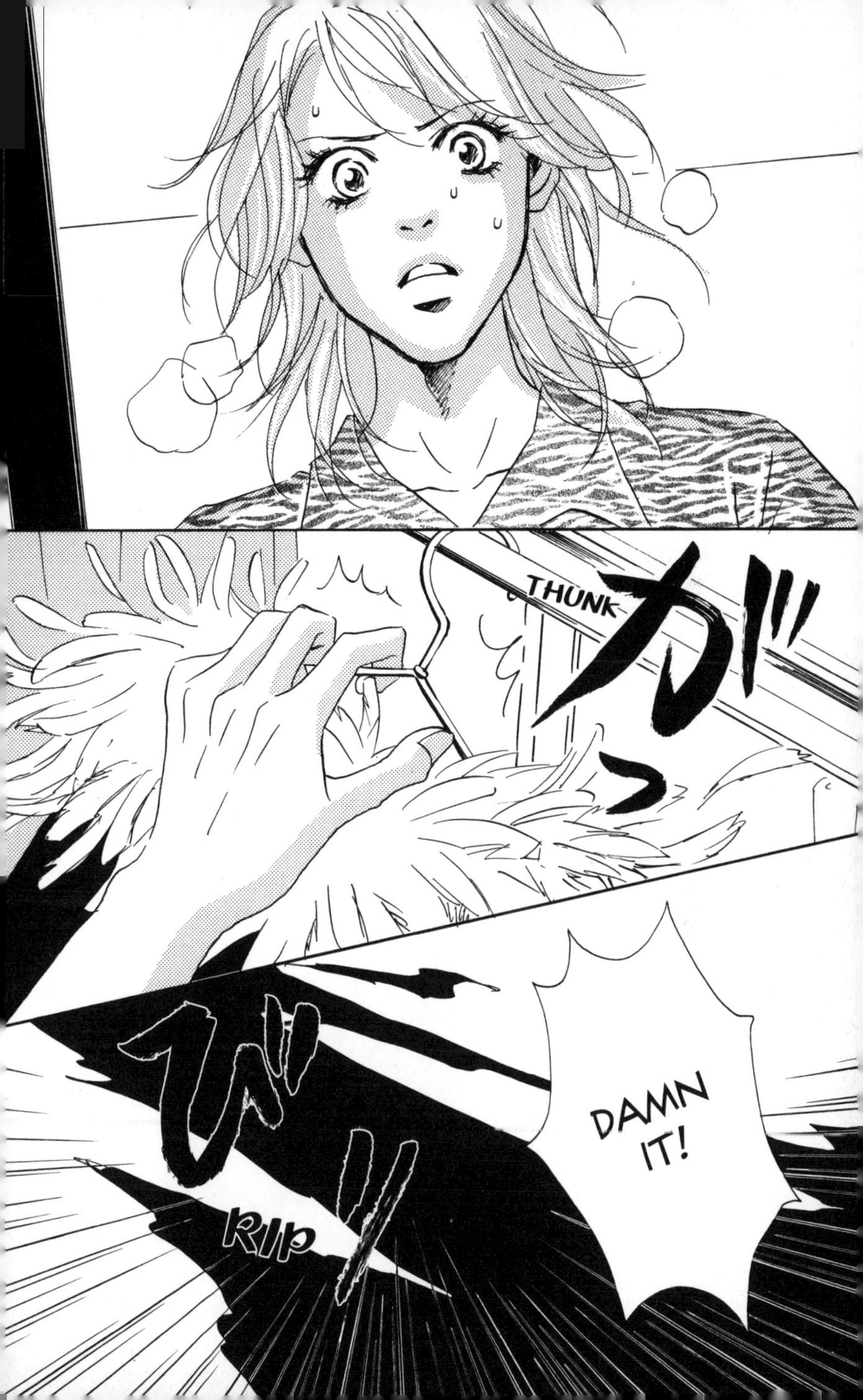
ガッ
THUNK
DAMN IT!
ビリ
RIP

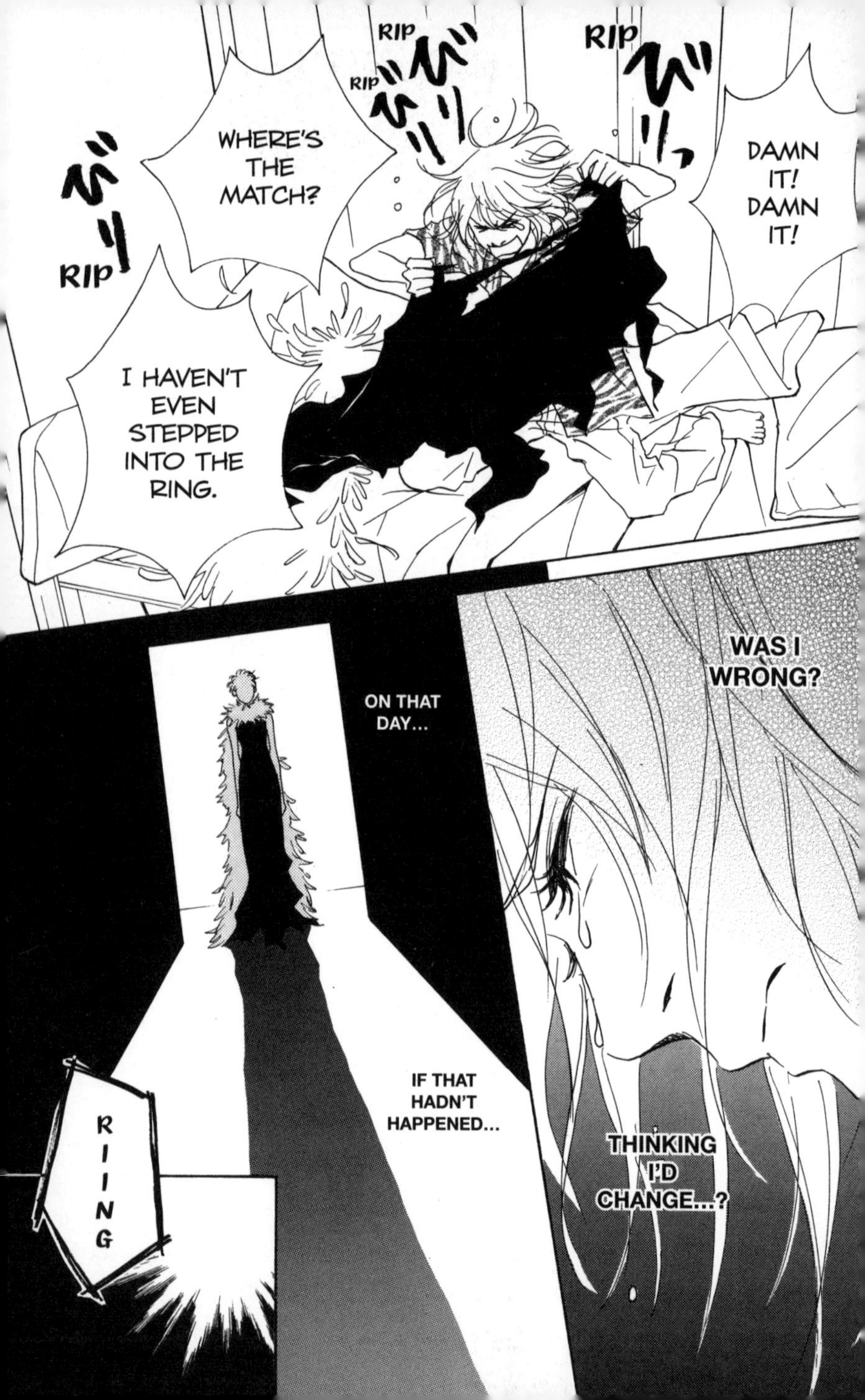
DAMN IT! DAMN IT!
RIP
RIP
RIP
WHERE'S THE MATCH?
I HAVEN'T EVEN STEPPED INTO THE RING.
RIP
WAS I WRONG?
THINKING I'D CHANGE...?
ON THAT DAY...
IF THAT HADN'T HAPPENED...
RIIING

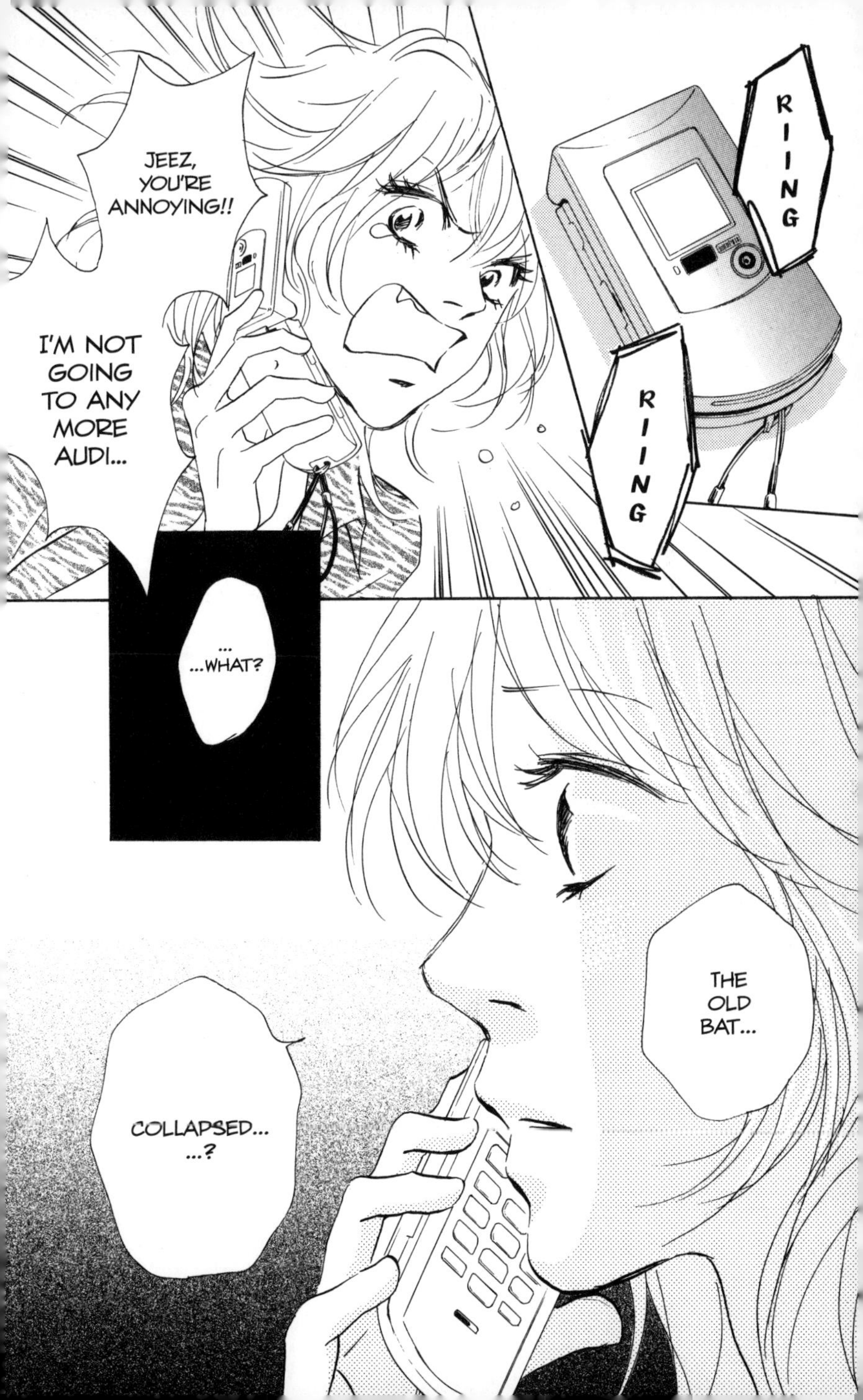
RIIING
RIIING
JEEZ, YOU'RE ANNOYING!!
I'M NOT GOING TO ANY MORE AUDI...
... ...WHAT?
THE OLD BAT...
COLLAPSED... ...?

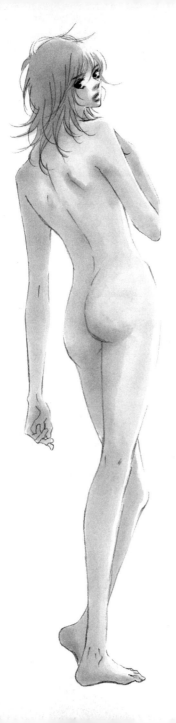

michiko's story
continues in
**walkin' butterfly
volume 3**

chihiro tamaki's

Sketchbook

W
B
ウォーキン・バタフライ
こんにちは。たまきちひろです。
178cmのくすぶり女・寅安ミチコ
の悪あがき白書・ここに参上！
人生が便秘のごとく行きづま
っているそこのアナタ！
明日への活力にこの一冊！
どうぞお試し下さいませ
たまきちひろ
宙出版. 790円(税別)

chihiro tamaki

photo by mattias westfalk

PROFILE: BORN IN AKITA PREFECTURE, JAPAN.
DEBUTED WITH *365-HO NO RYUTA (365-STEPS RYUTA)*
(SHOGAKUKAN) IN 2000. MAIN WORKS: *AI RABU YU
TO ITTEKURE! (SAY I LOVE YOU!)* (AKITA SHOTEN),
*SUKATO NO NAKA WA ITSUMO SENSO (IT'S ALWAYS
WAR INSIDE A SKIRT)* (ASAHI SONORAMA).

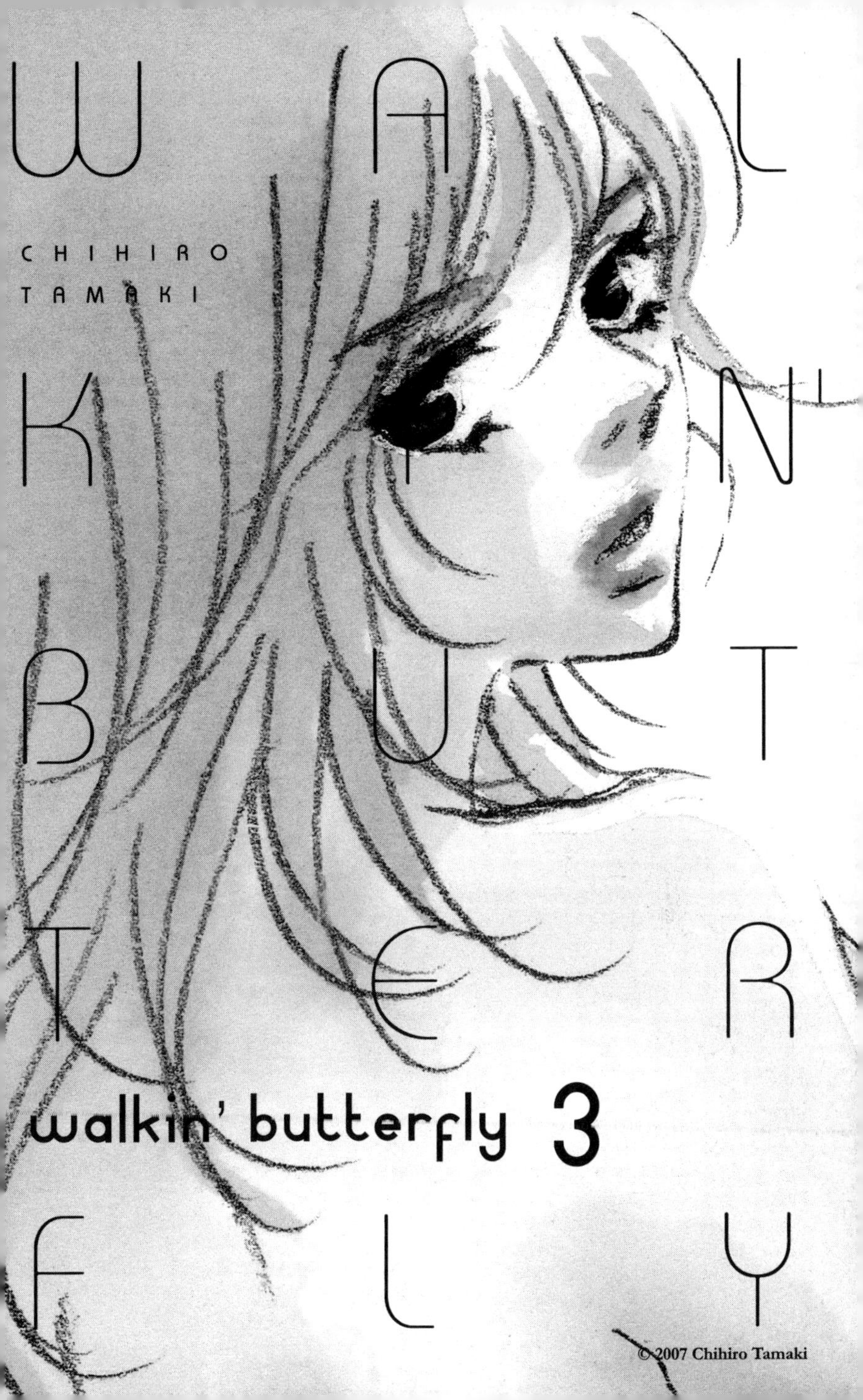
WALKIN' BUTTERFLY
CHIHIRO TAMAKI
walkin' butterfly 3
© 2007 Chihiro Tamaki

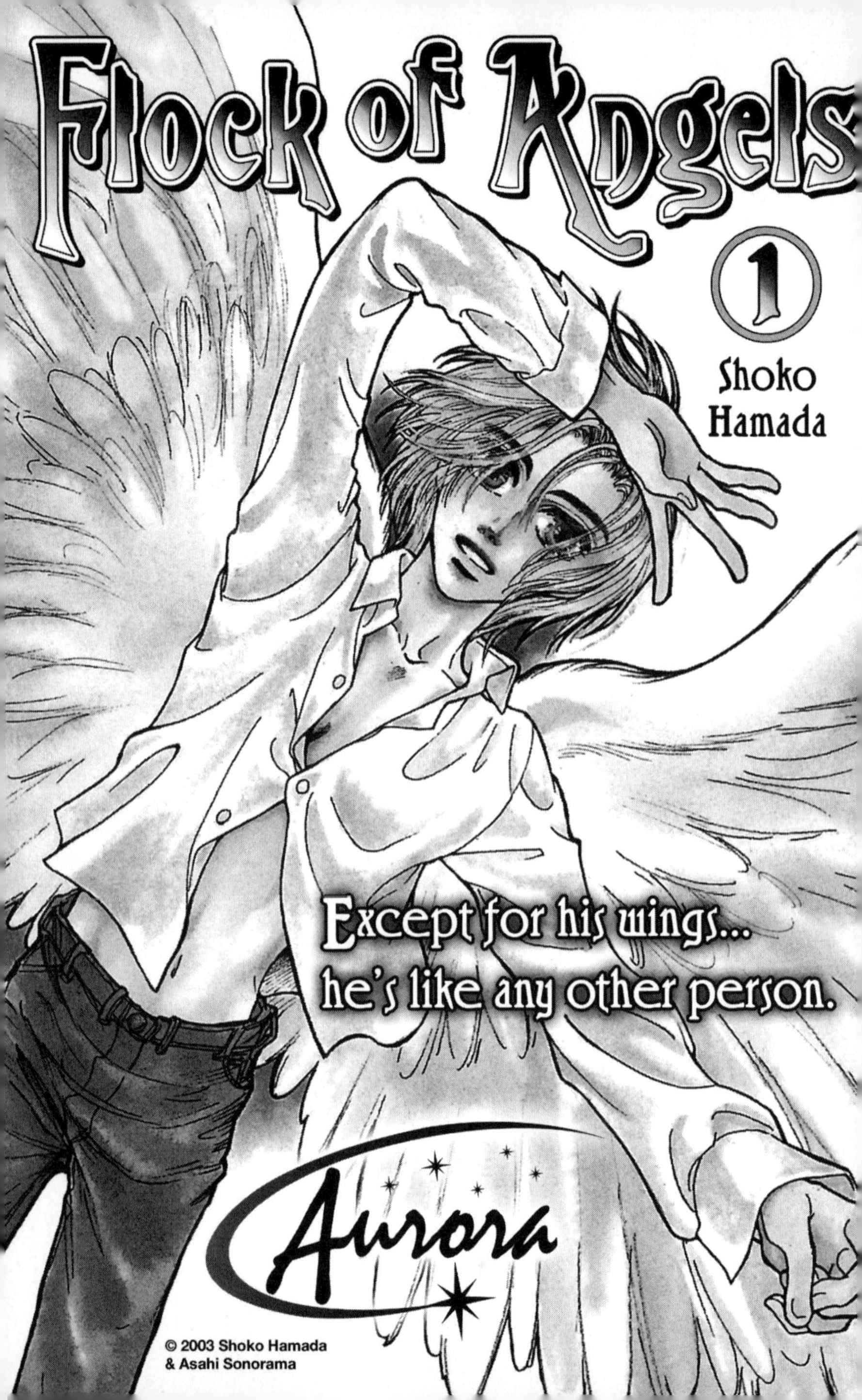
Flock of Angels
1
Shoko
Hamada
Except for his wings...
he's like any other person.
Aurora
© 2003 Shoko Hamada
& Asahi Sonorama

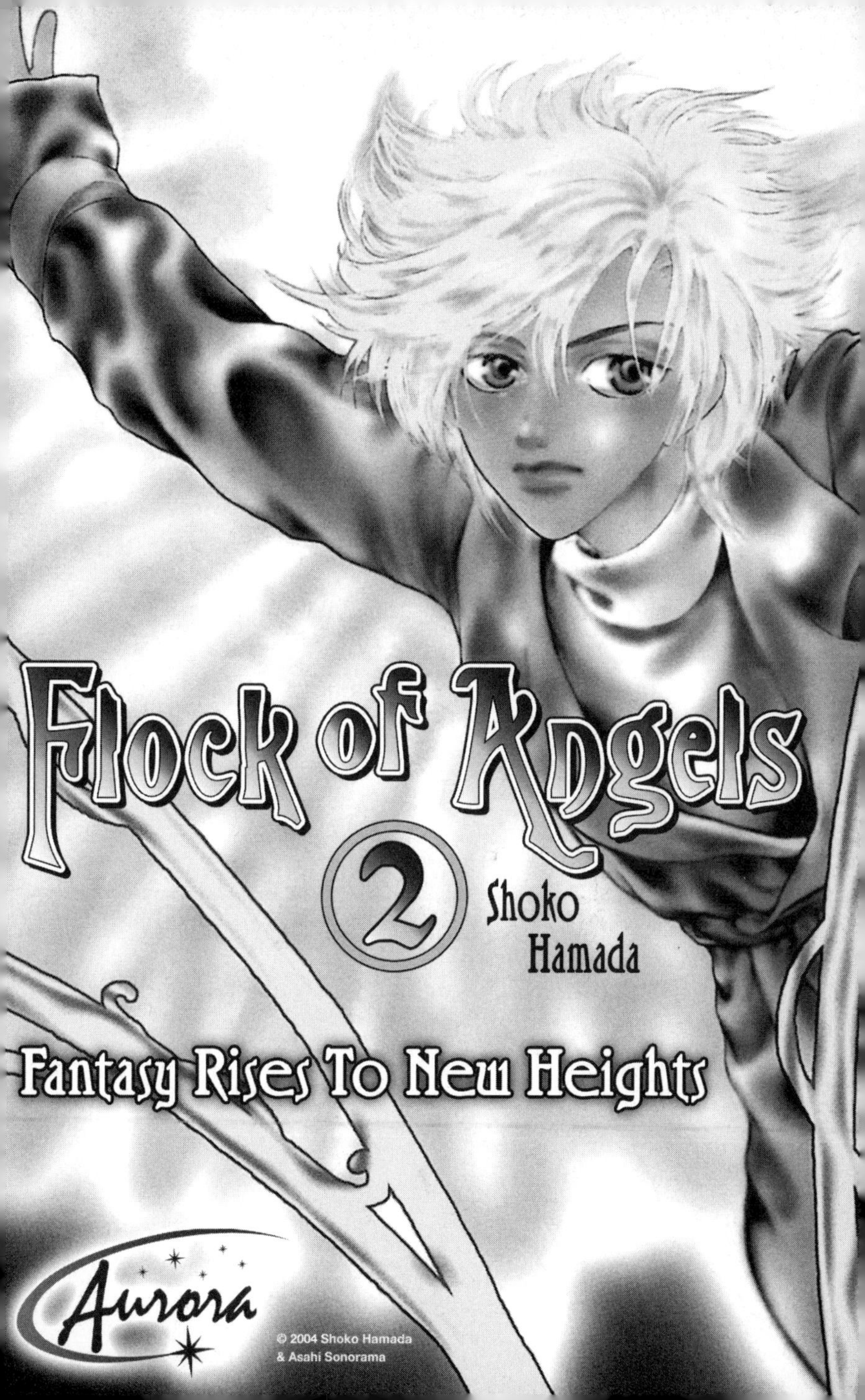
Flock of Angels
2
Shoko
Hamada
Fantasy Rises To New Heights
Aurora
© 2004 Shoko Hamada
& Asahi Sonorama

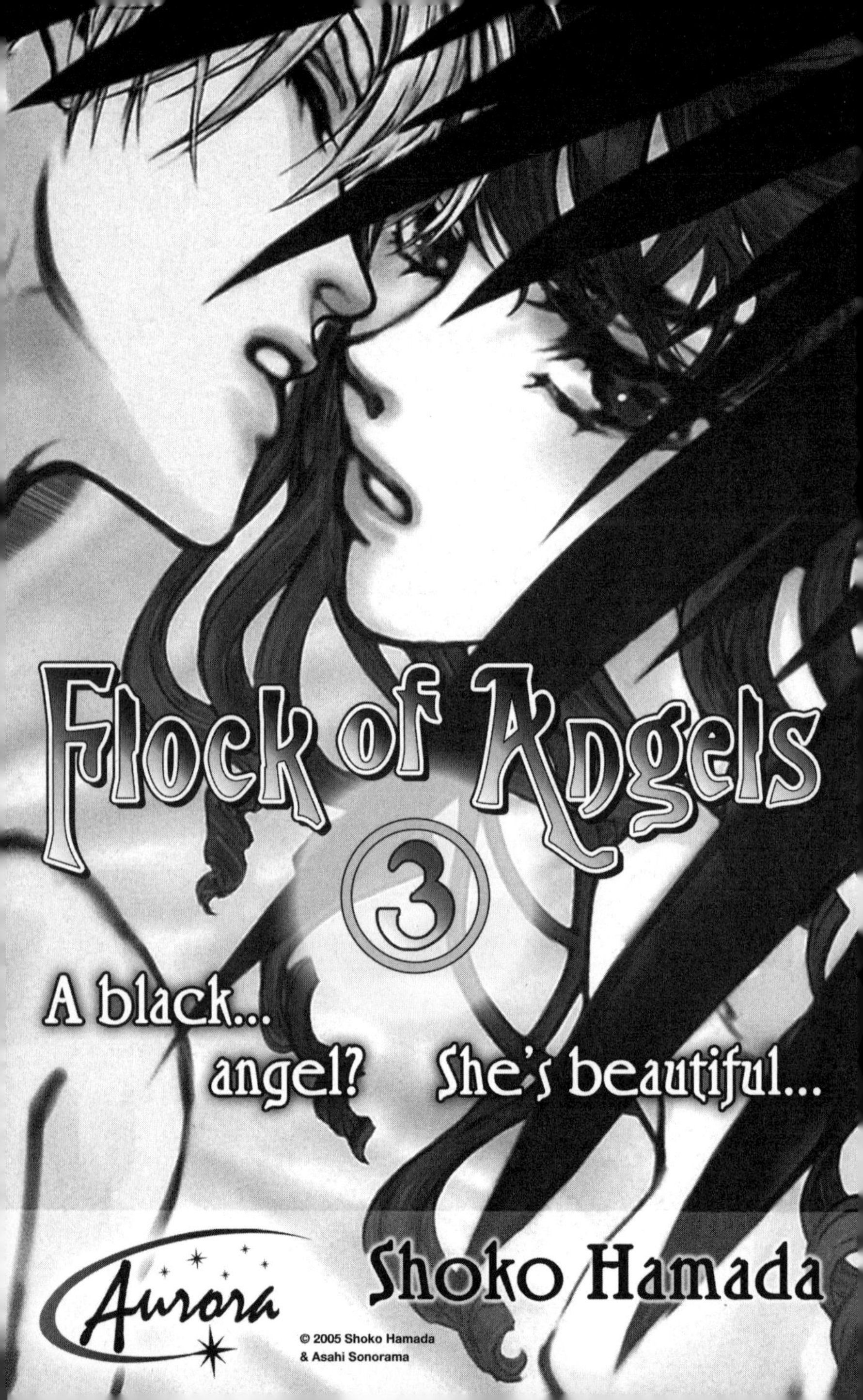
Flock of Angels
3
A black...
angel? She's beautiful...
Shoko Hamada
Aurora
© 2005 Shoko Hamada
& Asahi Sonorama

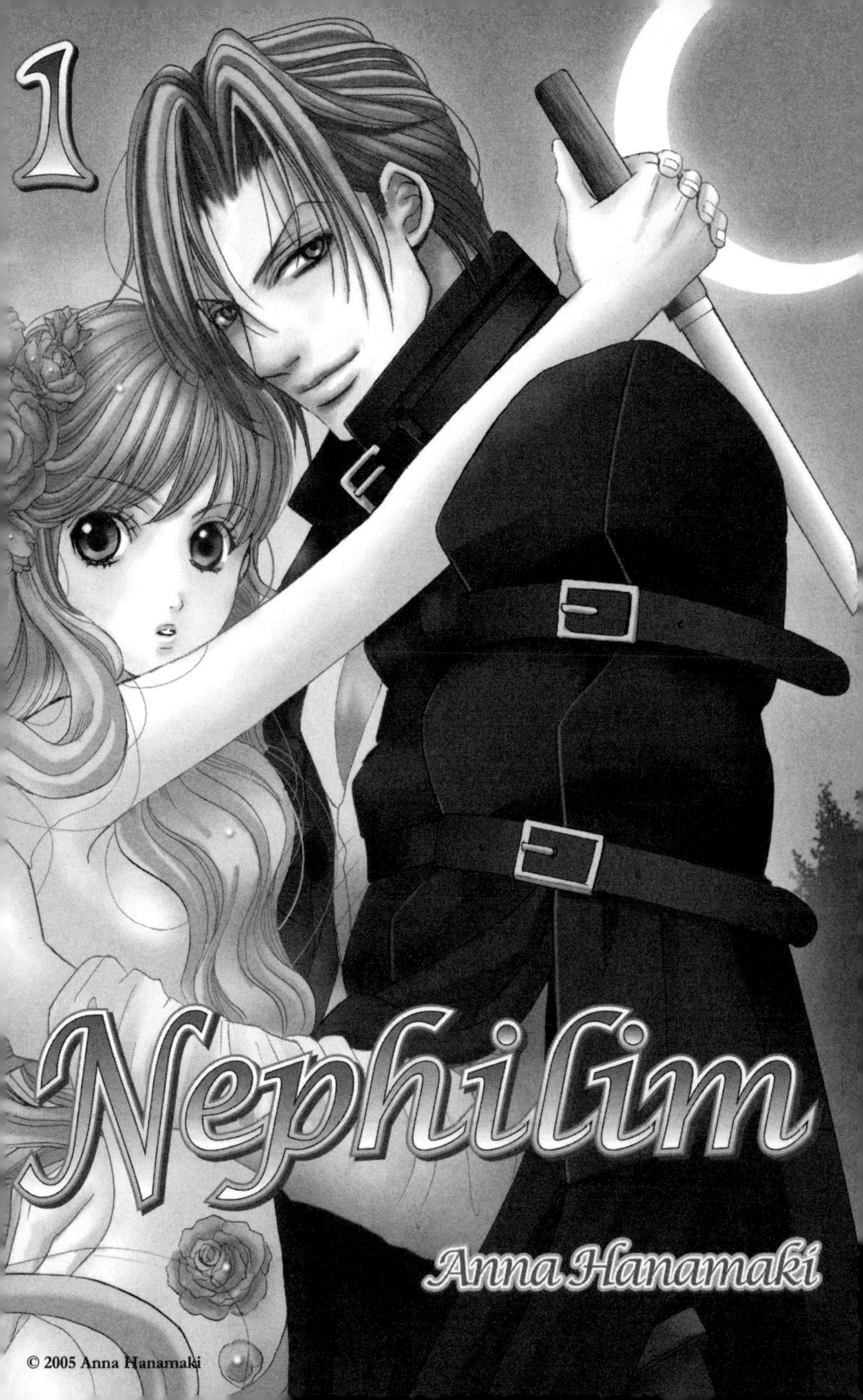
1
Nephilim
Anna Hanamaki

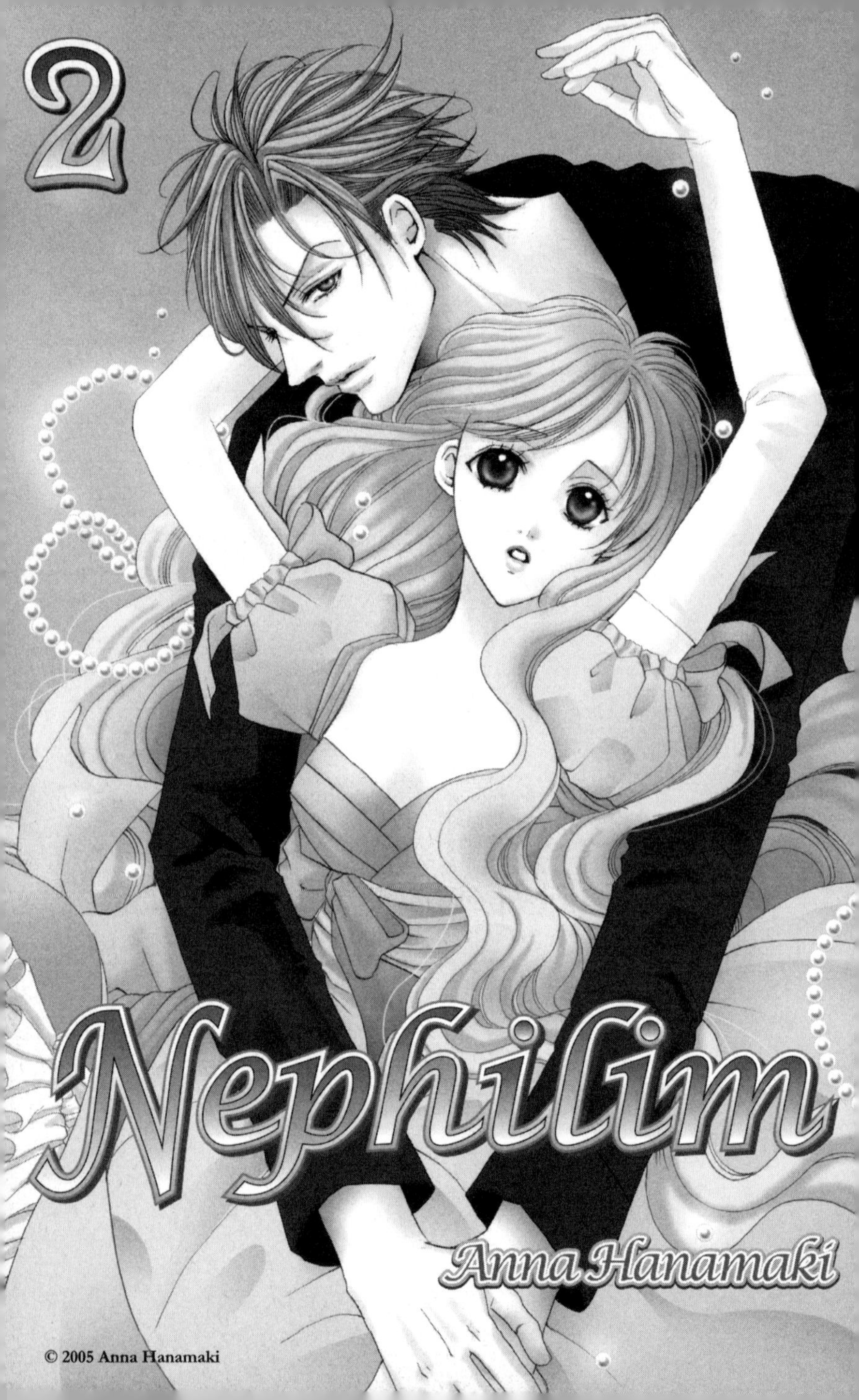
2
Nephilim
Anna Hanamaki

NIGHTMARES FOR SALE

1

Aurora

When you enter the Devil's pawnshop...
be careful what you wish for.

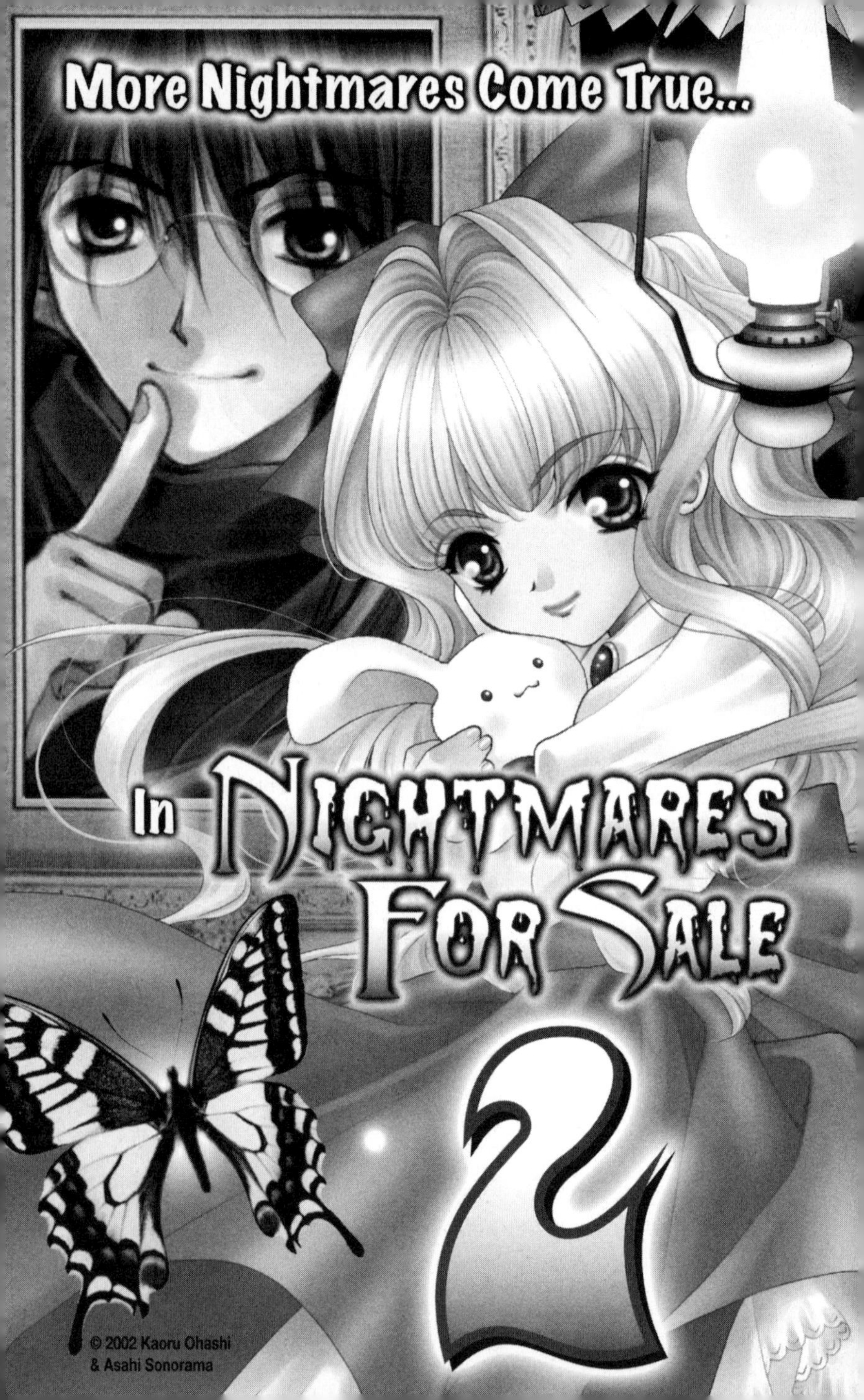
More Nightmares Come True...
In Nightmares For Sale
2
© 2002 Kaoru Ohashi
& Asahi Sonorama

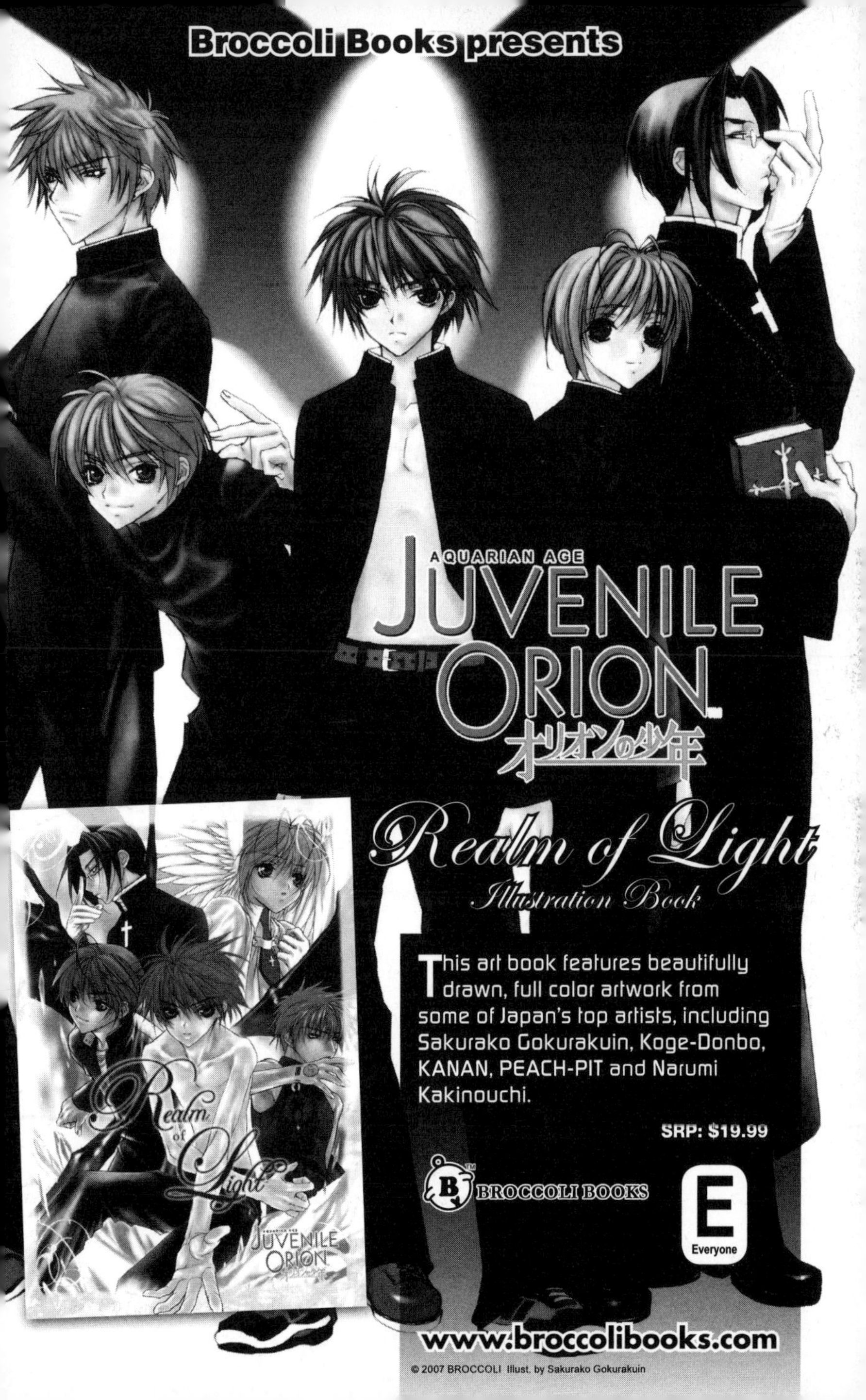
Broccoli Books presents
AQUARIAN AGE
JUVENILE
ORION
オリオンの少年
Realm of Light
Illustration Book
This art book features beautifully drawn, full color artwork from some of Japan's top artists, including Sakurako Gokurakuin, Koge-Donbo, KANAN, PEACH-PIT and Narumi Kakinouchi.
SRP: $19.99
BROCCOLI BOOKS
E
Everyone
www.broccolibooks.com
© 2007 BROCCOLI Illust. by Sakurako Gokurakuin

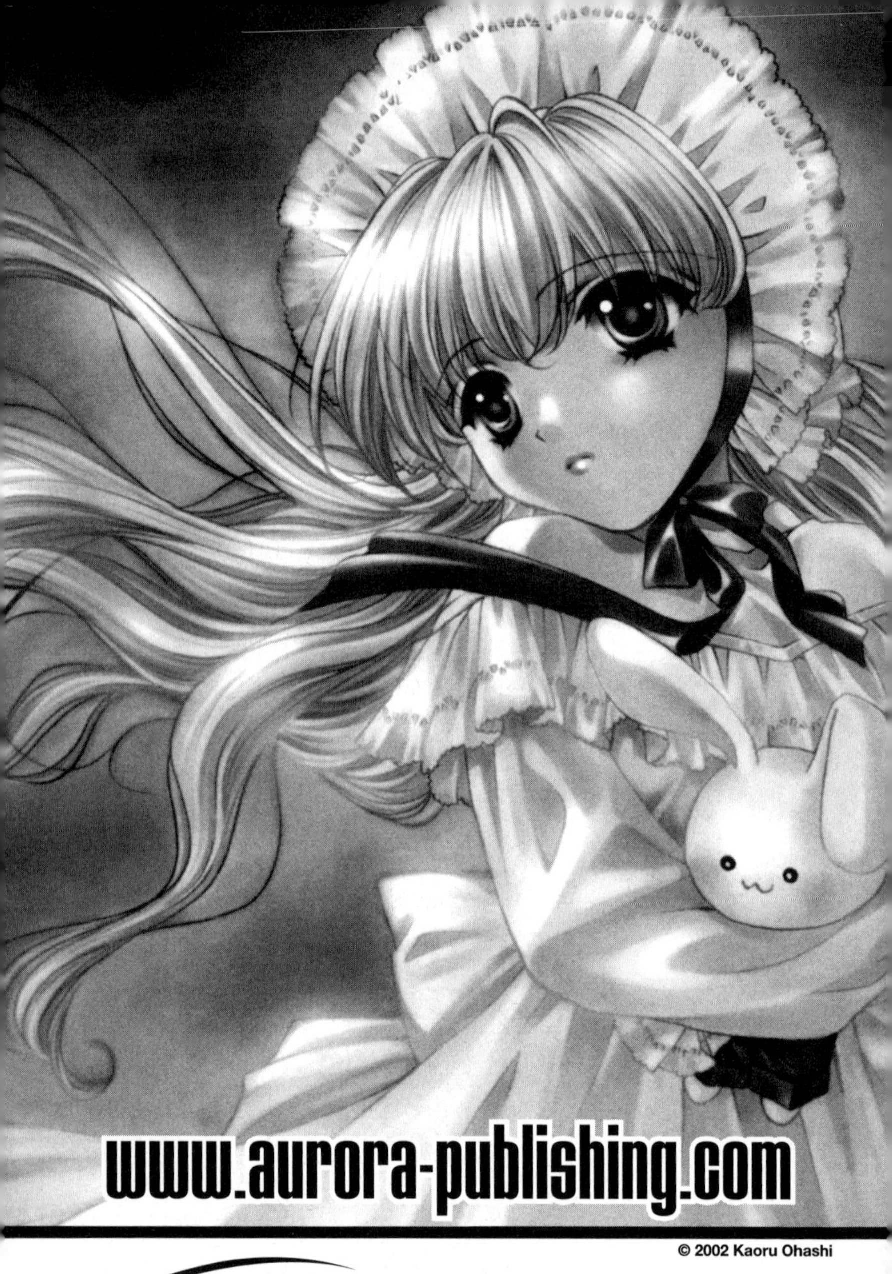
www.aurora-publishing.com

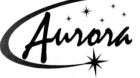

walkin' butterfly
volume 2

Walkin' Butterfly V...
Story and Art by Chihir...

© 2006 by Chihiro Tamaki. First publ... ...in 2006
by Ohzora Publishing Co. Ltd., Tokyo as *Walkin' Butterfly*.
English translation rights arranged with Ohzora Publishing Co. Ltd., Tokyo.

Translated by: Erin Brodhead
Edited by: K. Yukon
Translation & Editing Produced by:
Wowmax Media! LLC

WowmaxMedia!

Lettering: Thea Willis

Producer: Rod Sampson

Publisher: Nobuo Kitawaki

Published by Aurora Publishing, Inc.
www.aurora-publishing.com

Printed in Japan